GRAND CANYON

MONUMENT
TO CATASTROPHE

Edited by Steven A. Austin, Ph.D.

© 1994

Institute for Creation Research
Santee, California 92071

Grand Canyon is known internationally as the world's greatest natural wonder. Four-million people visit the Canyon each year and almost everyone who asks the question, "What mean these stones?" is given an evolutionary interpretation assuming slow processes operating for more than one-billion years. This is what the signs, museum displays, television documentaries, and textbooks present. In the minds of most people, Grand Canyon evokes an image of an evolving earth.

Christians, who have a strong commitment to the authority of Scripture, have wondered how Creation and Noah's Flood fit into the interpretation of Grand Canyon. They are usually told that such beliefs are myths which were incorporated into the Bible during "prescientific" times. Extraordinarily slow processes and organic evolution operated during "geologic ages," the public is told, to cause Grand Canyon to be as we see it today. Because of this teaching, many modern Christians fail to understand God's creation, and compromise in their commitment to Christ. Sadly, very few Christians can use Grand Canyon as an apologetic "to give an answer to every man" (I Peter 3:15) concerning God's actions either as a "faithful Creator" (I Peter 4:19) or as Revealer of a "lively hope" (I Peter 1:3).

Christian geologists have been challenged by the prophecy of the apostle Peter, when he wrote about scoffers who would come in the "last days" claiming "all things continue as they were from the beginning of the creation" (II Peter 3:3,4). According to Peter, these scoffers would deny that creation was by the Word of God, that the earth's surface was formed in a special way by water, and that the pre-Flood world was judged by a watery cataclysm (II Peter 3:5,6).

During the seventies and eighties, scientists with commitments to Christ discovered that Grand Canyon *does* provide a powerful testimony of Christ as Creator, Judge, and Coming King. Initial research projects proved especially beneficial in disclosing evidences of catastrophic, sedimentary, and erosional processes. Even many of the popular geologic evidences in Grand Canyon could be integrated well within the framework of a global Flood. Evidences in creationist biology flourished as well.

The success of creationist studies of Grand Canyon gave rise to field trips with graduate students and led to tours sponsored by two creationist organizations. During the first fourteen years that the Institute for Creation Research sponsored yearly tours, two thousand Christians discovered God's handiwork in the Canyon. A field guidebook was produced and distributed to participants of each of these yearly tours. The book you hold in your hand is the product of more than a dozen tours.

Fourteen creation scientists with recognized achievements in research and education were asked to contribute their understandings of Grand Canyon to this book. The result is the first distinctly creationist field guidebook to the geology, biology, and human history of the world's greatest natural wonder. The contributors were requested to write their experiences and understandings of Grand Canyon at the undergraduate college level, and to use nontechnical language. They were also encouraged, whenever possible, to include scholarly documentation so that the book would set a standard for Christian scholarship. Furthermore, they were requested to provide line illustrations and photographs to support their writings. Finally, the writers were asked to submit an extensive glossary of terms, so that the material could be comprehended by those without technical training in these specific sciences.

It was the desire of the authors that this book would make a lasting impact on Christians everywhere. We know that you will want to acquire your own understanding of Grand Canyon. Why not take a trip, yourself? The authors challenge you to integrate your study of Grand Canyon into the historical framework of Scripture. Grand Canyon is a significant monument to what God has done, and the authors hope you discover God's handiwork in the Canyon of canyons. When someone asks you, "What mean these stones?" you will be able to tell them. In the words of Joshua, ". . . these stones shall be for a memorial . . . that all the people of the earth might know the hand of the LORD, that it is mighty . . ." (Joshua 4:7,24).

Steven A. Austin
Santee, California
January 1994

CONTRIBUTORS

Fourteen creation scientists with recognized achievements in research and education helped write this book. Dr. Steven A. Austin, Chairman of the Geology Department at the Institute for Creation Research, served as general editor. The writers and their writing assignments are as follows:

Ralph E. Ancil, Ph.D., Resource Economics (Chapter 1, "Our Environment")

Steven A. Austin, Ph.D., Geology (Chapters 2, 3, 4, 5, and 6)

Walter R. Barnhart, M.S., Biology (Chapter 7)

Kenneth B. Cumming, Ph.D., Biology (Chapters 1 and 8)

Marcia L. Folsom, B.S., Geology (Chapter 7)

Michael P. Girouard, M.D., Surgery (Chapter 8)

Kenneth Ham, B. App. Sc., Dip. Ed., Science Education (Chapter 1)

William A. Hoesch, M.S., Geology (Chapter 11)

John R. Meyer, Ph.D., Biology (Chapter 8)

John D. Morris, Ph.D., Geological Engineering (Chapter 1 and Appendix A)

David E. Rush, M.S., Geophysics (Chapter 9)

Hannah Rush, B.A., Anthropology (Chapters 10 and 11)

Larry Vardiman, Ph.D., Atmospheric Science (Chapter 9)

Kurt P. Wise, Ph.D., Geology (Chapters 7 and 8)

In addition to the writers, numerous people have helped with illustrations and photography. Significant contributions have come from:

Marvin Ross

Marie Steinauer

J. Timothy Unruh

Arthur L. Battson, III

Ron Hight

Edmond W. Holroyd, III

Mark Looy

In review and design of the final manuscript, the following are particularly noteworthy:

Henry M. Morris (Review)

Andrew A. Snelling (Review)

Gary E. Parker (Review)

Pauline M. Colahan (Review)

George G. Kitchin (Review)

Jon Covey (Review)

David R. McQueen (Review)

Ruth Richards (Desktop Publishing)

Donald Rohrer (Publication)

Tom Rice (Review)

Marjorie Appelquist (Review)

TABLE OF CONTENTS

Figure 1.1 *Grand Canyon of northern Arizona.*

Chapter 1

THE GRANDEST OF CANYONS

". . . these stones shall be for a memorial. . . .
That all the people of the earth might know the hand of the LORD,
that it is mighty: that ye might fear the LORD your God for ever"
Joshua 4:7,24

Grand Canyon

There is no sight on Earth which matches Grand Canyon. There are other canyons, other mountains, and other rivers, but this Canyon excels all in scenic grandeur. Can any visitor, upon first viewing Grand Canyon, grasp and appreciate the spectacle spread before him? The ornate sculpture work and the wealth of color are like no other landscape. They suggest an alien world. The scale is too outrageous. The sheer size and majesty engulf the intruder, surpassing his ability to take it in.

The spectacle stretches 277 miles through northern Arizona (see figure 1.2). The main portion of Grand Canyon attains a depth of more than a mile and ranges from 4 to 18 miles in width. The north rim, somewhat higher than the south rim, reaches an altitude of 8,500 feet, while the Colorado River cascades along at about 2,400 feet.

Within the chasm is a host of pinnacles and buttes, canyons within canyons, and precipitous gorges and ravines. The most spectacular spires, or pinnacles, have been dubbed "temples," some towering a mile above the river. The

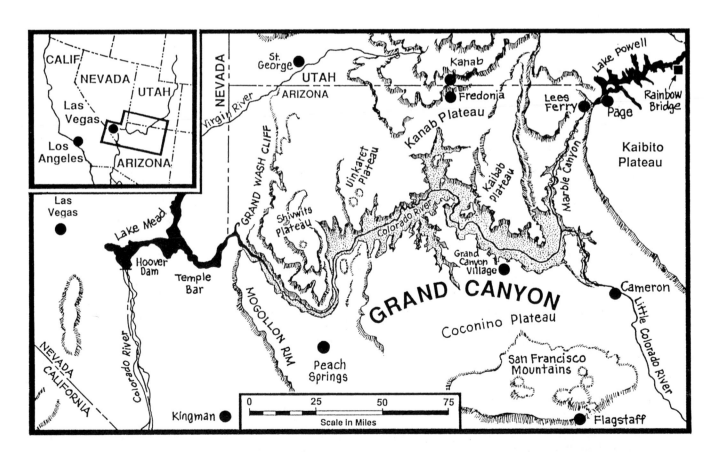

Figure 1.2 *Grand Canyon is 277 miles long, up to 18 miles wide, and almost a mile deep! Note that Grand Canyon (including its sixty-mile-long connection with Marble Canyon) isolates virtually the entire northwestern corner of Arizona from the rest of the state. High plateaus surround Grand Canyon.*

scarcity of vegetation allows the eyes to feast on delicate hues which come alive as the sun strikes the walls.

Surrounding Grand Canyon, throughout northern Arizona, New Mexico, and southern Utah, are spectacles made up of the same rock units found in the Canyon, as well as others which previously covered this area, now eroded away. A unique series of geologic events allows us to behold these various records of the past. This is "earth's strangest land," displaying the greatest variety of rock formations and erosional forms to be found in any area of comparable size.

The Christian can appreciate, as no one else, the wonders and beauty of God's creation. We can exclaim with David, "O LORD our LORD, how excellent is Thy Name in all the earth!" (Psalm 8:1,9). He has given us Grand Canyon and its environs as object lessons of His majestic power. Let us not fail to return to Him the praise, honor, and glory due Him for His wondrous works.

What Mean These Stones?

Our Lord understands that we are likely to forget the great things He has done for us. Not only are we likely to forget, we are also likely not to tell the next generation of the things of God as we ought.

The Lord has used a number of reminders or memorials on Earth to bring to memory vital matters that should never be forgotten. On a number of occasions, the Israelites were given specific memorials as reminders for each generation. One was to the generation of Israelites who escaped Egypt by a miraculous crossing of the Red Sea on dry ground, and who saw the pursuing Egyptians drowned behind them, but themselves died during the 40-year Exodus because they failed to remember God's sufficiency.

As recorded in Joshua 3 and 4, now the next generation stood facing the Promised Land, halted by the Jordan River at floodstage. Again, God provided a miracle. As the priests, bearing the Ark of the Covenant, stepped into the water, the Jordan's flow was stemmed. The priests proceeded to midstream and "stood firm," while all the people "passed over on dry ground." Next, 12 men, one from each tribe, picked up a stone from where the priests stood, and carried his to the far shore. The priests followed. Then, "the waters of Jordan returned unto their place, and flowed over all his banks, as they did before" (Joshua 4:18).

As a witness to future generations, the 12 stones were set up to be a memorial. "When your children ask their fathers in time to come, saying, What mean ye by these stones? Then ye shall answer them . . . these stones shall be for a memorial . . ." (Joshua 4:6,7). But, what is the purpose of this memorial? Scripture tells us, ". . . that all the people of the earth might know the hand of the LORD, that it is mighty: That ye might fear the LORD your God forever" (Joshua 4:24).

Consider, though, a far greater memorial! Crystalline rocks deep in Grand Canyon are covered by countless billions of tons of strata that remind us of God's intervention. In Genesis, chapter 1, we are told of a perfect earth created at God's command. In Genesis, chapters 6 through 9, we read of a later, worldwide catastrophe by which God judged the earth with a global flood.[1] If this catastrophic event, involving water scouring and the depositing of countless billions of tons of sediment, of the drowning and burying of millions of animals and plants really did occur, one would expect to discover massive evidences of the event. We would expect to find remains of billions of dead organisms buried in rock layers, laid down by water, all over the earth. That is exactly what we do find! The strata and fossils of the earth, and Grand Canyon in particular, could very well be intended as reminders that this judgment was carried out just as the Bible states. These are subjects for later chapters of this book.

As one stands on the rim of Grand Canyon or walks among the rocks displayed so prominently (figure 1.3), the question might be asked, "How is this a memorial of the mighty things our Lord has done?" First of all, many of those deeply buried crystalline rocks suggest God's activity during Creation Week. The fossil-bearing rock layers of Grand Canyon seem to have been laid down during the time of Noah's Flood.[2] The Canyon itself appears to have been eroded sometime after this catastrophic event.[3] Thus, the Canyon and layers of sedimentary rock may, in fact, offer an obvious reminder that God is omnipotent Creator and that He has sovereignly judged this world.

Secondly, Grand Canyon should be of interest to us because of the important controversy it has started. Most people who look at Grand Canyon and ask, "What mean these stones?" are told that scientists believe these layers are the results of millions of years of earth's history—that these layers are *not* a colossal memorial or reminder that God is both Creator and Judge. Instead, many people are being taught evolutionary ideas regarding the origin of Grand Canyon, and thus, in their minds, the Bible has been undermined. Even many Christians have been influenced by this teaching.

Thirdly, the Bible teaches that physical death and bloodshed came only after Adam sinned (Romans 5:12; I Corinthians 15:21). Not just man, but the whole creation, was subjected to the judgment of sin and death (Romans 8:22). This is a most important doctrine from the first three chapters of Genesis.[4] God instituted death and bloodshed because of sin, so that man could be redeemed. The redemption includes not only man, but the whole creation (Romans 8:19–23; II Peter 3:12,13). Though we leave this body because death and bloodshed have been introduced into the world, we know that God, Himself, came in the person of Jesus Christ, suffering death and shedding His blood for our sin—conquering death so that we can spend eternity with Him. However, if death and bloodshed existed before Adam sinned, then the whole foundation of the Gospel message has been nullified. If the Bible is true, then these billions of dead things (fossils) should not have formed until after Adam sinned. Noah's Flood offers a good explanation of these strata and the fossils they contain. What we believe concerning the origin of Grand Canyon is very important, because millions are being told that death during millions of years was a part of what happened to form strata of Grand Canyon. This means millions of people are being told that the foundation of the Gospel message has been destroyed.

Fourthly, II Peter, chapter 3 tells us that in the last days people will deny the message of Creation, Noah's Flood, and of the coming judgment by fire. Why should people listen when Christians teach about coming judgment, when they deny there was a past judgment? Each time a scientist or a guide teaches that Grand Canyon is the result of millions of years of slow and continuous processes, that person is questioning the past judgment by God.

Figure 1.3 *Grand Canyon commands our attention and prompts us to ask, "What mean these stones?"*

Evolutionary teaching puts a stumbling block in people's way regarding any future judgment.

The question could then be asked, "If the evidence of Grand Canyon fits with Noah's Flood, why have not the majority of scientists recognized it?" The answer to this can be found in II Peter 3:5,6 where we read: "For this they willingly are ignorant of, that by the Word of God the heavens were of old, and the earth standing out of the water and in the water: Whereby the world that then was, being overflowed with water, perished." The Bible teaches that people are willingly ignorant—that is, they deliberately choose to reject the evidence. As explained later in this book, the evidence from Grand Canyon *does* fit with Creation and Noah's Flood. That means that the Bible is true, and that God is Creator and Judge. To accept that God is Creator means that He has a right over each person's life because He owns each person. Thus, right and wrong are set by God, because He is the absolute authority.

On the other hand, to assume an evolutionary philosophy of origins leads to the belief that everything was formed by chance produced by random processes during billions of years. The evolutionary philosophy leads to the notion that each person owns himself, and is the master of his own destiny. This is contrary to the Bible teaching that mankind is in rebellion against God, because of the fact that we all sin after the likeness of Adam. Adam's sin was rebellion! He decided to write his own rules and not accept what God had stated. Thus, the real battle in regard to understanding Grand Canyon is founded not just upon Creation and Noah's Flood versus evolution, but upon Christianity versus humanism.

Each time we see Grand Canyon or hear people ask concerning this massive chasm, "What mean these stones?" let us hasten to explain the evidence for His past judgment and, as well, His future judgment. At the same time, we can also tell them of God's provision. Just as God preserved Noah and his family after they went through the door of the Ark to be saved from the judgment of the Flood, so God introduced death and bloodshed into the world, that we could have a doorway through which we could walk in order to be saved. The Lord Jesus Christ is that doorway. Because of what He did on the cross, those who trust in Him can spend eternity with Him. Let us, therefore, never forget that death and bloodshed are not the means by which we have evolved, but the means by which we can be redeemed. We chose to live in separation from God; God chose to have us live with Him!

Grand Canyon provides ample opportunity to reflect on the meaning of stones. The layers of beauty on all sides are, in all likelihood, the grim reminder of sin, judgment, and destruction. Peter tells us that "the world that then was, being overflowed with water, perished" (II Peter 3:6). All that remains of the pre-Flood world is rock laid down by Flood waters and fossils encased in these rocks—inhabitants of a world so sinful it had to be destroyed.

On the other hand, we are assured that the world will be restored to its former glory one day; with the effects of sin and judgment obliterated. The Bible describes the coming age in glorious terms, and God has left us a few additional clues in Grand Canyon, the destroyed remnant of the former world. Imagine how majestic the world must have been, for its destruction to exhibit such grandeur. Furthermore, ponder the surpassing glory of the coming new earth!

The true Gospel of Jesus Christ includes far more than His marvelous redemptive work, although that is the focal point of all history. The complete "good news" rightly includes the entire person and work of Jesus Christ, starting with His work of creation and culminating in His final vanquishing of all sin and reigning over His creation made perfect once again. Let us not only ponder His works of judgment and salvation at the time of Noah's Flood, let us more fully grasp the complete work of our Creator, Savior, and King—our Lord Christ Jesus!

Five Themes

A myriad of impressions and observations come to our attention as we observe and study Grand Canyon. It is, no doubt, for this reason that Grand Canyon has been called one of the earth's greatest natural wonders. But how do we recognize which impressions and observations are important? Can we *classify* those that are important? How do we incorporate our significant thoughts about the Canyon into an organized body of knowledge? Scientists at the Institute for Creation Research frequently speak of five themes which form the framework for our thinking about Grand Canyon. These five themes are: (1) hierarchy, (2) zonation, (3) relict forms, (4) degradation, and (5) history.

Hierarchy

We notice that things at Grand Canyon, as elsewhere, can be organized in a graded or ranked series called a hierarchy. Some of the things we observe are large and all-encompassing, while other things are rather small and specialized. We can place those things which are more

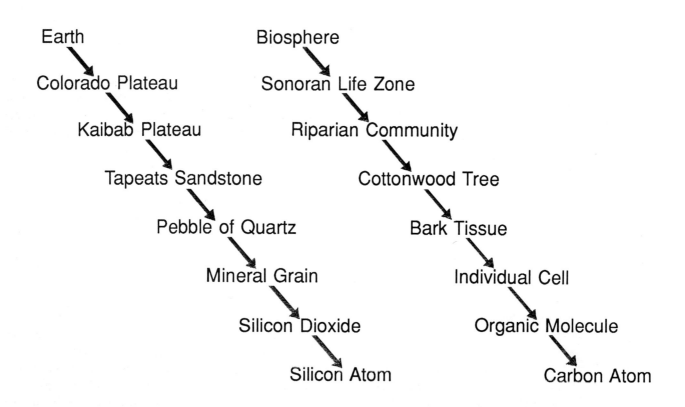

Figure 1.4 *Hierarchy can be illustrated at Grand Canyon by two examples: one from geology and one from biology.*

restricted as contained within the more inclusive. This applies to the major geological and biological wonders of the Canyon.

Figure 1.4 shows two examples illustrating the theme of hierarchy. For the geological world, we recognize the hierarchy shown on the left of figure 1.4. We can begin a geological hierarchy by considering the entire earth. That portion of the earth which we observe is its outer layer, called the "crust," which, in the southwestern United States, includes the large geographic province called the "Colorado Plateau." The Colorado Plateau can be divided into several smaller structural units. One of the smaller units is the Kaibab Plateau, which has an elevation of from 6,000 to 9,000 feet. It forms the upwarped crust in north-central Arizona (the eastern Grand Canyon region). Within the upwarped earth are strata of sandstone, limestone, and shale. One of the deeply buried sandstone formations is called the Tapeats Sandstone which, near its base, contains quartz pebbles. An individual quartz pebble is composed of mineral grains which are made up of the chemical compound silicon dioxide. An individual atom of silicon exists within the chemical compound.

In a similar fashion, we can arrange biological entities as the right side of figure 1.4 illustrates. The biosphere includes all living things on earth. A particular life zone in the southwestern United States is known as the "Sonoran Life Zone," which includes the living things within Grand Canyon. We recognize within the Canyon various ecological communities, one of which is the "Riparian Community"—a group of organisms inhabiting the wet stream banks. One conspicuous species of the Riparian Community is the cottonwood tree. This prominent tree is composed of different organs, one of which is the bark tissue, which, in turn, is composed of individual cells. A myriad of organic molecules is contained within a single living cell, with the carbon atom being a significant component of these molecules.

At Grand Canyon, as elsewhere, we notice that our geological and biological entities can be positioned in a hierarchy. It is very important that we be able to define the various entities we see, and be able to understand how to classify them within a hierarchy. We build our knowledge of Grand Canyon as we increase our awareness of these entities, and comprehend the relationships between these things as we organize and place them into a ranked or graded structure.

The Bible tells us of man's unique position within God's creation. We are natural (or physical) the same as other creatures, but we are also transnatural (or spiritual), in that we bear "the image of God" (Genesis 1:27). Because of our relationship with God, we occupy a seat of authority and responsibility over God's creation. The psalmist speaks of our position as "a little lower than the angels" (Psalm 8:5) for the purpose of having "dominion over the works of (His) hands" (Psalm 8:6).

Zonation

Things in Grand Canyon are not randomly distributed, but seem to be grouped together in distinct zones. The most striking geological observation is that the rocks occur as strata. Formations of the Canyon have different quantities of sand, lime mud, and clay, which impart different composition and color. Not only does this apply to the *mineral* constituents, but also to *fossils*. Each formation is itself strongly stratified with different textures of grains in regular beds and laminae. Usually the layered appearance can be distinguished within a single hand-sized rock. Geologists have sought to understand the agents of water sorting and transport which have distinctly separated these materials. The stratified structure at Grand Canyon has allowed each formation to be identified. Once you know the order of the strata sequence, you can train your eye to distinguish it over the entire extent of the Canyon—a distance of more than 200 miles.

The property of zonation is no less apparent, when we study the distribution of organisms in Grand Canyon. The extreme changes in elevation cause the organisms to occur in distinct ecosystems within the Canyon. At 7,000 feet elevation on the south rim of Grand Canyon, we encounter conifer forests, whereas near the Colorado River at 2,400 feet elevation, only sparse desert vegetation occurs. In between these two extremes is a variety of ecological communities. Biologists pay special attention to recognizing and classifying the different component species of these zones. They have endeavored to understand the different extremes of temperature and the different amounts of moisture which determine where each species lives.

Our observation is that each organism within Grand Canyon has its own place where it prevails or flourishes. That reminds us that we have a dwelling place provided by God. The words of our Lord Jesus Christ call men and women everywhere to "abide" in Him and "bear much fruit" (John 15:4,5). Our place is to be "rooted and built up in Him" (Colossians 2:7).

Relict Forms

A relict is a feature, object, or living thing which has remained essentially unchanged after other parts have changed or disappeared. The concept of relict forms has wide application in Grand Canyon. Consideration of the fossil record contained within the strata and the organisms in the world which survive today, emphasizes in our minds these unchanged entities. The basic types of organisms appear to be conserved. Life persists. Thus, living things at the Canyon can be viewed as the enduring remnant of otherwise extinct flora and fauna. This has special significance to the creationist, who views the present assembly of organisms of the Southwest as survivors of the Flood. The land-dwelling, air-breathing organisms survived on the Ark, and their descendants are able to make the best of the difficult conditions in today's desert. They are fulfilling the Genesis mandate to reproduce "after their kind" and to "fill the earth."

The landforms of Grand Canyon also illustrate the concept of relict forms. Many of the slopes within the Canyon appear to be precisely adjusted to preserve the stability of the entire profile of the Canyon, but the extant agents of erosion do not appear to have formed them. Many side canyons, for example, appear to have formed by failure of the base of the slope where water oozed out. The process is known technically as "sapping." But most side canyons today do not have enough water to cause the effect. They appear to be remnants formed in wetter conditions. Many cliffs in Grand Canyon are coated with a reddish-brown stain called "desert varnish," which indicates that slopes are long enduring, not continually evolving. Cliffs often do not have a significant talus at their base, indicating that the cliff has not been altered by a continuous process of rock falls. Many geologists have suspected that the present action of the Colorado River did not erode Grand Canyon through the uplifted plateau lands of northern Arizona. Thus, the entire Canyon, itself, may be a relict form.

Our biological observations also reveal that processes of conservation act to preserve the form and character of living things. Perhaps the most amazing component of living things is the DNA molecule, which forms the genetic code distinctive of each organism. While numerous varieties are evident within a single species, we recognize that the degree of variation has distinct limits. Natural selection, a process which limits the varieties which exist, is recognized by biologists to *restrict* change and *preserve* the character of the type. Biologists have even coined a word to describe this condition. They call it "stasis." The Bible calls it "after its kind."

Degradation

Although there are processes and properties at work in Grand Canyon which tend to maintain and conserve form and type, we recognize also certain processes which tend to degrade and destroy. The genetic stability of living things is interrupted, on rare occasion, in an adverse way, by a random rearrangement of the DNA molecule, a process called mutation. Rocks, likewise, cannot endure unchanged. Chemical and mechanical weathering break them into finer particles. Once divided into small fragments, the agents of erosion can remove them. In both biological and geological systems, we observe processes which lower grade, rank, or status.

The Bible describes these degradation processes we see around us. These processes are contrasted with the unchanging nature of God:

> *And thou, Lord, in the beginning hast laid the foundation of the earth; . . . They shall perish; but thou remainest; and they all shall wax old as doth a garment; and as a vesture shalt thou fold them up, and they shall be changed: But thou art the same, and thy years shall not fail (Hebrews 1:10–12).*

History

Earth's most colossal display of strata causes us to contemplate the issue of origins. Layers of sandstone, shale, and limestone along with contained fossils impel our minds to consider Grand Canyon, ultimately, as a monument to Earth history. Our question is, "What mean these stones?" We recognize, by the principle of superposition, that older strata are buried beneath younger strata. Beneath strata within the inner gorge are even older crystalline rocks. They cause us to ponder Earth's initial condition. We also recognize that the strata were once continuous across the present form of the Canyon. This indicates that the erosion of the Canyon occurred *after* the strata were deposited.

Whereas the relative *sequence* of events responsible for forming Grand Canyon appears to be well established, exactly *how* and *when* these events occurred is far from obvious. We cannot see or scientifically test Earth history, but can only decipher it by interpreting clues preserved within the rocks. Here is where models are necessary. If we assume a Biblical model, we can interpret Grand Canyon in relation to Creation and the Flood. If we assume an evolutionary model, we might suppose that slow processes during billions of years formed Grand Canyon. At issue, is which model for Earth history is correct. These are subjects to be explored in later chapters of this book.

Our Environment

Creationists recognize that mankind was originally created perfect and was placed in a perfect, friendly environment. Our mandate was to have dominion over the earth. Agriculture is not seen as destructive, for our God intended the earth to be cultivated (Genesis 2:5,15). In this perspective, each element of creation has its own rightful place. God pronounced His whole creation to be "very good" (Genesis 1:31). Therefore, respect for the Creator requires respect for His creation. It is with a sense of respect, humility, gratitude, and obligation that we creationists assume our role as stewards of our Master's estate. We care for God's handiwork, not to please ourselves with personal comfort, but to please our Creator. We are to have fellowship with Him. Creationists acknowledge men's unique position as stewards: We rule creation, and yet we, ourselves, are created.

Evolutionists also recognize man's unique position in respect to the natural world. They, however, face a distinct contradiction. How can man, who has arisen by an evolutionary process *from* nature, assert himself in dominion *over* it? As Rene Dubos so aptly observed:

> *We must learn to live with a paradox inherent in the human condition. On the one hand, man is still of nature, but he has lived outside nature in artificial environments since the agricultural revolution. Human ways of life must of course be compatible with natural laws, but they cannot be the ways of nature.*[5]

In other words, from the evolutionist's view, man is a product of nature. But, unlike any other "animal," he has evolved to a point where he stands outside of, and in opposition to, the very nature which supposedly produced him.

The evolutionist faces this contradiction because he defines nature (including man) in terms of itself. Man, the evolutionist asserts, must be understood apart from God. In 1931, Kurt Goedel gave a mathematical proof that a system of axioms can never be based on itself. In order to prove the system's validity, statements from *outside* that system must be used. This concept has been applied to science, i.e., science is possible only within a larger context of non-science issues and concerns.[6]

The creationist perspective, unlike the evolutionist's, is fully rational. This enables us to understand ourselves and nature. We can explain our unique position within the creation. We are natural (or physical) just as are all other creatures. However, we are also transnatural (or spiritual), in that we are created "in the image of God." We have the power to comprehend and rule over nature. The closer that image is to God, the better our understanding and rule of nature will be. The more intimate our fellowship is with our Maker, the better we can care for what was created. Thus, man's dominion is reflected in our relationship with God. It is an avenue, a primary activity, whereby we can become more like our Maker, for it requires us to exercise our highest faculties. It is, then, God's dominion over man which necessarily defines, delimits, and rationalizes man's dominion over nature. Thus, the physical and the spiritual, the body and the soul, are harmonized into one. Instead of an inexplicable "paradox," creationists recognize a marvelous duality.

C. S. Lewis likewise seems to have recognized this principle, for he wrote:

> *As long as one is a Naturalist, "Nature" is only a word for "everything." And everything is not a subject about which anything very interesting can be said or (save by illusion) felt. . . . And then, because we falsely take her for the ultimate and self-existent Fact and cannot quite repress our high instinct to worship the Self-existent, we are all at sea and our moods fluctuate and Nature means to us whatever we please as the moods select and slur. But everything becomes different when we recognize that Nature is a creature, a created thing, with its own particular tang or flavour. . . . It is not in her, but in Something far beyond her, that all lines meet and all contrasts are explained.*

Lewis later added:

> *The Englishness of English is audible only to those who know some other language as well. In the same way and for the same reason, only Supernaturalists really see Nature. You must go a little away from her, and then turn around, and look back. Then at last the true landscape will become visible. You must have tasted, however briefly, the pure water from beyond the world before you can be distinctly conscious of the hot, salty tang of Nature's current. To treat her as God, or as Everything, is to lose the whole pith and pleasure of her. Come out, look back, and then you will see. . . .*[7]

Of course, the original Edenic perfection no longer exists. Nature can be harsh; life is not always pleasant. Creationists understand that the single biggest reason for environmental degradation is our sin. The willful disobedience of man spoiled the original perfect harmony. Because our relationship with God was tainted, our ability to rule the earth wisely was also spoiled. In order to become reconciled to creation, we must become reconciled to God. This reconciliation occurs through the medium of Jesus Christ. The harshness of nature is, therefore, not a justification for ruthless reciprocity, but a reminder of sin and a call to repentance.

As an antithesis to conventional evolutionism, our creation concept has two features: closure and theism. By closure is meant the idea that God created a complete, perfect, and purposeful universe, with a definite beginning and end; it has temporal, spatial boundaries. By theism is meant the belief that God, though external to His creation, is nevertheless everywhere immanent and transcendent, lovingly sustaining and operating the world.

These two features are noticeable also in the moral sphere. Creationists believe that God has given us a set of moral values which are final and complete and which serve as an external standard for human conduct, thus providing moral boundaries. Furthermore, God's loving care and sustenance are necessary for our continuous moral and spiritual life. By contrast, the nontheistic evolutionist holds moral issues to be without closure or bounds—open-ended, and subject to continuous change. Man must sustain himself; he must save himself.

Creationists have demonstrated environmental awareness. For instance, one of the founders of the conservation movement was a creation scientist. While Charles Darwin and others were searching for materialistic explanations of life in the 1850's, one of America's best-known scientists, Louis Agassiz, was lecturing at Harvard University on the need for conservation of our land's resources.[8] How long was this form of environmental concern, initiated by a creation scientist, delayed, because of a preoccupation with evolution and materialism?

Certainly Christians have not always lived up to Biblical standards, and, to the extent that we have not, we have contributed to environmental problems. This is especially true of liberal churches which have led the way in compromising Scripture with evolutionism and other secular ideas. But, the Biblical basis for environmental concern is still there. By recognizing the historicity of the Genesis account, the Bible-believing Christian has a firm foundation for articulating a sound philosophy of ecology. It is a

philosophy which does not suffer from the extremism of "doom-and-gloom" projections which demand radical social change, nor from "hysterical optimism" in technology, as man's omnipotent savior.

Creationists recognize severe environmental problems which require our attention. We know our primary purpose. It is not the pursuit of material comfort or the service of nature; it is, rather, to be obedient to our Creator and Redeemer in all things. We recognize that true prosperity is a gift of God, not ultimately of market mechanisms or government control. We know that when individuals or nations serve Him, He blesses. Creationists welcome technological and industrial development, but not at the expense of God's creation, for stewardship is part of our duty to our Maker. It is a philosophy which allows us to prioritize and ameliorate many environmental problems while preserving Biblical Christian values.

What do creationists see at the Grand Canyon? Do we visualize a directionless process which, after the passage of geologic ages, has given rise to an animal which can finally control physical and social evolution? No! We see purpose, completeness, and constancy in both the physical and moral worlds. Salvation comes neither from man nor nature, but from the Creator and Redeemer of both. Indeed, the conservation of Biblical principles and values is indispensable to the conservation of creation.

NOTES—Chapter 1

1. For an extensive analysis of Biblical reasons why Noah's Flood was global, see John C. Whitcomb, Jr., and Henry M. Morris, *The Genesis Flood* (Philadelphia: Presbyterian and Reformed Publishing Co., 1961). A recent rebuttal to claims that the Bible describes a local flood is found in John C. Whitcomb, *The World that Perished* (Grand Rapids: Baker Book House, second edition, 1988), pp. 19–46. Also see the strong Scriptural and geological arguments in Ronald F. Youngblood, ed, *The Genesis Debate* (New York: Thomas Nelson, 1986), pp. 210–229.

2. For geologic evidences for Flood deposition of Grand Canyon strata, see chapters 3 and 4.

3. For geologic evidences for catastrophic post-Flood erosion of Grand Canyon, see chapter 5.

4. An excellent discussion of the deeper theological and Biblical issues of death, pain, and suffering with respect to God's creation is found in Nigel M. de S. Cameron, *Evolution and the Authority of the Bible* (Exeter, UK: The Paternoster Press, 1983) pp. 61–71.

5. Quoted in G. Tyler Miller, Jr., *Living in the Environment: Concepts, Problems, and Alternatives* (Belmont, CA: Wadsworth Publishing Company, 1975), p. 40.

6. Victor F. Weisskopf, "Frontiers and Limits of Science," *American Scientist* 65 (1977): 405–411. See also Ernest Nagel and James R. Newman, *Goedel's Proof* (New York University Press, 1958). From the foregoing definition, a violation of Goedel's Theorem would involve an attempt to prove or define a system in its own terms (i.e., using statements from *inside* the system).

7. C. S. Lewis, *Miracles: A Preliminary Study* (New York: MacMillan, 1947), pp. 65–67.

8. J. Edwin Becht and L. Belzung, *World Resource Management: Key to Civilization and Social Achievement* (Englewood Cliffs, NJ: Prentice-Hall, 1975), p. 35.

Chapter 2

GEOLOGIC STRUCTURE OF GRAND CANYON

"Where wast thou when I laid the foundations of the earth?
Declare, if thou hast understanding.
Who hath laid the measures thereof, if thou knowest?
Or who hath stretched the line upon it?
Whereupon are the foundations thereof fastened?
Or who laid the cornerstone thereof?"
Job 38:4–6

Graphic Tools

The earth is a three-dimensional object. It contains geologic structures such as strata, faults, and folds which have orientation and inclination in space. The topographic form of the earth's surface is often determined by these structures. Figure 2.1 shows some of the important topographic forms of the Grand Canyon region drawn as a block diagram. We see the plateau, mesa, butte, and pinnacle (also called a "spire" or "temple"). These highland features, which have formed by erosion in the flat strata, are common in the Grand Canyon region. More-resistant strata (sandstone or limestone) tend to endure as caps to elevated platforms (plateaus, mesas, and buttes), whereas less-resistant strata (shale) tend to be incised deeply to form slopes and valleys.

Sometimes three-dimensional structures are difficult to visualize, so geologists often plot them, using two-dimensional graphic tools. The most commonly employed graphic tools are the geologic map, geologic cross section, geologic block diagram, and strata column diagram.

Geologic Map - The accurate representation of the distribution of rock units and/or geologic structures of an area forms a geologic map. Such a map is drawn to scale, with distances shown by a simple scale bar or by a representative fraction. The fraction 1:62,500 means that one foot on the map equals 62,500 feet over the earth's surface (one inch equals one mile). Geologic maps also show very precise location information, such as a land-survey coordinate system of some type. Geologists take great care in plotting data on these maps, using standardized symbols. Geologic maps almost always have marginal notes which describe the symbols being used.

Geologic Cross Section - Once the geologic map of an area has been made, a line is drawn along the map, and the geologist attempts to sketch the rock units and structures

on the vertical plane *under* the line. The geologic cross section shows the distribution and orientation of rock units and structures at depth inside the earth. These are sometimes the geologist's best guess. If drill-core data are available, the interpretation of the underground structure can be more certain. Sometimes the geologic cross section is drawn with vertical exaggeration, so that the rock strata and structure can be visualized more easily.

Geologic Block Diagram - A six-sided block of the earth can be used to visualize geologic structures. A two-dimensional drawing of the block shows three sides of the block viewed in perspective from above and to one side. One surface of the block depicts the surface of the earth or "map view." The two other surfaces of the block show two vertical-plane, geologic cross sections oriented at right angles to each other. Figure 2.1 is an example of a geologic block diagram.

Figure 2.2 shows five geologic block diagrams which help us to visualize important geologic structures.[1] Block "a" shows a *fault*: a surface within the earth along which movement of adjacent rocks has occurred. Grand Canyon rocks, in many areas, exhibit the mismatch of strata, which

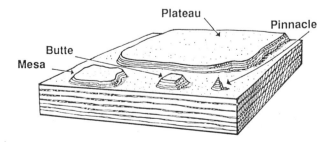

Figure 2.1 *Important topographic forms of the Grand Canyon region. The plateau, mesa, butte, and pinnacle are erosional features which developed in flat strata due to different resistances to erosion.*

is the proof that a fault exists. Geologists often measure the displacement which has occurred on a fault and carefully note the mass of earth which has moved upward relative to the mass of earth which has moved downward. In Block "a," the right side has moved upward relative to the left side.

Block "b" of figure 2.2 shows a *monocline*: a fold structure in which the strata flex only in one direction from the horizontal. Strata of the Kaibab and Coconino Plateaus were uplifted more than 2,000 feet above surrounding areas, by monoclines on the east end of Grand Canyon. In fact, many plateaus in northern Arizona were upwarped along monoclines. Geologists believe that monoclines were caused by the flexing of strata over deeply buried faults in crystalline rocks which lie concealed beneath the strata.

Blocks "c" and "d" of figure 2.2 show fold structures in which strata flex in two directions. The *anticline*, or arch structure, is a fold in which strata flex in two directions, dipping *away* from the center of the fold. Upwarp of rock in the center forms the anticline. The opposite structure is the *syncline*, or downwarp structure, where the fold flexes strata in two directions, dipping *toward* the center of the fold. Downwarp of rock in the center forms the syncline. In Grand Canyon, anticlines and synclines are very subtle structures with only very gentle flexing of strata from the horizontal orientation.

Block "e" of figure 2.2 shows an *unconformity*: a surface of erosion or nondeposition which is buried within the earth. Strata in the lower part of the diagram were flexed to form a plunging syncline, the rocks were later eroded, and, finally, horizontal strata in the upper part of the diagram were deposited. An unconformity also can occur where stratified rocks cover nonstratified rocks. Specific types of unconformities are the *angular unconformity, disconformity, paraconformity* and *nonconformity* Definitions are found in the Glossary (Appendix E) and discussion is found in chapter 3.

Strata-Column Diagram - The geologic map and cross section of an area can be used to show the strata sequence in a diagram. Usually, strata are drawn to scale by superimposing them on one another as if no tilting or disruption had moved them. A strata-column diagram usually has a description of the strata, beginning with the oldest at the base and proceeding to the youngest at the top. The strata-column diagram is very useful for interpreting the historical sequence of events which occurred to form the strata and other structures.

Grand Canyon Structures

Geologic maps, geologic cross sections, geologic block diagrams, and strata column diagrams make invaluable tools for visualizing the earth's crust in three dimensions. Faults, folds, unconformities, and the orientation of strata are better

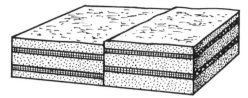
a. FAULT

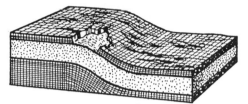
b. MONOCLINE

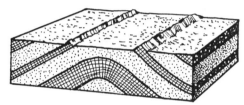
c. ANTICLINE

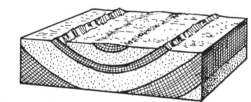
d. SYNCLINE

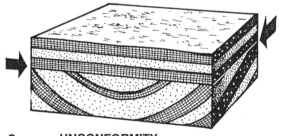
e. UNCONFORMITY

Figure 2.2 *Geologic block diagrams comparing important rock structures.*
a. *Fault with upward displacement on its right side relative to its left side.*
b. *Monocline with upward flexure on its left side.*
c. *Anticline or upwarp structure with older strata in the center.*
d. *Syncline or downwarp structure with younger strata in the center.*
e. *Unconformity (buried erosion surface) where flat strata overlie eroded strata, which form a syncline.*

understood by using these geologic tools. Geologists even use these to prospect for oil, gas, coal, and minerals. Sometimes special maps are drawn to show just one type of geologic data (e.g., rock structure symbols are plotted without geologic formations).

The following pages contain many geologic maps and cross sections. Each of the geologic maps needs symbols with which to help you interpret each map. These have been included to help you picture, in three dimension, the earth's structure at Grand Canyon. Take some time to study them. An amazing amount of information has been packed into geologic maps and cross sections!

The Colorado Plateau is a major physiographic region of the United States. It occupies 130,000 square miles of the Four Corners states. The plateau stretches northward from central Arizona into Utah and eastward to the Rocky Mountains in Colorado and New Mexico.

Figure 2.3 is a summary map which shows the main geologic structures of the southwestern part of the Colorado Plateau. Grand Canyon in northern Arizona is eroded through smaller plateaus, which together compose the larger plateau. These smaller plateaus have been uplifted as much

as 9,000 feet above sea level. They are bounded by faults on the west and by monoclines on the east. The faults on the west (Grand Wash, Hurricane, and Toroweap faults) have uplift on their east side. The East Kaibab Monocline on the east is a fold structure uplifting strata on its west side. San Francisco Mountains are a large complex of volcanoes. The eroded canyon country in southern Utah includes Zion Canyon and Bryce Canyon.

A north-to-south geologic cross section of the Grand Canyon area is shown in figure 2.4. The cross section begins in the north near Cedar City, Utah (city's location in figure 2.3) and proceeds southward to Grand Canyon.[2] Up to 13,000 feet of strata are believed to overlie crystalline basement rock in southern Utah. Many of these strata have been drilled while exploring for oil. In Utah, at Cedar City, the strata are broken by the Hurricane Fault, which has more than 6,000 feet of displacement. There, the same strata as at Grand Canyon are buried under more recent strata. The upwarp structure which forms the Kaibab Plateau is also obvious from the geologic cross section. Deep within the Grand Canyon, the cross section exposes tilted and eroded strata which lie below flat strata. The boundary

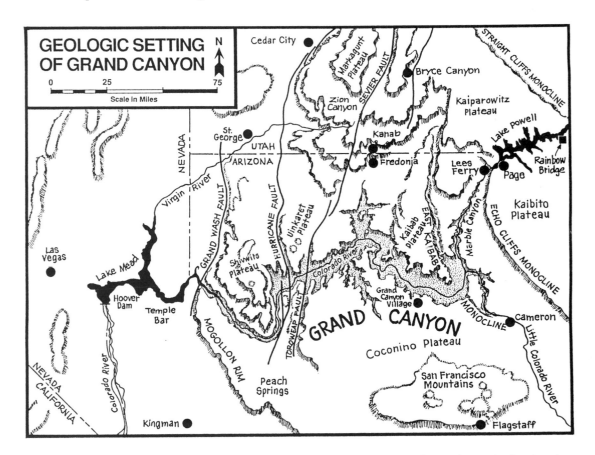

Figure 2.3 *Geologic setting of Grand Canyon. This summary map shows the main geologic structures of the southwestern part of the Colorado Plateau. Grand Canyon in northern Arizona is eroded through uplifted plateaus bounded by faults on the west and by monoclines on the east. The faults on the west (Grand Wash, Hurricane, and Toroweap faults) have uplift on their east sides. The East Kaibab Monocline on the east is a fold structure uplifting strata on its west side. San Francisco Mountains are a large complex of volcanoes. The eroded canyon country in southern Utah includes Zion Canyon and Bryce Canyon. Grand Wash Fault and the Mogollon Rim define the southwestern edge of the Colorado Plateau.*

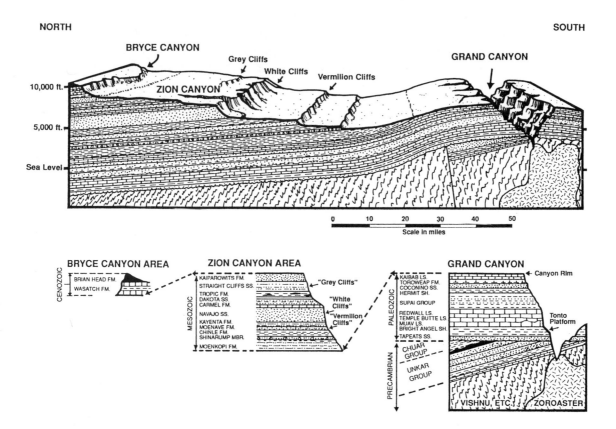

Figure 2.4 *North-south geologic cross-section from southeast of Cedar City, Utah to Grand Canyon, Arizona. The local area strata are shown with names of formations outcropping at the surface. The vertical exaggeration is twelve times horizontal scale. Abbreviations used: FM. = formation; SS. = sandstone; SH. = shale; LS. = limestone; MBR. = member.*

between the tilted and flat strata is known as an angular unconformity. Names applied to the strata are shown in strata column diagrams below the geologic cross section.

A more detailed representation of Grand Canyon strata is shown in figure 2.5. This figure is a block diagram depicting the eroded strata which occur along the Colorado River and under the north rim of Grand Canyon. Again, the rocks are shown with vertical exaggeration, which allows the compositions of different formations to be represented by symbols. Sedimentary rocks, which accumulated at the earth's surface by the action of water or wind, are shown by a pattern of dots, bricks, or dashed lines. The dot pattern represents *sandstone*, the brick pattern represents *limestone*, and the dashed-line pattern represents *shale*. The combination of dots and dashes represents *siltstone*. Igneous rocks, which crystallized from a molten condition, are shown in solid black (representing lava flows of basaltic composition) and as randomly oriented dashes (representing molten materials which appear to have cooled underground, with granitic composition). Metamorphic rocks (schist and gneiss), which have been changed by heat and pressure, are represented by short, bent lines. Definitions of these various rocks are found in the Glossary (Appendix E) at the end of this book.

The naming of rock strata by geologists follows certain guidelines. Geologists try to divide all rock strata of a region into vertically successive units of distinctive composition. The fundamental strata unit is what geologists call a "formation." The formation is the fundamental strata unit of distinctive rock composition, usually a few hundred feet in thickness. The unit is important to geologists because it can be mapped on a scale of one inch equaling one mile, and because it can be shown on most geologic cross sections.

Almost all of the names shown on strata in figure 2.5 are formally described-and-recognized formations in Grand Canyon. Sometimes two or more vertically contiguous formations are classified as a "group." This term is the next higher category above the formation. The Supai Group, shown in figure 2.5, is composed of four vertically successive formations.

Because figure 2.5 shows the layers of rocks so well, we can appreciate the organization and structure of rocks in Grand Canyon. The non-stratified "basement" rocks of Grand Canyon include the Zoroaster Granite (igneous rocks) and the Vishnu Schist (metamorphic rocks). An *unconformity*, a buried surface of erosion, occurs between the first stratified rock body, the Bass Limestone, and Vishnu Schist beneath it. The package of strata named Bass through Cardenas is inclined, and lies buried beneath the

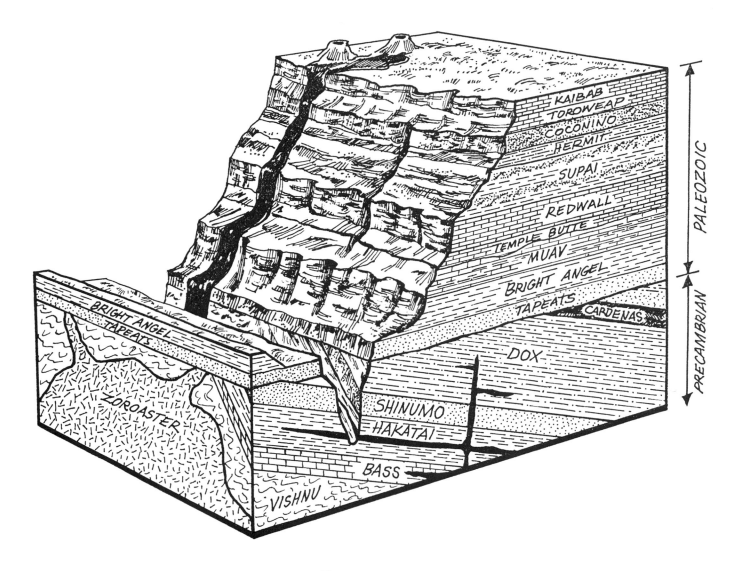

ROCK TYPES

SEDIMENTARY ROCKS

- Sandstone
- Siltstone
- Shale
- Limestone

IGNEOUS ROCKS

- Basaltic Rocks
- Diabase (sills & dikes)
- Granite

METAMORPHIC ROCKS

- Schist & Gneiss

Figure 2.5 *Geologic block diagram showing rock structure and topographic form below the north rim of Grand Canyon.*

flat-lying strata named Tapeats through Kaibab. Again, the tilted strata are separated from the flat-lying strata by an *unconformity*—a buried surface of erosion. Volcanic rocks of the composition of basalt issued from local volcanoes on the north rim, and are also found deeply buried (Cardenas Basalt). The Bass, Hakatai, Shinumo, and Dox formations are penetrated at intervals by black rocks of basaltic composition, called diabase. These basaltic-composition rocks have been called *dikes* (which cross-cut strata) and *sills* (which penetrate along stratification between the layers). They are believed to have been molten material which was injected into cracks within the strata.

Figure 2.5 also conveys something of the topographic form associated with Grand Canyon rocks. This form is accentuated by vertical exaggeration. The flat plateau surface is generally concordant with the upper surface of the Kaibab Limestone, and suggests the resistance of limestone to erosion. The broader portions of the Canyon, below the rim, have a depth of 4,000 feet and a width of from 4 to 18 miles. The broadest parts of the Canyon occur in the flat strata, with resistant limestone and sandstone strata tending to form cliffs, and less-resistant shale strata tending to form slopes. The narrowest part of the Canyon, with the steepest cliffs, is the inner gorge near the Colorado River. This inner gorge, with a depth of about 900 feet and a width of often less than one-half mile, is best expressed within the diagonally tilted strata and the crystalline basement rocks. It is noteworthy that the block diagram shows no fault or fold structure parallel to the direction along which Grand Canyon has been eroded. Thus, there does not appear to be any direct structural cause or control for the location of Grand Canyon.

Figure 2.6 is a generalized geologic map of northern Arizona and an east-west geologic cross section through the area just north of Grand Canyon. The map and geologic cross section have a very small horizontal scale: one inch equals thirty-eight miles. Because of the small scale of the geologic map in figure 2.6, only groups of formations can be shown. The map depicts only those formations which appear at the surface of the earth. The northwestern Arizona region shown on the map is dominated by the Kaibab Limestone (map abbreviation "Pk") which forms the surface of many of the plateaus. Grand Canyon is eroded through these plateaus and exposes formations beneath the Kaibab Limestone. Several of the plateaus in northwestern Arizona have a surface covering of volcanic rocks (map abbreviation "QTv").

Both figures 2.5 and 2.6 use nomenclature which suggests the correlation of Grand Canyon strata to strata in the rest of the world. figure 2.5 uses the words "Precambrian" and "Paleozoic;" figure 2.6 uses the words "Precambrian," "Cambrian," "Pennsylvanian," "Permian," "Triassic," "Jurassic," "Tertiary" and

"Quaternary." This nomenclature indicates the strata correlation, especially correlations with "type systems" of strata in Europe. Use of these words suggests the belief of the geologist who composed the map or diagram, as to how the strata correlate between continents. It should be pointed out that no strata system is physically continuous between North America and Europe.

While it is proper for geologists to seek to correlate strata over wide areas, there is some objectionable "baggage" which has been attached to strata-system nomenclature.[3] When we hear the word "Cambrian," for example, we are supposed to recall the strata of the type system located in Cambria, in Wales, Great Britain. However, the word may also bring to mind a popular "picture" promoted by either books, films, schools, or museums. This "picture" for *Cambrian* at the Smithsonian Institution in Washington, D.C., for example, shows supposed primitive earth conditions, specific environments with sediments being slowly deposited, inferred "transitional organisms" evolving toward familiar forms, and whole communities of organisms "at home," with other organisms absent. In short, the museum is asking us to contemplate a picture of a "geologic age" of 100 million years' duration which, supposedly, occurred 500 million years ago. This picture, an obvious *interpretation* of Cambrian strata, is offensive to creationists. How the strata were deposited is the subject of chapter 3. The ages assigned to strata systems are the topic of chapter 6, and the fossils of strata systems are the subject of chapter 7.

Returning to figure 2.6, we note that it also contains a geologic cross section showing where the plateaus in northern Arizona have been uplifted along faults and folds. The base of the cross section is below sea level. Major displacement along the Grand Wash Fault has uplifted, by thousands of feet, the Shivwitz Plateau above the Lake Mead area on its west. Other faults with vertical displacements define the Uinkaret, Kanab, and Kaibab Plateaus. The most significant total vertical uplift occurred to form the Kaibab Plateau, which has an elevation of as much as 9,000 feet above sea level. It has the general form of an anticline. It is bounded by faults on its west side, and folded strata on its east side. Because the highest uplift occurred in association with the Kaibab Plateau, it is frequently referred to as the "Kaibab Upwarp." Some concept of the fold structure known as the East Kaibab Monocline is seen in the lower diagram of figure 2.6. Here inclined strata are shown on the east side of the Kaibab Plateau. The vertical exaggeration of the cross section, however, makes the inclination appear greater than it actually is.

The geologic cross section shown in figure 2.6 is drawn with the vertical axis exaggerated ten times the horizontal axis. Such vertical exaggeration of the cross section is

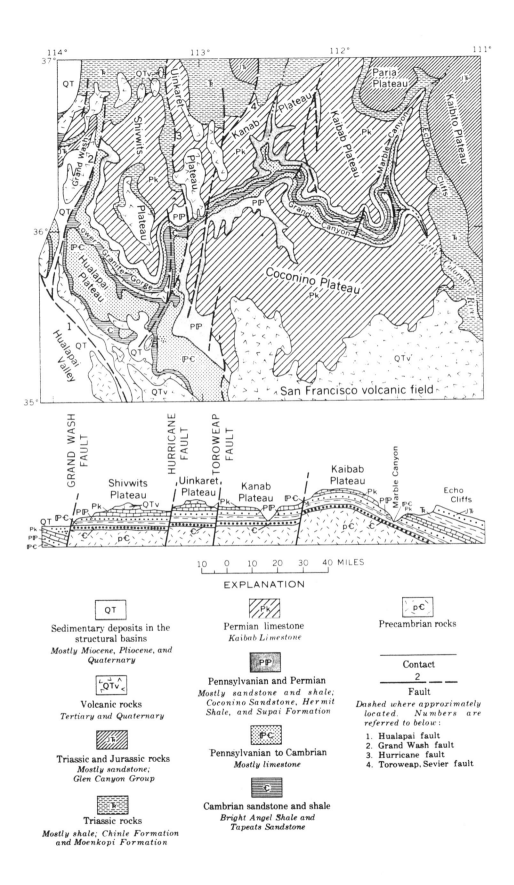

Figure 2.6 *Geologic map and east-west geologic cross section of northwestern Arizona (modified from C. B. Hunt).*[4]

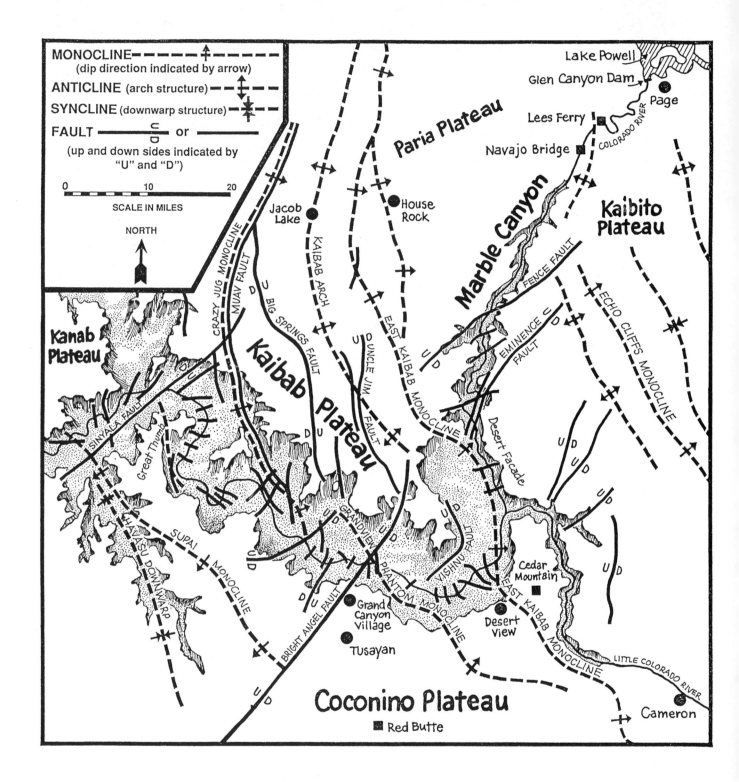

Figure 2.7 *Geologic structure map of eastern Grand Canyon. The area is dominated by north-northwest-trending fold structures (especially monoclines) and northeast-trending faults.[5] The East Kaibab Monocline marks the eastern boundary of the Kaibab Upwarp, the most elevated plateau in Arizona. Geologists are astonished by the fact that the Canyon is perpendicular to the geologic structure. Solid circles (●) on the map indicate small towns or villages, whereas solid squares (■) indicate noteworthy man-made or natural features. Geologic structure symbols are defined in the legend of the map in the upper left corner.*

Figure 2.8 *The East Kaibab Monocline in the extreme eastern Grand Canyon. This northward, aerial view from above the extreme eastern Grand Canyon shows inclined strata coming off the north rim. Three thousand feet of upwarping (called the "Kaibab Upwarp") has occurred on the left (west) side relative to the right (east), which has caused limestone strata of the Kaibab Formation in the center of the photo to be tilted. (Photo by Steven A. Austin.)*

necessary, if the stratification is to be shown. Without the exaggeration, the thickness of strata and the depths of canyons would be virtually indistinguishable. If no vertical exaggeration were shown, however, we could better appreciate the level nature of the uplifted plateau. It is a source of wonder, among geologists, that uplift of such magnitude over an enormous area (more than 100,000 square miles) could be accomplished so uniformly. We marvel at the resulting high tableland of the Colorado Plateau which is crossed by just a few folds and faults.

Figure 2.7 shows the eastern Grand Canyon in more detail, with some of its principal geologic structures. Four important north-trending monoclines are the Echo Cliffs Monocline, the East Kaibab Monocline, the Grandview-Phantom Monocline, and the Crazy Jug Monocline. It is significant that Marble Canyon opens abruptly to form the Canyon, where it is crossed by the East Kaibab Monocline. For a distance of 15 miles, the course of the Colorado River follows the East Kaibab Monocline, and then the Canyon deviates from the structure. Through the major uplifted area between the Kaibab and Coconino Plateaus, the Grand Canyon cuts *across* the principal geologic structure. Hundreds of smaller faults cross the river and influence side-canyon development.

Figure 2.8 shows the geologic structure of the East Kaibab Monocline in the extreme eastern Grand Canyon. In the upper right corner of figure 2.8, strata of the Kaibab

Formation have an elevation of 6,000 feet. These same strata rise to 9,000 feet elevation in the upper left corner of figure 2.8. The 3,000-foot change in elevation of the once-horizontal formation was not accomplished by a fault, but by a fold structure (monocline), by tilting of the strata in the center of figure 2.8. The structure formed is the East Kaibab Monocline on the eastern boundary of the Kaibab Upwarp.

The limestones of the Kaibab Formation were not the only strata affected by the tremendous upwarping in eastern Grand Canyon. All rocks beneath the Kaibab Formation were flexed, as well. Figure 2.9 shows remarkable bending of the Tapeats Sandstone in a deep canyon near the Colorado River. Here, in figure 2.9, we see where deep erosion has revealed lower strata within the East Kaibab Monocline. Intense buckling forces caused once-horizontal sandstone strata to be turned into vertical orientation. Such strata give us a better appreciation of the magnitude and scale of geologic forces which have deformed the earth.

Why should the *westward* course of the Colorado River and the *westward* orientation of the Canyon deviate so strongly from the *northward* geologic structure? That is an observation causing wonder and amazement among geologists. There is, for example, no fault or downwarp structure directing the position of the Colorado River or the orientation of Grand Canyon. It and the river clearly *cut across* that structure. Furthermore, the cross-cut of the

Figure 2.9 *Geologic structure within Carbon Canyon in the extreme eastern Grand Canyon. The uplift associated with the East Kaibab Monocline has caused strata of the Tapeats Sandstone to be tightly flexed into vertical orientation. The view is toward the south, and the upwarp is on the right (west) side. People provide scale for this figure. (Photo by Steven A. Austin.)*

structure is not merely local, it extends 200 miles along the river westward through northern Arizona! The Canyon's position relative to the geologic structure has inspired a great debate concerning how Grand Canyon was eroded, which is the topic of chapter 5.

Summary

Geologists use graphic tools to depict the three-dimensional geologic structure of the earth. The most common graphic tools are the geologic map, the geologic cross section, the geologic block diagram, and the strata-column diagram. The Grand Canyon of northern Arizona occurs among a series of immense plateaus uplifted as much as 9,000 feet above sea level along north-trending faults and along north-trending monoclines. The level nature of this uplift is indicated by its flat blanket of 4,000 feet of sandstone, limestone, and shale strata. How such great uplift could be so uniform over an enormous area continues to be a source of wonder. Even more amazing is the westward orientation of Grand Canyon within the plateau. Grand Canyon, Earth's most amazing erosional wonder, *cuts across* the geologic structure to a depth of a mile, through a distance of 200 miles!

NOTES—Chapter 2

1. Definitions of geologic structures are in accordance with generally accepted geologic practice as given by R. L. Bates and J. A. Jackson, eds., *Glossary of Geology* (Washington, D. C., American Geological Institute, 1980, second edition), 749 pp.

2. The geologic cross section is modified from *Geologic Cross Section of the Cedar Breaks—Zion—Grand Canyon Region* (Springdale, Utah, Zion Natural History Association, 1975), single sheet.

3. S. A. Austin, "Ten Misconceptions About the Geologic Column," *Institute for Creation Research Impact* 137 (November 1984): 1–4.

4. C. B. Hunt, "Geologic History of the Colorado River," *in* "The Colorado River Region and John Wesley Powell," *U.S. Geological Survey Professional Paper* 669–C (1969): 114.

5. The primary data sources for figure 2.7 are:

    P. W. Huntoon, "Phanerozoic Structural Geology of the Grand Canyon," *in* S.S. Beus and M. Morales, eds., *Grand Canyon Geology* (New York, Oxford University Press, 1990), pp. 261–309.

    P. W. Huntoon, *et al.*, *Geologic Map of the Eastern Part of the Grand Canyon National Park, Arizona* (Grand Canyon, Arizona, Grand Canyon Natural History Association, 1986), scale 1:62,500, one sheet.

    R. T. Moore, E. D. Wilson, and R. T. O'Haire, *Geologic Map of Coconino County* (Tucson, Arizona, Arizona Bureau of Mines, 1960), scale 1:375,000, one sheet.

Chapter 3

INTERPRETING STRATA OF GRAND CANYON

". . . the thought grew in to my mind that the canyons of this region would be a Book of Revelations in the rock-leaved Bible of geology. . . . I determined to read the book"

John Wesley Powell, 1870

Reading the Book

John Wesley Powell, the first geologist to explore Grand Canyon, began in 1869 what geologists will never finish—the complete description and deciphering of the rocks of Grand Canyon. The rock strata of Grand Canyon were regarded by Powell as "a Book of Revelations in the rock-leaved Bible of geology." He wrote, "I determined to read the book." For more than 120 years, geologists, by the thousands, have been visiting Grand Canyon for the purpose of "reading" the same book.

A few years ago, two more geologists came to Grand Canyon. Both geologists had Ph.D. degrees from American universities, both were familiar with the explorations of previous geologists before them, and both were personally involved in the study of the rocks of Grand Canyon. In spite of their common education, background, and research, the two geologists had different conclusions concerning Grand Canyon strata. One geologist said, "I see no evidence of a great flood forming Grand Canyon." The other geologist said, "I see evidence for powerful flood processes forming Grand Canyon." It is obvious that these two geologists had come to different conclusions!

When the first geologist said, "I see no evidence of a great flood forming Grand Canyon," what did he mean? Were geologists there to witness the formation of Grand Canyon? No, they were not there when strata were deposited or erosion occurred. Thus, in the strictest sense, geologists do not "see" or "observe" the history of Grand Canyon. They only decipher the clues remaining in the earth concerning that history. They simply "see" data for or against a particular interpretation.

A geologist's conclusion concerning the ancient events that formed Grand Canyon is, therefore, an *interpretation*, not an observation. What is interesting concerning the two geologists, is that both had the *same data* on which to base their interpretations of the history of Grand Canyon. How could they possibly come to mutually exclusive, directly opposing conclusions?

The answer to this rather disturbing question is found by recognizing that "data" (rock strata and fossils of Grand Canyon) *do not* dictate or determine the conclusions of geologists. Rock strata and fossils are *used* by geologists to build their interpretations of history. How, then, do geologists "use" data?

As in other fields of study, data of interest to the geologist are evaluated by placing them into some type of interpretive framework. This framework consists of a series of premises or postulates, from which conclusions concerning the meaning of the raw data are derived, using logic. The logic used is deductive. The premises or postulates are assumed; then, logic leads from data to conclusions. Figure 3.1 shows the geologist's method of interpreting data. It is important to notice that conclusions drawn using deductive logic, can be only as valid as the original premises. These premises that form the interpretive framework are held to a large degree in faith by the individual geologist.

The use of the interpretive framework, composed of a set of premises, can be illustrated by the method used by a geologist as he studies a sedimentary rock stratum in

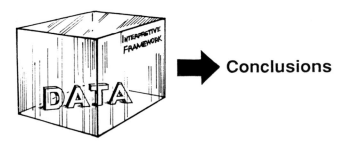

Figure 3.1 *The interpretive framework is used to draw conclusions from the data.*

Grand Canyon. One of the most basic premises held is that the stratum under investigation has *historical* significance—it represents the results of processes which operated during a past interval of time, and, therefore, is worthy of historical study. This assumption rejects two other premises, which suppose that the stratum either was created instantly or has existed eternally. Geologists, universally, recognize the historic significance of strata.

A second premise, dependent on the first, which the geologist may hold as he studies the stratum, is that its origin can be explained by sedimentary processes of the same *kind* as those which occur today. The geologist might assume that the stratum was accumulated as particles settled from water. This assumes that certain laws of nature (gravity, momentum, molecular bonds, etc.) were the same in the past as when the stratum is observed.

A third, much more controversial premise which the geologist *may* hold, is that the origin of the stratum can be best explained by sedimentary processes whose *rates* approximate those observed today. This premise maintains that two other explanations—(1) the stratum was deposited very rapidly (e.g., a one-foot stratum being deposited in minutes), and (2) the stratum was deposited very slowly (the one-foot stratum being deposited over a period of several million years)—are not to be preferred over the explanation that is more consistent with presently observed rates (the one-foot stratum being deposited over a period of about 1 to 1,000 years). This premise assumes that process and material conditions of the past are substantially of the same rate, scale, or intensity as those of the present. What is "normal" or "average" today, is being assumed also for the past.[1]

Many other premises are used by the historical geologist as he interprets the significance of the stratum. Some are trivial, and are accepted by all rational people (example: the geologist must believe his senses give him an accurate perception of the stratum). Other premises may be very specific and controversial (example: the geologist may have a bias concerning the stratum because of cultural, political, religious, or philosophical background). In order to be consistent, the geologist attempts to select those premises which are in agreement with his total world view. The sum total of these premises forms the interpretive framework.

The important point to notice is that conclusions we draw using deductive logic, can be only as valid as the original premises which form the framework. As figure 3.2 shows, it is possible to draw very different conclusions concerning particular data, or even from all of the data, if different frameworks (initial premises) are used. Only then can we understand why geologists "see" different things, when they look at Grand Canyon rocks.

Evolution and creation form different interpretive frameworks that geologists use to interpret Grand Canyon.

Both acknowledge that *water* was the primary agent which has formed Grand Canyon. Evolutionists frequently make the uniformitarian assumption that strata of Grand Canyon formed during long ages, as oceans slowly advanced and retreated over the North American continent. Sediment accumulated during millions of years, according to evolutionists, in or next to great calm and tranquil seas. Lime mud was supposed to have settled out extremely slowly in the quiet tropical seas, forming limestone strata. Evolutionists believe that clay and sand were added to the ocean by rivers, which, over enormous periods of time, built up prograding delta deposits of shale and sandstone. Each strata formation of Grand Canyon is thought to have accumulated in response to slow changes in the level of the sea.

Creationists usually make the catastrophist assumption that a global flood was responsible for depositing a great thickness of Grand Canyon strata. Different strata (sandstone, shale, and limestone) were accumulated as flood waters changed depth, velocity, and direction of movement. Some strata may have accumulated during many hundreds of years before the catastrophe, but creationists suppose that most of the Grand Canyon strata, exposed so obviously today, were deposited rapidly, during a single advancing and retreating flood.

We know why both evolutionist and creationist explanations of Grand Canyon strata exist. These *interpretations* of strata are determined by the *presuppositions* or *bias* of the interpreter. If one begins with the uniformitarian model, that sedimentation occurred in calm and placid seas, an evolutionary interpretation of thick strata sequences will be derived. However, if one

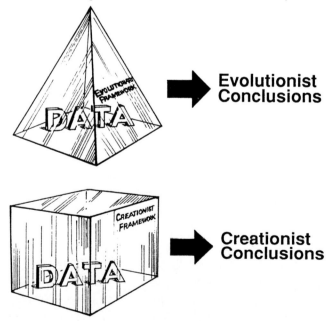

Figure 3.2 *Illustrations showing how two different interpretive frameworks can be used to derive **opposing** conclusions from the **same** data.*

starts with a catastrophist framework, that sedimentation has occurred in response to catastrophic agents, a creationist interpretation is given to thick strata sequences. Conclusions, therefore, are derived from assumptions.

Researchers are often afflicted with a serious malady: *they rarely recognize the tentative and controlling natures of their interpretive frameworks.* This is especially apparent in the creation/evolution controversy.

Davis A. Young, a Christian geologist, adopts the uniformitarian framework, and does not acknowledge a legitimate alternative. Young writes:

> *If rocks are historical documents, we are driven to the related conclusion that the available evidence is overwhelmingly opposed to the notion that the Noahic flood deposited rocks of the Colorado Plateau only a few thousand years ago. . . . The Christian who believes that the idea of an ancient earth is unbiblical would do better to deny the validity of any kind of historical geology and insist that the rocks must be the product of pure miracle rather than try to explain them in terms of the flood. An examination of the Earth apart from ideological presuppositions is bound to lead to the conclusion that it is ancient.*[2]

It is clear that Young believes rocks are "historical documents" that speak for themselves. His writing does not tell us that rocks need to be interpreted. He believes that their history is apparent, and is understood "apart from ideological presuppositions." He supposes that *his* interpretive framework is free from ideological presuppositions. Therefore, he can dismiss all other frameworks as illegitimate, or biased. In his thinking, that includes the concept of a recent creation and a global, dynamic flood.

It is imperative that we examine *both* uniformitarian and catastrophist frameworks for Grand Canyon strata.[3] We need to evaluate the consistency of these interpretive frameworks with all relevant data. Which framework explains the greatest number of facts with the fewest assumptions? Which makes more correct predictions, to promote further study? Appendix A of this book contains several principles for interpreting geological facts.

Principles for Interpreting Strata

Strata, especially those so well exposed in Grand Canyon, need to be understood and interpreted as a historical record of sedimentary processes. Over the years geologists have agreed on five major principles for interpreting strata:

1. Principle of Superposition:
    In any undisturbed succession of strata, the oldest stratum is at the base and the youngest is at the top.

    Superposition does not apply where strata have been completely overturned by folding, or where deep strata have been uplifted and faulted over a near-surface stratum. Usually such disturbances to superposition can be easily recognized. It is important to note that the principle of superposition gives the *relative* age of strata, not the *absolute* age, or duration.

2. Principle of Original Horizontality:
    Strata, when they were deposited, were horizontal, or nearly horizontal.

    Our experience with natural and laboratory sedimentation confirms that materials accumulate by gravity in horizontal, or nearly horizontal strata. Deviations from horizontality include local cross-bedding in sand dunes and accumulation of volcanic ash on slopes. However, in any thick accumulation of strata, the original horizontal orientation is easily recognized. This allows us to recognize strata which have been tilted and folded, from those which have not. If tilting or folding of strata has occurred, it must have occurred *after* the strata were deposited.

3. Principle of Original Continuity:
    Strata continue horizontally in all directions until ending by progressive thinning, or by being blocked against an obstruction.

    If a stratum ends by progressive thinning, the thinning is usually very gradual, and is indicated by the trend in the decreasing thickness of the stratum. If a stratum is terminated abruptly against an obstruction, there is usually good evidence for the obstruction. It is exceedingly rare that we encounter a thick stratum ending abruptly. We recognize their horizontal continuity.

4. Principle of Cross-cutting Relationships:
    Any feature which breaks the continuity of structure or cross-cuts strata must postdate the structure or strata.

    This means that canyons, dikes, faults, or folds, which break or disrupt the original horizontality or continuity of strata, must have formed within the strata *after* the strata were deposited. It is important to recognize that this principle gives sequence in time, *not* the absolute age or duration.

5. Principle of Process-Product Analogy:
   Geologists should prefer explanations for the origin of strata which are consistent with the kinds of geologic processes forming strata today.

This principle directs geologists as to how to think about strata, not about how all strata are necessarily deposited. Geologists should seek analogies between the *kinds* of processes which form strata, not the *rates* of processes which form strata. They should seek analogies with modern processes which obey natural laws. Water, wind, and ice today form strata. We should seek to explain ancient strata by reference to these agents, without assuming correspondence in the rate, scale, or intensity of modern and ancient processes. This does *not* make the extreme generalization that only known, modern processes, *operating at modern rates,* formed strata (uniformitarianism), or that only present natural laws explain all geologic features (naturalism).[4]

These five principles find direct application to our understanding of Grand Canyon strata. Of the sedimentary strata shown in the block diagram (figure 3.3), the oldest, by the principle of superposition, is the deeply buried formation named the Bass Limestone. Both superposition and cross-cutting relationships indicate that the horizontal Tapeats Sandstone is younger than the tilted and eroded Precambrian strata beneath it. Thus, tilting of the Precambrian must have occurred *after* the Precambrian strata were deposited but *before* the still-horizontal Tapeats Sandstone was deposited. Cross-cutting relationships and original continuity indicate that the profile of the Grand Canyon was eroded *after* the sedimentary strata were

deposited. The most recent strata to form in the block diagram are from the volcanoes on the north rim; lava flows even spilled over the rim after the main erosion of the Canyon had occurred. Other generalizations about Grand Canyon rocks can be made from figure 3.3.

Limestones of Grand Canyon

Lime Mud Layers

Shallow-water lime muds in today's tropical oceans accumulate at a rate of one-foot thickness per one thousand years. These muds are formed mainly by mechanical breakdown of carbonate-containing sea creatures. Modern muds are believed by evolutionists to provide an excellent example of how ancient lime mudstones ("micritic limestones") were accumulated in Grand Canyon. Even some creationists purport that the evidence from lime muds is so convincing, one must certainly believe in long ages of slow deposition for Grand Canyon limestones.

The cliff-forming Redwall Limestone (figure 3.4) is the most obvious Grand Canyon formation needing to be interpreted. Dan Wonderly, for example, insists that all one has to do is compare the modern lime muds with the texture of the Redwall Limestone of Grand Canyon, to be convinced that the Canyon strata required millions of years to be deposited.[5] He claims that young-earth creationists, in a very deliberate way, ignore or neglect these data, which, he says, prove slow deposition.

There are strong dissimilarities, however. Modern, shallow-water lime muds are dominated by *silt-sized crystals* (approximately 20 microns in diameter) of the mineral *aragonite* (most contain 60–95% aragonite, and 0 to 10% calcite), derived from disaggregation or abrasion of skeletons of marine organisms.[6] Ancient lime mudstones ("micritic limestones") are abundant in the Canyon, and are dominated by *clay-sized crystals* (less than 4 microns in diameter) of the mineral *calcite* (nearly 100% calcite and/or dolomite), with sand-size and larger skeletal (shell) fragments floating in the fine crystal matrix.[7]

Geologists emphasize the textural, mineralogical, and chemical *differences* between modern lime muds and many ancient limestones:

> *Micritic limestones, composed essentially of calcite, have textures quite different from those of the aragonite-dominated modern lime muds that have long been regarded as their precursors.[8]*

And again:

> *Modern carbonate sediments contrast sharply in their chemistry and mineralogy, with ancient carbonate rocks.[9]*

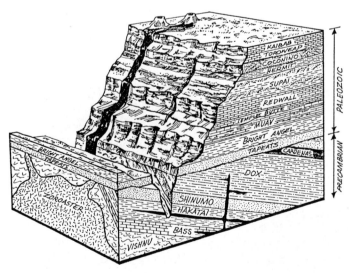

Figure 3.3 *Block diagram of Grand Canyon showing the relationships of different rocks.*

Even the *shapes* of the grains are strongly discordant between the modern-and-ancient lime muds:

> *Furthermore, the grain (crystal) size distribution and grain (crystal) shape characteristics of modern lime-mud sediment are very different from their lithified counterparts.*[10]

Could some process of recrystallization have been responsible for transforming these modern, coarser-textured, aragonite muds into the finer-textured calcite muds which compose limestones? This is a much disputed question. The process of recrystallization, it has been recognized, makes *larger crystals* from smaller crystals; *not smaller crystals* from larger ones. How could such a process form the predominantly fine-grained muds which now compose limestones? Early workers on the microcrystalline-calcite ("micrite") ooze of ancient limestone argued that it formed by direct precipitation from sea water,[11] not from recrystallization or even extensive abrasion of skeletons of marine organisms. This process, believed to form ancient lime muds, is much different from slow processes in modern oceans. The "lime-mud problem" has become more apparent in recent years, as the compositions and textures of modern lime muds and fine-grained limestones have been more thoroughly investigated.

At the present time, it would be inappropriate to suppose that the scientific evidence requires that ancient fine-grained limestones were derived from lime muds resembling the muds being deposited slowly in modern, tropical seas. Evolutionists make that assumption but the facts do not justify it. In the words of F. J. Pettijohn, "The origin of micrite is far from clear."[12]

Rapid Deposition of Lime Mud

Whereas many modern lime mud deposits are recognized to be accumulating very slowly, some modern examples of *rapid* lime mud accumulation are known. Modern hurricanes in the Florida-Bahama area have been observed to move and redeposit large quantities of fine, laminated, carbonate mud. Flats above normal high-tide level receive carpets of laminated mud after hurricanes, and offshore mud deposits have been observed to form rapidly.[13]

Of special interest are layers of creamy, white mud, of the consistency of toothpaste, found in tidal channels between islands in the Bahamas. These lime muds are dominated by silt- and clay-sized needles of aragonite occurring as beds one to two inches thick within a deposit, reaching a thickness of three feet. Two scientists report these lime mud beds occurring within "a high-energy bank margin environment not usually considered to be the site of mud-sized particle deposition."[14] Several scientists have suggested that these lime mud layers, associated with tidal

Figure 3.4 *The Redwall Limestone, the most prominent limestone formation of Grand Canyon, directs our thinking toward the ancient processes which accumulated lime sediment.*

channels, have formed by direct precipitation of aragonite during storms.[15]

The observation of lime mud deposits within environments of rapid accumulation has created a mystery. How can such fine mud particles settle quickly, from turbulent, fast-flowing waters? Our normal observations of modern mud-sized particles show that they settle very slowly, and only in quiet water.

The mystery appears to have been solved recently by microscopic study of modern lime muds. Muds from the tidal channels in the Bahamas were washed by a gentle stream of water revealing mud particles aggregated into pelletoids.[16] Evidently, pelletoids of flocculated aragonite particles exhibit the hydraulic characteristics of sand, which allows aggregates of particles to settle quickly. Two scientists report these new discoveries that "mandate caution when using these features as indicators of shoreline or quiet water in ancient carbonate deposits."[17]

The evidence of rapid accumulation of lime mud in modern sedimentary environments helps to interpret many ancient limestone deposits. Probably most significant are the so-called "lithographic limestones" with extremely fine texture, but with extraordinary fossil preservation. These limestones appear to have formed as animals were smothered in lime mud.[18] Perhaps the most famous example includes fossils of the bird *Archaeopteryx* from the Solnhofen, a lithographic limestone of Germany. The "world's most perfect fossils" may come from the fine-grained limestone of the Santana Formation of northeast Brazil. One geologist, describing the fossil fish of the Santana Formation wrote, ". . . lithification was instantaneous and fossilization may even have been the cause of death."[19] Clearly, catastrophic processes are needed to make these fine-grained limestones.

Fossil Reefs?

An important problem to be faced by Bible-believing geologists is the existence of alleged limestone "reefs."[20] Critics of the Flood theory say that many abundantly fossiliferous limestones are organically constructed "reefs," which were accumulated slowly along the edges of an ancient sea. The Flood, some critics say, could not have deposited such structures, because it took thousands of years to construct a huge, wave-resistant framework, as innumerable generations of marine organisms chemically cemented themselves one on top of the other. If Grand Canyon limestones were accumulated slowly, in tranquil seas, we might expect to have large, organically bound structures ("reefs") buried with the lime mud. Do large, organically bound structures occur within Grand Canyon limestones? Can these be proven to represent *in situ*, slowly accumulated sea floor? This would appear to be an ideal test for the Flood model.

The most extensive study of Grand Canyon limestone was by McKee and Gutschick. They admit, "Coral reefs are not known from the Redwall Limestone."[21] Concerning laminated algal structures (stromatolites) in the Redwall, which might form slowly in tidal flat environments, they say, "The general scarcity or near absence of bottom-building stromatolites suggests that places generally above low tide are not well represented."[22] These cautious statements concerning algal structures in Redwall Limestone were used by Dan Wonderly to argue against the Flood. He used these statements to imply that the presence of *some* algal structures indeed represent *in situ* ocean floor.[23] A careful study of McKee and Gutschick's work shows that the laminated algal structures typically show concentric structure (oncolites), and are best interpreted as algal masses which have been transported by rolling. These authors *believe* that the Redwall Limestone represents *in situ* ocean-floor deposits, but they have not proven their case with empirical evidence.

Sponges, as well as corals and algae, are responsible for building rigid-growth frameworks in many modern reefs. Do we find sponge frameworks in Grand Canyon limestones? Small broken fragments of sponges have been described in the Redwall, but the largest sponges occur in the lower part of the Kaibab Limestone. However, a recent report on the Kaibab admits, "Discrete organic build-ups, such as sponge patch reefs, have not been documented."[24]

Coral or sponge-reef structures are not known from any of the limestones of Grand Canyon. Because corals and sponges today build rigid frameworks in modern, slowly accumulated sea floor, they would be expected to have built reefs in the limestones of Grand Canyon. The absence of coral and sponge reefs is an added mystery, not well explained by the uniformitarian theory of *in situ* ocean floor.

Rapid Deposition of Limestone

In the year 1966, at a very small side canyon just a hundred yards off of the Colorado River, a geologist made a remarkable discovery. One thin layer of the lowest member of the Redwall Limestone reveals numerous, large, cigar-shaped fossils. On close inspection, these fossils are recognized to be calcium carbonate shells of large marine mollusks. The shapes are very distinctive. Some of the fossils approach two feet in length, yet are just several inches in diameter. News of the discovery spread rapidly.

Figure 3.5 shows an excellent example of these fossils. They are all a type of marine mollusk known as a nautiloid. Technically, they are of the class Cephalopoda (which includes the living octopuses, squids, and cuttlefishes), and of the variety called "orthocone nautiloids." These straight-shelled animals resemble the modern cephalopod called nautilus, the free-swimming, coiled, deep-sea mollusk found today in the Indian Ocean. The fossils in

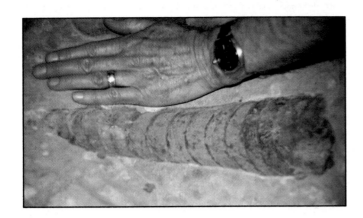

Figure 3.5 *Fossil of nautiloid from Redwall Limestone. The cross section of the fossil seen in the limestone (top) allows the complex anatomy of the chambered shell and fleshy parts to be sketched (bottom).*

the Redwall Limestone differ from the modern nautilus by being straight, not coiled. Like its modern counterpart, the fossil nautiloid had the squid-like animal living at one end of a chambered shell. The pressurized chambers in the shell were used to compensate for buoyancy in the fashion similar to a submarine. This construction allowed the animal to swim freely, probably at great speed, through the deep ocean. They must have been an important predator in the ancient sea.

Nautiloids of the Redwall Limestone are among the largest and finest examples found in the United States. They have increased our understanding of these unique animals. Because of these extraordinary fossils, the small, and otherwise obscure side canyon, is now enshrined on Colorado River maps as Nautiloid Canyon. River travelers frequently stop to observe and ponder these unusual fossils.

The observation of numerous straight-shelled nautiloids, buried in very fine-grained limestone, is fascinating. How did so many of these free-swimming, deep-sea animals become fossilized in one location? How did the fine-grained lime mud accumulate, as it buried these animals? These important questions come to us, as we consider the deposit.

The orientations or alignments of one dozen nautiloids from a single bed of limestone are shown in figure 3.6. This figure is called a "rose diagram," because it shows the compass-direction alignment of the long axes of the slender shells.[25] For the twelve measured shells, ten lie within the limestone layer with their long axes aligned within three, 30-degree sectors. These are the west-northwest sector (four shells), the north-northwest

sector (three shells), and the north sector (three shells). Only two of the twelve nautiloids occur with their long axes in the remaining three sectors. Simple probability analysis shows that there is less than a ten-percent chance that such an arrangement of shells could be generated by random fall of dead nautiloids onto a motionless and static, deep ocean floor.[26] Does this deposit represent a calm ocean floor where lime mud accumulated very slowly?

We know that long, cigar-shaped objects tend to align themselves in the direction of minimum resistance to flowing water. That is the observation made for logs in the floodplains of rivers devastated by the 1980 floods from the eruptions of Mount St. Helens. Therefore, we infer that the long axes of nautiloid shells in the Redwall Limestone were aligned in the direction of the prevailing current. However, any current able to induce orientation of large shells on the deep ocean floor would also be able to move and deposit fine-grained lime mud. Therefore, the deposit indicates that lime mud was moved and accumulated by current. What is amazing about this Redwall Limestone example is that the limestone bed which contains the nautiloids, except for the nautiloids, resembles many other limestone beds in the Redwall Limestone and other limestones of Grand Canyon. It is noteworthy that the fine-grained composition and bedded structure of the nautiloid deposit is typical of the Redwall generally! We can infer that many other fine-grained limestone layers were accumulated also, as lime mud was moved by water currents. We question the uniformitarian notion that

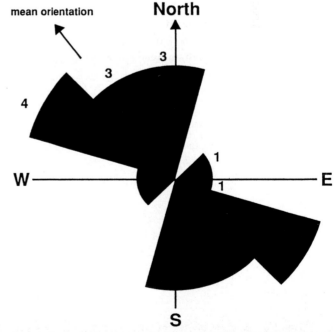

Figure 3.6 *Orientation diagram showing the directions of the long axes of twelve fossil nautiloids in a bed of limestone at Nautiloid Canyon. The nautiloid bed occurs in the uppermost limestone beds of the Whitmore Wash Member of the Redwall Limestone. (Measurements by Steven A. Austin, April 1991.)*

fine-grained limestone beds of Grand Canyon usually accumulated by the slow but steady rain of fine lime debris in a calm and placid sea. Close inspection of a fossiliferous limestone deposit causes us to propose a catastrophist model.

Not all limestones of Grand Canyon are fine-grained. Some contain coarse, broken fossil debris, which appears to have been sorted by strong currents. The Redwall Limestone contains coarse, circular disks (columnals) from the stems of crinoids—marine animals which lived in a cup, or head, attached to the stem. Evidently, vigorous current-washing of marine animal fragments occurred, which winnowed the finer sediment away, leaving a "hash" of crinoid debris. Occasionally, the heads of crinoids are found embedded in the coarse, circular disks. Sometimes these occur in deposits of inclined bedding (cross beds), which imply strong currents. Because modern crinoid heads in today's ocean are susceptible to rapid breakdown when these organisms die,[27] we conclude that rapid burial is needed to produce fossil-crinoid heads.

Limestone containing inclined bedding (cross beds) sometimes reaches great thickness. In the Redwall Limestone (upper third of the Mooney Falls Member), cross beds have been reported from several locations in Grand Canyon.[28] One package (set) of cross beds in Redwall Limestone at Kanab Creek has a vertical thickness of 30 feet. It appears that these beds represent the remnants of large sand waves (underwater dunes) composed of coarser lime sediment, which were shaped by vigorous and sustained ocean currents moving at three to five feet per second. Thick cross beds also occur within limestone members of the Esplanade Sandstone in the western Grand Canyon.

Evidence of current transport of lime sediment is also provided by quartz sand grains, which are found embedded in the fine-grained matrix of many limestones. These quartz sand grains are common in the Kaibab Limestone and limestones of the Supai Group of Grand Canyon. Because quartz sand grains cannot be precipitated from sea water, they must have been transported from some other location. Any water current fast enough to move sand grains would be able to move lime mud, as well. These quartz sand grains give rise to the opinion that the Kaibab Limestone and Supai Group limestones were accumulated from sediment which was being transported by moving water, not simply deposited from a slow, steady rain of carbonate mud on the floor of a calm and placid sea.

Source of Lime Sediment

We ultimately come to the question, "From where did the lime sediment come?" No doubt, some of the lime sediment was derived simply by precipitation of calcium carbonate from sea water. This may explain some of the very fine micrite particles. However, it appears that most of the lime sediment composing important limestones in Grand Canyon was derived from preexisting sediment supplies simply by transportation. This may explain, especially, the sources of the broken fossil fragments that compose an important part of these limestones. Most limestones in the Canyon show considerable thickening northwestward in Grand Canyon. Also associated with thickening to the northwest is increase in the purity of the lime sediment. These trends indicate that there was an important source or sources of lime sediment to the northwest of Grand Canyon which contributed its sediment to northern Arizona during the Flood.

Sandstones of Grand Canyon

River Sand Deposits?

If sedimentary strata of Grand Canyon were deposited by advancing-and-retreating seas during millions of years, we would expect clay-rich mud and quartz sand to be introduced to these oceans by rivers. The deposit formed today where a river enters the ocean is called a delta. It is a triangular-shaped deposit (map view) which thins abruptly and becomes finer grained under the sea in the direction of deep water. The clay, silt, and sand deposited at a river's delta would, if buried and cemented, form strata of shale, siltstone, and sandstone, with rather distinctive geometry. The entire deposit would be wedge-shaped in cross-section, and individual sandstone beds would represent the distributary channels of the river on the delta or the delta-front sand bars, formed where sand is deposited as the river enters the ocean.

Has good evidence of river delta accumulation of sand been found in Grand Canyon? We might best expect to see the evidence of a delta where "marine limestone" is interlayered with "terrestrial sand." In Grand Canyon, the most obvious and voluminous deposit that comes to our attention is the Supai Group (see figure 3.7). Repeating layers of sandstone, shale, and limestone dominate the Supai Group. Furthermore, these strata contain both *marine* and *terrestrial* fossils, as might be anticipated in an ancient river delta.[29]

Although the river-delta model for accumulation of the Supai has been considered by geologists for more than 60 years, most geologists remain skeptical. E. D. McKee, the geologist who has published the most data relevant to the Supai, wrote an entire paper on these strata, without once using the word "delta."[30] R. C. Blakey, who has also extensively studied these strata, questioned the delta model:

> *Numerous previous workers have loosely assigned Supai deposition to a deltaic environment. Both stratigraphic and sedimentological data gathered in this study contradict these earlier findings. Vertical*

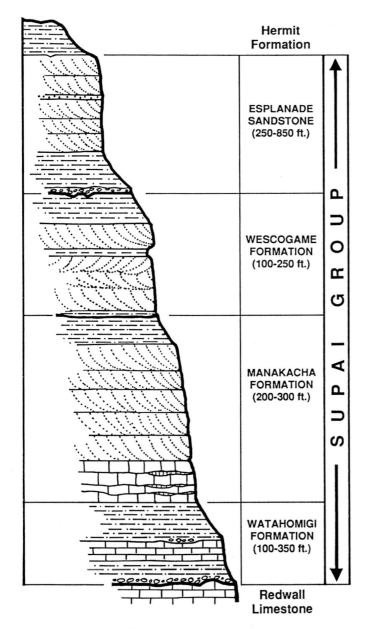

Hermit
Formation

ESPLANADE
SANDSTONE
(250-850 ft.)

WESCOGAME
FORMATION
(100-250 ft.)

MANAKACHA
FORMATION
(200-300 ft.)

WATAHOMIGI
FORMATION
(100-350 ft.)

SUPAI GROUP

Redwall
Limestone

ROCK TYPES:

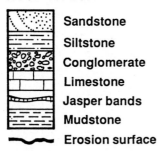

Sandstone
Siltstone
Conglomerate
Limestone
Jasper bands
Mudstone
Erosion surface

Figure 3.7 *The Supai Group of Grand Canyon is dominated by sandstones with very thick cross bedding with a thickness of almost 1,000 feet.*

sequences typical of deltaic environments are not abundant and paleogeography and basin analysis do not support major deltaic episodes of deposition. . . . The sand was probably distributed, deposited, and reworked by shallow marine currents.[31]

The discovery of the exceptionally extensive nature of the individual sandstone strata is perhaps the most obvious problem with the delta model.[32] Sandstone units within the Supai are remarkably thin, and some extend the whole length of Grand Canyon! These units are not wedge-shaped, as are sands in modern deltas. Furthermore, channels which might represent rivers or distributary channels of a river system are unknown.

The failure of the delta model for the Supai Group sandstones has only served to heighten the mystery concerning their origin. Among geologists, controversy prevails. Some purport that these sandstones represent shallow marine sand deposits,[33] perhaps moved by intense tides, storms, or floods. Other geologists have suggested accumulation as terrestrial sand dunes in a desert.[34] It has not been possible to obtain agreement among geologists concerning the deposition of these important sandstones. Most, however, would question the delta model and the notion of river accumulation.

Wind Deposits?

Among geologists, an important controversy has developed on the origin of Grand Canyon sandstones. Were they deposited by wind, or water?

Very early in the study of Grand Canyon sandstones, geologists noticed, within the large-scale horizontal beds of many sandstones, distinctly inclined layers of sand called cross beds. The property of cross bedding is most obvious in the Coconino Sandstone (figure 3.8), but it also has been noted as the dominant property of Supai Group sandstones. Over 60 years ago, geologists began to interpret cross bedding within Grand Canyon sandstones by analogy with the sand deposits with which they had direct experience—the desert-dune deposit. Sand dunes in modern deserts are dominated by quartz sand and have inclined internal sand beds.

It was proposed, therefore, that the Coconino Sandstone also accumulated in an immense windy desert by migrating sand dunes. The cross beds accumulated over many thousands of years on the down-wind side of the dune, as sand was deposited there.

The Coconino Sandstone is also noted for the large number of fossilized footprints, usually in sequences called trackways. These appear to have been made by four-footed vertebrates moving across the original sand surfaces (see figure 3.9). These fossil-footprint trackways were compared

Figure 3.8 *Enormous cross beds within the Coconino Sandstone. The man in the lower left corner provides the scale of this cliff along the Bright Angel Trail.*

to the tracks made by reptiles on desert sand dunes,[35] so it was then assumed that these fossilized footprints in the Coconino Sandstone must have been made in dry desert sands which were then covered up by wind-blown sand, and subsequently cemented into the sandstone, effectively fossilizing the prints.

Yet another feature that evolutionary geologists have used to argue that the Coconino Sandstone represents the remains of a long period of dry desert conditions, are the sand grains themselves. Geologists have studied the sand grains from modern desert dunes and, under the microscope, these grains often show pitted, or frosted surfaces. Similar grain-surface textures also have been observed in sandstone layers containing very thick cross beds such as are found in the Coconino Sandstone. So, again, this comparison has strengthened the argument that the Coconino Sandstone was deposited as dunes in a desert.

At first glance, this interpretation would appear to be an embarrassment to Bible-believing geologists who have suggested that Noah's Flood deposited the flat-lying beds of what were once sand, mud, and lime, but which are now exposed as the rock layers in the walls of the Canyon.

Above the Coconino Sandstone is the Toroweap Formation and below is the Hermit Formation, both of which, geologists agree, are made up of sediments that were deposited in water.[36] How could there have been a

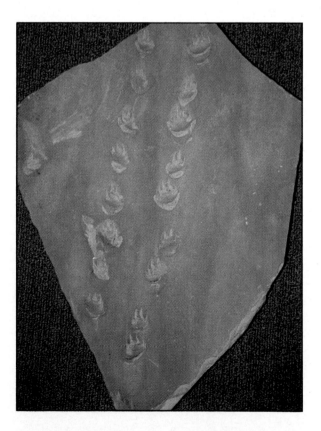

Figure 3.9 *Trackway of a four-footed vertebrate fossilized on an inclined cross bed within the Coconino Sandstone.*

period of dry, desert conditions in the middle of the Flood year, when "all the high hills that were under the whole heaven, were covered" (Genesis 7:19) by water?

This seeming problem certainly has not been lost on those (even from within the Christian community) opposed to Flood geologists and creationists in general. For example, Dr. Davis Young, Professor of Geology at Calvin College in Grand Rapids, Michigan, in a recent book being marketed in Christian bookstores, has merely echoed the interpretations made by evolutionary geologists, of the characteristics of the Coconino Sandstone, arguing against the Flood as being the agent for depositing the Coconino Sandstone. He is adamant in his consideration of the desert dune model:

> *The Coconino Sandstone contains spectacular cross bedding, vertebrate track fossils, and pitted and frosted sand grain surfaces. All these features are consistent with formation of the Coconino as desert sand dunes. The sandstone is composed almost entirely of quartz grains, and pure quartz sand does not form in floods . . . no flood of any size could have produced such deposits of sand. . . .*[37]

Footprint Experiments

The footprint trackways in the Coconino Sandstone recently have been re-examined in the light of experimental studies by Dr. Leonard Brand of Loma Linda University, in California.[38] His research program involved careful surveying and detailed measurements of 82 fossilized vertebrate trackways discovered in the Coconino Sandstone along the Hermit Trail in Grand Canyon. He then observed and measured 236 experimental trackways made by living amphibians and reptiles in experimental chambers. These tracks were formed on sand beneath the water, on moist sand at the water's edge, and on dry sand. The sand surface was mostly sloping at an angle of 25°, although some observations were made on slopes of 15° and 20°, for comparison. Observations also were made of the underwater locomotion of five species of salamanders (amphibians) both in the laboratory and in their natural habitat, and measurements were again taken of their trackways.

A detailed statistical analysis of these data led to the conclusion, with a high degree of probability, that the fossil tracks of the Coconino Sandstone must have been made under water. Whereas the experimental animals produce footprints under all test conditions, both up and down the 25°-slopes of the laboratory "dunes," all but one of the fossil trackways could have been made only by the animals in question climbing "uphill." Toe imprints were generally distinct, whereas the prints of the soles were indistinct. These and other details were present in over 80% of the fossil's underwater and wet-sand tracks, but less than 12% of the dry-sand and damp-sand tracks had any toe marks. Dry-sand, uphill tracks were usually just depressions, with no details. Wet-sand tracks were quite different from the fossil tracks in certain features. Added to this, the observations of the locomotive behavior of the living salamanders indicated that all spent the majority of their locomotion time by walking on the bottom, underwater, rather than by swimming.

Putting together all of his observations, Dr. Brand came to the conclusion that the configurations and characteristics of the animals' trackways made on the submerged sand surfaces most closely resembled the fossilized quadruped trackways of the Coconino Sandstone. Indeed, when the locomotion behavior of the living amphibians is taken into account, the fossilized trackways are best understood as suggesting that the animals were entirely under water (not swimming at the surface) and moving upslope (against the current), in an attempt to get out of the water. This interpretation fits with the concept of a global Flood, which overwhelmed even four-footed reptiles and amphibians that normally spend most of their time in the water.

Not content with these initial studies, Dr. Brand has continued (with the help of a colleague) to pursue this line of research. He recently published further results,[39] which were so significant that brief reports of their work appeared in *Science News*[40] and *Geology Today*.[41]

His careful analysis of the fossilized trackways in the Coconino Sandstone, this time not only from the Hermit Trail in Grand Canyon but from other trails and locations, again revealed that all but one had to have been made by animals moving up cross-bed slopes. Furthermore, these new tracks often show that the line of the trackway was in one direction, while the animals' feet and toes were pointing in a different direction. It would appear that animals were walking in a current of water, not air. Other trackways start or stop abruptly, with no sign that the animals' missing tracks were covered by some disturbance such as shifting sediments. It appears that these animals simply swam away from the sediment.

Because many of the tracks have characteristics that are "just about impossible" to explain unless the animals were moving under water, Dr. Brand suggested that newt-like animals made the tracks while walking under water and being pushed by a current. To test his ideas, he and his colleague video-taped living newts walking through a laboratory tank with running water. All 238 trackways made by the newts had features similar to the fossilized trackways in the Coconino Sandstone, and their video-taped behavior, while making the trackways, thus indicated how the animals that made the fossilized trackways might have been moving.

These additional studies confirmed the conclusions of his earlier research. Thus, Dr. Brand concluded that all his data suggest that the Coconino Sandstone fossil tracks should not be used as evidence that desert-wind deposition of dry sand formed the Coconino Sandstone, but, rather, point to underwater deposition. These evidences, from such careful experimental studies, overturn the original interpretation by evolutionists of these Coconino Sandstone fossil footprints, and, therefore, call into question their use by Young and others as an argument against the Flood.

Desert "Dunes?"

The desert sand-dune model for the origin of the Coconino Sandstone also has been challenged recently by Glen Visher,[42] Professor of Geology at the University of Tulsa in Oklahoma, and who is not a creationist geologist. He noted that large storms, or amplified tides, today produce submarine sand dunes called "sand waves." These modern sand waves on the sea floor contain large cross beds composed of sand with very high quartz purity. Visher has thus interpreted the Coconino Sandstone as a submarine sand-wave deposit accumulated by water, *not* wind. This, of course, is directly contrary to Young's claims, which, after all, are just the repeated opinions of evolutionary geologists.

Furthermore, there is other evidence that casts grave doubts on the view that the Coconino Sandstone cross beds formed in desert dunes. The average angle of slope of the Coconino cross beds is about 25° from the horizontal, less than the average angle of slope of sand beds on the down-wind side of most modern-desert sand dunes. Those sand beds usually slope at an angle of more than 25°, with some beds inclined as much as 30° to 34°—the angle of "rest" of dry sand. On the other hand, modern oceanic sand waves do not have "avalanche" faces of sand as commonly as desert dunes do, and, therefore, have lower average dips of cross beds.

Visher also points to other positive evidence for accumulation of the Coconino Sandstone in water. Within this sandstone is a feature known, technically, as "parting lineation," which is commonly formed on sand surfaces during brief erosional bursts beneath fast-flowing water.[43] Parting lineation is not known from any desert sand dunes. Thus, Visher also uses this feature as evidence of vigorous water currents accumulating the sand which forms the Coconino Sandstone.

Similarly, he has noted that the different grain sizes of sand within any sandstone are a reflection of the process that deposited the sand. Consequently, he performed sand grain-size analyses of the Coconino Sandstone, desert sand dunes, and modern sand waves. Visher found that the

Coconino Sandstone does *not* compare as favorably to dune sands from modern deserts.

Figure 3.10 shows grain-size distributions of four sand samples obtained by Visher.[44] Dune sand plots in figure 3.10 as a straight line on the graphical plot, indicating to Visher a *single* log-normally distributed population of grains moved by saltation (the bouncing process induced by wind). Coconino Sandstone, however, does not compare favorably to dune sand. Visher notes distinct straight-line segments to its grain-size plot indicating at least *two* distinct log-normally distributed populations. Visher sees the bimodal character of Coconino Sandstone as resembling the sand accumulated underwater as sand waves. Two sand samples from Altamaha Estuary in Georgia (figure 3.10) compare favorably to the Coconino Sandstone. This evidence indicated to Visher that Coconino Sandstone accumulated from water, not wind.

The pitting and frosting of sand grains, claimed by some to prove wind deposition, has also been investigated further. It now has been found that not only is the pitting *not* diagnostic of the last process to have deposited the sand grains (pitting can, for example, form first by wind impacts, followed by redeposition by water), but pitting and frosting of sand grains can form outside a desert environment.[45] For example, geologists have described how pitting on the

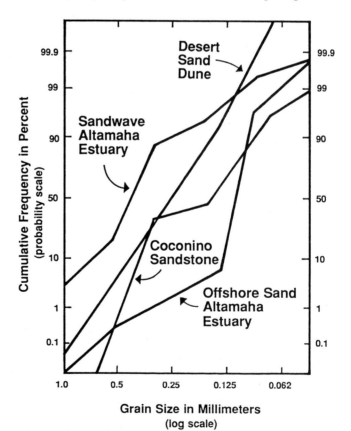

Figure 3.10 *Grain-size plots of sand provide a "fingerprint" of the agent of deposition. Glen S. Visher argued that the Coconino Sandstone was deposited by water, not wind.*

surface of sand grains can form by chemical processes during the cementation of sand.

Sand-Wave Deposits

A considerable body of evidence has appeared which indicates that most sandstones of Grand Canyon were deposited by the ocean. This appears to be the case for the Tapeats Sandstone, the Supai Group sandstones, the Toroweap sandstones, the sandstones within the Kaibab Limestone, and even the Coconino Sandstone. These sandstones are characterized by cross bedding (inclined beds of sand within horizontal strata) which is best understood to be evidence of ocean currents. The evidence indicates that cross beds in many Grand Canyon sandstones formed by water currents on dunelike mounds called sand waves.[46]

Figure 3.11 shows the way sand waves have been observed to produce cross beds in sand. The water current moves over the sand surface, building up the mound of sand. The current continues to erode sand from the up-current side of the sand wave, and deposits it in the

zone of reverse flow as inclined layers on the down-current side of the sand wave. The current causes the form of the sand wave to move in the down-current direction, as the inclined strata continue to be deposited. Erosion of sand by the current removes both the up-current side of the sand wave and the top of the sand wave. The only part of the sand wave usually preserved is the down-current side, and usually just the lower half of the down-current side. Thus, the height of the cross beds preserved is just a fraction of the original sand-wave height. If the current and sediment supply continue, migration of a second sand wave over an area will occur, producing a second layer of sand containing the inclined cross beds.

Observations of sand waves have been made under laboratory conditions in large flumes. Sand waves have been observed also on certain parts of the ocean floor and in rivers. J. R. L. Allen[47] used the experimentally produced sand waves to demonstrate that sand-wave height is related to the water depth. As water depth increases, so does the height of the sand wave which is produced. The empirically derived relationship between sand-wave height and water

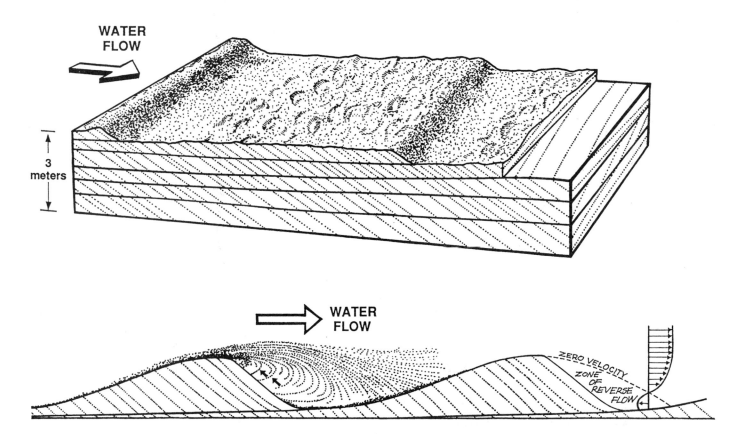

Figure 3.11 *Formation of cross beds on a sandy ocean floor, from the migration of sand waves in response to sustained water flow.*
   a. *Block diagram shows the form of small sand waves observed on the floor of the shallow ocean. Tabular cross beds are produced beneath the sustained water flow by down-current migration of sand waves.*
   b. *Cross-sectional diagram shows how a sand wave moves and accumulates. Erosion of sand occurs on the up-current surface of the sand wave. Sand grains accumulate as inclined beds on the down-current surface of the sand wave in the "zone of reverse flow." (This diagram was drawn with vertical exaggeration, in order to show detail.)*

depth is shown graphically in figure 3.12, on the left side. Sand-wave height is approximately one-fifth of the water depth.

Laboratory studies, using sand in large flumes, have helped delimit the hydrodynamic conditions under which sand waves and cross beds form. As a water current is initiated in a flume over a flat sand bottom, no sand movement occurs until a certain critical velocity is reached. Just above this critical velocity, sand begins to form small ridges, called "ripples." As the water velocity is increased, the ripples grow into the larger mounds, called sand waves. It is at this velocity that cross beds begin to form in the sand on the down-current side of the sand wave. As the velocity of water is increased further, the sand waves disappear, and the sand surface again becomes flat. At this high velocity, flat beds form in the sand.

D. M. Rubin and D. S. McCulloch[48] have made observations of sand waves in San Francisco Bay and have related these to sand waves produced in flumes. The right side of figure 3.12 is a graph of the stable-bed forms which have been observed in fine sand at various water depths and water velocities. Also included on the graph, within the stability field of each bed form, is a cross-sectional

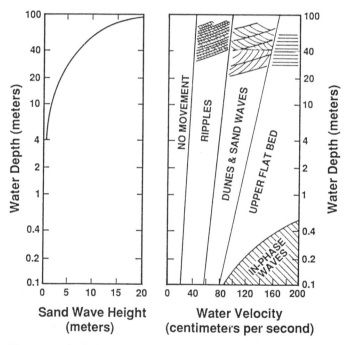

Figure 3.12 *Graphs of water depth versus sand-wave height, and water depth versus water velocity, showing bedforms in fine sand expected under different water conditions. The thickness of cross beds observed in fine-grained sandstone is used to estimate sand-wave height. Then, sand-wave height is entered into the graph on the left to estimate the water depth where the sand wave formed. After a water depth is estimated on the left graph, that depth is transferred to the right graph, where the minimum-and-maximum velocities of water are indicated for the specific water depth.*

diagram of the type of stratification produced. We note that cross beds occur within the stability field of sand waves.

Geologists have reported very thick cross bed sets in the fine-grained sandstone strata of Grand Canyon. Cross bed sets in Supai sandstones up to five meters (16 feet) thick have been reported.[49] Just east of Grand Canyon, the Kaibab Limestone has quartz sand at its base, with individual cross beds up to six meters (20 feet) thick.[50] Among the thickest sets of cross beds are those in the Coconino Sandstone, where a thickness of nine meters (30 feet) is reported.[51] Even coarse-grained lime sediment contains thick cross bedding. The most extraordinary examples come from the Redwall Limestone, where nine-meter-thick cross beds, composed of lime sediment, have been described.[52]

These great thicknesses of individual cross beds in Grand Canyon imply enormous heights of sand waves. Because erosion has removed the sand which formed the top of each sand wave, the true height of each sand wave could have been double the present cross bed thickness. In the case of the sand waves which formed cross beds in the Supai sandstones and Kaibab sandstone mentioned above, we suggest sand-wave heights of ten meters (33 feet). If the Coconino Sandstone was deposited under water, its sand waves could be easily 18 meters (60 feet) high.

Using the sand wave deposits of the Supai and Kaibab sandstones (the ones with strongest evidence for marine sand-wave deposition), we can estimate the current velocity which deposited the sand. Here is how it is done: The sand-wave height of 10 meters (33 feet) for the Supai and Kaibab sandstones is selected on the left graph of figure 3.12, and a *vertical* line is drawn upward, which intersects the curved line. Next, we draw a *horizontal* line from the point of intersection with the curved line, to the vertical axis on the left of the graph. The logarithmic scale on the vertical axis indicates that the sand wave formed in water at a depth of 54 meters (180 feet). Now, we can continue the horizontal line, representing a depth of 54 meters, to the right graph in figure 3.12, so that the stability field of sand waves is intersected twice, at the depth of 54 meters. The first intersection with the sand-wave field indicates the *minimum* current velocity which is needed to make sand waves in fine sand in water at a depth of 54 meters. The *minimum* velocity of 90 centimeters per second (three feet per second) is read off the horizontal axis at the bottom of the graph. The second intersection of the 54-meter-depth line with the sand wave field indicates the *maximum* current velocity, which would make sand waves in water at a depth of 54 meters. The *maximum* velocity of 155 centimeters per second (five feet per second) is also read off the horizontal axis.

Our analysis of large-scale cross beds in Grand Canyon sandstones indicates that high velocity currents formed enormous sand waves. Sustained, unidirectional currents of 90 to 155 centimeters per second (three to five feet per second) must have occurred in deep water. Modern tides and normal ocean currents do not have these velocities in the open ocean. Deep-sea currents have been reported to attain velocities of 150 centimeters per second in the Norwegian Sea, more than 100 centimeters per second out of the Mediterranean Sea, and more than 50 centimeters per second out of the Red Sea.[53] On the bottom of San Francisco Bay at the Golden Gate, currents have been measured at over 250 centimeters per second.[54] These high velocities, however, are caused by the flow of tides through restrictions of the ocean within straits. The Grand Canyon strata provide no evidence of geographic restriction.

Catastrophic events provide the mechanism which can make high-velocity ocean currents. Hurricanes are thought to make modern sand waves of smaller size than the Grand Canyon examples. No measurements have been reported of hurricane-driven currents approaching 100 centimeters per second in water over 50 meters deep. The most severe modern-ocean currents known have been generated during a tsunami ("tidal wave"). In shallow oceans, tsunami-induced currents have been reported, on occasion, to exceed 500 centimeters per second, and unidirectional currents have been sustained for hours.[55] Such an event would be able to move large quantities of sand, and, in its waning stages, build huge sand waves in deep water. A tsunami provides the best modern analogy for understanding how large-scale Grand Canyon cross beds form. We can imagine how the Flood would cause similar sedimentation in strata of Grand Canyon.

Source of Sand

A natural question to ask is, "From where did the sand come, which forms Grand Canyon sandstones?" We recognize that quartz and feldspar grains, which constitute most of the Grand Canyon sandstones, could not have been precipitated from water. These grains were derived by erosion of crystalline basement rocks (granite, gneiss, or schist), or by reworking from earlier sand deposits. These two sources of grains need to be evaluated for Grand Canyon formations.

In the case of the Tapeats Sandstone in Grand Canyon, grains appear to have been derived from both sources. This sandstone rests directly, with erosional contact, on crystalline basement (Zoroaster granites and gneisses of the Vishnu Group) and beveled sandstones (Nankoweap, Dox, and other sandy formations). We can visualize deep erosion to both the crystalline and sedimentary rocks as being especially dominant near the beginning of the Flood. Such erosive processes would create great sources of sand grains. The mechanics of erosion and deposition of the Tapeats Sandstone is discussed in chapter 4.

The Supai Group sandstones provide very interesting insight into the sources of sand grains. The cross beds within this group dip southeast, showing that the current which moved sand, flowed southeast.[56] Yet, detailed studies of the Supai strata to the northwest of Grand Canyon show no acceptable source of quartz sand grains. There is no basement complex of granite or gneiss to provide quartz sand; only sedimentary strata are associated laterally with Supai sandstones. Everywhere north and west of Grand Canyon, the Supai Group occurs above the Redwall Limestone—an extraordinarily pure carbonate with extremely rare sand grains. Furthermore, detailed mapping of the lateral change within the Supai strata show that the sandstones grade laterally northwestward into *limestone.*[57] The Esplanade Sandstone (uppermost Supai formation) intertongues with the Pakoon Limestone to the west, in the extreme western end of Grand Canyon. To the north, the Esplanade also intertongues with Pakoon Limestone in southern Utah, as is seen at Zion National Park. Similar limestone, intertonguing west and north, occurs with other Supai Group sandstones. There is, therefore, no nearby source for quartz sand to the west or north of the Canyon.

John S. Shelton, who considered the Supai to have been deposited "on the upper part of a delta or the lower part of a flood-plain," recognized the sand-source problem:

> *Full interpretation of the Supai-Hermit sequence is thwarted by some puzzles. For example, throughout the Grand Canyon region the typically aqueous cross-bedding in the Supai consistently dips toward the south and southeast, indicating that this was the general direction of the depositing currents. Yet, it is difficult to find an adequate northern or northwestern source for such quantities of sand and mud; those that lie in the right direction seem either to have been under water or composed predominantly of limestone at the appropriate time.*[58]

If we take the evidence at face value, it would appear that Supai sand grains came from the ocean, not from a river.

A truly great distance of transport must be postulated for Supai Group sand grains. Blakey[59] suggested that the nearest source for Supai sand was northern Utah, or Wyoming. There, sedimentary sand sources occur beneath the Supai-equivalent strata, and crystalline-basement sources of sand were exposed at that time. However, we have not found geologic evidence for a great, ancient river system which eroded and transported Supai sand grains from Wyoming. Instead, we find limestone, the deposits of an ocean, directly on the path from Wyoming to Grand Canyon!

The source of the Coconino Sandstone presents a similar problem. Figure 3.13 shows that the Coconino Sandstone is part of a vast blanket of sand extending eastward from Arizona into New Mexico, Colorado, Kansas, Oklahoma, and Texas. Drill data obtained by the oil industry has helped produce this map.[60] The map area underlain by the Coconino and its correlating sandstones is 200,000 square miles, and the sand volume is estimated at 10,000 cubic miles! That's a colossal quantity of sand distributed over an incredibly extensive area. Cross beds within the Coconino Sandstone (and the Glorieta Sandstone of New Mexico and Texas) dip toward the south, indicating that the sand came from the north. Along its northern occurrence, the Coconino rests directly on the Hermit Formation. This formation has a finer texture than the Coconino and would not be an ample erosional source of sand grains for the Coconino.

Thus, we cannot look *underneath* the Coconino for a colossal quantity of sand, we must look *northward.* However, in southern Utah, where the Coconino thins to zero, the underlying Hermit Formation (and its lateral equivalent, the Organ Rock Shale) continues northward. No obvious, nearby source of Coconino sand grains is known. A very distant source area must be postulated.

As we think about the truly colossal quantities of sand grains occurring in Grand Canyon formations and the very distant source areas for those grains, we come to consider the Flood as an excellent mechanism for distributing those grains. A flood model for catastrophic, interregional erosion, transport, and sedimentation explains the evidences for long distances of sediment transport better than uniformitarian models of river erosion, transport and sedimentation.

Shales of Grand Canyon

Not all muds are rich in lime (calcium carbonate) sediment. Many muds are dominated by microscopic silicate minerals, called clays. Rivers are especially known for carrying enormous amounts of clay, much of which comes from weathered materials on the continents. Clay-rich muds are distinctive of continents, and evolutionists generally assume shale to be the sedimentary-rock counterpart. Evolutionists seem to favor the delta model for clay-rich shales, especially when the shale contains fossils of terrestrial plants and animals. The delta model for Grand Canyon shales has become unpopular, as the tremendously extensive nature of these strata has become evident and as sand-channel systems, suggestive of rivers, have not been discovered. Still, evolutionists persist in their belief that shales of Grand Canyon represent very slowly accumulated sediment. Even some creationists (e.g., Dan Wonderly and Davis Young)

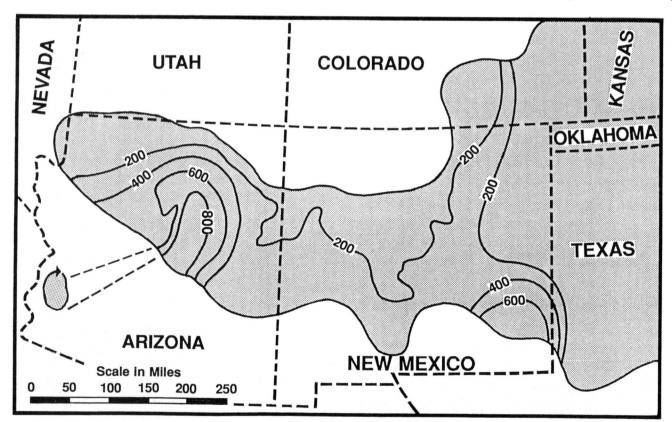

Figure 3.13 *Sandstone-thickness map. The Coconino Sandstone (Arizona) correlates with the Glorieta Sandstone (New Mexico and Texas), Cedar Hills Sandstone (Colorado and Kansas), and the Duncan Sandstone (Oklahoma). The area of sandstone shown on the map is 200,000 square miles, and the volume of sand is estimated at 10,000 cubic miles. Contour lines indicate sandstone thickness in feet.*

have endorsed uniformitarian assumption and suppose very quiet-water accumulation of muds.

Three main lines of evidence have been claimed to indicate very slow sedimentation of shale: (1) thin laminae; (2) burrows of organisms; and (3) shrinkage cracks. Each of these will be discussed and briefly refuted.

Thin Laminae

Laminae are sedimentary layers thinner than one centimeter. They are frequently abundant in fine-grained, clay-rich rocks such as shales. Evolutionists often make the assumption that great periods of time are required to build up thinly laminated sedimentary rocks. Usually, they regard each lamina (a single layer thinner than one centimeter) to represent a *seasonal* alternation of sedimentary conditions—a feature known in some modern-lake sediments. Thus, a single lamina, or pair of laminae, might be supposed to represent the alternation between summer and winter, a one-year period of time. The boundary between successive laminae could represent a break in sedimentation caused by a drought. Thousands of laminae, stacked one on top of each other in shale, may be supposed by evolutionists to represent thousands or even millions of years of slow accumulation. Furthermore, the classical thinking of evolutionists supposes that catastrophic

sedimentary action should homogenize fine clay-rich sediment, and should deposit a massive, nonlaminated formation.

Davis A. Young, Professor of Geology at Calvin College, endorses the uniformitarian way of thinking about thinly laminated sediments. He suggests that thin laminae of the Green River Formation of Colorado, Utah, and Wyoming represent varves (yearly alternations in sedimentation).

> *There are more than a million vertically superimposed varve pairs in some parts of the Green River Formation. These varve deposits are almost certainly fossil lake-bottom sediments. If so, each pair of sediment layers represents an annual deposit. . . . The total number of varve pairs indicates that the lakes existed for a few million years.*[61]

The uniformitarian notion of laminae formation has had a powerful impact on the interpretation of sedimentary deposits.

However, a large body of experimental and observational data refutes the notion that laminae, in shale, generally form slowly.[62] In fact, new evidence shows just

Figure 3.14 *Fine layering was produced within hours at Mount St. Helens on June 12, 1980, by hurricane-velocity surging flows from the crater of the volcano. The twenty-five-foot-thick, June 12 deposit is exposed in the middle of the cliff. It is overlain by the massive, but thinner, March 19, 1982, mudflow deposit, and is underlain by the air-fall debris from the last hours of the May 18, 1980, nine-hour eruption. (Photo by Steven A. Austin.)*

the opposite. Laminated, fine-grained sediments can, and do form by rapid sedimentation. We have even observed laminae deposition in some modern situations, and we can use laboratory experiments to document how extremely thin laminae form rapidly.

In 1960, Hurricane Donna created surging ocean waves which flooded inland up to five miles, for six hours, along the coast of southern Florida.[63] The hurricane deposited a six-inch-thick mud layer, with numerous thin laminae. In Colorado, a storm created flooding on Bijou Creek, and fine lamination was produced.[64] The June 12, 1980, eruption of Mount St. Helens produced a hurricane-velocity, surging-flow of volcanic ash, which accumulated in less than five hours, as twenty-five feet of laminated volcanic ash.[65] Figure 3.14 shows a portion of that laminated volcanic ash. A lake in Switzerland, which was thought to accumulate one lamina pair each year, was shown to accumulate up to five laminae pairs per year, by a rapid, turbid-water, underflow process.[66] One layer within the Swiss lake dates from the year 1811, but was observed in 1971 to be buried beneath 300 to 360 varvelike silt laminae.

Not only do we have numerous modern examples where natural catastrophic events accumulate laminae rapidly, but we have laboratory experiments that allow researchers to see the remarkable process. Horizontal laminae in fine-grained sediment were produced by P. H. Kuenen[67]

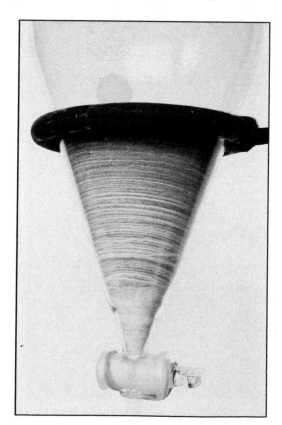

Figure 3.15 *Laboratory experiment shows rapidly produced laminae, which resemble the structure of many sedimentary rocks. (Photo by Guy Berthault.)*

by high-velocity current (upper-flow regime, flat-bed field). Using a circular flume, Kuenen was able to demonstrate that high-velocity currents had the ability to sort and deposit sedimentary grains by weight, density, and shape. The grain segregation occurs as a turbidity current loses velocity, producing a succession of thin, parallel laminae.

Laboratory experiments have not only shown that currents rapidly deposit laminae, they also show that no current is needed to form laminae. In a series of laboratory experiments, Guy Berthault[68] rapidly deposited homogenized, heterogranular clay and silt, both in water and air. He found that the homogenized sediment was indeed deposited in mass, but separated, just after deposition, to form very thin laminae (see figure 3.15). Evidently, the laminae form rapidly just below the sediment-water or sediment-air interface, by a grain-penetration process. The coarse silt particles have a tendency to penetrate downward a certain distance through the clay until they meet the resistance of more compacted sediment.

Berthault demonstrated that this rapid grain-segregation was responsible for forming laminae in some ancient rocks. He carefully disaggregated two laminated sedimentary rocks, then rapidly *redeposited* them with his sedimentation apparatus in his laboratory. These experiments reproduced the laminae of the original rocks, without requiring long periods of time.

Many geologists who have researched laminated shales have disputed the notion that such laminated structures formed slowly. In their classic study of marine black shales of Scotland, E. B. Bailey and J. Weir[69] showed that the shale intertongues with large boulders. They supposed that the boulders were moved during a submarine earthquake, and that an enormous tsunami ("tidal wave") rapidly deposited shallow marine organisms in clay-rich muds on top of the boulders. Large boulders are also reported within the Bright Angel Shale of the Grand Canyon, and would appear to require rapid accumulation of the shale. Rapid deposition of laminated shales and mudstones from Ireland, England, and Canada was documented by D. J. W. Piper.[70] He proposed deposition of laminae from high-velocity, dense suspensions of sediment and water which moved over the ocean floor. In Washington State, thin laminae and beds of clay, silt, and sand up to 300 feet thick, called the "Touchet beds," were once supposed by evolutionists to have been deposited slowly by gradual water fluctuations in an ancient lake, but were later reinterpreted as slack-water sediments associated with the catastrophic floods which formed the famous Channeled Scabland[71] of eastern Washington.

The Green River Formation (Eocene) of Wyoming is dominated by "oil shale" containing very thin laminae. The popular geologic opinion has been that each pair of laminae represents a "varve," the unit of sediment deposited during a one-year period of time. That is the interpretation of Davis Young and others who argue for a very old earth.[72] The very thick laminated oil shales have been supposed to represent deposits formed in the bottom of a lake during millions of years. Has the "varve" interpretation been justified?

Buchheim and Biaggi[73] have devised a test of the "varve" interpretation of very slow oil-shale accumulation. Evidently, this is the first geologic test of the "varve" interpretation. Near Kemmerer, Wyoming, the Green River Formation contains two tuff beds, each two to three centimeters thick, representing the synchronous deposit of a volcanic eruption. The two tuff beds are separated by 8.3 to 22.6 centimeters of laminated oil shale. According to the "varve" interpretation, the number of years between the two tuff beds is exactly the same over the wide area the tuff beds are observed. The number of varves between the tuff beds should be equal in all areas. Furthermore, the average thickness and composition of laminae should be nearly constant, over the wide area of occurrence. Buchheim and Biaggi discovered that the number of laminae between the two tuff beds varied from 1160 to 1568, with an overall increase of laminae number (up to 35%) and laminae thickness, from basin center to basin margin. They also observed that the kerogen content of the oil shale decreased, from basin center to basin margin.

These observations of the Green River Formation are inconsistent with the "varve" model of deposition in a stagnant lake. The authors say:

> *The differences in laminae count, laminae thickness, unit thickness, and kerogen content can be accounted for by a model evoking more voluminous sedimentation and more frequent sedimentation "events" nearer the lake margins than center. The "varve" model is not adequate to explain these differences because it would predict the same number of laminae lake-wide as well as consistent unit thicknesses and kerogen content.*[74]

Burrows of Organisms

Burrows are the tubes left by organisms that live within sediment. Many terrestrial and marine organisms occupy burrows, and, because of this activity, leave obvious evidence by disrupting layering, especially lamination in clay-rich muds. Modern marine and terrestrial organisms are "biological bulldozers," which so thoroughly rework and burrow recent sediments, that stratification is often completely homogenized. An example comes from the sedimentary deposit from Hurricane Carla, which, in 1961,

devastated the central Texas coast. Miles Hayes published an extensive study of a distinctive, two-inch-thick, graded sand, silt, and mud layer deposited off shore by the hurricane. Yet, 20 years later, the layer had been so thoroughly burrowed by marine organisms that it was unrecognizable.[75]

The intensity of burrowing in sediments on land and under the sea causes us to ask a fundamental question. How could any laminae be preserved in the strata record, if sediment accumulates very slowly and is in contact with burrowing organisms for so long? Some evolutionists proposed that the deep-burrowing activity of organisms had not yet evolved, when most Grand Canyon strata were deposited.[76] However, this opinion was strongly challenged by more recent investigators who documented deep-burrow structures even in Cambrian strata.[77] Creationists would propose that the reason that major laminae are not severely burrowed, is because thick sequences of strata were deposited rapidly, not slowly. Therefore, the sediments were in contact with burrowing organisms for only short periods of time, and the probability of burrowing was low.

Burrows and trackways in the Bright Angel Shale (Cambrian) of Grand Canyon were studied by D. K. Elliott and D. L. Martin.[78] They noted obvious evidences of rapid sedimentation in the sandstones and shales, but supposed that long time periods might be represented by some horizons where trackways and burrows occur. Burrows and trackways might be regarded as features produced by normal life activities of organisms. We might suppose that some burrows represent feeding, while others represent resting. Because burrows and trackways might be supposed to indicate cessation of sedimentation, evolutionists have used their presence to argue against a single flood forming great thicknesses of strata.

The trackways of trilobites occur in the Bright Angel Shale. It is doubtful that a trackway, or even several trackways on a bedding surface would require a long period of time to form. Modern marine arthropods can move rapidly across sediment, and can form a short trackway in seconds.

Burrows in the Bright Angel Shale are of two types: horizontal and vertical orientations. Three types of horizontal burrows (*Palaeophycus*, *Phycodes*, and *Teichichnus*) were observed by Elliott and Martin in the Bright Angel Shale. Each of these horizontal burrows was recognized by the researchers to have been formed by marine organisms burrowing, and which were entirely buried within the sediment. Because these horizontal burrows had no connection with the overlying water column, the organisms which produced them did not require cessation of sedimentation, and their activity would have little restriction by the overlying sedimentation, whether slow or fast.

Two types of vertical burrows (*Dipolocraterion* and *Skolithos*) were observed by Elliott and Martin in the Bright Angel Shale. These burrows have direct reference to the rate of sedimentation question, because they connected vertically to the water column which overlays the sediment. We might suppose that these vertical burrows are the *dwellings* of organisms, and that they represent occupation levels upon which marine burrowers lived and died. A long time period might be suggested—an interpretation which might be favored by evolutionists, and which would call into question the model of flood sedimentation.

An alternate interpretation can be proposed for vertical burrows. Instead of representing occupation, or dwelling-sites of organisms, they may have been excavated by organisms escaping vertically from rapid sediment burial. The modern wormlike organism *Phoronopsis viridis* constructs burrows which closely resemble *Skolithos*.[79] Laboratory experiments show that burial induces an escape response from the organism which can produce either vertical or horizontal burrows.[80] *Dipolocraterion*, the commonest vertical burrow in the Bright Angel Shale, could have been made also by upward movement of an organism in response to rapid sedimentation. Two geologists admit, ". . . *Dipolocraterion* cannot be dismissed as an escape trace."[81] If vertical burrows in shale are regarded as the traces of animals *escaping* from sediment which was burying them, then the long time period needed for their formation disappears. Instead, they become evidence for rapid burial.

Shrinkage Cracks

Another evidence, claimed by evolutionists to indicate great periods of time within the sedimentary layers, is shrinkage cracks. Clay-rich muds often shrink when they lose water, and form cracks on the surfaces of bedding. Many different strata surfaces within Grand Canyon display irregular and polygonal cracks (see figure 3.16). Shrinkage cracks are especially abundant within the Hakatai Shale, Supai Group, and Hermit Formation. The cracks resemble those commonly seen in the beds of dry lakes and ponds, or on mud flats on modern deltas. Evolutionists propose that the Grand Canyon shales, like a modern delta or mud flat, were alternately wet and dry. When the surface was wet, water brought in clay-rich muds. Then, when drying of the mud began, shrinkage of mud occurred, and a layer of cracks formed. Repeated wetting and drying is proposed to have formed the different layers of cracks in the Supai Group and Hermit Formation.

Daniel Wonderly[82] supposes such desiccation processes would require an enormous period of time. He proposes that evolutionists are correct in their allegation that no single flood could be responsible for depositing such a formation. Recently, Davis Young restated the case:

> *Mudcracks commonly develop on tidal flats or the shores of lakes when mud dries out. As the mud dries, it shrinks and cracks into individual plates that curl up with increased*

Figure 3.16 *Shrinkage cracks in the Hakatai Shale of Grand Canyon. The shale that was above this silty, and sandy layer has been removed to reveal the pattern formed, as the layer was intruded into cracks.*

drying. Obviously, mudcracks could not have formed during flood conditions, but only afterward. The Supai Group within the Grand Canyon contains numerous layers with abundant mudcracks, as do the Moenkopi, the Chinle, and the Morrison Formations. Each of these formations had to experience several episodes of wetting and extended drying out. They cannot be global flood deposits.[83]

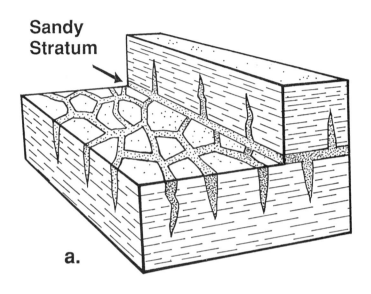

Sandy Stratum

a.

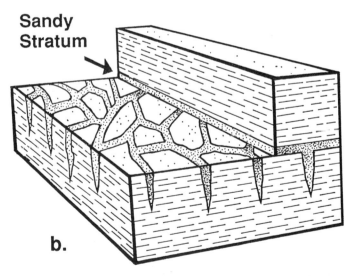

Sandy Stratum

b.

Figure 3.17 *Shrinkage cracks are shown in block diagrams, where sandy or silty laminae or beds have been injected into cracks in clay-rich layers.*
a. *Shrinkage cracks seen in the Hermit Formation have both downward and upward penetration, and document the syneresis process, not shrinkage caused by drying.*
b. *Shrinkage cracks with only downward penetration would be expected to form in Hermit Formation if the clay-rich strata were subjected to drying before the overlying sandy or silty stratum was deposited. Such cracks are doubtful in the Hermit Formation.*

The familiar patterns of cracks in shale is best studied in cross section. The cross-sectional view of shrinkage cracks from the Hermit Formation (figure 3.17a) shows that the cracks frequently occur in clay-rich shale, where they contact thinner silty or sandy layers. After the clay-rich layer contracted and cracked, silty or sandy material, which had not shrunk as much, filled in the cracks. The reason why the shrinkage cracks are apparent in the Hermit Formation is that the silty or sandy material which fills in the crack is of a different color and resistance to erosion.

The desiccation hypothesis commonly accepted for the origin of these shrinkage cracks in the Hermit Formation would require that each clay-rich layer dried and cracked *before* the silt or sand layer was deposited on top of it. The desiccation hypothesis requires that the infilling of cracks was *from above* and that the cracks only penetrate downward, as illustrated in figure 3.17b.

Closer study of the Hermit Formation shrinkage cracks requires the desiccation model for their origin to be challenged. The silty and sandy material fills cracks in clay-rich layers both *from above* and *from below*. This downward *and* upward filling of cracks is indicated in figure 3.17a, where two clay-rich shale layers have been penetrated by a sandy layer which lies between them. Logic would seem to require that the lower and upper clay-rich layers shrank and cracked simultaneously. The principle of cross-cutting relationships appears to require that the sandy layer and upper clay-rich layer were on top of the lower clay-rich layer when the layers cracked. No period of desiccation of the lower clay-rich layer is required to shrink and crack it *before* the sandy layer infilled and buried it. The evidence seems to require that the cracks in Hermit Formation formed while they were buried within sediment, not while they were drying at the surface.

A large body of geologic literature has appeared, which recognizes that shrinkage cracks can be formed in clay-rich sediment *without* desiccation.[84] Both modern subaqueous natural environments and laboratory experiments have demonstrated that wet, clay-rich sediment commonly develops shrinkage cracks. The evidence has been used to document the process of *syneresis*, a process of volume reduction occurring as clay-rich sediments lose water in a subaqueous or subsurface environment.

Geologists have described numerous examples of shrinkage cracks in shales, which have been filled from above and below. P. S. Plummer and V. A. Gostin,[85] who have recently summarized this literature, observe that the "from-above-and-below" filling is diagnostic of syneresis cracks, and document that such features are common in the geologic record. Plummer and Gostin recognize that such cracks commonly form in a "substratal" environment, without the desiccation process. The body of research and experiment, along with the field observations of shale, argues that the long-age interpretation of Hermit Formation shrinkage cracks in Grand Canyon is incorrect. Creationists have an adequate model to explain cracks in clay-rich sedimentary rocks.

Long Ages *Between* Strata?

Creationists and evolutionists recognize significant erosion surfaces between Grand Canyon strata, but come to different conclusions as to the amount of time they represent. Evolutionists currently assign more time to the erosion of missing strata at unconformities than they do for the deposition of all the strata present in Grand Canyon. They suppose that significant and widespread erosion surfaces between strata (which are technically known as *unconformities*) have time durations representing from tens of millions to even several hundreds of millions of years. Figure 3.18 shows one of the most prominent erosion surfaces within Grand Canyon strata. According to most evolutionists, the erosion occurred after the ocean, which had been depositing strata, retreated, leaving a land surface exposed for millions of years to chemical and mechanical weathering and to erosion by wind and water. The erosion surface later became submerged, as the ocean again advanced over the land surface. Sedimentation began again, as new strata were deposited over the erosion surface.

Creationists suggest that erosion on many unconformities in Grand Canyon was very rapid, and, in some cases, they suspect that the underlying sediments may

not have been lithified. Rather than have the land surface exposed for enormous periods of time after the ocean retreated, creationists have proposed that the same flood processes responsible for depositing sediment, were also capable of eroding significant thicknesses of both loose sediment and consolidated rock.

The nature of the debate concerning unconformities is evident from the different interpretations made by observers. Davis Young, who adopts a uniformitarian assumption, wrote of the great ages of time he believes are represented by these erosional surfaces:

> *The presence of each unconformity is physical evidence that the Colorado Plateau experienced consolidation of sediments, uplift and possibly gentle tilting, weathering of the uplifted surface to form soil, and erosion by streams and wind before the sediments of the next formation were deposited. There must have been several of these episodes of consolidation, uplift, weathering, and erosion—a conclusion clearly at variance with the theory that the sediments were deposited during a year-long global flood.*[86]

We can contrast the statement of Davis Young with that of Ariel Roth. Dr. Roth adopts a catastrophist framework, and takes issue with the evidences for great "ages" of time often assumed at unconformities.

Figure 3.18 *The "Great Unconformity" in eastern Grand Canyon. Here, tilted Precambrian strata of the Unkar Group occur beneath flat Cambrian strata. (Photo by Steven A. Austin.)*

The difficulty with the extended time proposed for these gaps is that one cannot have deposition, nor can one have much erosion. With deposition, there is no gap, because sedimentation continues. With erosion, one would expect abundant channeling and the formation of deep gullies, canyons and valleys; yet, the contacts are usually "nearly planar." Over the long periods of time envisioned for these processes, erosion would erode the underlying layers and much more. One has difficulty envisioning little or nothing at all happening for millions of years on the surface of our planet. The gaps seem to suggest less time. . . . The assumed gaps in the sedimentary layers witness to a past that was very different from the present. In many ways, that difference is readily reconciled with catastrophic models such as the Genesis flood that proposes the relatively rapid deposition of these layers.[87]

Types of Unconformities

Figure 3.19 shows four types of unconformities recognized by geologists: the *nonconformity* (where strata cover nonstratified rock), the *angular unconformity* (where strata cover tilted and eroded strata), the *disconformity* (where parallel strata occur above and below, but where discordance of bedding is noteworthy), and the *paraconformity* (a surface between parallel strata, where no discordance of bedding is noticeable).[88]

The *paraconformity*, the last of the four types of unconformities, is often proposed to exist between strata, for the sole reason that appropriate fossils from the intervening "geologic strata system" do not occur at the boundary between the adjacent strata. In the evolutionary explanation, the "geologic strata system" represents an associated "geologic age," so there must be a *hiatus* of millions of years' duration between the strata. Such paraconformities are often admitted to show virtually no physical evidence of subaerial exposure, and display no evidence of millions of years between strata.

Interpreting Unconformities

Norman Newell, an evolutionary paleontologist, is committed to the belief that gaps of millions of years' duration occur between strata, but he honestly admits that the physical evidence is often weak:

A remarkable aspect of paraconformities in limestone sequences is general lack of evidence of leaching of the undersurface.

a. nonconformity

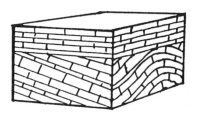

b. angular unconformity

c. disconformity

d. paraconformity

Figure 3.19 *Four block diagrams illustrate the types of unconformities. Erosion surfaces, or suspected erosion surfaces, buried within the earth, take on several appearances. The most pronounced is the nonconformity (a) where stratified rock rests upon nonstratified rock. The most common type of unconformity is the disconformity (c) or its close associate, the paraconformity (d). Paraconformities continue to be debated by geologists.*

Residual soils and karst surfaces that might be expected to result from long subaerial exposure are lacking or unrecognized.[89]

In a later publication, Newell made general application of the characteristics he observed at paraconformities:

A puzzling characteristic of the erathem boundaries and of many other major biostratigraphic boundaries [boundaries separating differing fossil assemblages] is the general lack of physical evidence of subaerial exposure. Traces of deep leaching, scour, channeling, and residual gravels tend to be lacking, even where the underlying rocks are cherty limestones (Newell, 1967b). These boundaries are paraconformities that are usually identifiable only by paleontological evidence.[90]

These characteristics of paraconformities have application to many disconformities, angular unconformities and even nonconformities of Grand Canyon. Important real-or-suspected unconformities in Grand Canyon are indicated in figure 3.20. In fact, Dunbar and Rodgers, who coined the word *paraconformity*, found immediate applications to Grand Canyon:

The relative importance of a hiatus is immediately evident if the beds above and below bear fossils by which they can be assigned their proper position in the geologic column. In most instances this is the final and the only criterion that gives quantitative

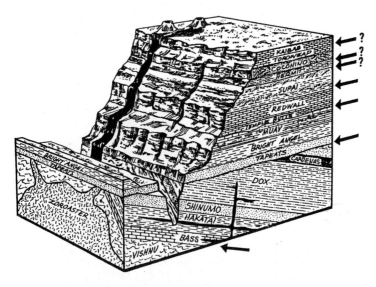

Figure 3.20 *Block diagram of Grand Canyon rocks, showing the positions of important unconformities. Some of these unconformities are real, but others remain doubtful.*

results for the large unconformities. In the Grand Canyon walls, for example, where Redwall limestone can be dated as Lower Mississippian and the underlying Muav limestone as Middle Cambrian, we know that the paraconformity represents more than three geologic periods, yet the physical evidence for the break is less obvious than for that which separates the Toroweap and the Kaibab limestones, both of which are Middle Permian. Many large unconformities would never be suspected if it were not for such dating of the rocks above and below.[91]

From the preceding discussion, it is obvious that geologists often use an interpretive framework to discern the amount of time that may be missing along a particular surface of erosion. Ronald Blakey, an evolutionary geologist, acknowledged this when he wrote:

Unfortunately, presence or absence of conglomerate, relief, or contrast in lithology has little to do with the extent or amount of time missing at a given unconformity. Regional unconformities are determined by regional paleontologic, stratigraphic, and sedimentologic data.[92]

When Blakey wrote of regional paleontologic data determining major unconformities, he was referring to evolutionary notions of the time significance of fossils, especially certain "index fossils," which may be missing between superimposed formations. A particular "index fossil" could be interpreted in an evolutionary context as representing an "age" of millions of years. Absence of the "index fossil" might be assumed to require missing millions of years.

Regional stratigraphic data can delineate major unconformities if an angular relationship is found over a wide area with various formations below an erosional surface. If a formation is supposed to have been deposited over millions of years, its absence at a particular erosion surface might argue for missing strata representing millions of years. Obviously, one's bias enters here, as well.

Blakey also acknowledged that regional sedimentologic data determines regional unconformities. By this, he was referring to the sedimentologic interpretation of the formations above and below a suspected erosion surface. If a fine-grained limestone, interpreted to be a deep ocean deposit, is overlain by a sandstone, interpreted to be a river flood-plain deposit, one might imagine transitional sedimentary deposits (delta, shallow marine shales) to have existed between the limestone and sandstone. The absence of the transitional formation might be used to argue for erosion during millions of years, *if* the uniformitarian assumptions of slow deposition of the transitional formation can be justified.

From the foregoing discussion, it is obvious that the evaluation of the time significance represented by erosion between strata is tied ultimately to one's assumptions. If uniformitarian assumptions are entertained, one's conclusion may indicate a time period of millions of years. If catastrophist assumptions are considered, one's conclusion may be very short periods of time.

The Great Unconformity

The most noteworthy unconformity of Grand Canyon is the "Great Unconformity," which occurs between the Precambrian rocks and the overlying Tapeats Sandstone. Figures 3.18 and 3.21 show typical exposures. Concerning the Great Unconformity, Davis Young wrote, "Scientific creationists, on the other hand, assert that there is no physical evidence for erosional removal of rock."[93] This is an incorrect statement. Creationists have for many years recognized very significant evidence for erosion on the Great Unconformity in Grand Canyon. At issue is not *whether* erosion occurred on the Great Unconformity, but *how* it occurred. Davis Young adopts the uniformitarian notion that significant erosion of Precambrian rocks occurred during many millions of years, by slow processes. Creationists with catastrophist assumptions have suspected

that rapid erosion of rock occurred on the Great Unconformity by catastrophic agents related to Noah's Flood.

Davis Young, however, disputes the Flood. He attributes the deep erosion at the Great Unconformity to gentle weathering and slow erosion:

> *The observed features indicate that the unconformity is an ancient land surface that experienced gentle weathering and erosion over a long period of time before being submerged beneath a gradually encroaching sea. The weathering and erosion effects could not have been produced by a catastrophic flood.*[94]

Davis Young supposes that Precambrian rocks were exposed at the earth's surface for an enormous period of time, while mountains were being gently eroded to sea level. We would expect extensive chemical weathering of minerals by oxidation and acid-leaching processes in the rock directly beneath the Great Unconformity. Furthermore, we would expect the weathered residue, a soil, to exist at this surface.

Has evidence of "gentle weathering" been documented at the Great Unconformity? Geologists have been divided on this point. Robert Sharp[95] maintained that extensive chemical weathering occurred on the Great Unconformity and argued, from field evidences, that chemical weathering

Figure 3.21 *The Great Unconformity. Here, stratified Tapeats Sandstone (Cambrian) rests directly on nonstratified Vishnu Schist (Precambrian). In this photo, the contact represents a "nonconformity," while the contact in figure 3.18 is an "angular unconformity." (Photo of Zoroaster Temple area by Steven A. Austin.)*

Figure 3.22 *Detail of the Great Unconformity in Grand Canyon. At this location, Tapeats Sandstone (Cambrian) overlies Dox Sandstone (Precambrian). Evidences of extensive chemical weathering are not obvious. Instead, feldspar-rich pebbles of Tapeats overlie the unaltered surface of Dox Sandstone. Does the surface of erosion represent one-half billion years? We marvel at the fresh appearance of the contact.*

in a humid climate prevailed. However, Sharp described the very granular detritus at the boundary as "structureless." Evidence for the different chemical weathering zones of a residual soil was not observed. Detail of a typical exposure of the unconformity is shown in figure 3.22.

N. E. A. Hinds[96] disputed the notion of extensive chemical weathering on the Great Unconformity. He could not find significant evidence of chemical weathering of bedrock, or of the debris incorporated into the base of the Tapeats Sandstone. Indeed, in some areas, minerals occur within the bedrock below the unconformity that would be unstable in a humid climate during long exposure. Hinds argued that considerable *physical* disintegration occurred, but without *chemical* effects. It would be appropriate to say, therefore, that widely divergent interpretations have been offered concerning the weathering effects at the Great Unconformity.

How much erosion, even erosion of solid rock, could be performed by a catastrophic flood? That was the subject of a 40-year debate that centered on erosional channels in lava flows in eastern Washington State.[97] In 1923, J Harlen Bretz proposed that deeply incised channels, within solid basalt, were erosional features from a 400-foot-deep flood. Some of the greatest uniformitarian geologists of the present century claimed that Bretz was in error, and that catastrophic flooding could *not* deeply erode bedrock, as Bretz had

Figure 3.23 *Stratum of boulders at the base of the Tapeats Sandstone in the bottom of Grand Canyon. The large boulder above and to the left of the man in the lower right corner has a diameter of fifteen feet and weighs nearly two hundred tons. The staid and sluggard boulder does not move, unless it is given a kick. How much energy would be required to move the fifteen-foot-diameter boulder? It is difficult for the mind to comprehend. The entire boulder-bearing stratum, including the two-hundred-ton boulder, is believed to have been deposited from a catastrophic, underwater mass flow. The boulders are of Shinumo Quartzite, which rest on Hakatai Shale at this location, on the east side of Clement Powell Butte. (Photo by S. A. Austin.)*

proposed. They failed to appreciate the processes of cavitation (implosion of vacuum bubbles which inflict hammerlike blows on rock) and hydraulic plucking (the impact force of water which removes blocks of rock on joint surfaces). By 1960, some of the greatest geologists of the twentieth century had been proven wrong. Bretz's theory of catastrophic erosion of solid rock was vindicated! Geologists have learned that catastrophic floods *do* cause significant erosion of bedrock.

Is there evidence for catastrophic erosion on the Great Unconformity? Many creationists believe there is. Large boulders of Shinumo Quartzite fill great channels of boulders which, in places, occur directly above the Great Unconformity in the base of the Tapeats Sandstone (figure 3.23). These loose boulders and sand have been interpreted by some geologists to be "fossil soils." Arthur Chadwick surveyed hills of bedrock covered with boulder and sand beds. These were interpreted by Chadwick[98] as catastrophic underwater debris flows, which were able to move boulders ten feet in diameter more than a quarter mile. Such processes require conditions which would be very erosive to bedrock. This would not be evidence of "gentle weathering and erosion," as stated by Davis Young. The best theory seems to be that significant erosion occurred on the Great Unconformity while it was under water, *not* while it was elevated out of the sea. Creationist ideas seem to be in line with the facts.

The Kaibab-Toroweap Boundary

Dunbar and Rodgers (cited earlier in this chapter) wrote that we should look at the contact between the Toroweap and Kaibab Formations for obvious physical evidence of paraconformity. When we look at *local* exposures of the contact (figure 3.24 is an example), we usually see no obvious physical evidence of paraconformity. However, many geologists have suggested that *regional* study of the boundary between Toroweap and Kaibab Formations provides an argument for significant paraconformity.

Indeed, the Kaibab-Toroweap contact was studied more than 50 years ago by E. D. McKee[92] and classified as a disconformity. His interpretation was based on two facts. First, east of Grand Canyon, the Kaibab Formation is known to rest directly on the Coconino Sandstone, without the presence of the intervening Toroweap Formation. Why is the Toroweap absent, east of Grand Canyon? McKee assumed that the Toroweap had been eroded from the area east of Grand Canyon before the Kaibab Formation was deposited. The regional stratigraphic study, therefore, gave reason to suspect a regional unconformity. Second, detailed study, by McKee, of the contact between Kaibab and

Figure 3.24 *The Kaibab-Toroweap boundary at Lees Ferry, Arizona. The contact of the Kaibab Formation (above) with the Toroweap Formation (below) at this location on the Colorado River, is not marked by physical evidence of unconformity. Does this boundary represent a paraconformity, with a significant time gap of millions of years between the two formations? (Photo by Steven A. Austin.)*

Toroweap did reveal, at rare locations, small, channel-like "erosional structures" filled with broken clasts of Toroweap lithology. These channels (evidence of disconformity) were at the precise level where the regional unconformity should occur! Thus, the unconformity interpretation of the boundary seemed very secure.

For fifty years, geologists have been repeating the evidence for a regional unconformity between the Kaibab and Toroweap Formations. Thousands of geologists have pondered the signs just below the rim, which give the interpretation of *two different* "ages" of marine deposition forming the limestones. The "Toroweap sea" deposited the first limestone, then the ocean is supposed to have slowly retreated. There is believed to have followed an epoch of subaerial exposure which first caused cementation, then weathering and erosion to the lithified, uppermost surface of the Toroweap. Later, according to the signs, the "Kaibab sea" advanced over the region, depositing the Kaibab Limestone. There is no doubt that this model has had a profound impact on geologists. It continues to be enshrined on signs at Grand Canyon.

Has detailed stratigraphic analysis corroborated the physical evidence for an epoch of subaerial erosion *between* the Kaibab and Toroweap? Doubts about the regional unconformity started to develop in the 1970s. A Ph.D. dissertation by Mather[100] dealt with the Kaibab-Coconino contact east of Grand Canyon. That location is where the deepest erosion of the formations beneath Kaibab should have occurred. Mather was not able to substantiate any erosional channels at the top of the Coconino. This observation was later confirmed by Lapinski[101] and Cheevers,[102] who interpreted the Kaibab-Coconino contact as "conformable." Further studies of the Kaibab-Toroweap contact in Grand Canyon, by Cheevers and Rawson,[103] showed that the channel erosion at the top of the Toroweap was very localized and limited. Studies of the broken clasts of Toroweap lithology at the top of the Toroweap showed that they, and associated "erosional channels," were formed by underground solution and collapse of limestone, *not* by subaerial weathering and channel erosion.[104] No *intervening* epoch of subaerial erosion was needed to form the broken Toroweap fragments or the "erosional channels" they occupied.

We have witnessed a revolution in geologists' thinking concerning the Kaibab-Toroweap contact. Ralph Hopkins[105] now calls the contact "conformable or only locally disconformable." Cheevers and Rawson[106] say the contact is "conformable." The signs at the Canyon, however, still tell the discredited story of *two different oceans* depositing the Toroweap and Kaibab Formations. Where is the evidence for a geologic age *between* these formations?

The Supai-Redwall Boundary

The uppermost strata of the Redwall Limestone are usually very level and continuous. These strata are often overlain by ten-feet thicknesses of siltstone (recently called the Surprise Canyon Formation) or a thick limestone sequence which forms the base of the Supai Group strata (called the Watahomigi Formation of the Supai Group). The upper surface of the Redwall Limestone has been recognized to be a disconformity. In places, a slight degree of relief exists on top of the Redwall, and broad channels, as much as 200 feet deep occur. This surface of erosion is of considerable interest to both creationists and evolutionists.

Evolutionists have supposed that very significant chemical weathering occurred on this surface of Redwall Limestone after the ocean retreated. Evolutionists have suggested that, as the continent was exposed, acids dissolved the top of the Redwall Limestone, producing a so-called "karst" feature. It is often supposed that, as the ocean again advanced over the surface, accumulating the lowest Supai limestones, that it buried caves and solution deposits formed by the long period of chemical weathering and erosion.

The evidence of buried and infilled caves is found at the top of the Redwall Limestone, which contains within it lenticular deposits of red siltstone, clays, or chert breccia resembling the overlying Supai lithology. E. D. McKee and R. C. Gutshick[107] assumed that this solution occurred *between* the times the Redwall and Supai were deposited. Other geologists have assumed the same. However, many hundreds of solution and collapse structures (breccia pipes) occur in strata above the top of the Redwall Limestone in the Grand Canyon region.[108] Many of the solution and collapse structures have filled horizontally, radiating solution drainage channels in the uppermost Redwall, but contain fragments of formations overlying the Supai. Many solution collapse structures have been mined for copper and uranium, and have been documented to contain breccia fragments of Coconino Sandstone and even Kaibab Limestone. Thus, we should conclude that significant solution of the Redwall Limestone occurred *after* the rest of the Grand Canyon strata were deposited. The evidence for solution occurring in the time interval *between* Redwall and Supai remains doubtful. This is a topic worthy of further study.

We might again ask ourselves if tens of millions of years of chemical weathering and erosion would leave so little evidence of solution obviously assignable to the boundary between Redwall and Supai. In many places, it is difficult to locate the disconformity exactly, and it is hard to prove that it exists, especially where limestone overlies limestone. In some places, only a few inches of chert breccia can be found, without any soil evidence.

A channelized flow of water appears to have occurred as the waters of the Flood became very shallow and erosive. Most of the solution and infilling features appear to have formed *after* the Flood. Thus, it is conclusive that solution *has* occurred, but inconclusive as to *when* it occurred. Evidence of extensive pre-Supai solution is doubtful.

The Coconino-Hermit Contact

Another contact between Grand Canyon formations has excited wonder and amazement among geologists. This is the Coconino-Hermit contact, shown in figure 3.25. Thousands of geologists have a vivid impression of the abrupt boundary between the cream-colored Coconino Sandstone above, and the red siltstone of the Hermit Formation beneath, along the Bright Angel Trail. What does this contact represent? Is it an unconformity? Geologists have long pondered this classic locality.

Most geologists have recognized the extraordinarily flat surface to be free of any channel erosion. Furthermore, pebbles of lithified Hermit siltstone are not known, from the base of the Coconino. No soil-or-weathering profile is known at the top of the Hermit Formation. Instead, the Hermit Formation contains elongated cracks (clastic dikes) filled with white Coconino Sandstone at the uppermost surface. It would appear that the uppermost Hermit was not lithified, when deposition of the Coconino began.

Concerning the contact, Shelton writes, ". . . there is no evidence of prolonged weathering or extensive erosion. . . ."[109]

Interest in the Coconino-Hermit contact has been increased recently, by discovery of a thick formation *between* the Coconino Sandstone and Hermit Formation in central and eastern Arizona. This formation, the Schnebly Hill Formation, is composed of sandstone, shale, and limestone, which approaches a thickness of 2,000 feet beneath Holbrook, Arizona.[110] Evolutionists who adopt the uniformitarian assumption of slow sedimentation, might suggest more than ten million years to deposit the Schnebly Hill Formation. Therefore, evolutionists would be inclined to insert a significant paraconformity between the Coconino Sandstone and the underlying Hermit Formation. Indeed, Blakey wrote:

> *The sharp contact may be a major regional unconformity though sufficient paleontological evidence to confirm this hypothesis is not yet available.*[111]

Is there significant *physical* evidence of subaerial erosion (channeling, residual soil, weathering, etc.) at the contact? No, it is just uniformitarian theory that would like to place millions of years between the Coconino Sandstone and Hermit Formation.

Figure 3.25 *Contact of the Coconino Sandstone (above) with the Hermit Shale (below), along the Bright Angel Trail. Geologists wrote that this contact did not seem to be an unconformity. However, recently, a very thick formation has been found **between** Coconino and Hermit, in eastern Arizona.*

The Hermit-Esplanade Contact

The base of the Hermit Formation was first recognized as distinct from the underlying Supai Group by L. F. Noble. Sixty-five years ago, he described the boundary between shale of the Hermit Formation and sandstone of the Esplanade Sandstone (uppermost formation of the Supai Group) as an unconformity of regional extent.[112] The evidence was later reviewed by E. D. McKee[113] and mentioned by Davis Young[114] as incompatible with a Flood interpretation.

In his review of several unconformities, Davis Young cited "the unconformity between the Supai Group and the overlying Hermit Shale" as an example of an unconformity which "marks an extended period of the consolidation of underlying strata, uplift, weathering, erosion, and renewed sedimentation."[115] He argues that these "weathering and erosion effects could not have been produced by a catastrophic flood."[116] Young is relying on the detailed studies of E. D. McKee.

The report by E. D. McKee contains many honest admissions. McKee even considers the possibility that the Esplanade Sandstone was not lithified when Hermit deposition began:

> *The general lack of conglomerate on the erosion surface at the Esplanade-Hermit contact is notable. . . . Possibly the scarcity of conglomerate is the result of the hiatus being so short that the Esplanade did not become lithified prior to Hermit Shale deposition.*[117]

If such a possibility is considered, then Davis Young's argument against Noah's Flood loses significance.

Further comments by McKee illustrate that Davis Young may be overstating his case:

> *In many of the areas studied, in which exposures were reasonably good, the unconformity is not represented by any obvious relief. Massive beds of sandstone in the Esplanade are overlain by shaly siltstone or mudstone of the Hermit with an even, flat contact.*[118]

McKee continues:

> *Subsequent to Noble's investigation in the eastern part of the Grand Canyon, studies of the Hermit-Supai contact have been made in many other parts of the region. In a number of areas no evidence of a physical break has been detected, and at these places a boundary between formations can be established only by placing it arbitrarily where a lithologic*

change occurs. Thus, the significance of the surface as a record of regional erosion seemed questionable.[119]

Figure 3.26 shows an excellent exposure where the boundary is extremely difficult to locate.

One gets the impression that McKee was struggling to defend the unconformity interpretation in the face of admittedly weak evidence. In spite of these statements, McKee persisted in his belief that, indeed, a regional unconformity exists at the Hermit-Esplanade contact.

Recently, however, a regional strata synthesis of Hermit Formation has been completed by Ronald Blakey. He expresses doubts concerning the regional unconformity.

> *At many locations, there is a definite transition between the Esplanade below and the Hermit above. . . . Still other locations exhibit channeling into the Esplanade, but the channels originate from within the Hermit and not from the base. This suggests that the*

Figure 3.26 *Contact between the Hermit Formation (above) and Esplanade Sandstone (below) at Soap Creek Rapid on the Colorado River. At this location, no definite break can be seen between the two formations. The contact appears to represent an intertonguing change in the grain size of sediment. (Photo by Steven A. Austin.)*

erosion surfaces formed after the deposition of the Hermit began. In a few places (such as near Toroweap, in the Shivwits area, and around Sedona), cross-stratified sandstone typical of the Esplanade occurs as much as 100 feet (30 m) above the Hermit/Esplanade contact. This suggests that the contact is variable from place to place and that it represents a zone of transition. The erosional relief also may be related to channel cut-and-fill sequences and not to a major regional unconformity. Obviously, there is a great deal that geologists do not know about this contact zone.[120]

Again, Blakey disputes the unconformity:

A relatively sharp contact is between the two units in some areas, whereas gradation and probable intertonguing is observed elsewhere.[121]

Blakey's strata-correlation diagrams even show the intertonguing and transitional gradation between Hermit and Esplanade. Such stratigraphic analysis does not allow for a regional unconformity.

Can it be stated conclusively that an interval of millions of years separates Hermit from Esplanade? Does this boundary mark "an extended period of the consolidation of underlying strata, uplift, weathering, erosion, and renewed sedimentation," as Davis Young maintains? Are we sure that these "weathering and erosion effects could not have been produced by a catastrophic flood," as Davis Young insists? Many geologists, even some of uniformitarian bias, consider the unconformity interpretation of the Hermit-Esplanade to be doubtful.

Summary

In this chapter, we have explored some of the basic ways of interpreting geologic facts from both creationist and evolutionist perspectives. Specifically, we have reviewed what creationists and evolutionists have supposed concerning the origin of limestone, sandstone, and shale. Evolutionists usually approach the evidence with a presupposition that sedimentation occurred slowly. Creationists usually presume rapid sedimentary processes. Catastrophic-flood processes appear to explain the most common strata of Grand Canyon. The long ages that are supposed to have occurred between Grand Canyon strata are recognized to be doubtful. In many ways, these erosion surfaces (unconformities) between strata can best be reconciled with a catastrophic flood model with rapid deposition of thick strata sequences.

Our investigations of Grand Canyon strata allow seven generalizations to be stated:

1. **Importance of the Interpretive Framework.** The sedimentary strata and fossils of Grand Canyon do not tell us directly of their history. Their history must be inferred. The strata and fossil data are evaluated by placing them into an interpretive framework. This framework for interpreting Grand Canyon data consists of a series of premises or postulates, from which conclusions concerning the meaning of the raw data (strata and fossils) are derived, by using deductive logic. Conclusions drawn are only as valid as the original premises. These premises are held, to a large degree, by faith by the individual geologist. Uniformitarian and catastrophist interpretive frameworks lead to different conclusions concerning the significance of the Grand Canyon strata and fossil data.

2. **Ocean Over the Continent.** Marine-shell fossils are contained in limestones of Grand Canyon. The evidence indicates that limestones, which today are as much as 9,000 feet above sea level, were deposited beneath sediment-charged ocean waters, which stood over northern Arizona. Geologists continue to be amazed at the evidences of marine deposition in Grand Canyon.

3. **Rapid Burial.** Marine shell fossils, large-scale cross beds in limestone and sandstone, thinly laminated shales, and coarse boulders above erosion surfaces all indicate catastrophic sedimentation by water, not by slow accumulation. Deposits which would be diagnostic of slow accumulation (coral or sponge reefs, mudcracks formed by desiccation, varves, and fossil soils) have not been documented in the Canyon.

4. **Widespread Strata.** The amazing horizontal continuity of strata argues against a local site for sedimentation (beach, river, flood plain, or delta), but favors a widely acting agent. Supai sandstones, limestones, and shales are so thin and continuous through the Canyon, they cannot represent a river delta. Catastrophic interpretations of sedimentation find direct application to widespread Grand Canyon strata.

5. **Long Distance of Sediment Transport.** Most of the materials that compose Grand Canyon strata did not come from local erosion and transportation of immediately underlying strata, but from distant erosion and interregional transport. Thousands of cubic miles of Coconino Sandstone, covering tens of thousands of square miles of Arizona, could not be derived from the erosion of underlying Hermit Formation. Supai shales and sandstones, which everywhere overlie Redwall Limestone, could not be derived from the limestone. A flood model for catastrophic, interregional erosion, transport, and sedimentation explains the evidences for long distances of sediment transport.

6. **Rapid Erosion Between Strata.** While geologists continue to debate the locations of Grand Canyon

unconformities and the amount of time they represent, evidences continue to be amassed, which indicate short time periods between successive strata. Regional unconformities *do* exist between some strata in Grand Canyon, but the evidences favor rapid erosion. Has anyone documented millions of years *between* Grand Canyon strata?

7. **Success of the Flood Model**. Catastrophist concepts of sediment erosion, transportation, and deposition have proven especially beneficial for interpreting Grand Canyon strata. The idea that a widely acting flood was involved in accumulating the strata coordinates and integrates a large body of geologic data into a satisfying and coherent package. Catastrophist geology is alive and well in Grand Canyon.

NOTES—Chapter 3

1. For a thorough discussion of the use and abuse of the uniformitarian doctrine, see Steven A. Austin, "Uniformitarianism—A Doctrine That Needs Rethinking," *Compass of Sigma Gamma Epsilon*, 56 (1979): 29–45.

2. Davis A. Young, "The Discovery of Terrestrial History," *in* Howard J. Van Till, Robert E. Snow, John H. Stek, and Davis A. Young, *Portraits of Creation* (Grand Rapids, Michigan: William B. Eerdmans, 1990), pp. 80,81.

   The apostle Peter wrote about the importance of interpretive frameworks. In II Peter, chapter 3, he warned that "in the last days" scoffers would come. According to Peter, the essential interpretive framework of these scoffers will be, "all things continue as they were from the beginning of creation" (II Peter 3:4). The proposition of slow and gradual change will allow these scoffers to question the future intervention of God in human affairs, and ultimately deny the evidence for creation. Peter reprimanded the scoffers for denying two facts: (1) that God spoke and the world was created, and (2) that the world was overflowed by an enormous flood (II Peter 3:5,6).

3. A "two-model approach" to the issue of origins requires that we evaluate both frameworks.

4. For further discussion, see Austin, op. cit.

5. D. E. Wonderly, *God's Time-Records in Ancient Sediments* (Flint, Michigan, Crystal Press, 1977), pp. 138–140.

6. R. P. Steinen, "On the Diagenesis of Lime Mud: Scanning Electron Microscopic Observations of Subsurface Material from Barbados, W.I.," *Journal of Sedimentary Petrology* 48 (1978): 1140.

7. E. D. McKee and R. G. Gutschick, *History of the Redwall Limestone in Northern Arizona* (Boulder, Colorado, Geological Society of America, Memoir 114, 1969), p. 103.

8. Z. Lasemi and P. A. Sandberg, "Transformation of Aragonite-dominated Lime Muds to Microcrystalline Limestones," *Geology* 12 (1984): 420.

9. R. M. Garrels and F. T. Mackenzie, *Evolution of Sedimentary Rocks* (New York, W.W. Norton, 1971), p. 215.

10. Steinen, op. cit., p. 1139.

11. R. L. Folk, "Practical Petrographic Classification of Limestones," *American Association of Petroleum Geologists Bulletin,* 43 (1959): 8.

12. F. J. Pettijohn, *Sedimentary Rocks* (New York, Harper & Row, 3rd ed., 1975), p. 334.

13. M. M. Ball, E. A. Shinn, and K. W. Stockman, "The Geologic Effects of Hurricane Donna in South Florida," *Journal of Geology* 75 (1967): 583–597. R.D. Perkins and P. Enos, "Hurricane Betsy in the Florida-Bahamas Area—Geological Effects and Comparisons with Hurricane Donna," *Journal of Geology* 76 (1968): 710–717. E. A. Shinn, R. P. Steinen, R. F. Dill, and R. Major, "Lime-mud Layers in High-energy Tidal Channels: A Record of Hurricane Deposition," *Geology* 21 (1993): 603-606.

14. R. F. Dill and R. P. Steinen, "Deposition of Carbonate Mud Beds Within High-Energy Subtidal Sand Dunes, Bahamas," *American Association of Petroleum Geologists Bulletin* 72 (1988): 178,179.

15. E. A. Shinn, R. P. Steinen, B. H. Lidz, and P. K. Swart, "Whitings, a Sedimentologic Dilemma," *Journal of Sedimentary Petrology* 59 (1989): 147–161. For geochemical evidence that recent aragonic muds are inorganically precipitated, see J. D. Milliman, D. Freile, R. P. Steinen, and R. J. Wilber, "Great Bahama Bank Aragonitic Muds: Mostly Inorganically Precipitated, Mostly Exported," *Journal of Sedimentary Petrology* 63 (1993): 589-595.

16. R. F. Dill, C. G. S. Kendall, and E. A. Shinn, "Giant Subtidal Stromatolites and Related Sedimentary Features," *American Geophysical Union, Field Trip Guidebook* T373 (1989): 33. See also Dill and Steinen, op. cit., p. 179.

17. Dill and Steinen, op. cit., p. 179. For further caution statements concerning fine, laminated carbonate muds as indicators of slow deposition see Shinn, Steinen, Dill, and Major (op. cit., pp. 605–606).

18. C. E. Brett and A. Seilacher, "Fossil Lagerstätten: A Taphonomic Consequence of Event Sedimentation," *in* G. Einsele, W. Ricken, and A. Seilacher, eds., *Cycles and Events in Stratigraphy* (New York, Springer-Verlag, 1991), p. 296.

19. D. M. Martill, "The Medusa Effect: Instantaneous Fossilization," *Geology Today* 5(1989):201. Another excellent example of rapid accumulation of fine lime

mud comes from Mexico. See D. M. Martill, "A New 'Solenhofen' in Mexico," *Geology Today* 5 (1989): 25–28.

20. S. E. Nevins, "Is the Capitan Limestone a Fossil Reef?" *Creation Research Society Quarterly,* 8 (1972): 231–248.

21. McKee and Gutschick, op. cit., p. 557.

22. Ibid., p. 546.

23. D. E. Wonderly, *Neglect of Geologic Data: Sedimentary Strata Compared with Young-Earth Creationist Writings* (Hatfield, Pennsylvania, Interdisciplinary Biblical Research Institute, 1987), p. 17.

24. R. L. Hopkins, "Kaibab Formation," *in* S.S. Beus and M. Morales, eds., *Grand Canyon Geology* (New York, Oxford University Press, 1990), p. 243.

25. Observation of Steven A. Austin in Nautiloid Canyon, April 1989 and April 1991.

26. Analysis of directional data was performed by Steven A. Austin using the methods of John C. Davis, "Statistics and Data Analysis in Geology" (New York, John Wiley & Sons, 1986), pp. 314–330. A much simpler way of appreciating the preferred orientation of the nautiloids in the Redwall Limestone is by the analogy of tossing of a coin. The alignment of ten out of twelve shells in one 90°-sector is similar to the probability of tossing a coin twelve times and getting heads on ten of the tosses. That is easily appreciated to be a small probability.

27. D. L. Meyer and K. B. Meyer, "Biostratinomy of Recent Crinoids (Echinodermata) at Lizard Island, Great Barrier Reef, Australia," *Palaios* 1 (1986): 294–302.

28. McKee and Gutschick, op. cit., p. 111.

29. W. J. Breed, V. Stefanic, and G. H. Billingsley, *Geologic Guide to the Bright Angel Trail, Grand Canyon, Arizona* (Tulsa, American Association of Petroleum Geologists, 1986), 42 p. "The four Supai groups represent river, delta, estuary, lagoon and shallow marine deposits," p. 20.

30. E. D. McKee, "Characteristics of the Supai Group in Grand Canyon, Arizona," *in* S. S. Beus and R. R. Rawson, eds., *Carboniferous Stratigraphy in the Grand Canyon Country, Northern Arizona and Southern Nevada* (Falls Church, Virginia, American Geological Institute, 1979), pp. 105–113.

31. R. C. Blakey, "Stratigraphy of the Supai Group (Pennsylvanian-Permian), Mogollon Rim, Arizona," *in* S. S. Beus and R. R. Rawson, eds., *Carboniferous Stratigraphy in the Grand Canyon Country, Northern Arizona and Southern Nevada* (Falls Church, Virginia, American Geological Institute, 1979), pp. 102, 103.

32. E. D. McKee, "The Supai Group of Grand Canyon," *U. S. Geological Survey Professional Paper* 1173 (1982): 1–504.

33. Ibid.

34. R. C. Blakey, "Supai Group and Hermit Formation," *in* S. S. Beus and M. Morales, *Grand Canyon Geology* (New York, Oxford University Press, 1990), pp. 167, 168.

35. E. D. McKee, "Experiments on the Development of Tracks in Fine Cross-bedded Sand," *Journal of Sedimentary Petrology* 17 (1947): 23–28.

36. For a discussion of evidences of water deposition of the Toroweap and Hermit Formations, see chapters 9 and 11 of S. S. Beus and M. Morales, eds., *Grand Canyon Geology* (New York, Oxford University Press, 1990), 518 p.

37. Young, op. cit., pp. 72, 73.

38. L. R. Brand, "Field and Laboratory Studies on the Coconino Sandstone (Permian) Vertebrate Footprints and Their Paleoecological Implications," *Palaeogeography, Palaeoclimatology, Palaeoecology* 28 (1979): 25–38.

39. L. R. Brand and T. Tang, "Fossil Vertebrate Footprints in the Coconino Sandstone (Permian) of Northern Arizona: Evidence for Underwater Origin," *Geology* 19 (1991): 1201–1204.

40. R. Monastersky, "Wading Newts May Explain Enigmatic Tracks," *Science News* 141 (1992): 5.

41. Anonymous, "Wet Tracks," *Geology Today* 8 (1992): 78, 79.

42. Glen S. Visher, *Exploration Stratigraphy* (Tulsa, Oklahoma, Penn Well Publishing Co., 2nd ed., 1990), pp. 211–213.

43. John R. L. Allen, *Sedimentary Structures: Their Character and Physical Basis* (New York, Elsevier Science Publishers, 2nd. ed., 1984), pp. 259–266.

44. Visher, op. cit., p. 213. W. E. Freeman and G. S. Visher, "Stratigraphic Analysis of the Navajo Sandstone," *Journal of Sedimentary Petrology* 45 (1975): 651–668. G. S. Visher and J. D. Howard, "Dynamic Relationship Between Hydraulics and Sedimentation in the Altamaha Estuary," *Journal of Sedimentary Petrology* 44 (1974): 502–521.

45. P. H. Kuenen and W. G. Perdok, "Experimental Abrasion—Frosting and Defrosting of Quartz Grains," *Journal of Geology* 70 (1962): 648–658.

46. For a recent summary of sand waves, see C. L. Amos and E. L. King, "Bedforms of the Canadian Eastern Seaboard: A Comparison with Global Occurrences," *Marine Geology* 57 (1984): 167–208.

47. J. R. L. Allen, *Physical Processes of Sedimentation* (New York, American Elsevier, 1970), p. 78.

48. D. M. Rubin and D. S. McCulloch, "Single and Superimposed Bedforms: A Synthesis of San Francisco Bay and Flume Observations," *Sedimentary Geology* 26 (1980): 207–231. For a recent survey of flume studies of bed configuration, see J. B. Southard and L. A. Boguchwal, "Bed Configuration in Steady Unidirectional Water Flows. Part 2. Synthesis of

Flume Data," *Journal of Sedimentary Petrology* 60 (1990): 658–679.

49. E. D. McKee, "Characteristics of the Supai Group in Grand Canyon, Arizona," *in* S. S. Beus and R. R. Rawson, eds., *Carboniferous Stratigraphy in the Grand Canyon Country, Northern Arizona and Southern Nevada* (Falls Church, Virginia, American Geological Institute, 1979), pp. 110, 112.

50. J. W. Brown, "Stratigraphy and Petrology of the Kaibab Formation Between Desert View and Cameron, Northern Arizona," *Geology and Natural History of the Grand Canyon Region* (Four Corners Geological Society Guidebook, 5th Field Conference, 1969), p. 172.

51. S. S. Beus, "Trail Log—Third Day: South Kaibab Trail, Grand Canyon, Arizona," *in* S. S. Beus and R. R. Rawson, eds., *Carboniferous Stratigraphy in the Grand Canyon Country, Northern Arizona and Southern Nevada* (Falls Church, Virginia, American Geological Institute, 1979), p. 16.

52. McKee and Gutschick, *History of the Redwall Limestone in Northern Arizona*, p. 111.

53. P. Lonsdale and B. Malfait, "Abyssal Dunes of Foraminiferal Sand on the Carnegie Ridge," *Geological Society of America Bulletin* 85 (1974): 1697–1712.

54. Rubin and McCulloch, "Single and Superimposed Bedforms . . ." p. 207.

55. P. J. Coleman, "Tsunami Sedimentation," *in* R. W. Fairbridge and J. Bourgeois, eds., *The Encyclopedia of Sedimentology* (Stroudsburg, Pennsylvania, Dowden, Hutchison & Ross, 1978), pp. 828–831.

56. McKee, *The Supai Group of Grand Canyon*, pp. 218–242.

57. Ibid., pp. 335–359.

58. J. S. Shelton, *Geology Illustrated* (San Francisco, W. H. Freeman, 1966), p. 280.

59. Blakey, "Stratigraphy of the Supai Group . . ." p. 102.

60. R. C. Blakey and R. Knepp, "Pennsylvanian and Permian Geology of Arizona," *in* J. P. Jenney and S. J. Reynolds, eds., *Geologic Evolution of Arizona* (Arizona Geological Society Digest, vol. 17, 1989), pp. 313–347. D. L. Baars, "Permian System of Colorado Plateau," *American Association of Petroleum Geologists Bulletin* 46 (1962): 200,201. J. M. Hills and F. E. Kottlowski, *Correlation of Stratigraphic Units of North America—Southwest/Southwest Mid-Continent Region* (Tulsa, Oklahoma, American Association of Petroleum Geologists, 1983).

61. Young, op. cit., p. 77.

62. See summary of literature in S. A. Austin, *Catastrophes in Earth History* (El Cajon, California, Institute for Creation Research, 1984), 318 p.

63. M. M. Ball, E. A. Shinn, and K. W. Stockman, "The Geologic Effects of Hurricane Donna in South Florida," *Journal of Geology* 75 (1967): 583–597.

64. E. D. McKee, E. J. Crosby and H. L. Berryhill, Jr., "Flood Deposits, Bijou Creek, Colorado, June 1965," *Journal of Sedimentary Petrology* 37 (1967): 829–851.

65. S. A. Austin, "Mount St. Helens and Catastrophism," *Proceedings of the First International Conference on Creationism* (Pittsburgh, Creation Science Fellowship, volume 1, 1986), pp. 3–9.

66. A. Lambert and K. Hsu, "Non-annual Cycles of Varve-like Sedimentation in Walensee, Switzerland," *Sedimentology* 26 (1979): 453–461.

67. P. H. Kuenen, "Experimental Turbidite Lamination in a Circular Flume," *Journal of Geology* 74 (1966): 523–545.

68. G. Berthault, "Experiments on Lamination of Sediments, Resulting from a Periodic Graded-bedding Subsequent to Deposit," *C. R. Academie des Sciences, Paris* 303 (1986): 1569–1574. G. Berthault, "Sedimentation of a Heterogranular Mixture. Experimental Lamination in Still and Running Water," *C. R. Academie des Sciences, Paris* 306 (1988): 717–724.

69. E. B. Bailey and J. Weir, "Submarine Faulting in Kimmeridgian Times, East Sutherland," *Transactions of the Royal Society of Edinburgh* 57 (1932): 429–454.

70. D. J. W. Piper, "Turbidite Origin of Some Laminated Mudstones," *Geology Magazine* 109 (1972): 115–126.

71. R. J. Carson, C. R. McKhann, and M. H. Pizey, "The Touchet Beds of the Walla Walla Valley," *in* V. R. Baker and D. Nummedal, eds., *The Channeled Scabland* (Washington, D.C., National Aeronautics and Space Administration, 1978), pp. 173–177.

72. Young, op. cit., p. 77.

73. H. P. Buchheim and R. Biaggi, "Laminae Counts within a Synchronous Oil Shale Unit: A Challenge to the 'Varve' Concept," *Geological Society of America Abstracts with Programs* 20 (1988): A317.

74. Ibid.

75. R. H. Dott, Jr., "Episodic Sedimentation—How Normal is Average? How Rare is Rare? Does it Matter?" *Journal of Sedimentary Petrology* 53 (1983): 12.

76. C. W. Thayer, "Biological Bulldozers and the Evolution of Marine Benthonic Communities," *Science* 203 (1979): 458–461.

77. M. F. Miller and C. W. Byers, "Abundant and Diverse Early Paleozoic Infauna Indicated by the Stratigraphical Record," *Geology* 12 (1984): 40–43. P. M. Sheehan and D. R. J. Schiefelbein, "The Trace Fossil *Thalassinoides* from the Upper Ordovician of the Eastern Great Basin: Deep Burrowing in the Early Paleozoic," *Journal of Paleontology* 58 (1984): 440–447.

78. D. K. Elliott and D. L. Martin, "A New Trace Fossil from the Cambrian Bright Angel Shale, Grand Canyon, Arizona," *Journal of Paleontology* 61 (1987): 641–648.

79. Miller and Byers, "Abundant and Diverse Early Paleozoic Infauna . . . ," p. 40.

80. T. E. Ronan, Jr., *Structural and Paleoecological Aspects of a Modern Marine Soft-Sediment Community: An Experimental Field Study* (Davis, University of California, Ph.D. dissertation, 1975), 220 p.

81. Miller and Byers, "Abundant and Diverse Early Paleozoic Infauna . . ." p. 41.

82. D. E. Wonderly, *Neglect of Geologic Data: Sedimentary Strata Compared with Young-Earth Creationist Writings* (Hatfield, Pennsylvania, Interdisciplinary Biblical Research Institute, 1987), pp. 6–10.

83. Young, op. cit., p. 74.

84. W. A. White, "Colloid Phenomena in Sedimentation of Argillaceous Rocks," *Journal of Sedimentary Petrology* 31 (1961): 560–570. L. Dangeard, C. Migniot, C. Larsonneur, and P. Baudet, "Figures et Structures Observées au Cours du Tassement des Vases sous L'eau," *C. R. Academie des Sciences, Paris* 258 (1964): 5935–5938. J. F. Burst, "Subaqueously Formed Shrinkage Cracks in Clay," *Journal of Sedimentary Petrology* 35 (1965): 348–353. P. H. Kuenen, "Value of Experiments in Geology," *Geologie en Mijnbouw* 44 (1965): 22–36. P. S. Plummer, "The Upper Brachina Subgroup: A Late Precambrian Intertidal Deltaic and Sandflat Sequence in the Flinders Ranges, South Australia" (Adelaide, University of Adelaide, Australia unpublished Ph.D. dissertation, 1978).

85. P. S. Plummer and V. A. Gostin, "Shrinkage Cracks: Desiccation or Synaeresis?" *Journal of Sedimentary Petrology* 51 (1981): 1147–1156.

86. Young, op. cit., pp. 70,72.

87. A. A. Roth, "Those Gaps in the Sedimentary Layers," *Origins* 15 (1988): 90.

88. C. O. Dunbar and J. Rodgers, *Principles of Stratigraphy* (New York, John Wiley, 1957), pp. 116–120.

89. N. D. Newell, "Paraconformities," *in* C. Teichert and E. L. Yochelson, eds., *Essays in Paleontology and Stratigraphy* (Lawrence, Department of Geology, University of Kansas Special Publication 2, 1967), pp. 349–367.

90. N. D. Newell, "Mass Extinction: Unique or Recurrent Causes?" *in* W. A. Berggren and J. A. Van Couvering, eds., *Catastrophes and Earth History: The New Uniformitarianism* (Princeton, New Jersey, Princeton University Press, 1984), pp. 115–127.

91. Dunbar and Rodgers, *Principles of Stratigraphy*, p. 127.

92. R. C. Blakey, "Stratigraphy and Geologic History of Pennsylvanian and Permian Rocks, Mogollon Rim Region, Central Arizona and Vicinity," *Geological Society of America Bulletin* 102 (1990): 1201.

93. H. J. Van Till, D. A. Young, and C. Menninga, *Science Held Hostage* (Downers Grove, Illinois, InterVarsity Press, 1988), p. 104.

94. Young, op. cit., p. 68.

95. R. P. Sharp, "Ep-Archean and Ep-Algonkian Erosion Surfaces, Grand Canyon, Arizona," *Geological Society of America Bulletin* 51 (1940): 1235–1270.

96. N. E. A. Hinds, *Ep-Archean and Ep-Algonkian Intervals in Western North America* (Carnegie Institution of Washington Pub. 463, vol. 1, 1935), 52 pp.

97. The history of the debate over the Channeled Scabland of eastern Washington is summarized by V. R. Baker, "The Spokane Flood Controversy and the Martian Outflow Channels," *Science* 202 (1978): 1249–1256. Further discussion of rapid erosion is found in chapter 5.

98. A. V. Chadwick, "Megabreccias: Evidence for Catastrophism," *Origins* 5 (1978): 39–46.

99. E. D. McKee, "The Environment and History of the Toroweap and Kaibab Formations of Northern Arizona and Southern Utah" *Carnegie Institute, Washington Publication* 492 (1938): 1–268.

100. T. Mather, *Stratigraphy and Paleontology of Permian Kaibab Formation, Mogollon Rim Region, Arizona* (Boulder, Colorado, University of Colorado, unpublished Ph.D. dissertation, 1970), 164 pp.

101. P. W. Lapinski, *The Gamma Member of the Kaibab Formation (Permian) in Northern Arizona* (Tucson, Arizona, University of Arizona, unpublished M.S. thesis, 1976), 138 pp.

102. C. W. Cheevers, *Stratigraphic Analysis of the Kaibab Formation in Northern Arizona, Southern Utah, and Southern Nevada* (Flagstaff, Arizona, Northern Arizona University, unpublished M.S. thesis, 1980), 144 pp.

103. C. W. Cheevers and R. R. Rawson, "Facies Analysis of the Kaibab Formation in Northern Arizona, Southern Utah, and Southern Nevada," *Permianland* (Durango, Colorado, Four Corners Geological Society, Guidebook for 9th Field Conference, 1979), pp. 105–113.

104. Hopkins, op. cit., p. 228.

105. Ibid.

106. Cheevers and Rawson, op. cit., p. 106.

107. McKee and Gutschick, op. cit., pp. 74–85.

108. K. J. Wenrich and P. W. Huntoon, "Breccia Pipes and Associated Mineralization in the Grand Canyon Region, Northern Arizona," *in* D. P. Elston, G. H. Billingsley, and R. A. Young, eds., *Geology of Grand*

Canyon, Northern Arizona* (Washington, D.C., American Geophysical Union, 1989), pp. 212–218.

109. Shelton, op. cit., p. 283.

110. Blakey, "Stratigraphy and Geologic History of Pennsylvanian Rocks . . .", p. 1206.

111. Blakey, "Supai Group and Hermit Formation," p. 164.

112. L. F. Noble, "A Section of Paleozoic Formations of the Grand Canyon at the Bass Trail," *U.S. Geological Survey Professional Paper* 131–B (1923): 63, 64.

113. McKee, *Supai Group of Grand Canyon*, pp. 169–171.

114. Young, op. cit., p. 69.

115. Ibid.

116. Young, op. cit., p. 68.

117. McKee, *The Supai Group of Grand Canyon*, p. 171.

118. Ibid.

119. McKee, *The Supai Group of Grand Canyon*, p. 202.

120. Blakey, "Supai Group and Hermit Formation," pp. 159, 161.

121. Blakey, "Stratigraphy and Geologic History of Pennsylvanian Rocks . . ." p. 1205.

Chapter 4

A CREATIONIST VIEW OF GRAND CANYON STRATA

". . . the waters were on the face of the whole earth"
Genesis 8:9

After the initial amazement of viewing Grand Canyon diminishes, our attention becomes fixed on the strata so marvelously exposed. This enormous chasm reveals a sequence of strata displayed more prominently than on any other spot on earth. We realize that this Canyon shows us the "inside story" concerning the ground beneath our feet. How did the layers form? Which sedimentary processes were responsible for depositing these strata? How do these processes relate to the historical framework of Scripture? In what ways do these strata provide evidence of rapid deposition and a young earth? Our minds become focused on such questions.

Five Divisions of Grand Canyon Rocks

Creationists have divided the rocks of Grand Canyon into five major groups, according to their association with the historical framework of Scripture. The sequence of strata and the corresponding epoch of earth history are suggested in figure 4.1, the cross section of the strata of the Grand Canyon region. This is presented as a model, so that the reader may evaluate the correspondence of geology to the statements of Scripture.

The first, oldest, and most deeply buried rocks are crystalline, igneous, and metamorphic rocks (Zoroaster Granite and the Vishnu Group) which lie below the various stratified rocks of the Canyon. These deeply buried rocks are believed by many creationists to represent the crust of the early earth during the first part of Creation Week. These rocks have been altered severely by temperature and pressure. Great faults have broken these rocks.

The second division, which includes the oldest stratified rocks, is the tilted and faulted sedimentary rocks (Grand Canyon Supergroup) buried, in most places, below horizontal strata. These deeply buried, tilted strata seem to provide evidence of sedimentary and tectonic processes which occurred during and after Day Three of Creation Week. That was the time when God said, "Let the waters

under the heaven be gathered together in one place, and let the dry land appear" (Genesis 1:9). Some of the uppermost strata within this division may represent normal sedimentation in the post-Creation, but pre-Flood ocean. Everywhere in northern Arizona these strata occur, they are bounded above by a very conspicuous planar surface of erosion (the "Great Unconformity"), believed to represent early erosion and the onset of Noah's Flood. Geologists often call these tilted rocks of the Grand Canyon the "Precambrian strata," or the "Grand Canyon Supergroup."

The third division of strata comprises the Canyon's characteristic, horizontally stratified layers (the so-called "Paleozoic strata"), which are four thousand feet thick. These are understood to be broad sedimentary deposits in northern Arizona from the early part of Noah's Flood.

The fourth division consists of strata and erosion surfaces representing erosion and deposition as floodwaters retreated during the last half of the Flood year. These deposits (the so-called "Mesozoic strata") are poorly preserved at the rim, but can be seen north, east, and south of the Canyon. They are associated with the tectonics which lifted the Colorado Plateau more than one mile above sea level.

The fifth division, and youngest group of strata, were deposited in response to various processes after the major erosion of the Canyon had been formed. These most recent strata include river terrace gravels, lake sediments, landslide deposits, and lava flows of the post-Flood period.

Beginning with the lowest and earliest rock units and climbing up the strata sequence, we can discern the order of formation of the Grand Canyon region. The sequence described below can be seen in figure 4.1, a geologic cross section. This cross section involves considerable vertical exaggeration, and the horizontal distances between formations have been shortened to show their vertical position more clearly. Most of these formations can be seen in the eastern Grand Canyon, the focus of our study.

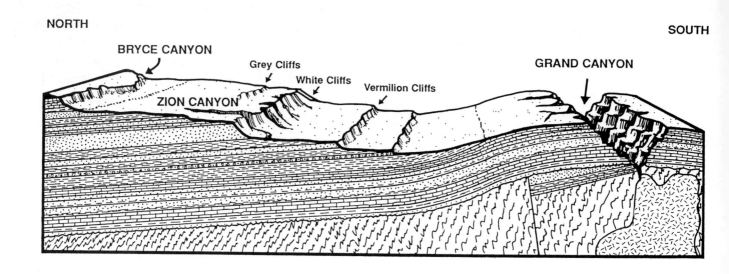

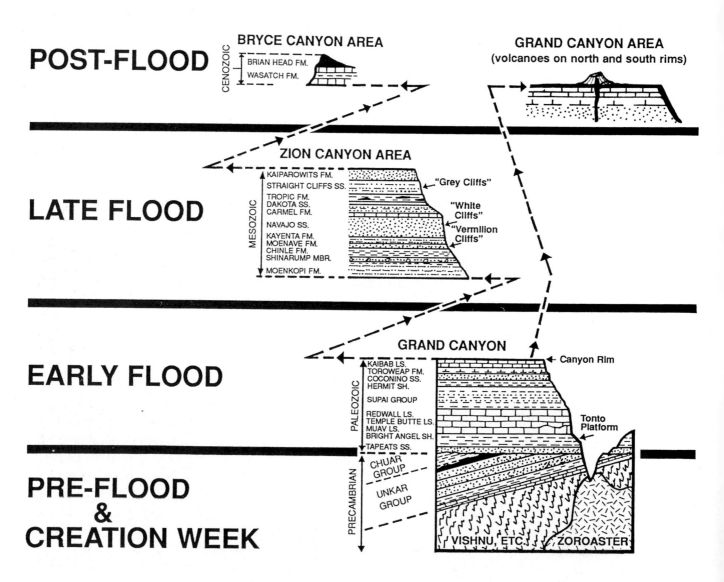

Figure 4.1 *Geologic cross section through Grand Canyon region, showing different rock units and a creationist-strata interpretation. Abbreviations used: FM = Formation, SS = Sandstone, MBR = Member, LS = Limestone, and SH = Shale.*

Knowledge of the rock units of figure 4.1 is required, to understand the origin of Grand Canyon rocks and to relate them properly to the framework of Scripture. Using our "principles for interpreting strata" (see chapter 3), we can "read" these strata like pages of a book. They provide the data from which we can weave our theories and discussion. We begin with the rock layers and build our interpretation of them around the sequential, literal understanding of Genesis, Chapter 1, and a dynamic, global Flood.

Early Creation Week Rocks

What was the original earth like on Day One of Creation Week? The text of Scripture says the earth was "without form and void" (Genesis 1:2). Does this suggest a rocky earth covered with water, or formless matter not yet bound and energized into the three familiar states—solid, liquid, and gas? What does God's command, "Let the dry land appear" (Genesis 1:9), on Day Three suggest? Was there an unveiling of the preexisting rock to reveal continents as the ocean basins formed? Or was Day Three the time when water first became distinct from rock?

A majority of conservative Christian Hebrew scholars understand that an original rocky earth existed on Day One. Dr. John C. Whitcomb speaks for this majority view, interpreting "without form and void" as implying that the original condition of the earth was a waste and desolate place, "not yet complete as far as God's ultimate purposes were concerned." He describes the earth in Genesis 1:2 as composed of rock, water, and atmosphere, with the earth, itself, differentiated into core, mantle, and crust.[1] God's command, "Let the dry land appear," is interpreted as an unveiling of previously created crustal rock suggesting that continents were uplifted on Day Three out of water which had previously covered the whole, rocky earth.[2] Other Hebrew scholars have adopted similar interpretations.[3]

A minority of scholars suggest an alternate view—that it was not until Day Three, when God said, "Let the dry land appear," that dissolved elements precipitated and combined to form the vast complex of the first minerals and rocks which composed the earliest solid earth.[4]

In the analysis of Grand Canyon rocks offered in the following pages, we adopt the majority view. Solid rock is assumed to have existed on Day One of Creation Week.

Vishnu and Related Rocks—A complex group of metamorphic rocks (specifically, chlorite-mica schist, with minor amounts of amphibolite, gneiss, and calc-silicate rock) are exposed by deep erosion along the Colorado River, deep within the Canyon. These metamorphic rocks are among the oldest rocks of Grand Canyon. The oldest rocks may be the Elves Chasm Gneiss and the Trinity Gneiss, which are associated with the Vishnu. Creationists relate these rocks to the first events of Creation Week.

Figure 4.2 *Zoroaster Granite occurs as narrow, vertical dikes penetrating Vishnu rocks deep within the inner gorge of Grand Canyon. (Photo by Steven A. Austin.)*

What the Vishnu and associated rocks in their present form were derived from remains uncertain.

Zoroaster Granite—Nonstratified, crystalline rocks rich in pink feldspars (the mineral orthoclase), sometimes richer in dark minerals (mafic minerals, especially biotite, hornblende, and pyroxene), occur with intrusive contact with Vishnu rocks (see figure 4.2). Pegmatite dikes of the Zoroaster composition are common as distinct pink-colored "veins" which penetrate Vishnu Schist. Some of Grand Canyon's most spectacular minerals come from these pegmatites—tourmaline, apatite, beryl, and feldspar crystals up to eight inches long. Molten material appears to have been injected into large vertical cracks during an upheaval of colossal scale.

Could molten Zoroaster Granite have been injected as dikes into Day-One rock as a large continent and ocean basin formed on Day Three? Such an explanation seems reasonable. Vertical uplift of the continent or downsinking of ocean floor would be an efficient way to cause gravity to collect waters into ocean basins. If this uplift or downwarping occurred, then faults and cracks would have formed in Day-One rocks. Molten material from beneath could be injected into those cracks. The primary region of

cracks in the crust would have been along the line dividing the Creation Week continental mass from the ocean basin. Thus, we might suppose that northern Arizona was directly adjacent to the uplifted continent on Day Three of Creation Week. We might suppose that northern Arizona did not experience as significant an uplift as the Creation Week continental mass. Arizona, therefore, remained seafloor during Creation Week. Sedimentary evidence, from overlying formations, suggests that the continental mass was to the east of Grand Canyon.

Nonconformity—A buried, very-low-relief surface of erosion occurs above Vishnu and Zoroaster rocks and below sedimentary strata of the Unkar Group, giving us our first glimpse of the earth's original solid surface. This surface is shown in figures 4.3 and 4.4. What does that surface suggest?—that erosion was the dominant process. It would appear that the uplift of continents and the "gathering together" of the waters on Day Three initiated the process of erosion. This location in Grand Canyon appears to have remained underwater.

That the erosion process occurred on Day Three is suggested by the Old Testament scholar E. J. Young, in his analysis of Genesis 1:9,10:

Figure 4.3 *Nonconformity between sedimentary strata of the Unkar Group (above) and the crystalline rocks of the Vishnu Group (below). The surface of erosion was horizontal when erosion and deposition of Unkar Group rocks began. Tilting of the strata probably occurred very early during the year of the Flood. (Photo by Steven A. Austin.)*

Figure 4.4 *Tilted sequence of Unkar Group strata in eastern Grand Canyon overlies the Vishnu Schist. View is toward the east from above Sockdolager Rapids. (Photo by Larry Vardiman.)*

*If process is here involved, Scripture does
not mention that fact; the entire stress
appears to be upon the directness with which
the task was accomplished. At the same time,
it could well be that in this work of division
there were tremendous upheavals, so that
the mountains were formed and the processes
of erosion set in motion.[5]*

Creation Week and Pre-Flood Strata

A thick sequence of tilted strata overlies Vishnu and Zoroaster crystalline rocks. These strata are called the Grand Canyon Supergroup, and include rocks of the Unkar Group, Nankoweap Formation, and Chuar Group. Many creationists have suggested that these lowest stratified rocks represent the sedimentary deposits which occurred late in Creation Week and continued into the pre-Flood period. Figure 4.5 is a model suggesting the configuration of the southwest United States during the pre-Flood period.

Unkar Group—Strata of conglomerate, limestone, shale, sandstone, and lava flows appear to represent the deposits of Day Three of Creation Week, and residual accumulation which prevailed after Day Three (see Genesis 1:9–13). These strata indicate that northern Arizona remained as ocean floor on Day Three and for many years

after Day Three. The ocean floor appears to have sunk, as it received a thick carpet of sediment. Current indicators in the sandstones suggest that sediment was transported from the east. The main continental mass was to the east of the northern Arizona seafloor, following Creation Week.

Direct mineralized remains of plants or animals from rocks of the Unkar Group have not been documented. This is a subject discussed in detail in chapter 7. Only *possible* algae-stabilized laminations, known as *stromatolites*, have been noted. Whether these structures within the Unkar Group strata are organic in origin will be a matter for further research. However, it is worth noting that the first living things created on Day Three were plants (Genesis 1:11–13).

There are five geologic formations superimposed in the Unkar Group, with a total thickness of about 5,320 feet.[6] Beginning with the lowest unit and moving up, we have the Bass Formation, Hakatai Shale, Shinumo Quartzite, Dox Formation, and Cardenas Basalt. There are also intrusive rocks called Diabase Sills which are also assigned to the Unkar Group.

The **Bass Formation** is composed of impure, sandy limestone and interbedded shales 250 feet thick. Locally, the Bass contains the Hotauta Conglomerate Member at its base, which contains pebbles of Vishnu Schist and Zoroaster Granite. Dolomite casts of gypsum crystals have been described from the Bass, indicating that the water which

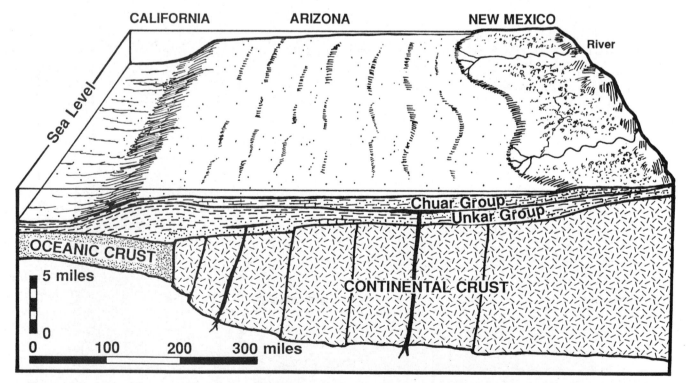

Figure 4.5 *A model suggesting the configuration of the southwestern United States on the day before Noah's Flood began. The area which is today Arizona, was then shallow ocean floor along the pre-Flood continental margin. Thick sedimentary deposits of the Unkar and Chuar Groups had accumulated during the Creation Week and pre-Flood periods. Vertical exaggeration is 15 times horizontal.*

deposited the limestone and shale was rich in oxygen. The presence of oxidized minerals in the lowest Grand Canyon strata contradicts the evolutionist's supposition that the original earth had a reducing atmosphere (i.e., an atmosphere devoid of oxygen, but with reducing gases).

A creationist model is consistent with the evidences of oxygen and calcium carbonate in the ocean when the Bass Formation was deposited. Scripture tells us that the atmosphere became distinct on Day Two (Genesis 1:6–8), and that it had a composition suitable for an enormous variety of plants by Day Three (Genesis 1:11–13). To make calcium carbonate (with gypsum), the dominant sedimentary deposit requires both oxygen and carbon dioxide to be dissolved in the ocean. Limestone of the Bass Formation, therefore, indicates the normal composition of the ocean, and, by association, the normal composition of the atmosphere.

The Bass Formation contains some problematic structures which were once described as "organic remains." Three structures originally attributed by Raymond Alf [7] to jellyfish, sponge, and worm, were critically reviewed by Preston Cloud.[8] He considered the three structures to be inorganic, and that they were formed by sedimentary and compactional processes. Some concentrically laminated structures the size of biscuits were supposed to have been formed by blue-green algae. However, a critical review of the biscuit-like structures by Matthew Nitecki,[9] failed to reveal any organic morphologic structures. Nitecki

concluded: "There are a number of distinct structures in the Bass Limestone, but none of these can be considered unquestionably organic."[10]

The **Hakatai Shale** is brown-to-red, sandy shale, 600 to 1,000 feet thick. The upper part of the formation is bright vermilion and is one of the most conspicuous colors in Grand Canyon. The red coloration is due to oxidized iron. The formation contains ripple marks, shrinkage cracks, and cross-bedding. The presence of fossils is doubtful. In many areas, the Hakatai Shale has been intruded by igneous dikes and sills of diabase (figure 4.6). The heat from the igneous material cooling nearby may have caused the oxidation and red color of the Hakatai Shale. Three subdivisions of the Hakatai have been recognized: red mudstone at the base, orange mudstone in the middle, and purple sandstone toward the top. The formation thickens westward.

The **Shinumo Quartzite** is dominated by quartz sand firmly cemented by silica, with very little clay or silt. It produces a red, brown, or purple sandstone that is a dominant cliff-forming unit within the inner gorge of Grand Canyon. The sandstone commonly contains cross-bedding and ripple marks, which indicate water-current action during deposition in deeper water. No fossils have been found in the Shinumo Quartzite. The formation averages 1,200 feet thick, with thickness increasing westward.

An unusual disruption structure occurs at several levels within the uppermost Shinumo beds. Figure 4.7 is an

Figure 4.6 *Diabase dike at Hance Rapids. The dike was once molten material which was intruded diagonally through the Hakatai Shale (lower part of photo), but did not penetrate the overlying Shinumo Quartzite (upper part of photo). (Photo by Steven A. Austin.)*

example. Sandstone beds have been deformed into a series of complex folds. The deformation appears to have been induced by overloading flat beds of rapidly deposited, loose, water-saturated sand. Evidently, earthquake energy shook the loose sand as it was being deposited on a slope, expelling the water that was contained between the grains. The resulting deformation and associated sediment compaction produced upthrusting convolutions within the sandstone, which can be called "fluid evulsion structures."[11] In the Grand Canyon, faults are known to occur beneath the Shinumo Quartzite.[12] Therefore, the formation provides a vivid example of concurrent sedimentation and tectonics, probably on Day Three of Creation Week.

The **Dox Formation** is the thickest formation in Grand Canyon, recently measured to be over 3,100 feet. The Dox is composed of red, thin-bedded siltstone and shale, with less-abundant beds of reddish sandstone. Characteristic rounded hills in the eastern Grand Canyon below Desert View Tower, are distinctively Dox. There, Dox strata are inclined between five and ten degrees. The lower, sandy beds of the Dox contain the style of contorted bedding abundant in the Shinumo Quartzite (the "fluid evulsion structures"). The upper shale and siltstone beds have ripple laminae, cross beds, and shrinkage cracks suggestive of water accumulation. As we study the Dox Formation, we

get the impression of a downwarping basin, or continental margin, receiving a thick carpet of sediment.

Diabase Sills occur in many Unkar-Group formations. Dark, coarse-grained, gray-to-black diabase (the intrusive equivalent of basalt) was frequently intruded as sills and dikes in the Bass Formation, Hakatai Shale, or Dox Formation. Some of the wider diabase dikes may represent the cracks through which molten rock was erupted to form the overlying Cardenas Basalt. The dike shown in figure 4.6 reveals no indication that it broke to the surface causing a lava flow.

The **Cardenas Basalt** (formerly known as the Cardenas Lavas) is composed of brownish-gray basalts and basaltic andesites, with a maximum thickness of about 980 feet.[13] Lava flows poured out over the ocean floor, as indicated by pillow basalts and interbedded sandstone layers. The basalts overlie the Dox Formation, without obvious scour or erosion to the top of the Dox.

Dating of the basalt is described in chapter 6. The Cardenas Basalt was dated using the rubidium-strontium-isochron method at 1.07 billion years. The basaltic rocks of the Uinkaret Plateau (described later) gave an age of 1.3 billion years by the same method, but are clearly much *younger* than the Cardenas Basalt. The potassium-argon-isochron method gave a discordant date of 715 million years

Figure 4.7 *Shinumo Quartzite in Seventyfive Mile Canyon. Overloading and probable earthquake-shaking of rapidly deposited, loose, water-saturated sand, caused significant deformation of the beds. Rapid deposition and tectonics are indicated in the formation of Shinumo Quartzite! Man's hat provides scale. (Photo by Steven A. Austin.)*

for the Cardenas Basalt. These radioisotope dates cannot be the true ages for these rocks.

Nankoweap Formation—White, brown and purple sandstones average 330 feet thick in this formation. The sandstones contain ripple marks, shrinkage cracks, and cross-bedding. The Nankoweap rests with disconformity on the Cardenas Basalt of the Unkar Group, and has recently been assigned formation status above the Unkar Group and below the Chuar Group.

Chuar Group—In a very remote section of the extreme eastern portion of the Canyon, on the north side of the Colorado River, shale, sandstone, limestone, and breccia overlie the Nankoweap Formation and the Unkar Group. Figure 4.8 shows typical outcrops of these strata. Called the Chuar Group, assigned to the uppermost Precambrian, and divided into three formations (Galeros, Kwagunt, and Sixtymile), the group has a measured maximum thickness of 6,610 feet.[14]

An extensive search for fossils has been conducted in Chuar Group rocks. However, the finds of fossils have not been extraordinary. No indisputable, multicellular fossils are known in these eastern Grand Canyon rocks. Evolutionists suppose that these Precambrian rocks should contain fossils revealing how the complex multicellular organisms of the Cambrian were derived from "simple" organisms of the Precambrian. No evolutionary ancestry is evident.

Creationists have been interested in Chuar Group strata because they may represent pre-Flood ocean floor. These strata may be interpreted as having accumulated offshore between Creation and the Flood, as erosion occurred on the adjacent continental area and brought sediments into the shallow sea. Indeed, large laminated structures, called *stromatolites*, do suggest *in situ*, ocean floor. The massive, 12-foot-thick limestone at the base of the Awatubi Member of the Kwagunt Formation, indicates that organisms known as cyanophytes ("blue-green algae") did build large *in situ* structures. In other limestones of Grand Canyon, stromatolites are known, but those in other limestones (e.g., Redwall) are small, with no obvious binding to the substrate. Evidently, a shallow ocean covered northern Arizona before the Flood, and a remnant of the sea floor is preserved.

Chuar Group strata provide ample evidence of tectonic catastrophism. The Sixtymile Formation, which forms the uppermost 120 feet of the Chuar Group, is composed of sedimentary breccia formed by rapid tectonic disruption and breakage of the underlying, poorly consolidated limestone and shales. Evidently, as the

Figure 4.8 *Oblique aerial photograph of Chuar Group shales and sandstones in eastern Grand Canyon, at Nankoweap Butte. The top of the butte contains the Sixtymile Formation, with breccia beds indicating catastrophic tectonic process. (Photo by Steven A. Austin.)*

Flood began, the Precambrian strata in the eastern Canyon were downwarped into a huge, north-trending trough structure ("syncline"), which lowered them into the earth to the extent that subsequent Flood erosion did not completely remove them. At the same time, the enormous limestone and shale clasts now composing the Sixtymile Formation were redeposited by slumping and sliding, after great masses of Chuar limestone and shale were eroded. The evidence seems to favor the interpretation that most of the Chuar Group is pre-Flood (most representing, perhaps, the first 1,656 years after Creation), with only the uppermost strata representing redeposition by the initial upheaval beginning the Flood. More study on these strata is needed.

The **Galeros Formation** is the lowest formation of the Chuar Group. This is composed of shale and limestone, with minor amounts of sandstone. The formation has a measured maximum thickness of 4,272 feet,[15] and is defined by its four members: Tanner, Jupiter, Carbon Canyon, and Duppa. The base of the Jupiter member contains stromatolitic limestone, with undulating and domal forms embedded in a fine carbonate matrix. These structures appear to have been deposited by growth of algae.

The **Kwagunt Formation** is composed of shale and sandstone, with minor dolomite and chert. The formation has a measured maximum thickness of 2,218 feet, and is defined by its three members: Carbon Butte, Awatubi, and Walcott. The bottom of the Awatubi Member contains a massive limestone stromatolite layer 12 feet thick, with domes up to 12 feet in height and width, and with branching columns possessing thin laminae. Black shales of the Awatubi Member contain small circular impressions of the problematic fossil *Chuaria*, which is discussed in chapter 7. Chert from the Awatubi contains microscopic filaments and spheroids possibly related to cyanophytes ("blue-green algae").

The **Sixtymile Formation** is composed of reddish beds of sandstone with minor amounts of chert, which are interstratified with breccia.[16] The breccia (figure 4.8) consists of angular fragments of reddish sandstone, blocks of shale (from the Kwagunt Formation), and blocks of limestone (from the Kwagunt Formation). Kwagunt Limestone blocks, 20 feet thick, within the Sixtymile Formation, indicate massive landslides from a nearby fault. Breccia beds with finer sand matrix appear to indicate large mudflows. The entire formation has a measured thickness of 120 feet, but may have been much thicker before erosion.

The Great Unconformity—This most important erosion surface in Grand Canyon overlies both the tilted, stratified Precambrian rocks and the Vishnu and Zoroaster rocks. Many regard this unconformity as the best example of an unconformity visible anywhere in the world. Without

Figure 4.9 *The Great Unconformity as it is most often seen in Grand Canyon. Here Tapeats Sandstone overlies the eroded upper surface of Vishnu Schist. (Photo by John D. Morris.)*

doubt, this is the most prominent unconformity in Grand Canyon. Geologists have discovered that this surface of erosion exists through a major portion of the North American continent, and perhaps on other continents, as well.

The magnitude and scale of the erosion which has occurred on the Great Unconformity is staggering. The erosion appears greatest in the western and central Grand Canyon, where Tapeats Sandstone above the unconformity most often rests directly on schist, gneiss, and granite (Vishnu, Trinity, and Zoroaster). There, the structure would be called a nonconformity (see figure 4.9). The depth of erosion is least in the eastern Grand Canyon where Tapeats rests directly on tilted strata of the Unkar and Chuar Groups. There, the structure is called an angular unconformity (see figure 4.10).

Most creationist geologists regard the Great Unconformity as the feature formed during the tectonic and erosive catastrophe at the onset of Noah's Flood. Massive erosion occurred as the upheaval moved and flexed great bodies of earth's crust including Unkar and Chuar strata. The Unkar Group strata were solidly cemented, as is evidenced by rounded cobbles and boulders of Shinumo Quartzite contained in the Tapeats Sandstone. Some of the

uppermost Chuar Group strata, however, were not solidly cemented, as is apparent from plastic deformation of large blocks of Chuar Group strata within the Sixtymile Formation. Overall, when viewed on a regional scale, the Great Unconformity is a very flat surface. Locally, however, the Great Unconformity displays as much as 300 feet of topographic relief around resistant ridges of Unkar Group rocks (Shinumo Quartzite, Cardenas Basalt, and Diabase sills).

Early Flood Strata

Grand Canyon's characteristic horizontal, sedimentary strata are 4,000 feet thick (figure 4.11). These are interpreted as the broad sedimentary deposits from the advance of floodwaters into northern Arizona.

Tapeats Sandstone—The lowest horizontal formation of enormous lateral extent in Grand Canyon is the Tapeats Sandstone (figure 4.9). It is medium- to coarse-grained, quartz-rich sandstone, with a thickness usually between 125 and 325 feet. The base of the formation is often dominated by pebbles and coarse sand in flat beds or cross beds. In some areas, the base is dominated by large boulders up to 30 feet in diameter. Everywhere, these beds overlie the Great Unconformity. The central portion of the formation

Figure 4.10 *The Great Unconformity in eastern Grand Canyon is the noteworthy boundary between tilted Precambrian strata (below) and flat Paleozoic strata (above). Here Tapeats Sandstone overlies tilted Unkar Group strata. (Photo by Larry Vardiman.)*

Figure 4.11 *The extreme eastern wall of Grand Canyon ("Palisades of the Desert"). Here a 3,600 feet thickness of flat strata is exposed. The strata sequence begins with Tapeats Sandstone and continues through the Kaibab Limestone. (Photo by Steven A. Austin.)*

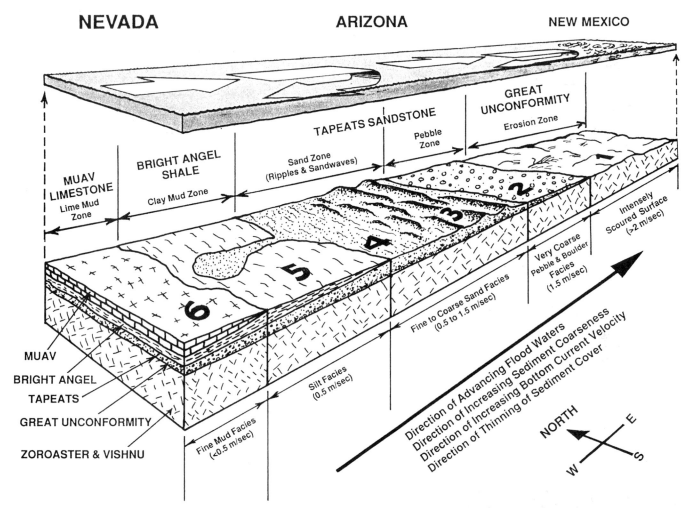

Figure 4.12 *A model for the formation of sedimentary deposits beneath advancing floodwaters in Nevada, Arizona, and New Mexico. The water mass advancing eastward over Arizona has been "lifted" off the surface of the earth to reveal, underneath, the erosion and sedimentation occurring during the Flood. The Flood model explains erosion of the Great Unconformity and simultaneous deposition of the Tapeats Sandstone, Bright Angel Shale, and Muav Limestone. The waters from the Flood have advanced eastward through Nevada (lower left of diagram), finally reaching the more elevated area in Arizona and New Mexico (upper right of diagram). As the Flood advances eastward, it produces horizontally segregated deposits (facies) and vertically stacked sediments (strata).*

Zone 1 is the highest elevation area of the continent, where shallow, fast floodwaters are causing intense scouring and erosion of the pre-Flood rocks.

Zone 2 is the adjacent shallow-water area, where coarse pebbles and lag boulders are accumulating at the base of the Tapeats Sandstone. All finer sand, silt, and mud are being winnowed from Zone 2, and moved westward into Zones 3 and 4 by intense bottom-surging current (velocity about 1.5 meters per second).

Zone 3 is composed of sand waves forming thinly cross-bedded sands, which compose the middle of the Tapeats. Here, the water velocity is about 1.0 meter per second.

Zone 4 is plane beds of sand, with ripples representing the deepest and lowest-velocity waters depositing the uppermost Tapeats.

Zone 5 is located in still deeper and slower-moving waters. The silicate clay- and silt-size particles are accumulating as graded silt and clay beds. These deposits are the residue winnowed from Zones 1 through 4, and compose the Bright Angel Shale. Here, the water velocity is about 0.5 meter per second.

Zone 6 is farthest to the west, in the deepest and slowest-moving water, where there is a deficiency of silicate clay and silt-sized particles. Lime mud, apparently the dominant type of pre-Flood sediment to the west, is accumulating, in Zone 6, as rhythmically laminated and bedded flat strata, where the water current velocity is less than 0.5 meter per second.

The continuous advance of the Flood over Arizona caused the deeper-water, slower-velocity sediment facies to be stacked above the shallower-water, faster-velocity sediment facies. The result is the vertical sequence, consisting of the Great Unconformity, Tapeats Sandstone, Bright Angel Shale, and Muav Limestone. Each has enormous horizontal extent, which can be measured in hundreds of miles. (Diagram by Steven A. Austin.)

is dominated by coarse-grained sandstone having cross beds with westward and southwestward dips (indicating water current flowing westward). The top of the formation is dominated by plane beds of sand, with ripples, and by thinner, fine-grained sand and silt beds which form a gradational contact with the overlying Bright Angel Shale.

The Tapeats Sandstone directly overlies the Great Unconformity, except in restricted areas, where the sandstone thins to zero against elevated Precambrian bedrock. In those places, Bright Angel Shale directly overlies the unconformity. The uppermost beds of the Tapeats contain trackways of trilobites (marine arthropods), especially in those areas where the sand beds intertongue with Bright Angel Shale. Therefore, geologists believe that the Tapeats is a marine sand deposit. It has been assigned to the Cambrian System.

The intertonguing relationship at the top of the Tapeats Sandstone indicates that deeper, slower-moving water was to the west. Creationists have suggested that the formation represents the first deposits from the eastward-advancing Flood in northern Arizona. A Flood model which would account for the Great Unconformity, Tapeats Sandstone, Bright Angel Shale, and Muav Limestone, is shown in figure 4.12.

Bright Angel Shale—Here, greenish-buff, silty-to-sandy shale is 350 to 400 feet thick. Prominent beds of sandy dolomite and silty limestone are very persistent within the shale, throughout the Canyon. Green sandstones, containing glauconite and dark-brown ironstone are also common. The Bright Angel Shale is very easily eroded (figure 4.13) and forms the widest bench at any level in the Canyon (the Tonto Platform). Marine fossils include trilobites (*Olenellus* and *Glossopleura* common), trails, burrows, and thin-shelled brachiopods (*Lingulella* and *Paterino*). It is assigned to the Cambrian System.

As indicated by figure 4.12, the Bright Angel Shale represents deeper water and slower currents than does the Tapeats Sandstone. The model proposes the Bright Angel was deposited in a more offshore area. The top of the Bright Angel Shale intertongues with Muav Limestone.

Muav Limestone—Yellowish-brown, impure, silty and sandy limestone is from 350 to 1,000 feet thick. It is distinguished from underlying Bright Angel Shale by the lack of greenish color. The Muav Limestone usually forms cliffs. Small, irregular inclusions of mud within Muav occur above the Bright Angel Shale. It is assigned to the Cambrian System.

Waters from the Flood were deeper when Muav was deposited, than for Tapeats Sandstone or Bright Angel Shale (see figure 4.12), and current action in deep water was slower. The Muav Limestone would represent the deposit farthest offshore. The calcium carbonate sediment source

was located west of the Canyon, as is indicated by increasing limestone thickness and purity toward the west. Because the Tapeats, Bright Angel, and Muav are not separated by unconformities but grade into each other, they have been collectively called the Tonto Group.

Unnamed Dolomite Above Muav—Detailed measurements have shown that silty and sandy dolomite occurs above, and separate from, the Muav Limestone. This as-yet-unnamed unit, up to 425 feet thick and of high purity, is best displayed at the extreme western end of Grand Canyon in the Grand Wash Cliffs area. Eastward in Grand Canyon, the unit thins and becomes richer in silt and sand. In the extreme eastern end of Grand Canyon, the unit is dolomite, siltstone, and sandstone, with a thickness of 160 feet. Ripple lamination and small-scale cross beds are common. The unit has been tentatively assigned to the Cambrian System and may be named formally the Grand Wash Dolomite, in the future.

Disconformity Beneath Temple Butte Limestone—This type of unconformity displays a surface of slight topographic relief where sedimentary rock strata overlie sedimentary rock strata without evidence of tectonic tilting or faulting. About 30 feet of channeling of Muav can be seen in excellent exposures in Marble Canyon, but this disconformity has been interpreted to include the erosion of the Ordovician and Silurian Systems, supposedly accumulated and eroded over a period of 100 million years! Is such a long interval justified by the

Figure 4.13 *Hikers from an Institute for Creation Research activity examine the Bright Angel Shale for fossils of trilobites. (Photo by John D. Morris.)*

physical evidence? Does the surface represent a period when the marine strata below were uplifted out of the ocean, lithified, and then eroded to a plain? Might the disconformity represent a surface of erosion of soft sediment, rather than a surface of erosion of lithified rock? Evidently, the Flood waters got shallower and bottom-current velocity increased, allowing soft sediments to be eroded in channels as sedimentation stopped.

Temple Butte Limestone—Sandy, dolomitic limestone displays a distinct purplish color. It is usually absent in the extreme eastern Grand Canyon, but, where present, frequently occupies low areas on the disconformity above the Muav Limestone. The Temple Butte Limestone rarely is more than a few tens of feet thick, and is the only formation of Grand Canyon which has been assigned to the Devonian System. This limestone contains few fossils, but rare corals, brachiopods, and gastropods can be found.

Disconformity Above Temple Butte Limestone—A surface of incredible flatness occurs above the Temple Butte Limestone. It generally lacks even the minor channeling of the disconformity below, however, and no karst topography has been found. This disconformity above the

Temple Butte Limestone in many places in the eastern Grand Canyon, merges with the underlying disconformity. There, the Redwall Limestone above it rests directly on Muav Limestone. Concerning this surface, L. F. Noble wrote:

> *In brief, if an unconformity separates the Temple Butte Limestone and the Redwall Limestone in the region which I have examined, it is so obscure and exhibits so little irregularity that it can be detected only by obtaining determinable fossils in the strata within which it lies.[17]*

Later, E. D. McKee and R. C. Gutschick wrote:

> *At 11 of 21 localities examined, including most of those in eastern Grand Canyon, no evidence of an erosion surface could be detected at the contact: the surface appeared even and flat.[18]*

Those places considered to show evidence of erosion by McKee and Gutschick, were where channels of Temple Butte occur (see previous discussion).

Figure 4.14 *Redwall Limestone forms the prominent cliff along the Colorado River gorge in Marble Canyon. In ascending order from the level of the river, the order of limestone members within the Redwall is the Whitmore Wash Member (only upper part exposed), the Thunder Springs Member (dominated by thin gray chert beds), the Mooney Falls Member (massive limestone beds), and the Horseshoe Mesa Member (thin beds of limestone at top of cliff). Here, the thickness of Redwall Limestone is about 540 feet. (Photo by Steven A. Austin.)*

Is there evidence, above the Temple Butte, of tens of millions of years of erosion occurring after the continent was uplifted out of the ocean? The lenticular infillings of Temple Butte Limestone have not been found to contain stream gravels, and, so, are not the deposit expected for prolonged uplift of the continent and river erosion. Could this surface, instead, be better explained by submarine erosion and removal of sediment by water currents?

Redwall Limestone—Very pure, fine-to-coarse-grained limestone and dolomite (light gray in unweathered samples) occur throughout Grand Canyon. The limestone is usually stained red, by seepage and coating of red clays from overlying shales. This limestone forms a prominent 500-foot cliff almost exactly midway in elevation between the Colorado River and the south rim, at Grand Canyon Village. Spectacular displays of the limestone are seen along the Colorado River in Marble Canyon (figure 4.14). The Redwall Limestone averages less than one percent silicate minerals (clay and quartz), although levels are rich in chert and dolomite. Marine fossils of ribbed brachiopods, gastropods, foraminifera, crinoids, and corals occur at certain levels. The Redwall Limestone has been assigned to the Mississippian System. The formation thickens toward the northwest into Nevada, where it reaches a thickness of 800 feet, and thins eastward into New Mexico.

Creationists might suppose that a source of pure calcium carbonate sediments, to the west, was introduced over the Canyon at the same time the Flood waters became hot from the "fountains of the great deep." Coarse-grained carbonate detritus (organic and inorganic) brought in by Flood waters, would have mixed with directly precipitated, fine-grained calcite and dolomite from hot water. Chert also may have been deposited from hot water as a silica gel, which rapidly lithified. Rapid accumulation of lime mud is demonstrated by fossils of crinoid heads (a fossil structure which breaks apart quickly after death), by oriented nautiloids (a marine animal resembling a squid which show current action during deposition), and by enormous cross-bed sets up to 30 feet thick (described in chapter 3).

Four members have been recognized in the Redwall Limestone (figure 4.14). Thicknesses and descriptions given below are from along the Kaibab Trail. From top to bottom (youngest to oldest), the four members are: Horseshoe Mesa Member, Mooney Falls Member, Thunder Springs Member, and Whitmore Wash Member.

The **Horseshoe Mesa Member** contains very fine-grained, light olive gray, thin bedded limestone which forms the top of the cliff at a thickness is 67 feet. Fossils are rare.

The **Mooney Falls Member** is composed of fine-to-coarse-grained, very thick-bedded, light-olive-gray limestone, with fossils of foraminifera and brachiopods. Some gray chert occurs near the top. At several locations,

the upper third contains enormous cross beds, which form the most massive cliff of the formation, with a thickness of 245 feet.

The **Thunder Springs Member** contains very fine-grained, pale, yellowish-brown dolomite or limestone, alternating with gray chert. The gray chert is the most noteworthy feature of the Thunder Springs Member, making it distinguishable from other members of the Redwall. Fossil brachiopods, bryozoans, and crinoids have been found. Its thickness is 90 feet.

The **Whitmore Wash Member** is composed of fine-grained, pink-to-brown dolomite and coarse-grained, light, olive-gray limestone, containing fossils of nautiloids, crinoids, horn corals, foraminifera, and brachiopods. Its thickness is 88 feet.

Disconformity Above the Redwall Limestone—A slight degree of relief exists on top of the Redwall where broad channels as extensive as 200 feet deep occur. This surface of erosion is of considerable interest to both creationists and evolutionists. It is described in chapter 3.

Surprise Canyon Formation—Recently, geologists have recognized some of the deposits directly overlying the disconformity above the Redwall as a new formation. It has been called the Surprise Canyon Formation, and is reported to consist of dark, red-brown siltstones, sandstones, and conglomerates, which are usually less than ten feet thick. It is poorly exposed as a slope at the top of the Redwall cliff. More study needs to be conducted on this formation. It has been assigned to the uppermost Mississippian or lowermost Pennsylvanian Systems.

Supai Group—This sequence of four formations contains sandstone, siltstone, shale, and limestone (figure 4.15). From top to bottom (youngest to oldest), the four formations are given Indian names: Esplanade Sandstone, Wescogame Formation, Manakacha Formation, and Watahomigi Formation.[19]

The **Esplanade Sandstone** is composed of pale red sandstone and siltstone, with large-scale, cross-bedding indicating rapid accumulation from rapidly flowing ocean water. Evidences of marine deposition include lateral intertonguing to the west with marine limestone (Pakoon Limestone), gypsum beds within the sandstone, and fossils of fusulinids (marine planktonic animals) and crinoids. It is assigned to the Permian System, and forms a ledge and cliff with thicknesses usually over 300 feet.

The **Wescogame Formation** contains alternating pale red sandstone and siltstone, with occasional tracks of vertebrate animals. Sheetlike geometry of thick, cross-bedded bodies argues for marine flooding, not river sedimentation. The formation is dominated by cross-bedded limestone in the extreme western Canyon. Assigned to the Pennsylvanian System, it forms a slope 240 feet thick.

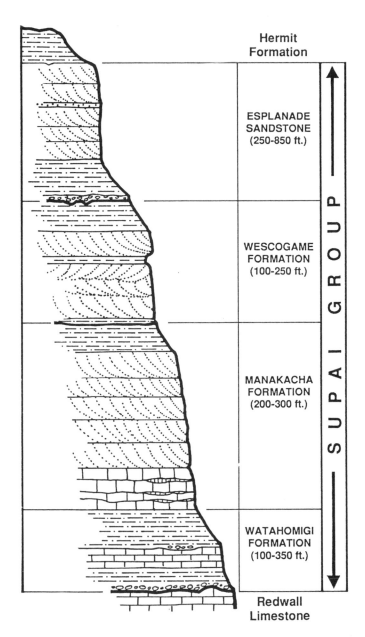

Hermit
Formation

ESPLANADE
SANDSTONE
(250-850 ft.)

WESCOGAME
FORMATION
(100-250 ft.)

MANAKACHA
FORMATION
(200-300 ft.)

WATAHOMIGI
FORMATION
(100-350 ft.)

Redwall
Limestone

SUPAI GROUP

ROCK TYPES:

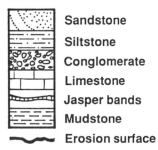

Sandstone
Siltstone
Conglomerate
Limestone
Jasper bands
Mudstone
Erosion surface

Figure 4.15 *The Supai Group contains four formations, and is dominated by sandstone, shale, and limestone.*

The **Manakacha Formation** contains orange-red-and-brown sandstone and mudstone above shale with limestone with red chert (jasper) beds. Horizontal sand beds within this formation are extremely rare. Most of the formation is dominated by large-scale cross beds of sandstone, with some sets 30 feet thick (Havasu Canyon) and 12 feet thick (Bright Angel Trail). The largest cross-bed sets of the Manakacha were deposited by sand waves much larger than those generated in the ocean today by large storms. Strong current, flowing southward, is indicated. Assigned to the Pennsylvanian System, this cliff-forming unit is 300 feet thick.

The **Watahomigi Formation** is composed of gray-and-red limestone, with some red chert beds, sandstone, and shale, indicating ocean deposition. Assigned to the Pennsylvanian System, this slope-forming unit is the thinnest Supai Group formation, usually at thicknesses of 160 feet.

The four Supai Group formations total about 1,000 feet thick in the eastern Grand Canyon. The red shales have been supposed, in classical geologic theory, to contain oxidized iron weathered in a continental environment. However, the very uniformity of the red shales and sandstones over tremendous areas (without a local source area or channel system) argues against continental origin, and for marine origin. Throughout its extent, the Supai Group lies on top of the Redwall Limestone, which, because of its purity, is not an acceptable source of clay and sand. Furthermore, the marine limestones of the Manakacha and Watahomigi formations are interlayered with red sandstone and shale. Could these represent continental exposure? The case appears very weak. Thus, we have evidence for marine deposition of red sand.

The Supai limestones thicken toward the west into southern Nevada, where they have been given formation status (called the Callville Limestone and the Pakoon Limestone). Supai sandstones and limestones have water-deposited cross-bedding, which consistently dips toward the south and southeast. This indicates a northerly source of sand, but it must be very far away. The very thick cross beds in marine sandstones and limestone appear to have been deposited as sand waves moved in deep water by fast currents. One geologist has suggested that the nearest quartz-sand-source area was in northern Utah and Wyoming.[20]

The heterogeneous lithology of the Supai Group makes it distinguishable from homogeneous formations above and below it. Uniformitarian geologists might argue that the Supai Group represents an enormous delta, deposited where a river entered the ocean, but the thin, widespread sandstone beds, without evidence of much channelized sand, argue against it (see discussion in chapter 3). The origin of the red color of Supai sand grains continues to be debated by

Figure 4.16 *Paraconformity between Hermit Formation (below), and Coconino Sandstone (above). (Photo from the Grandview Trail, by John D. Morris.)*

geologists. Some creationists have supposed that hot Flood waters may have oxidized the sand grains.

Conformity Between Hermit and Supai—The boundary between the Esplanade Sandstone (uppermost Supai Group) and the Hermit Formation was interpreted as a regional unconformity, for over 50 years. Recent analysis by Blakey[21] suggests the boundary is conformable with only local channeling of sandstones of the Hermit into the Esplanade. A boundary that once was thought to prove significant time missing between strata has now been reinterpreted. Further discussion is found in chapter 3.

Hermit Formation—Thin red layers of red siltstone alternating with some very fine-grained sandstone and claystone total 300 feet in thickness. Originally, the formation was called the "Hermit Shale," but, because of the dominance of silt-size particles, is mostly siltstone. The Hermit Formation contains amphibian, or reptile footprints, shrinkage cracks, and fossils of ferns. A five-inch-long fossil wing of a fly was found in the shale. The formation thickens westward into Nevada, where it intertongues with limestone. Limestones are also found in the Hermit Formation near Sedona, 75 miles south of Grand Canyon.[22]

Uniformitarian geologists recognize that water deposited the Hermit Formation, but they suppose it accumulated in a continental environment such as a river floodplain, or delta. But a river delta would also contain much more sand, and distinctive channels of sand would be predicted. Again, uniformitarians might suppose the red color came from oxidation of iron on a continent exposed to weathering, but no *red* sedimentary units are being deposited in modern river floodplains and deltas. From where did the red silt and clay come? The underlying Esplanade Sandstone could not be the source, as it has little clay and silt, and is not deeply channeled or eroded. Thus, a very distant source of silt and clay must be supposed. This Hermit Formation has been assigned to the Permian System.

Paraconformity Between Hermit and Coconino—The Hermit Formation has *not* been significantly channeled, and very little evidence exists for an extensive period of erosion between the Hermit Formation and the overlying Coconino Sandstone. Figure 4.16 shows one outcrop of the contact. With considerable interest, we note that almost 2,000 feet of sandstone, shale, and limestone (the Schnebly Hill Formation) occur *between* the Hermit Formation and the Coconino Sandstone, near Holbrook, in eastern Arizona.[23] The Schnebly Hill strata may have never been deposited at Grand Canyon, or were deposited, but uniformly eroded away. In the uniformitarian way of thinking, the time break between Hermit and Coconino might be assumed to represent more than ten million years, yet we marvel at the flat and nearly conformable nature of

Figure 4.17 *The Coconino Sandstone contains enormous, southward dipping, cross beds which provide evidence of sand accumulation under deep, fast-moving water. (Photo by Steven A. Austin of the east side of Crystal Creek Canyon.)*

the contact. Geologist J. S. Shelton writes: ". . . there is no evidence of prolonged weathering or extensive erosion. . . ."[24]

Coconino Sandstone—This noteworthy formation is composed of white or cream-colored quartz sandstone which forms one of the most prominent cliffs in Grand Canyon (see figure 4.17). The sandstone has enormous cross-bedded units sometimes 30 feet thick. Individual cross beds typically have dips averaging 25 degrees, and contain footprint fossils of four-footed animals (reptiles or amphibians). Because of its unique color and internal structure, the Coconino Sandstone is one of the most easily recognized formations in the Canyon. At Grand Canyon Village, the Coconino is 300 feet thick, but thickens to 1,000 feet, 100 miles south of the Canyon. North of the Canyon, along the Utah border, and west of the Canyon, along the Nevada border, the Coconino Sandstone is less than 100 feet thick. In New Mexico and Texas, the equivalent of the Coconino Sandstone is called the Glorieta Sandstone. The area covered by Coconino Sandstone (including correlation to Glorieta in New Mexico and Texas) exceeds 100,000 square miles. The volume of this sandstone is conservatively estimated at 10,000 cubic miles.[25]

The cross beds dip consistently toward the south or southeast, indicating that sand came from the north, or northwest, yet the underlying Hermit, Supai, and Redwall are as persistent as the Coconino, and no angular unconformity below the Coconino is known. From where did 10,000 cubic miles of sand come? Evidently, it came from a very great distance to the north. No local source area is known.

Uniformitarian geologists have proposed that the Coconino sand was moved by wind from the north, and that the enormous cross beds represent sand-avalanche surfaces on the downwind (southern) slopes of desert sand dunes. In chapter 3, a number of problems are presented to question the desert-dune model. Instead, evidence is presented for water deposition.

If the cross beds were deposited as sand waves in water, the water would have had to be more than 100 feet deep, moving southward, with current velocity of greater than three feet per second (see discussion in chapter 3). One finds it possible to visualize a water catastrophe on a scale of Noah's Flood forming the Coconino Sandstone in Nevada, Arizona, New Mexico, and Texas. The Coconino Sandstone has been assigned to the Permian System.

Toroweap Formation—This gray, fossiliferous limestone has considerable clastic impurities, particularly quartz sand. The Toroweap is about 250 feet thick, with the central 75 feet consisting of purer limestone, with reddish, sandy limestone at the top and bottom (see figure 4.18). The Toroweap Formation thins toward the east and contains more sand, becoming indistinguishable from the underlying Coconino Sandstone southeast of the Canyon. The limestone purity increases toward the west, suggesting a westerly source for lime sediment. Brachiopods are the most common fossils (especially *Derbya*, *Meekella*, and the group known as productids). The sand in the Toroweap appears to have been eroded from the Coconino, suggesting that substantial water currents, not a sluggish sea, were important in depositing the Toroweap. The fact that quartz sand grains are dispersed throughout the limestone would indicate that currents prevailed throughout deposition. The abrupt and flat contact with the Coconino, and, in places, an intertonguing relationship, indicates that no long period of time separated the two formations. The Toroweap has been assigned to the Permian System.

Conformity Between Kaibab and Toroweap—For fifty years, geologists have been telling the story of how *two different oceans* deposited the Toroweap Formation

and the Kaibab Limestone. A long period of subaerial weathering and erosion was thought to have occurred *after* Toroweap, but *before* Kaibab. As discussed in chapter 3, the notion of a regional unconformity between Kaibab and Toroweap has been questioned. Most recent geologists identify the contact as "conformable," or "locally disconformable." Only *one ocean* is needed to deposit both the Kaibab and Toroweap Formations. Creationist ideas of a single oceanic flood, depositing both Kaibab and Toroweap, are consistent with the strata boundary.

Kaibab Limestone—Light-gray to cream-colored, sandy and cherty limestone is approximately 250 feet thick. The Kaibab Limestone forms the prominent rim strata at the Canyon (see figure 4.19). The lower part is dolomitic limestone, the middle part is cherty limestone, and the upper part is dolomitic limestone with silty and sandy zones. This limestone contains marine fossils similar to those of the underlying Toroweap. The Kaibab, like the Toroweap, becomes richer in sand toward the east. Just east of Grand Canyon, the base of the Kaibab contains 20-feet-thick cross

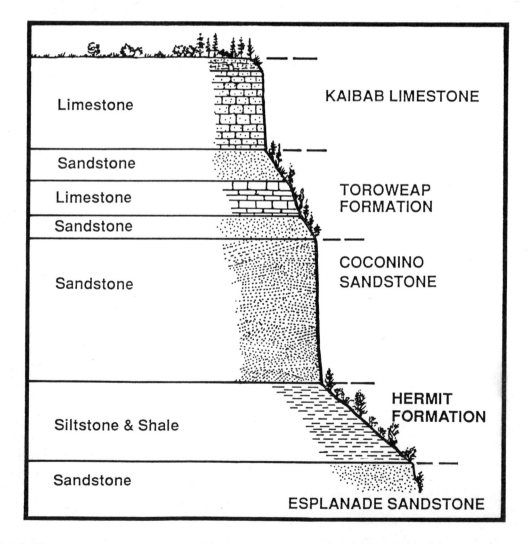

Figure 4.18 *The uppermost one thousand feet of strata in eastern Grand Canyon. Cliffs are caused by the outcrop of durable sandstone or limestone strata. Slopes are caused by weaker strata of shale.*

Figure 4.19 *The Kaibab Limestone forms the dominant rim strata at Grand Canyon. Above the Kaibab Limestone is the widespread erosion surface beveled by sheetlike erosion during the retreat of the Flood. This photo from the south rim, in the extreme eastern Grand Canyon, shows the strata sequence all the way down to the Colorado River (left center of photo). (Photo by Ruth Painter.)*

beds of quartz sand,[26] indicating accumulation from sand waves by south-flowing water currents of from three to five feet per second. Sixty miles east of the Canyon, where the Toroweap Limestone is missing, the Kaibab Limestone rests on the Coconino Sandstone. Reddish zones in the upper Kaibab are caused by sandy siltstone. In the extreme eastern Canyon, the upper part of the Kaibab Limestone contains cross-laminated sandstone with fossils, indicating water-current action, transported quartz sand, and lime sediment.

The Kaibab Limestone forms the rim rock and surface of the Coconino and Kaibab plateaus, because it was overlain by easily erodable shales of the Moenkopi Formation. One does not find the Moenkopi or even the uppermost beds of the Kaibab Limestone at the north and south rims of the Canyon.

Late Flood Strata and Erosion Surfaces

The Bible describes the retreat of the floodwaters as beginning to occur 150 days after the onset of the Flood (Genesis 8:3), at which time the Ark rested on land (Genesis 8:4). However, the retreat of floodwaters continued to occur for another 74 days, before even the tops of mountains were seen from the Ark (Genesis 8:5). The receding of the floodwaters is described twice (Genesis 8:3a, 5a) by Hebrew phrases that are not properly translated in most English Bibles, many of which imply that the retreat was slow and steady. However, the King James II Version of 8:3a, 5a, is: "And the waters retreated from the earth, going and retreating, . . . And the waters were going and falling until the tenth month." The phrase "going and retreating" involves a Hebrew construction similar to that of the raven's motion (8:7), indicating that the waters were rushing back and forth with an action resembling tidal movement, as the overall level of water progressively declined. Such activity would produce distinctive strata. When the water was shallow and fast-moving, erosion surfaces would form; when the water was deep, sedimentary deposits would form. These erosion surfaces between strata would merge with each other as high ground was approached, and the strata would occur adjacent to high ground as an offlapping sequence.

Unconformity Above Kaibab Limestone—A very poorly exposed erosion surface occurs in the Grand Canyon region between the Kaibab and overlying Moenkopi. We see the unconformity displayed at Lees Ferry (figure 4.20). That an unconformity occurs is demonstrated by erosion of the underlying Kaibab Limestone in northeastern Arizona, where Moenkopi shales sit directly on Coconino

Sandstone and DeChelly Sandstone. Elsewhere, evidence of erosion is very difficult to see. H. J. Bissell comments on the nature of this unconformity:

> *Actually the surface of contact appears to be a paraconformity; yet, if true, why is there supposedly an hiatus of substantial time-gap? The surface between sediments that accumulated during Late Paleozoic and those of Early Mesozoic does not everywhere in the study area suggest an erosional vacuity. Is it possible to have very little evidence of physical erosion between the rocks of two geologic eras, yet have a substantial time gap?*[27]

This honest admission indicates that a great time gap may not be represented by this unconformity.

Evidently the waters of the Flood became shallower, and thus more erosive. This unconformity and others above it seem to mark a turning point in the Flood, when the waters began to decrease in northern Arizona. The present erosion surface on top of the Kaibab Limestone, which forms many of the plateaus in the Grand Canyon area, was caused by sheet-flood erosion, as northern Arizona became exposed later in the Flood. Evidently, many formations were poorly lithified as erosion of sediment occurred.

Moenkopi Formation—Strong evidence exists that the Kaibab Limestone, which forms the rim of the Canyon, was overlain everywhere by the Moenkopi Formation, a red-colored mudstone, siltstone, and sandstone deposit, almost 300 feet thick. The middle of the unit contains gray-to-buff claystone, with lenses and veins of gypsum. The formation is very soft, and is often poorly exposed due to its ease of erosion. Erosionally isolated remnants of Moenkopi occur at Red Butte (sixteen miles south of Grand Canyon Village) and at Cedar Mountain (three miles east of Desert View Tower). Thus, we suppose that Moenkopi originally lay on top of Kaibab throughout the Grand Canyon region, before erosion removed the Moenkopi. The Moenkopi Formation is best exposed east of the Canyon, as at Wupatki National Monument, 30 miles north of Flagstaff. The Moenkopi has been assigned to the Triassic System.

Chinle Formation—The top of Cedar Mountain (east of Desert View Tower) and the top of Red Butte (south of Grand Canyon Village) are capped by a resistant layer of sandstone and conglomerate (the Shinarump Conglomerate Member of the Chinle Formation), which appears to be the erosional remnant of an enormously vast chert pebble and sandstone layer which can be found north, east, south and west of the Canyon. The chert pebbles have no source known from strata lying beneath the Chinle. The pebbles must have been transported by shallow, sheet flooding, from a very distant, exposed source area.

The bulk of the Chinle Formation above the conglomerate is reddish-purple and purple sandstones, with gray, green, and brown shales and volcanic ash beds. A

Figure 4.20 *The contact between the Kaibab Limestone (below) and the Moenkopi Formation (above), at Lees Ferry on the Colorado River. The boundary between the two formations has been called a paraconformity. (Photo by Steven A. Austin.)*

truly colossal quantity of volcanic ash (many thousands of cubic miles) occurs in the Chinle. Evidence suggest a massive source of volcanic debris south of Grand Canyon, as the Flood retreated. The volcanoes appear to have been located in Mexico.

The Chinle Formation contains large fossil logs, ferns, dinosaur fossils, and marine invertebrate fossils. The Petrified Forest National Park is famous for its petrified wood. The large fossil logs within the Chinle Formation are deposited with branches stripped off, and with the long axes of logs oriented in a dominant direction. Evidently, enormous masses of logs were floated and then deposited by a current on an exposed land surface, as the Flood was retreating. Burial of the logs with volcanic ash helped to petrify the wood.

Widespread Erosion Surface Above Grand Canyon Formations—An enormous, fairly flat erosion surface occurs above most Grand Canyon formations. It forms the upper surface of many of the most prominent plateaus of northern Arizona. Figure 4.21 shows the erosion surface in the extreme eastern Grand Canyon. At Grand Canyon, this erosion surface is most commonly seen as the upper surface of the Coconino and Kaibab Plateaus. In fact, most visitors stand on its surface as they view the Canyon. The Kaibab Limestone is the most prominent formation observed at this surface. Even formations above the Chinle, however, have been beveled by this extensive erosion. North of Grand Canyon, the Navajo Sandstone occurs beneath the erosional surface.

The physical evidence for extensive post-Chinle erosion in northern Arizona is best regarded as the product of sheet-flood erosion, as the waters of the Flood retreated off Arizona. As they retreated, poorly consolidated, recently deposited formations beneath were beveled. Exactly what the thickness of these formations was above Grand Canyon is not certain, as they no longer occur there. Today, many of the elevated plateaus of northern Arizona endure as uplifted monuments of sheet-flood erosion. This broad erosion is to be contrasted with the channelized erosion which forms the present topographic expression within the Canyon. This channelized erosion is more recent than the extensive sheet-flood erosion of the plateaus. Chapter 5 describes the evidence for post-Flood channelized erosion within the Canyon.

Post-Flood Deposits

A variety of post-Flood deposits occurs in direct association with Grand Canyon. These are volcanic strata, landslide deposits, river gravels, and lake deposits which accumulated in response to one mile of vertical uplift of northern Arizona.

Volcanic Rocks of Western Grand Canyon—In the Toroweap area, on the north side of the Colorado River, volcanoes flooded large areas of plateaus with lava, which cooled to form the rock called basalt. Some of these lava flows actually spilled over the north rim of the Canyon, forming frozen lava falls, descending to the level of the river (figure 4.22). Lavas even blocked the river, forming large lakes, which occupied the eastern Canyon area. Breaching of these lava dams caused recent catastrophic

Figure 4.21 *Widespread erosion surface on top of the Kaibab Limestone just northeast of Grand Canyon. (Oblique aerial photo by Steven A. Austin.)*

Figure 4.22 *Lava Falls area in western Grand Canyon. Lava flows spilled over the north rim of Grand Canyon (right) and blocked the Colorado River. The volcanic rock is basalt and has a very black appearance. (Photo by Steven A. Austin.)*

erosion, especially in the inner gorge of the Canyon. Many of these lava flows are attributed to the Pleistocene by geologists, but give anomalous radioisotope dates. These flows obviously post-date the erosion of the Canyon, and some appear to be as fresh as any erupted from modern volcanoes just hundreds of years ago. A rubidium-strontium isochron "age" of 1.3 billion years was generated for these rocks (see chapter 6)—an "age" which is geologically ridiculous. This shows that radioisotope dating methods do not give reliable ages for rocks.

Landslide Deposits—Following the major erosion of the Colorado Plateau and establishment of the Canyon, landslides have been a dominant mode of cliff retreat. Many significant, large landslide deposits are located in the eastern and western Grand Canyon. Landslides, no doubt, were more numerous in the past, when slopes were significantly wetter and more unstable, especially in the early post-Flood period.

River Gravels—Rather small deposits of river gravels occur within Grand Canyon, because the dominant process within the Canyon has been erosion. To the west, we find the recent river gravels from the Colorado River. No deep and massive accumulation of gravel is known, and an extensive history of continuous river erosion over tens of millions of years remains doubtful. The thickness of river deposits and other evidences for catastrophic erosion of the Canyon are discussed in chapter 5.

Lake Deposits—Silt and travertine deposits suggest brief intervals when post-Flood lakes existed within the Canyon. These lakes were formed behind large lava dams, which formed from lava flows from the north-rim volcanoes in western Grand Canyon. Evidence of an ancient large lake east of the Canyon is found in the Bidahochi Formation (Pliocene), which may have caused catastrophic drainage through the Canyon in the post-Flood period. That is a topic discussed in chapter 5.

Summary

In this chapter, we have explored some of the basic ways of interpreting strata from a creationist and catastrophist framework. Five main divisions of Grand Canyon rocks can be integrated well into the historic framework of

Scripture. The crystalline-basement rocks exposed deep within the Canyon (schist, granite, and gneiss) represent some of earth's oldest rocks, probably from early in Creation Week. Tilted, deeply buried strata (the "Grand Canyon Supergroup") show evidence of catastrophic-marine sedimentation and tectonics associated with the formation of an ocean basin midway through Creation Week, and may include ocean deposits from the post-Creation, but pre-Flood world. The Canyon's characteristic horizontally stratified layers (the "Paleozoic Strata") are up to 4,000 feet thick and are understood to be broad sedimentary deposits in northern Arizona dating from the early part of

Noah's Flood. Remnants of strata overlying the rim of Grand Canyon (the "Mesozoic Strata") are associated with a widespread erosion surface. These features suggest tectonics, sedimentation, and erosion during the last half of the Flood year as the Colorado Plateau was lifted more than a mile above sea level. The catastrophic erosion of Grand Canyon (probably a result of drainage of lakes) was associated with river-terrace gravels, lake sediments, landslide deposits, and lava flows of the post-Flood period. A detailed review of dozens of formations of northern Arizona indicates that they can be interpreted well within the framework of Scripture.

NOTES—Chapter 4

1. John C. Whitcomb, Jr., *The Early Earth* (Grand Rapids, Michigan, Baker Book House, revised edition, 1986), p. 149.

2. Ibid., p. 39.

3. Edward J. Young, *Studies in Genesis One* (Philadelphia, Presbyterian and Reformed Publishing Co., 1964), pp. 34, 35, 91. U. Cassuto, *From Adam to Noah* (Jerusalem, Magnes Press, Part One, 1978), p. 35. "The waters, which were still covering everything under the heavens, were to be concentrated in one place, and, as a result, the solid matter hidden beneath them would be revealed in the remaining areas." Elsewhere, in John C. Whitcomb and Henry M. Morris, *The Genesis Flood* (Philadelphia, Presbyterian and Reformed Publishing Co., 1961), pp. 229, 230, we read, "Then, on the third day, came the first appearance of 'dry land.' The waters under the firmament were gathered together into one common bed as the lands under them sank. In other parts, the lands rose and a great continent or continents appeared (Genesis 1:9,10)."

4. Henry M. Morris, *The Genesis Record* (San Diego, California, Creation-Life Publishers, 1976), pp. 50, 51, 61.

5. E. J. Young, *Studies in Genesis One*, p. 91.

6. T. D. Ford and W. J. Breed, "The Younger Precambrian Rocks of the Grand Canyon," *in* W. J. Breed and E. Roat, eds., *Geology of the Grand Canyon*, (Flagstaff, Museum of Northern Arizona, 2nd. ed., 1976), pp. 21–40.

7. R. M. Alf, "Possible Fossils from the Early Proterozoic Bass Formation, Grand Canyon, Arizona," *Plateau* 31 (1959): 60–63.

8. P. E. Cloud, Jr., "Pre-Metazoan Evolution and the Origins of the Metazoa," *in* E.T. Drake, ed., *Evolution and Environment* (Yale, Yale University Press, 1968), pp. 1–72.

9. M. H. Nitecki, "Pseudo-organic Structures in the Precambrian Bass Limestone in Arizona," *Fieldiana Geology* 23 (1971): 1–9.

10. Ibid, p. 3.

11. D. P. Elston, "Grand Canyon Supergroup, Northern Arizona: Stratigraphic Summary and Preliminary Paleomagnetic Correlations with Parts of Other North American Proterozoic Successions," *in* J. P. Jenny and S. J. Reynolds, eds., *Geologic Evolution of Arizona* (Tucson, Arizona Geological Society Digest 17, 1989), p. 264.

12. J. W. Sears, "Structural Geology of the Precambrian Grand Canyon Series, Arizona" (Laramie, Wyoming University, unpublished M.S. thesis, 1973), 100 p.

13. J. D. Hendricks, "Petrology and Chemistry of Igneous Rocks of Middle Proterozoic Unkar Group, Grand Canyon Supergroup, Northern Arizona," *in* D. P. Elston, G. H. Billingsley, and R. A. Young, eds., *Geology of Grand Canyon, Northern Arizona* (Washington, D.C., American Geophysical Union, 1989), pp. 106–116.

14. Ford and Breed, "The Younger Precambrian Rocks of the Grand Canyon."

15. Ibid.

16. D. P. Elston, "Late Precambrian Sixtymile Formation and Orogeny at the Top of the Grand Canyon Supergroup, Northern Arizona," *U. S. Geological Survey Professional Paper* 1092 (1979): 1–20.

17. L. F. Noble, "A Section of the Paleozoic Formations of the Grand Canyon at the Bass Trail," *U. S. Geological Survey Professional Paper* 131 (1923): 54.

18. E. D. McKee and R. G. Gutschick, *History of the Redwall Limestone in Northern Arizona* (Boulder, Colorado, Geological Society of America, Memoir 114, 1969), p. 16.

19.   E. D. McKee, "The Supai Group of Grand Canyon," *U. S. Geological Survey Professional Paper* 1173 (1982): 1–504.

20.   R. C. Blakey, "Stratigraphy of the Supai Group (Pennsylvanian-Permian), Mogollon Rim, Arizona," *in* S. S. Beus and R. R. Rawson, eds., *Carboniferous Stratigraphy in the Grand Canyon Country, Northern Arizona, and Southern Nevada* (Falls Church, Virginia, American Geological Institute, 1979), pp. 102, 103.

21.   R. C. Blakey, "Supai Group and Hermit Formation," *in* S.S. Beus and M. Morales, *Grand Canyon Geology* (New York, Oxford University Press, 1990), pp. 159, 161. See more extensive discussion of this contact in chapter 3.

22.   Blakey, "Stratigraphy of the Supai Group . . . ," p. 101.

23.   R. C. Blakey, "Stratigraphy and Geologic History of Pennsylvanian and Permian Rocks, Mogollon Rim Region, Central Arizona and Vicinity," *Geological Society of America Bulletin* 102 (1990): 1206.

24.   John S. Shelton, *Geology Illustrated* (San Francisco, W. H. Freeman, 1966), p. 283.

25.   See discussion of the area and volume of Coconino Sandstone and its correlating strata in chapter 3.

26.   J. W. Brown, "Stratigraphy and Petrology of the Kaibab Formation Between Desert View and Cameron, Northern Arizona," *Geology and Natural History of the Grand Canyon Region* (Four Corners Geological Society Guidebook, 5th Field Conference, 1969), p. 172.

27.   H. J. Bissell, "Permian and Lower Triassic Transition from the Shelf to Basin (Grand Canyon, Arizona to Spring Mountains, Nevada)," *Geology and Natural History of the Grand Canyon Region* (Durango, Colorado, Four Corners Geological Society, Guidebook for the 5th Field Conference, 1969), p. 156.

Chapter 5

HOW WAS GRAND CANYON ERODED?

*"The greatest of the Grand Canyon's enigmas is the problem of how it was made.
This is the most volatile aspect of Grand Canyon geological studies. . . .
Grand Canyon has held tight to her secrets of origin and age. Every approach to
this problem has been cloaked in hypothesis, drawing on the incomplete
empirical evidence of stratigraphy, sedimentology, and radiometric dating"*
Earle E. Spamer, 1989

*"In the inductive process, the more hypotheses the better. . . . Contrary to this essential . . .
the doctrine of uniformitarianism leads to poverty where riches are to be desired"*
Howard Bigelow Baker, 1938

Grand Canyon, the world's most awesome erosional wonder, captures our attention and causes us to contemplate the forces of nature which have excavated it. As we stand on the south rim, we see only a fraction of its true dimensions. Those who have flown over the Canyon have observed its full extent. Grand Canyon is 277 miles long, counting the 60 miles of Marble Canyon upstream on the Colorado River. The depth of the main segment of Grand Canyon varies between 3,000 and 6,000 feet and the width, from rim to rim, between 4 and 18 miles. At the south rim near Grand Canyon Village, the Coconino Plateau has an elevation of nearly 7,000 feet above sea level. The north rim, which is the southern part of the adjacent Kaibab Plateau, has an elevation of 8,000 feet, whereas the Colorado River below has an elevation of 2,400 feet.

Three Observations

To begin our discussion concerning the erosion of Grand Canyon, we make three important geologic observations. We then evaluate three theories which have been used to explain the erosion.

An Enormous Amount of Erosion

Our attention is drawn first to the colossal quantity of material which has been removed. Figure 5.1 shows the entire drainage basin of the Colorado River.[1] It comprises an area of one quarter million square miles. Sedimentary strata, the major rocks forming the surface of the broad area known as the Colorado Plateau, have been deeply incised, destroying the original continuity of the strata.

In Grand Canyon, we see the breached remnants of once-continuous strata. A simple calculation of the volume of the Canyon shows that almost 1,000 cubic miles (4,000

cubic kilometers) of sediment have been removed from northern Arizona to produce just the topographic form of the Canyon itself.

But this is not all the erosion. Beside the road, just 16 miles south of Grand Canyon Village, rises Red Butte, a prominent conical hill standing 1,000 feet above the present surface of the Coconino Plateau (see figure 5.2). Red Butte is composed of shale of the Moenkopi Formation overlain by Shinarump Conglomerate of the Chinle Formation (the same formations outcropping in southern Utah).[2] The very top of the butte is volcanic rock from an ancient lava flow. This small butte stands on top of the Kaibab Limestone,

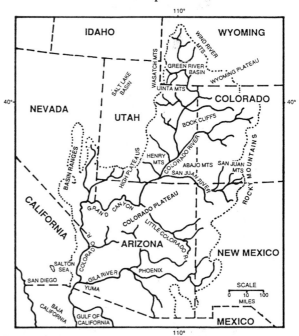

Figure 5.1 *The enormous drainage basin of the Colorado River includes parts of seven states plus Mexico.*

Figure 5.2 *Red Butte, just south of Grand Canyon. (Photo by Steven A. Austin.)*

which forms the present surface of the Coconino Plateau. Figure 5.3 is a geologic cross section through Red Butte, showing the small amount of Moenkopi and Chinle formations composing the butte and the connection of these formations with the outcrops in southern Utah.

The top of Red Butte is capped by a lava flow which has protected the underlying shale and conglomerate from erosion. We might ask how a lava flow could cover a butte, since lava does not usually flow *over* hills but *around* them. The answer is found by postulating that the lava flowed over a vast plain that existed 1,000 feet above the present south rim of the Canyon, and that the Moenkopi and Chinle formations covered the entire surface of the present Coconino Plateau and Kaibab Plateau above the Kaibab Limestone! This distribution of Moenkopi and Chinle is sketched in figure 5.3. Red Butte is simply interpreted as an erosional remnant providing evidence of broad, sheetlike erosion of the Coconino Plateau.

This plateau appears to have been buried even deeper than the 1,000 feet indicated by Red Butte. There is evidence above the Moenkopi and Chinle formations, which have now been eroded off the south rim, that the Glen Canyon Group (Navajo Sandstone, Kayenta Formation, Moenave Formation, and Windgate Sandstone)—another 2,000 feet of strata—were present, as well. Our minds are staggered in the attempt to imagine not just 1,000 cubic miles of canyon erosion, but many times that volume, indicated by thousands of feet of erosion off the plateaus which surround the Canyon.

Grand Canyon Cuts Through the Plateau

A second observation is even more startling than the first: Grand Canyon cuts *through*, not *around*, a great plateau land. The well-developed drainage basin of the Colorado River (see figure 5.1) has its headwaters in elevated areas, as all rivers do, but, unlike most rivers, it has high plateaus adjacent to it, one-third of its total length from the sea. Most rivers have broad lowland areas that close to the sea. We would expect the Colorado River to have established its course *around*, *not through* such an elevated area standing in its path to the sea.

Observation of the extreme eastern portion of the Canyon shows the magnitude of this river-location problem. At Grandview Point and Desert View Tower, we observe the Colorado Plateau north and east of Grand Canyon. The plateau, with its surface of Kaibab Limestone, to our astonishment, rises from an elevation of 5,000 feet near Glen Canyon Dam on Lake Powell to 7,400 feet at Grandview Point on the south rim. The north rim of the Canyon, across the Colorado River, represents the southern

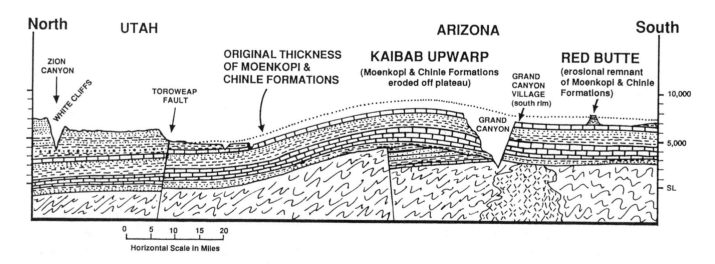

Figure 5.3 *Geologic cross section along a north-south line from southern Utah to northern Arizona. The extensive erosion of the plateau is indicated by the continuity of the Moenkopi and Chinle Formations, which are projected from Utah over Grand Canyon to Red Butte.*

portion of the Kaibab Plateau (also the upper surface of the Kaibab Limestone), which has an elevation over 8,000 feet above sea level. The rise in the plateau is caused by a north-south trending geologic fold structure called a *monocline*, which flexes up Grand Canyon strata and the plateau almost 3,000 feet on the west, relative to the east. This fold structure is called the East Kaibab Monocline. The elevated land surfaces to the west of the monocline are called the Kaibab and Coconino Plateaus. Geologists refer to these elevated areas also as the "Kaibab Upwarp."

Because of the upwarped surface in the river's path, the Colorado River might be expected to have chosen a different path to the sea. It could have flowed southeast from its present entrance to Grand Canyon onto the lower terrain of Painted Desert in east-central Arizona. From there, the Colorado River could have proceeded southeast to join the Rio Grande River, emptying into the Gulf of Mexico, or cut back toward the west through central Arizona to join the Gila River emptying eventually into the Pacific Ocean. The Colorado River, to our astonishment, does neither. Instead, the river is directed to the west, *straight through the plateau lands of northern Arizona*, to take a more direct route to the Pacific Ocean!

Uplift Occurred
Before Erosion of the Canyon

A third observation also has profound implications concerning the origin of Grand Canyon. It is the idea that the folding of the monocline on the east side of the Canyon and the associated uplift of the Kaibab and Coconino Plateaus are geologically "old," occurring *before* major landscape erosion.

That the East Kaibab Monocline is an "old" geologic structure, is illustrated by the strata which were affected, and, most importantly, those *not* affected by the folding action. At the northern-most occurrence of the East Kaibab Monocline near Canaan Peak (just east of Bryce Canyon, Utah), inclined strata within the East Kaibab Monocline are beveled and overlain by the flat-lying Wasatch Formation.[3] We note immediately that the Wasatch Formation was not folded. The structural association indicates that the fold was produced *after* the last inclined stratum was deposited, but *before* the flat-lying Wasatch was deposited.

Geologists refer to the uppermost inclined and beveled strata in the monocline as belonging to the Upper Cretaceous System. The unfolded Wasatch Formation, burying the monocline, has been assigned to the Eocene Series of the Tertiary System.[4] Geologists call this interval of deformation on the Colorado Plateau from the Upper Cretaceous to the Eocene the "Laramide Orogeny." This interval of uplift *preceded* the extensive erosion of the

Colorado Plateau, because the Wasatch Formation is itself severely eroded as in the spectacular exposures at Bryce Canyon.

We do not need to go to Utah to find evidence that the Kaibab Upwarp in northern Arizona is an "old" geologic structure. Gravel deposits occur within channels eroded into the surface of the Coconino and Kaibab Plateaus. These have been called "rim gravels," and have been the topic of intense study for twenty years. A major portion of the gravels have been assigned to the Paleocene and Eocene Series.[5] This means that the major uplift of the Coconino and Kaibab Plateaus was accompanied by the initial erosion of its surface during the Paleocene and Eocene—the time of the Laramide Orogeny on the Colorado Plateau.[6] These rim gravels, no doubt, provide the strongest evidence for the Laramide age of the Kaibab Upwarp.

Therefore, the geologic relationships between the fold structure, the strata, and the erosion make the uplift of the Colorado Plateau look "old." We can discard the hypothesis that the Kaibab Upwarp was uplifted *after* the major erosion occurred. The major uplift must have occurred *before* erosion.

Exactly how old is "old," is a point of debate between creationists and evolutionists. Conventional uniformitarian dating of the Upper Cretaceous is about 70 million years, and of the Eocene, is about 50 million years. The Laramide flexing of the Plateau is, thus, supposed to have occurred between about 50 and 70 million years ago. Almost every introductory geology text teaches both these great ages and their assignment to the Laramide Orogeny. Creationists, however, dispute the age assignment, but accept the observation that the monocline is deeply buried beneath strata of the Wasatch Formation.

The Antecedent River Theory

The first geologists, who studied Grand Canyon more than 120 years ago, had a pattern of thinking that was decidedly uniformitarian.[7] They conceived of great ages for the accumulation of strata, the erosion of canyons, and the establishment of river drainage basins. John Wesley Powell, the first geologist who rafted through Grand Canyon, described erosion as continuing for millions of years at imperceptibly slow rates, to excavate canyons. Geologists since that time, have been educated at major universities which teach that the uplift of the Colorado Plateau occurred during the Laramide Orogeny, supposedly 50 to 70 million years ago. As geologists have observed the Colorado River drainage basin, they have made the logically elegant conclusion that the river is older than the plateau uplift, and that Grand Canyon is an enormously old feature, which evolved directly as a result of the uplift.[8]

Figure 5.4 shows the theory that geologists have surmised.[9] The present course of the Colorado River was

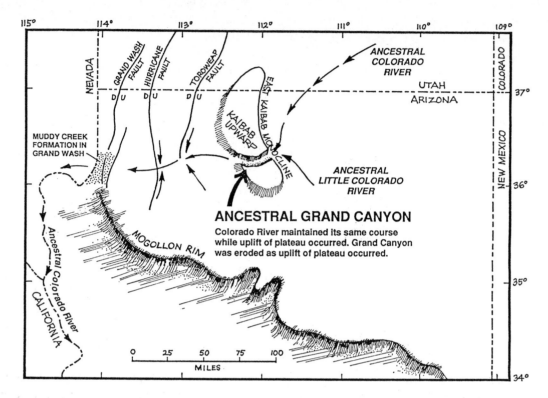

Figure 5.4 *Explanation of how the Grand Canyon was eroded, according to the antecedent river theory. Before the Kaibab Upwarp began, some seventy million years ago, the ancestral Colorado River was flowing westward through northern Arizona. According to the theory, the Grand Canyon was eroded by slow downcutting by the Colorado River as the Kaibab Upwarp occurred. The present course of the Colorado River was inherited from the ancestral river after tens of millions of years of uplift and erosion.*

inherited from the location it had before the plateau land was uplifted. Very slow uplift of the Kaibab Upwarp, beginning in late Cretaceous time, could have been accompanied by equally slow erosion. The rate of uplift is supposed to have been precisely balanced by the rate of downcutting. The theory maintains that the Colorado River was not diverted toward the southeast, but maintained its course, as the Kaibab Upwarp occurred. The river's erosion produced Grand Canyon. Essential to the theory, is the notion that the ancestral Colorado River was positioned in northern Arizona *before,* or *antecedent to,* the uplift of the plateau. That is why it is referred to as the "antecedent river theory."

The antecedent river theory has great explanatory power, and this may explain why so many geologists have favored it over the years. For example, the theory is able to explain the sheetlike erosion of the Moenkopi and Chinle Formations off the top of the Coconino Plateau. All we need to surmise is that the entire plateau was near sea level during late Cretaceous time, and that the ancestral Colorado River was a slow, sluggish, meandering river, which had beveled the uppermost formations. The notion of even planation is what geologists have called a "peneplain," the supposed end-product of millions of years of erosion.

The antecedent river theory is extraordinary in its simplicity. It explains things rationally and reasonably, by analogy with processes which geologists can see and understand going on today. The theory is consistent with uniformitarian dogma and the education which geologists have received during the last one-hundred years. All we need to do is assume that Grand Canyon evolved by the incessant action of the Colorado River, as the uplift of the plateau began 50 to 70 million years ago. The elegance of the theory is its simplicity.

The effect of the antecedent river theory on geologists' thinking is no less extraordinary. In 1869, John Wesley Powell rafted on the Green River (a tributary of the Colorado), in Utah's Uinta Mountains, and, later that year, explored Grand Canyon, in Arizona. The experience led Powell to coin the term "antecedence" in relation to the river's course, and enabled him to extend the explanation, ultimately, to the entire drainage of the Colorado River. Powell wrote:

> . . . *all the facts concerning the relation of the waterways of this region to the mountains, hills, canyons, and cliffs, lead to the inevitable conclusion that the system of*

drainage was determined antecedent to the faulting, and folding, and erosion.[10]

C. E. Dutton, another early geologist who explored the Colorado Plateau, was even more certain, in 1880, concerning the history of the river:

> *Now the grand truth which meets us everywhere in the Plateau Country, which stands out conspicuous and self-evident, which is so unmistakable even by the merest tyro [sic] in geology is this: The river is older than the structural features of the country.*[11]

These glowing praises of the antecedent river theory might appear to establish, beyond doubt, that the Colorado River did, indeed, erode Grand Canyon. Add to this the statements on signs at Grand Canyon and what public school textbooks teach, and the argument appears invincible!

Problems with the Antecedent River Theory

The theory of an antecedent river had some fatal flaws. Geologists could not rationally explain real and concrete data without contriving imaginary schemes which drew them away from explaining what they actually saw. Chief among these are two major problems.

Where Has All the Sediment Gone?

The muddy waters of the Colorado River remind us that the drainage basin is rapidly eroding. This erosion has been of special interest to engineers who need to measure the load of sediment carried by the river in order to estimate the life expectancy and filling of reservoirs. Before construction of Glen Canyon Dam, the sediment load at Grand Canyon was measured carefully over a 25-year period. For the period 1926 to 1950, the sediment load of the Colorado River at Grand Canyon averaged 168 million tons per year.[12] That is equivalent to just under 500,000 tons of sediment per day, or just over five tons of sediment per second, on the average, over the 25-year period. The sediment load, of course, increases much above the average during big floods on the river. In 1927, a flood on the river was estimated to have carried 55 times its average load, or about 23 million tons per day.

The antecedent river theory supposes that the Colorado River has been located in Arizona for some 70 million years, and has been eroding as it is today for that incredible length of time. We can estimate the weight (W) of sediment which should occur in the delta of the Colorado River. The answer is found by multiplying the load moved per year, times the supposed age of the river:

W = 168 million tons per year x 70 million years
  = 11.8 million billion tons.

Because river sediments have an average density of 9.3 billion tons per cubic mile (2.0 grams per cubic centimeter), the volume (V) of these sedimentary deposits can be estimated:

V = 11.8 million billion tons ÷ 9.3 billion tons per cubic mile
  = 1.3 million cubic miles.

This colossal quantity of sediment would have a volume 1,500 times that of Grand Canyon.

We would expect this enormous amount of material to be accumulated as gravel, sand, silt, and clay west of the Canyon. The 1.3-million-cubic miles of sediment are equivalent to the volume of a cube 110 miles on a side. It would be extremely difficult to hide such an impressive mass! Geologists should be able to locate this colossal deposit easily in the delta of the Colorado River. However, studies of the Colorado River delta have failed to reveal anywhere near this amount of sediment.[13] Something appears to be seriously wrong with the antecedent river theory.

Of special interest is the downfaulted basin just to the west of Grand Canyon at Pierce Ferry (see figure 5.5). Here is where the Colorado River issues out of Grand Canyon. We would expect thick sedimentary deposits to accumulate in the basin there, from the ancestral river. Thick sedimentary deposits occur, but not of the character that would be deposited by a long-enduring river. Called the Muddy Creek Formation (assigned Miocene age), these deposits have been intensely studied by C. R. Longwell:

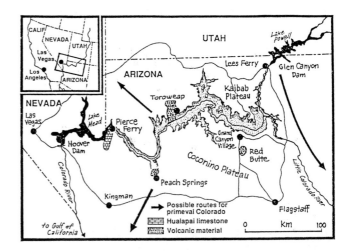

Figure 5.5 *Possible routes of the ancestral Colorado River, with locations of geologic features important to theories on how Grand Canyon was eroded (after R. J. Rice, 1983).*

. . . evaporites and fan-debris, many hundreds of feet thick . . . the thickness, areal extent, and character of this basin fill bear eloquent testimony to a long regime of interior drainage, under an arid climate, throughout the basins now crossed by the through-flowing Colorado River. . . . There is no possibility that the river was in its present position west of the Plateau in Muddy Creek time.[14]

One of the uppermost units of the Muddy Creek Formation is called the Hualapai Limestone, which is 600 feet thick (see figure 5.5). Relatively pure limestone (*not* gravel, sand, and silt deposited by the antecedent river), characterize the deposits just west of Grand Canyon. Gravel deposits beneath the limestone are dominated by granite pebbles from local sources, not exotic lithologies (gneiss, schist, etc.) as would come from distant areas via a large river. Geologists who have investigated the deposits west of Grand Canyon have almost universally discarded the antecedent river theory. A symposium of geologists reviewed the evidence in 1964, and unanimously rejected the antecedent river theory.[15] One geologist exclaimed in print, "Did the Colorado River exist anywhere in Pliocene time?"[16]

Some geologists have tried to imagine how the extreme western end of Grand Canyon could be young, allowing just limestone to accumulate at Pierce Ferry. It was proposed by Hunt,[17] that the ancestral Colorado could have departed its present path southwest from Peach Springs (see figure 5.5). Such thinking requires an underground course for the river. No cave system has been found southwest of Peach Springs.

Another hypothesis has been offered to explain how the western Grand Canyon could be young. Lucchitta[18] suggested that the Miocene Colorado River departed Grand Canyon near Toroweap and flowed northwest (see figure 5.5). Rather than postulate an "antigravity waterfall," Lucchitta proposed that the ancient river had not incised northern Arizona yet, to any depth. No gravel deposits, suggestive of a big-river system, have been located in extreme northwestern Arizona. It is, therefore, a hypothesis waiting for evidence to confirm it.

Another proposal offered, is that the entire drainage basin became extremely arid, and that no through-flowing Colorado River existed within Grand Canyon during Miocene and Pliocene time.[19] Thus, the Muddy Creek Formation was deposited west of Grand Canyon, after the Canyon was eroded, but when no river flowed through the Canyon!

We continue to marvel at the various proposals concerning the antecedent river. Is it possible that these proposals tell us more about geologists than they do about the history of the Colorado River? One generalization seems appropriate: *geologists are very adept at constructing*

theories which explain why we find no evidence for the antecedent river.

Could the Upper Colorado River Erode for 70 Million Years?

The theory of the antecedent river requires that the drainage basin of the Colorado River above Grand Canyon was established by the Laramide Orogeny, and, like Grand Canyon, has been eroding for 50 to 70 million years. Could Grand Canyon and the upper Colorado River be long-enduring features left over from Cretaceous uplift of the Colorado Plateau? Some calculations illustrate the order of magnitude of the problem.

As mentioned previously, scientists have measured the sediment load of the Colorado River at Grand Canyon. The load of its muddy waters over a twenty-five-year period (before the construction of Glen Canyon Dam) was an average of 168 million tons per year. This weight of gravel, sand, silt, and clay is equivalent to 0.015 cubic mile per year, of hard-rock erosion in the headwaters of the upper Colorado River. Using this erosion rate, we can estimate the volume (V) of rock which would be eroded from the upper Colorado River drainage basin in 70 million years. If we assume constant rate of erosion, the calculation is

$$V = 0.015 \text{ cubic mile per year} \times 70 \text{ million years}$$
$$= 1 \text{ million cubic miles.}$$

Thus, the ancestral upper Colorado River could have eroded one million cubic miles of rock, assuming a 70-million-year-old river.

Have one million cubic miles of rock been eroded from the drainage basin above Grand Canyon? We can convert the volume of rock supposed to have been eroded to an average thickness or depth of erosion. The drainage basin of the Colorado River above Grand Canyon has an area of 137,800 square miles.[20] Therefore, the average depth (D) of erosion above Grand Canyon should be:

$$D = 1 \text{ million cubic miles} \div 137,800 \text{ square miles}$$
$$= 7.3 \text{ miles.}$$

This colossal depth of erosion (7.3 miles) should have occurred since the Cretaceous strata were deposited.

Inspection of the drainage basin of the Colorado River shows that Cretaceous strata today underlie one half the drainage basin above Grand Canyon.[21] Thus, we can say with confidence, that not even one mile average depth of erosion has occurred over half the drainage basin—the half underlain by Cretaceous strata. The remaining half of the drainage basin of the upper Colorado River is dominated by Jurassic and Triassic strata at the surface.[22] We could make a case here for a few thousand feet of Cretaceous strata being removed, but *not* several miles' thickness of strata being removed. Thus, we must conclude that there is nowhere near the seven miles average depth of erosion anticipated by the antecedent river theory.

An illustration of the present rate of erosion in the Colorado River drainage basin can be seen in relation to the volume of Grand Canyon. How long would it take to erode the 1000 cubic miles of materials, to produce the topographic form of Grand Canyon? If all the erosive power were concentrated within the Canyon, the time (T) to erode the Canyon at the average yearly rate would be:

$$T = 1000 \text{ cubic miles} \div 0.015 \text{ cubic mile per year}$$
$$= 67,000 \text{ years.}$$

If the Grand Canyon erosion could be sustained at the 1927 high-water flood rate (55 times average rate), the time (T) to erode the Canyon would be:

$$T = 1000 \text{ cubic miles} \div 0.77 \text{ cubic miles per year}$$
$$= 1,300 \text{ years.}$$

These estimates illustrate the potential for just modern, slow erosion, when accumulated over just thousands of years. (Actually, most of the present erosion is occurring in the headwaters of the Colorado River, not on the present slopes of Grand Canyon. The Canyon, accordingly, can be viewed as a pipe transmitting most of its sediment delivered at its east end to its west end.)

No matter how we consider present rates of erosion and the present form of the Colorado Plateau, we find it very difficult to imagine that the Colorado River drainage basin and Grand Canyon have an age of 50 to 70 million years.

The "Precocious Gully Theory"

The demise of the antecedent river theory for the erosion of Grand Canyon caused distress in the minds of many geologists. By 1960, however, most experts on Grand Canyon geology were willing to discard the straightforward and elegant theory of the ancestral river.[23] Many geologists knew that a less logical, more empirical explanation needed to be found. The theory was proposed that Grand Canyon formed, *not* by the Colorado River over millions of years, but by greatly enlarged gully erosion very rapidly. The replacement theory was called the "stream capture theory," or the "precocious gully theory," somewhat disparagingly, even by its advocates.[24] This theory would have to explain how the upstream segment of the Colorado River could have the appearance of being long established in its drainage basin, while the Grand Canyon segment of the river would appear to be very young. Geologists would have to postulate a major adjustment in the course of the Colorado River, to allow it to erode Grand Canyon in less than a few million years before the present. They would also have to explain

how the Kaibab and Coconino Plateaus could endure in uplifted configuration for 70 million years, without having great canyons resembling Grand Canyon.

Figure 5.6 shows three block diagrams depicting how, according to the theory, the Colorado River became established through northern Arizona.[25] Originally (block diagram a), over 10 million years ago in the Miocene Epoch, the primeval Colorado River drained southward from Utah to the eastern Grand Canyon area, but continued to flow southeast along the present course of the Little Colorado River, east of the Kaibab and Coconino Plateaus. Erosion of the Kaibab and Coconino Plateaus, according to this theory, began just a few million years ago, and a westward-flowing stream eroded the Hualapai drainage

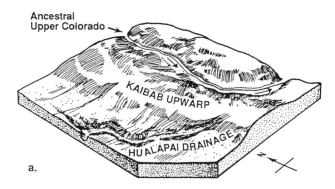

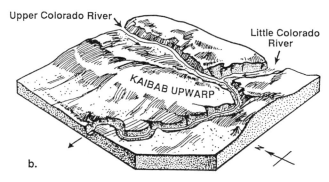

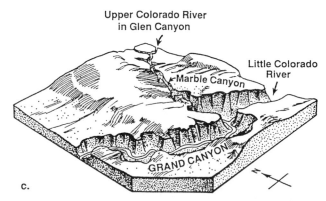

Figure 5.6 *Block diagrams showing three steps, surmising how Grand Canyon formed according to the "stream capture" or "precocious gully theory." The repositioning of the Colorado River through the Kaibab Upwarp is supposed to have been caused by a westward-flowing drainage which cut eastward, and captured the south-flowing Colorado River.*

system (block diagram b). The drainage extended eastward about 100 miles through what is today Grand Canyon. Because of energetic erosion, the Hualapai stream was somehow able to cut down the plateau enough to make an enormous gully almost the size of the present Grand Canyon. Finally (block diagram c), the Hualapai gully was able to "capture" the drainage of the Colorado River and divert it through the gigantic gully, adding some finishing touches, with further downcutting, to complete Grand Canyon.

Problems with the "Precocious Gully Theory"

The notion that a greatly enlarged gully could capture and divert the drainage of an entire river to form Grand Canyon has four major problems.

How Could the Gully Do It?

The explanation offered appears to create more problems than it does solutions. Chief among these is the lingering doubt about whether assigning the major excavation of Grand Canyon to enlarged gully erosion is possible. We instinctively realize that the theory is arguing a special case. There are many elevated plateaus in the world, but very few of them have Grand Canyon sized gullies through them. By arguing for the gully, *we know we are attributing Grand Canyon to one of the world's most remarkable natural accidents!*

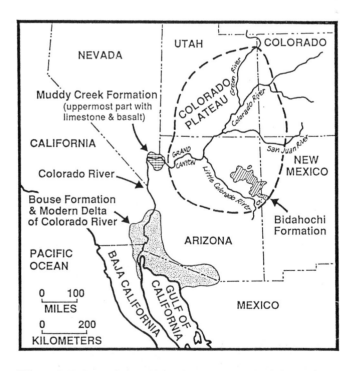

Figure 5.7 *Locations of the Muddy Creek Formation, the Bidahochi Formation, and the Bouse Formation. These three formations contain geologic evidence critical to our understanding of how and when Grand Canyon was eroded.*

Even more perplexing is the understanding that there is no major structural reason as to why a hundred-mile-long drainage would have been positioned where the Grand Canyon is today. There is, for example, no east-west trending fault or zone-of-rock weakness to guide the gully as it enlarged, and no trough-like sag in the plateau to straighten the gully or direct it eastward.[26] The major structural elements of the Grand Canyon region described in chapter 2 are aligned north-south (Hurricane Fault Zone, Toroweap Fault Zone, and Kaibab Upwarp) and would be expected to divert the gully in a north or south direction. Furthermore, the drainage must have been very long, straight, and deep, without much branching. These are all features we know are *not* characteristic of enlarged gullies. Lastly, the gully must enlarge to the east, through a sloping plateau which presently has drainage on its surface to the south.

These and other problems prompted C. B. Hunt to write:

> *It would indeed have been a unique and precocious gully that cut headward more than 100 miles across the Grand Canyon section to capture streams east of the Kaibab upwarp.*[27]

When Did the Gully Do It?

Radioisotope "ages" continue to baffle and amaze geologists desiring to understand how and when Grand Canyon was eroded. This is the subject of chapter 6. Dating of three formations (Muddy Creek Formation, Bouse Formation, and Bidahochi Formation) is especially important, if we are to solve this mystery. Locations of these three formations are shown in figure 5.7.

The Muddy Creek Formation (figure 5.7), in the Lake Mead area, as mentioned previously, provides no evidence for a through-flowing, large river in Miocene time. The lower part of the Hualapai Limestone Member of the Muddy Creek Formation contains volcanic ash beds, which gave a potassium-argon "age" of 8.7 ± 2.2 million years,[28] indicating that river sediment yet had not begun to be deposited. The uppermost part of the Muddy Creek Formation contains the Fortification Hill Basalt Member, which gave a potassium-argon "age" of 5.8 ± 0.2 million years,[29] and another "age" of 5.0 ± 0.4 million years.[30] In the Grand Wash area, at the west end of Grand Canyon, the Muddy Creek Formation is overlain by gravels no doubt from the Colorado River, which had eroded downward near to its present level. Two basalt flows (Sandy Point and Grand Wash Bay basalts) within these river gravel deposits, gave two potassium-argon "ages" of 3.8 ± 0.5 and 3.8 ± 0.1 million years.[31] Thus, the potassium-argon "ages" from the Lake Mead area suggests that the Grand Canyon was eroded between 5.0 and 3.8 million years ago.

The "age" of the Canyon evidence from the Lake Mead area, is, however, contradicted by potassium-argon "ages" from other areas. South of Lake Mead, in the area of the modern delta of the Colorado River, we find the Bouse Formation—an estuary deposit whose sediment content and configuration conform to the recent delta of the Colorado River (see figure 5.6). Thus, the association argues that the Bouse Formation contains Colorado River sediment deposited when sea level was higher.[32] However, the Bouse Formation gave a potassium-argon "age" of 5.3 million years,[33] suggesting that the Colorado River and Grand Canyon had already been established by that time.

Even more amazing is the relationship of Grand Canyon to the Bidahochi Formation (figure 5.7) east of Grand Canyon. Like the Bouse, the Bidahochi has been regarded to be of Pliocene age, but it contains lake sediments at very high elevations within the present drainage basin of the Little Colorado River. It appears that there was no through-flowing Colorado River or established Little Colorado River, when the Bidahochi Formation was deposited. The data suggest that the Bidahochi was deposited in an enclosed basin east of the Kaibab Upwarp. Yet, potassium-argon "ages," in a volcanic deposit from the middle of the Bidahochi, span the interval 10.85 ± 0.20 to 4.2 ± 0.0 million years.[34] A basalt flow at Black Point, on the present drainage of the Little Colorado River, dammed the Little Colorado. This basalt gave a potassium-argon "age" of 2.4 ± 0.3 million years.[35] Thus, the Little Colorado River would appear, on the basis of potassium-argon dating, to have been established between 4.2 and 2.4 million years ago.

Reflection on the "ages" obtained by the potassium-argon method leads to a contradiction. The deltaic deposits of the Colorado River (Bouse Formation) give an *older* age (5.3 million years) than the *maximum* ages for establishment of the Colorado River allowed by the Muddy Creek (5.0 million years) and Bidahochi formations (4.2 million years). If we discard the 5.3-million-year "age" for the Bouse Formation, the "age" interval for establishment of Grand Canyon by dating of Muddy Creek and Bidahochi deposits is 4.2 to 3.8 million years. This requires that the erosion of the Grand Canyon, along with the Little Colorado drainage, occurred in just a fraction of a million years! This is contrary to the ancestral river theory of Powell and the signs at Grand Canyon National Park, which imply that the Colorado River eroded the Canyon over many millions of years.

If the Canyon is to be attributed to rapid-gully erosion, we are amazed at both its speed and magnitude! How could an enormous canyon like Grand Canyon be eroded by a gully in just a fraction of one million years? Creationists,

who have no commitment to the accuracy of potassium-argon dating, simply point out this important contradiction in uniformitarian theory. A complete analysis of radioisotope dating is found in chapter 6. The "ages" assigned to these rocks are doubtful.

Could the Landscape Endure?

Although the gully theory does not require the Grand Canyon to be several tens of millions of years old, it supposes, as does the antecedent river theory, that river erosion and the Laramide uplift of the plateau can be dated to 70 million years ago. As mentioned previously, 70 million years of erosion should severely alter the uplifted plateau. There should have been intense erosion, generally, to the plateau lands, to a depth of several miles—not just deep erosion in one enlarged gully. Both theories leave this logical consequence unexplained.

Where Are the Evidences of the Ancestral Upper Colorado River?

Because the gully theory assumes that the Kaibab Upwarp began to occur about 70 million years ago, while the amazing stream capture was accomplished less than 5 million years ago, we are obligated to have the ancestral upper Colorado River, located east of the Kaibab Upwarp, for as much as 60 million years. We would expect significant erosional and depositional features to be obvious. No abandoned channel for the postulated ancestral Colorado River has been found southeast or northeast of the Grand Canyon.

The search for Miocene deposits from the ancestral upper Colorado River has been equally discouraging. Edwin Larson, William Bradley, and Minoru Ozima write:

> By contrast, unequivocal evidence for a Colorado River older than 10 m.y. has yet to be produced. It is a curious fact that older Colorado River sediments have not been recognized anywhere, even though Miocene deposits were accumulating in basins that now lie athwart or near the present river. For example, the Colorado River crosses Troublesome Basin in Middle Park, yet the only deposits which can be identified as belonging to the Colorado River are found near the top of the unit (Izett, 1968, and G.S.A. Memoir 144). Even if the Colorado had been transporting only sand and mud at that time, it should have left a recognizable record in the Troublesome Formation. Similarly, the 14 to 10 m.y. old sediments which are present in the State Bridge Syncline, now being dissected by the

Colorado River, have characteristics that belie the existence of a large river at that location and time (Brennan, 1969). Nor do the sediments farther to the northwest give any sign that a Miocene Colorado River might have flowed into a basin in that direction (Kucera, 1962, 1968). . . . A southwesterly course for a Miocene Colorado River, similar to today's course, is refuted by volcanic evidence. . . . The question remains: where was the Colorado River in Miocene time?[36]

One specific prediction of the stream capture theory is that deposits from the Miocene or Pliocene upper Colorado River would be found east of Grand Canyon in the Little Colorado River drainage basin. There we find the Miocene/Pliocene Bidahochi Formation, but its silt, sand, and volcanic ash layers have been interpreted as lake deposits, not as deposits from a through-flowing, large river. Carol Breed writes:

> *The capture hypothesis was not in disagreement with the known facts of Colorado Plateau geology in the early 1960's. But at least one difficulty should be noted: the Bidahochi Formation stands in relation to the postulated southeasterly ancestral upper Colorado in much the same way as the Muddy Creek Formation stands in the way of a pre-Pliocene westward flowing Colorado River. There is a notorious lack of pre-Muddy Creek Colorado River sediments in the west; there is a similar lack of proven pre-Bidahochi upper Colorado sediments in the east.*[37]

If the ancestral Colorado River remained on the eastern side of the Kaibab Upwarp, its connection with the Rio Grande River should have left traces of sand and gravel. M. Collier wrote of the absence of evidence:

> *No one has ever found the ancestral river bed of the Colorado where it was supposed to flow east and south across Arizona, New Mexico, and Texas.*[38]

Ivo Lucchitta also noted that evidence recently collected "argues against the Rio Grande connection."[39]

In summary, although the "stream capture" and "precocious gully theory" make fascinating mental exercises, they are deficient in empirical evidence.

The Breached Dam Theory

An Extraordinary Proposal

Both the antecedent-river and the precocious-gully theories for the erosion of Grand Canyon require that the agents of erosion, and specifically the Colorado River, have been in operation for tens of millions of years. That assumption, however, ultimately worked contrary to forming the very geologic structures that the theories were trying to explain. *Could geologists be laboring with a concept of geologic time that does not exist? Is it possible that the Kaibab Upwarp, the erosion of Grand Canyon, and the operation of the Colorado River do not date back tens of millions of years? Was there an ancestral Colorado River after all? Could catastrophic drainage have been responsible for most of the erosional features we see?*

Theories for erosion of Grand Canyon by catastrophic drainage are not new. We are amazed to learn that the idea of catastrophic drainage is contained in legend and is the oldest explanation for the origin of Grand Canyon. According to the Havasupai Indians, who still tell the story in their villages within Grand Canyon, the immense chasm formed after the world was covered by a great flood. Details of this legend are found in the discussion of "Early Peoples of the Southwest" (chapter 10). The Havasupai legend is immediately recognizable as one of hundreds of flood traditions which are known worldwide, of which the Biblical account of Noah's Flood is the most detailed and accurate. If catastrophic drainage was involved in forming Grand Canyon, then it would be a relict feature formed from erosive processes which had operated at rates and scales far greater than today. Grand Canyon would be a static monument to the action of intense ancient processes, not a dynamically evolving landform in equilibrium with slow, modern, erosive processes.

Of various catastrophic drainage models which can be proposed, the most fascinating is the theory of the catastrophic drainage of lakes.[40] Figure 5.8 shows the high plateau land of Utah, Colorado, Arizona, and New Mexico. Called the "Colorado Plateau," the region can be viewed as a saucer-shaped, uplifted basin, because around it are very high mountains. If Grand Canyon were blocked by material filling it to an elevation of 5,700 feet, an enormous lake would form on the saucer-shaped plateau. Figure 5.8 shows the outline of the lake which would form today if Grand Canyon was blocked and the basin to the northeast was allowed to fill with water.[41] The lakes would cover an area of more than 30,000 square miles.

A most extraordinary association is obvious, from our analysis of the Colorado Plateau. A drainage basin of enormous volume exists just east of Grand Canyon. That

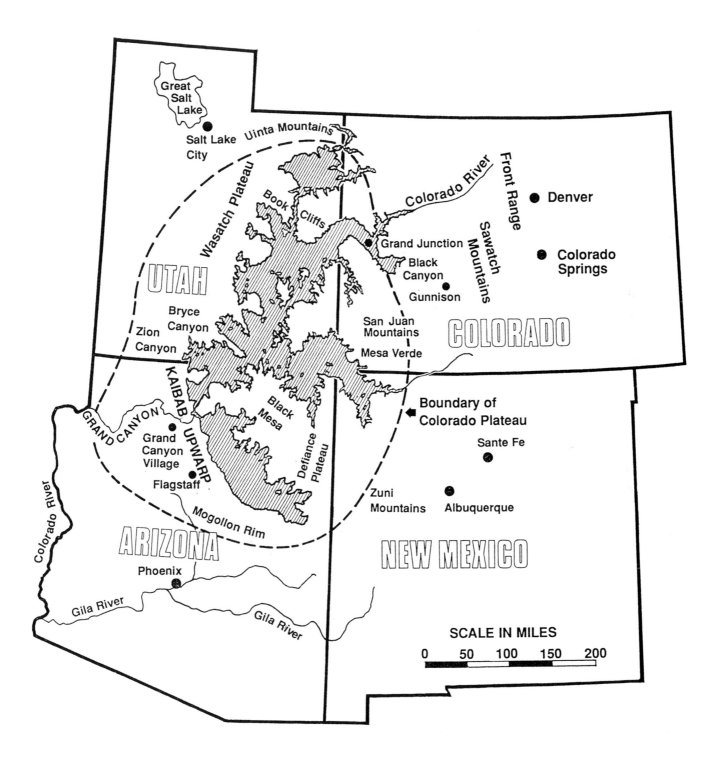

Figure 5.8 *The saucer-shaped surface of the Colorado Plateau. The surface of the plateau could be made to contain a giant lake (indicated by shaded pattern). A computer was used to draw the shoreline of the lake, which would form behind the Kaibab Upwarp today, if Grand Canyon was blocked at the 5,700-foot elevation. The lake would occupy an area of more than 30,000 square miles, and contain 3,000 cubic miles of water. The volume of the lake would be three times that of Lake Michigan. The computer-generated lake approximates the outline of ancient lakes (figure 5.22), which breached their dams to form Grand Canyon. (Plotted by Edmond W. Holroyd, III.)*

colossal drainage basin is associated with Grand Canyon, one of earth's largest and most distinctive erosional features. *Could Grand Canyon have been eroded by failure of a dam and catastrophic drainage of lakes?*

The breached dam theory for Grand Canyon is suggested in figure 5.9. Two large lakes (extreme west ends shown in figure 5.9a) are believed to have existed east of the Kaibab Upwarp. The catastrophic drainage of a lake in eastern Arizona (figure 5.9b) first created a notch and channel through the Kaibab Upwarp. Then, catastrophic drainage of a lake in southeastern Utah (figure 5.9c) established the connection with the upper Colorado River basin. The mechanisms for failures of these dams, and the causes of catastrophic erosion, are explained later in this chapter.

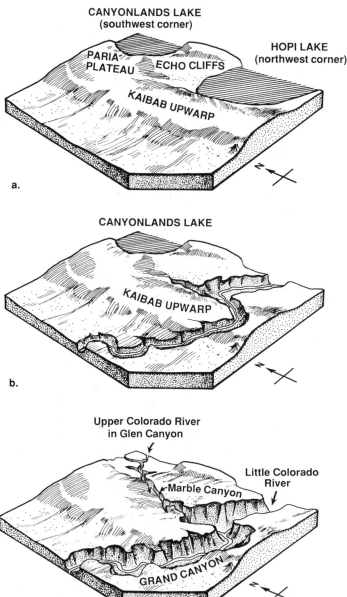

Figure 5.9 *Breached dam theory for catastrophic, post-Flood erosion of Grand Canyon.*

Examples of Failed Dams

The failure of both natural and man-made dams has been recognized as causing enormous erosion and deposition. The largest man-made dam to fail, in the history of the United States, was Teton Dam, in Idaho, on June 5, 1976. High water on the Teton River caused failure of the 275-foot-high earth dam, releasing less than one-tenth cubic mile of water. More than 3,700 homes were damaged or destroyed, but, because of early warning, only 11 people died in the flood. Erosion of bedrock was observed downstream in the Teton River valley, to a depth of 20 feet.

The largest, well-documented, prehistoric, natural-dam failure occurred during the time of continental glaciation in Washington, Idaho, and Montana. This is called the Lake Missoula Flood. Ancient, glacial Lake Missoula (figure 5.10) breached its ice dam in northern Idaho. Five hundred cubic miles of lake water from Montana scoured across eastern Washington to a depth of hundreds of feet, at speeds approaching 100 miles per hour.[42] In its wake, the flood left 16,000 square miles of scarred terrain and deeply cut valleys, which today are such a striking feature of the scabland of eastern Washington. Significant erosion occurred to depths of hundreds of feet, through solid rock.[43]

The most spectacular erosional feature which was caused by flood erosion from ancient Lake Missoula is Grand Coulee, in Washington (figure 5.11). It is a 50-mile-long trench, from one to six miles wide, with steep walls up to 900 feet high. The trench was chiseled into solid basalt and granite, southward from the Columbia River, just above Grand Coulee Dam, to Quincy Basin, just north of the town of Ephrata. It is estimated that almost ten cubic miles of basalt were eroded rapidly from Grand Coulee by catastrophic, Lake Missoula flooding.

One of the most interesting small canyons eroded by the Missoula Flood is Palouse Canyon (figure 5.12). It, too, was deeply incised into solid basalt. The gorge is up to 500 feet deep. It extends for six miles north of the Snake River, in southeastern Washington.

One particularly vivid recent example of a rapid breaching event comes from study of the eruptions of Mount St. Helens, also in Washington State. The valley of the North Fork of the Toutle River, northwest of Mount St. Helens, was blocked by a dam of landslide debris and volcanic ash on May 18, 1980. The valley was unblocked by a mudflow on March 19, 1982. The breaching event occurred when mud and water overtopped the landslide-debris dam.[44] The catastrophic event produced a wide assortment of canyons, some as much as 140 feet deep (see figure 5.13). Even solid, prehistoric lava flows were incised to depths of tens of feet at Mount St. Helens (figure 5.14).

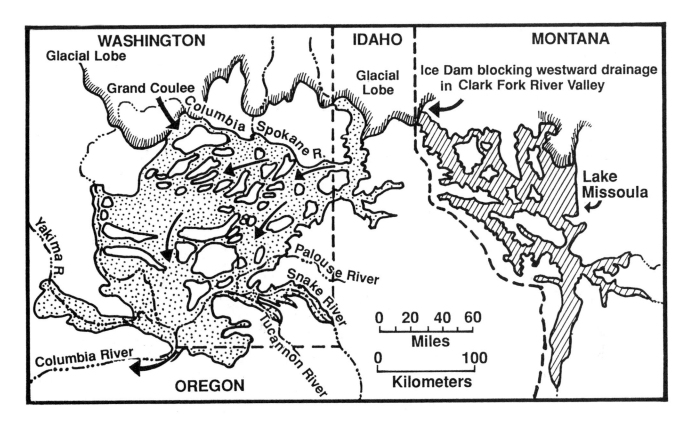

Figure 5.10 *Area devastated by the Lake Missoula Flood. This prehistoric glacier ice dam in northern Idaho was breached, allowing Lake Missoula in Montana to catastrophically flood Washington State with up to 500 cubic miles of water (half the present volume of Lake Michigan), eroding the Channeled Scabland of eastern Washington. Fifty cubic miles of sediment and bedrock were eroded, forming the elaborate network of channels.*

Evidences for the Breached Dam

If Grand Canyon was eroded largely by catastrophic drainage of large lakes as a breach occurred through the Kaibab Upwarp, four types of evidences would be expected. First, we would expect to find sedimentary strata diagnostic of a Pliocene lake east of Grand Canyon. Second, because major topographic features in Grand Canyon and also of the Colorado Plateau to the northeast were affected by catastrophic drainage, we would expect to see geomorphic evidence that increased water flow had occurred in ancient times. Third, we would anticipate finding evidences that many features of the present landscape are relict forms. These landscape elements which were formed by catastrophic agents would show a great degree of stability, rather than appearing to be in a process of continual change. Fourth, we would expect to observe unusual Pliocene delta deposits near the Gulf of California. These deposits would suggest rapid establishment and sedimentation of the Lower Colorado River.

Evidence for an Ancient Lake

Thin laminae of silt and mud are contained in Pliocene strata, within a mudstone and sandstone formation of eastern Arizona. Named the Bidahochi Formation, its thin, laminated silt and mud layers have been interpreted as deposits from "Hopi Lake."[45] The unusual sedimentary deposits of Hopi Lake contain fossils of freshwater fish (chub and squawfish), amphibians (salamanders and toads), and beavers.[46] The shoreline of the lake is not known, because the margins of the Bidahochi Formation (figure 5.7) have been severely eroded, but the elevation of the lake is indicated by the present elevation of the deposits above 6,000 feet, in the headwaters of the present Little Colorado River drainage basin.[47] Hopi Lake, a large Pliocene lake, existed at high elevation east of the Kaibab Upwarp. The lake could not exist there today, because of the enormous breach (Grand Canyon) which occurs through the Kaibab Upwarp.

Other deposits on the Colorado Plateau may be interpreted as ancient lake deposits. These occur at various places in the drainage basin of the Colorado River, but are

Figure 5.11 *Grand Coulee in Washington State. The severely eroded landscape is viewed toward the northeast, in this high-altitude, oblique, aerial photo. Water from the ice-blocked channel of the Columbia River was diverted southwestward, as a flood through the Upper Grand Coulee. The Flood eroded the trench now occupied by Bank Lake (the two-mile-wide lake in top center of photo). The flood proceeded southwest, forming the severely scoured landscape of the Lower Grand Coulee (lower half of photo). The western edge of the flood-scoured zone is the 1000-foot-high cliff on the west side of Park Lake (lower left corner of photo). The boundary between the upper and lower Coulee is Dry Falls—a broad vertical escarpment (center of photo) up to 350 feet high and **five times** the width of Niagara Falls. Water from this flood was estimated to have had a depth of over 200 feet, and velocity of over 60 feet per second. Imagine how puny Niagara Falls would appear next to Dry Falls in its prime! (Photo copyright by Leonard Delano.)*

Figure 5.12 *Palouse Canyon in southeastern Washington which was eroded through solid basalt by Lake Missoula floods. Cliffs are from 300 to 500 feet high. People on the right provide scale. (Photo by Steven A. Austin.)*

Figure 5.13 *The "Little Grand Canyon of the Toutle River" is a relict-canyon system on North Fork of the Toutle River, just north of Mount St. Helens volcano. The rockslide-and-pumice deposits from the 1980 eruptions were breached by mudflow, on March 19, 1982, to form a dendritic system of canyons up to 140 feet deep. (Photo by Steven A. Austin.)*

Figure 5.14 *Loowit Canyon, north of Mount St. Helens, which was eroded through solid rock after the summer of 1980. Note the small stream in the canyon and the waterfall in upper left. Depth of Canyon is 100 feet. (Photo by Steven A. Austin.)*

not as well understood. Do they represent the same lake, or disconnected lakes? The evidence allows at least one lake to be documented. We continue to explore the evidence and marvel at its association with the present Grand Canyon.

Evidence for Accelerated Drainage

Many of the valleys upstream from Grand Canyon have rather sluggish streams positioned on very broad flood

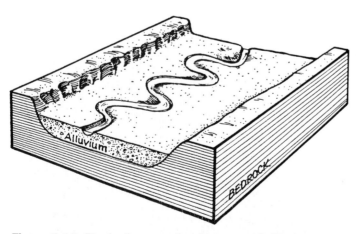

Figure 5.15 *Block diagram showing an underfit river in a wide valley. The present stream does not have enough velocity to move the coarse alluvium from its floodplain, and, as a result, is not actively eroding the bedrock.*

plains. These streams and rivers appear "underfit." The present discharge rates are insufficient to modify significantly these flood plains. Other streams above Grand Canyon have narrow bedrock channels, but the beds of these streams are filled with an accumulation of boulders and cobbles. Thus, these present streams do not have enough water velocity and water volume to remove the buffer of boulders and cobbles that cover their beds, in order to erode the bedrock beneath their channels (see figure 5.15). Again, this evidence indicates that these present streams are underfit, and that there was at least one episode of very high discharge.

Among the most amazing erosional forms in the drainage basin above Grand Canyon are incised river meanders. At the Goosenecks of the San Juan River (figure 5.16), for example, we see a meandering canyon which has been cut, vertically, hundreds of feet into sedimentary strata. Laboratory experiments have been conducted, using a large flume, which allowed a small stream of water to reproduce the conditions which erode incised meanders.[48] It was found that high discharge rate, and lowering of base level (the depth to which a stream seeks to erode), cause meanders to be incised vertically. Both causes would be initiated by breaching of a dam and drainage of a lake. When discharge is low, and the alluvium in the channel is not swept away,

Figure 5.16 *The Goosenecks of the San Juan River in southeastern Utah. Incised meanders indicate greater water flow rate in the past.*

the channel cuts horizontally, not vertically. Shepherd says:

> *The experimental results suggest that the vertically incised meanders of the San Juan may have resulted from downcutting during low-frequency discharges of large magnitude which entrained all of the alluvium in the channel.*[49]

Further evidence that incised meanders are eroded by catastrophic drainage comes from the Channeled Scabland of Washington State. We note that incised meanders occur on the Palouse River in southeastern Washington.[50] The Palouse River valley was very severely eroded into basalt by the catastrophic Lake Missoula Flood. The present Palouse River, with its characteristic low discharge, did not erode the incised meanders.

Evidence for Relict Landforms

If a lake, or series of lakes on the Colorado Plateau rapidly drained, the water trapped inside the rocks and soil along the shore and floor of the lake would escape quickly to the space previously occupied by the lake. Thus, along the former shore of the lake, we would expect to find large landslide scars and zones of failure, caused by water oozing out of the earth. This type of failure would be expected within the breached area of the dam, and along the spillway downstream, as well as along the shore of the lake. Such

features have been observed around modern lakes which have drained rapidly.

We immediately recall the severely eroded lip of the plateau which forms Bryce Canyon, and countless other topographic wonders of Canyonlands in southern Utah. Might the enormous "monuments" such as occur around

Figure 5.17 *Sapping structures eroded rapidly in sand. These modern structures resemble many larger side canyons on the Colorado Plateau. (Photo by Steven A. Austin.)*

Monument Valley be topography accentuated by such slope failure?

Hundreds of smaller side canyons branch off from the Colorado River in Grand Canyon. What is interesting, is that these side canyons are alcoves, typically with short, rather wide, and very deep, bowl-shaped heads ("amphitheater" or "theater" heads). These side canyons of this shape are not typical of enlarged gullies, which usually have narrow, V-shaped heads. We have difficulty conceiving of a very old river canyon having such short and wide features. Instead, such theater-headed side canyons remind us of collapse features formed where water oozes out of wet sediment, causing the supporting layers of sediment, or rock, to be removed so that collapse occurs. Technically, this process is known as "sapping," and would have been an important process, as greatly enlarged flow through the main canyon cut through the dam and caused material marginal to the canyon to dewater, and slump into the main canyon.

Sapping structures form rapidly as modern examples illustrate. Figure 5.17 shows sapping structures formed in sand along the bank of the Colorado River within Grand Canyon. In this example, the wake of a power boat was observed to hit the river bank causing a one-foot-high wave to run up on the river bank. As the wave receded abruptly, it caused erosion of the sloping sand surface just above the normal water level of the river. The characteristic theater-headed "canyons" in figure 5.17 required less than 30 seconds to be eroded.

Laboratory experiments also illustrate the ability of escaping fluids to modify sediments rapidly. Figure 5.18 shows a cross-sectional view of a ground-water-sapping chamber built by Alan Howard.[51] Sand is accumulated within a large tank, to form a sloping pile against a wire screen. The reservoir on the opposite side of the screen is filled with water, and a drain is opened at the base of the

sand slope. Water begins to saturate the sand, forming a water table within the sand (figure 5.18). The sapping zone occurs above the base of the sand slope, where water issues out of the sand. Failure of the sand slope occurs by sapping, and produces alcoves ("theater-headed canyons"), as seen in figure 5.19. These resemble some of the side canyons formed by catastrophic erosion at Mount St. Helens in 1982, and are similar to erosion which has occurred at man-made dams which have collapsed. An assortment of theater-headed canyons on Mars have been observed to issue into wide outflow channels. Carr[52] interpreted these sapping features as having formed by catastrophic release of Martian ground water.

We have found significant evidence that Grand Canyon and the region upstream have been eroded chiefly by catastrophic agents. Our interpretation is that many features of the present landscape are in an arrested stage of development. Many features were formed in the past by catastrophic agents, but are now being slowly remolded by gradual erosion. We would interpret these landforms to be relicts—features which are left over from the previous epoch of very significant erosion.

Examples of relict landforms in the Canyon and in the Canyonlands above Grand Canyon are abundant. Most of the theater-headed canyons or alcoves adjacent to Grand Canyon, and those in the Canyonlands, do not have active springs, so sapping processes which formed them have essentially stopped. Howard and Kochel say:

The number and extent of active seeps in alcoves in the Navajo Sandstone appear to be less than would be expected for active

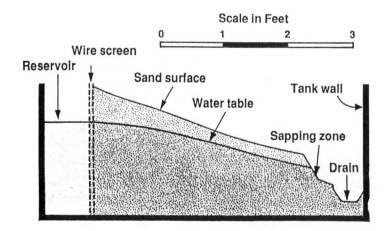

Figure 5.18 *Cross-section view of a tank used to produce sapping structures in the laboratory. (After A. D. Howard, 1988.)*

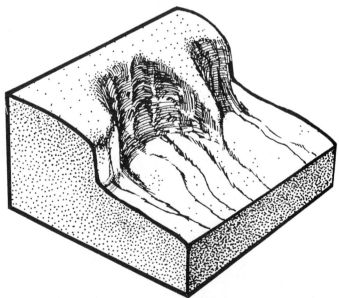

Figure 5.19 *Example of experimentally produced sapping structures made in the laboratory. These resemble theater-headed canyons of the Colorado Plateau.*

Figure 5.20 *A spectacular example of a cliff without active talus deposit is seen at Lees Ferry, upstream from Grand Canyon. If the sandstone cliff had a history of slow and continuous erosion, a much more significant quantity of boulders would be expected at the foot of the slope. (Photo by Steven A. Austin.)*

Figure 5.21 *Cliff stability in Grand Canyon is indicated by absence of recent talus at the base of many cliffs. (Photo by Mark Looy.)*

valley development by sapping processes. Many major alcoves are presently dry or have small seeps that occupy only part of the alcove. Most of the alcoves in which cliff dwellings were built 800–1000 years ago by the Anasazi have few or no seeps. Although a dry environment may have been a factor in alcove selection, seeps must have been active at some time in the past to create the alcove. Similarly, rockfalls have occurred over only a few cliff dwelling ruins since their occupation, and most of those are small. The paucity of fresh rockfalls in general within alcoves on the Colorado Plateau has already been discussed. [53]

Where modern springs do occur, the sapping forms are rather insignificant. Howard and Kochel say:

> *. . . the Weeping Wall at Zion National Park is an impressive seep emerging from the Navajo Sandstone, but the associated alcove and canyon are relatively small. Many other examples of fairly high discharge rates but only minor or nonexistent alcoves can be found throughout the Colorado Plateau.* [54]

Further evidence of the relict nature of the landscape comes from considering the stability of cliffs. Most major cliffs in Grand Canyon have only a small amount of talus, indicating that intermittent rock-fall accumulation over vast periods of time is not necessary. Figures 5.20 and 5.21 are examples. If such cliffs are the result of slow erosion over hundreds of thousands of years, we might expect a progressive increase in the decomposition of talus on the benches away from cliffs. [55] Such boulder-aging has not been demonstrated. Instead, we see shale benches which appear to have been swept clean of larger rocks by extensive flooding. Then, after significant flood modification, a recent talus has accumulated.

Another evidence of cliff stability in the Grand Canyon region comes from study of "desert varnish," an accretionary coating of minerals which attaches itself very slowly to stable rock surfaces. An excellent example is the cliff of Redwall Limestone, which has the accretionary, reddish coating derived from overlying Supai redbeds dominating its exposure. At present, this cliff is not eroding back slowly through a major extent of the canyon, or the coating would not be so obvious. Another example is the Vishnu Schist of the inner gorge, which is dominated by reddish-brown desert varnish.

Extraordinary Delta Deposits

If Grand Canyon was eroded by catastrophic drainage of lakes, we would expect the Pliocene deltaic deposits in the vicinity of the Gulf of California to provide data confirming the recent and rapid establishment of the Lower Colorado River. Two predictions can be made: (1) the Pliocene deltaic deposits should appear abruptly above non-deltaic deposits, and, (2) the deposits should show obvious evidences of rapid deposition, not characteristics typical of normal river deltas.

Charles D. Winker[56] recently surveyed the Pliocene sedimentary deposits associated with the delta of the Colorado River. The Bouse Formation (Lower Colorado River area along the California-Arizona border) and the Imperial Formation (Salton Trough area of California) do contain marine Pliocene deltaic deposits which appear abruptly above non-deltaic deposits. Pebbles within strata beneath the deltaic deposits do have local sources and indicate no large river system was present in the Lower Colorado River area before the Pliocene deltaic sands and muds were deposited. Thus, the Pliocene establishment of the Lower Colorado River seems confirmed.

Even more interesting is the character of the lowest deltaic deposits. The Imperial Formation west of the Salton Sea in San Diego County, California, contains a 3,000-foot-thick strata sequence dominated by rhythmically bedded mudstones.[57] These so-called "rhythmites" mark the introduction of deltaic sedimentation in the Salton Trough area. Winker recognizes that these deposits are *not* characteristic of modern delta deposits:

> *The striking lateral continuity of rhythmite bedding is unusual for shallow-water, traction-dominated deposits, but is quite common in fine-grained turbidites, which raises the possibility that deposition could have been primarily by sediment gravity flows.* [58]

Elsewhere, geologic researchers have argued that rhythmite deposition is a rapid, non-seasonal process, not characteristic of normal deltaic environments.[59] Therefore, the strata sequence in the earliest delta of the Colorado River does appear to be consistent with the breached-dam theory for Grand Canyon. This is a topic worthy of future research.

How the Breach Occurred

Failure of Dams

The weight of the evidence favors the theory that Grand Canyon was opened by a breaching event—probably failure of the natural dam formed by the Kaibab Upwarp. How and when the failure of the dam occurred is a subject for continued geologic study and speculation. What we *do* know about dams is that, when they fail, they fail catastrophically. Numerous historic examples of natural and man-made dams confirm that they rupture rapidly. There is no such thing as a *slow* dam failure!

A study of numerous historic dam failures showed that they fail in two major ways: either by overtopping or piping.[60] Overtopping occurs when water reaches a high-enough level behind the dam that water flows over the dam. Erosion occurs rapidly, as a spillway is formed, and the volume of flow increases enormously as the notch in the dam is lowered and the lake behind it is drained. Rapid erosion, even of solid rock and concrete occurs, as high-velocity flow causes cavitation (a rock-pulverizing process associated with fluid flows greater than 30 feet per second) and plucking (the yielding of jointed rock to macroturbulent flow). The volume of material that can be removed during overtopping is astounding.

Piping, the second way dams can fail, occurs when water pressure *within* the dam builds up to such a sufficient level that tunnels of water begin flowing through the dam. Usually, one tunnel system predominates, as a natural "pipe" is formed within the dam. The flow of water through the dam increases to such a high velocity that material within the dam is eroded, causing collapse of the dam into the piping channel. The collapse of the dam rapidly opens a spillway through the dam, and the lake drains catastrophically. Extreme volumes and velocities of water flow through the dam allow cavitation and plucking to accomplish significant erosion.

Configuration of Lakes

Outlines of large lakes, which appear to have existed east of the Kaibab Upwarp, are suggested in figure 5.22. Hopi Lake occupied a large area of the drainage basin of the present Little Colorado River. The deposits of Hopi Lake (the Bidahochi Formation) indicate that the elevation of the lake was above 6,000 feet, and that it extended into New Mexico.[61] It would appear that Hopi Lake failed, probably by piping, beneath a low point in the Kaibab Upwarp near Grand Canyon Village, in the extreme eastern Grand Canyon area. As an underground channel enlarged, collapse occurred, and catastrophic erosion carved a notch which began to form the Canyon. At the same time, the drainage of Hopi Lake downcut the present drainage basin of the Little Colorado River.

North of Hopi Lake, separated from Hopi Lake by the Echo Cliffs Monocline, was Canyonlands Lake.[62] It appears to have occupied a major area of the upper Colorado River drainage basin, including parts of the Green, Gunnison, and San Juan Rivers. Sedimentary deposits have yet to

prove the existence of Canyonlands Lake. Certain deposits (suggestive of the shore) and sapping structures (suggestive of structural collapse on the bed of the lake) indicate that Canyonlands Lake had an elevation above 5,800 feet. It appears that the catastrophic drainage of Hopi Lake caused instability and later failure of the dam for Canyonlands Lake. The Echo Cliffs Monocline, the structure impounding Canyonlands Lake, probably failed by piping.

The rapid drainage of Canyonlands Lake excavated Marble Canyon through its natural dam, added the connection of drainage with Grand Canyon, and caused further extensive erosion in the Canyon. The outline of Canyonlands Lake is indicated by spectacular topographic features, including cliffs at Bryce Canyon, Monument Valley, Mesa Verde, and Grand Junction. Because breaching of the Echo Cliffs dam for Canyonlands Lake caused significant lowering of the natural drainage, there was significant downcutting within this drainage, including The Canyonlands area, the Goosenecks of the San Juan, and the Black Canyon of the Gunnison River. Many of the most spectacular sapping features of southeastern Utah appear to be related to the rapid drainage of this lake.

A third lake, Lake Vernal, appears to have been located north of Canyonlands Lake, within the Green River drainage in northeastern Utah. Drainage of Canyonlands Lake could

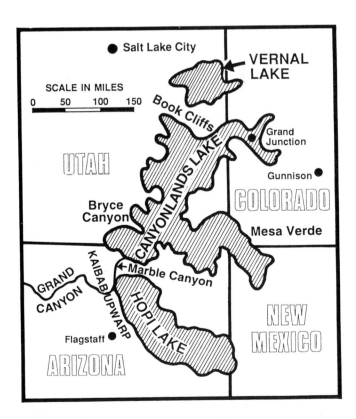

Figure 5.22 *Former locations of Hopi, Canyonlands, and Vernal Lakes on the Colorado Plateau. These lakes breached their dams, causing catastrophic drainage and erosion of Grand Canyon.*

have initiated failure of the dam holding Vernal Lake. The breach through the Book Cliffs lowered the elevation of the upper Green River, and caused remarkable downcutting on the Green River in Flaming Gorge, in Utah and Wyoming.

Together, Hopi, Canyonlands, and Vernal Lakes would occupy about one-fourth of the drainage basin above Grand Canyon (an area of over 30,000 square miles). The volume of water contained in these lakes is estimated to have been about three times the volume of Lake Michigan (over 3,000 cubic miles).[63] The drainage of these lakes through Grand Canyon would have caused the significant downcutting through the plateaus of northern Arizona. As catastrophic erosion of the dam proceeded, large landslides from side canyons, and sapping, caused by outflow of water from wet strata, would enlarge the Canyon. The drainage of these three lakes through the Canyon would keep it free of obstructions.

The breached dam theory for the origin of Grand Canyon can be integrated into a Biblical Flood model. Late in the Flood, and in the immediate post-Flood, the Kaibab Upwarp was formed. This upwarp blocked the drainages of the Colorado Plateau. In the post-Flood period, possibly hundreds of years after the Flood, enough water had built up in these lakes, that dam failure could occur. Forests and animals appear to have been living on the plateau when the dam was breached. This breaching event may explain the unusual distribution of the tassel-eared squirrels on the Kaibab and Coconino Plateaus (see chapter 8).

Rapid Erosion of Bedrock

How much erosion could occur as these three lakes, containing 3,000 cubic miles of water, breached their dams?

Could significant erosion of hundreds of cubic miles of both strata and crystalline basement rock occur within Grand Canyon? Many people, no doubt, will question the breached dam theory because of the inability to conceive of such massive erosion in so short a period of time. Can solid rock be eroded rapidly?

The question concerning the magnitude and speed of erosion of solid rock has already been the subject of an intense geologic debate, which lasted over 40 years (1923-1962). The flood controversy for the Channeled Scabland of eastern Washington centered on whether catastrophic water flows could create enough scouring and irregular plucking of basalt bedrock to form what are today dry, deeply incised channels.[64]

J Harlen Bretz proposed, in 1923, that channels hundreds of feet deep were eroded by a catastrophic flood. The controversy became especially heated, after Bretz[65] provided evidence, in 1932, that Grand Coulee, of Washington State, (figure 5.11) was eroded by catastrophic drainage of Lake Missoula, in Montana. He proposed that Grand Coulee, a 50-mile-long trench from one to six miles wide and up to 900 feet deep, was eroded catastrophically! That would involve rapid erosion of *many cubic miles* of basalt from Grand Coulee.

There were many critics of the Lake Missoula Flood between 1930 and 1960. Even some of the most famous geologists of that time remained solidly uniformitarian, and refused to believe in massive-flood erosion in eastern Washington. That controversy formed one of the most interesting episodes in the history of geology. V. R. Baker wrote:

> *The role of floods in the erosion of stream channels has been one of the most*

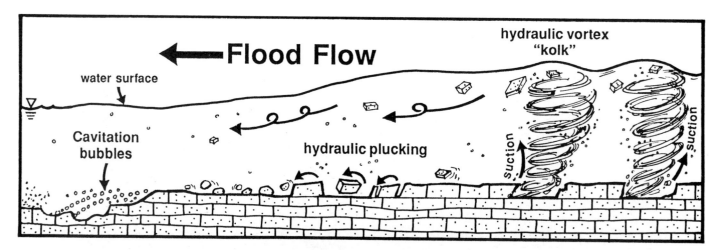

Figure 5.23 *Major agents of erosion of solid bedrock during a large flood. High-velocity flow produces cavitation downcurrent from an obstruction, as vacuum bubbles implode, inflicting hammerlike blows on the bedrock surface. Streaming flow impacts bedrock surface, causing hydraulic plucking, especially along joint surfaces. Hydraulic vortex action causes a "kolk," which exerts intense lifting force, removing blocks of bedrock.*

Figure 5.24 *Cavitation damage in left spillway tunnel at Glen Canyon Dam. The enormous erosional hole (32 x 40 x 150 feet) penetrated through steel-reinforced concrete into sandstone bedrock in June 1983. The hole is shown here during the process of repair, below the undamaged 40-foot-diameter tunnel. Men provide scale. (Bureau of Reclamation photo.)*

controversial topics in fluvial geomorphology. . . . Indeed, the famous Spokane flood debate, concerning the effects of the greatest known freshwater floods on the planet, . . . centered on the issue of the erosive capability of running water. . . . Those who disbelieved the flood theory of J Harlen Bretz did so out of their experience that rivers did not behave as Bretz proposed. Subsequent work showed that their experience, not Bretz's theory, was inadequate.[66]

The debate concerning the magnitude and speed of flood erosion of bedrock was resolved, largely by investigations of cavitation and plucking, two processes which dominate erosion during catastrophic floods. Figure 5.23 shows these processes. Cavitation, the rock-pulverizing process associated with fluid flows greater than 30 feet per second (20 miles per hour), occurs as the fluid detaches from irregularities in the bedrock channel. The detachment of the fluid produces vacuum cavities ("bubbles"), which implode. The cavitation process inflicts explosive, hammerlike blows on the bedrock surface, with pressures ranging as high as 30,000 atmospheres (440,000 pounds per square inch).[67] The extreme pressure which can be delivered by cavitation is many times greater than the compressive strength of rocks. Therefore, rocks are literally converted to powder by the cavitation process. Because of its obvious catastrophic effects, engineers take deliberate steps to avoid the conditions which cause cavitation.

Plucking is the second erosive process which causes extremely rapid erosion in bedrock channels. High-velocity flows are able to rip loose large blocks of bedrock along bedrock-joint surfaces (figure 5.23). Once a large block of bedrock is dislodged, the high-velocity flow is able to move and abrade it.

Perhaps the most energetic phenomenon associated with macroturbulent flow is the production of a "kolk," the underwater equivalent of a tornado.[68] The vortex of water (figure 5.23) producing a kolk has very low pressure beneath the flowing water. The suction power of the kolk exerts intense hydraulic lifting forces and can remove or pluck slabs of bedrock from the channel.

A number of features eroded by the Lake Missoula Flood, as well as those eroded by modern catastrophic floods, have been attributed to macroturbulent flow processes.[69] Close study of some of the hard-rock erosion features which formed recently at Mount St. Helens also gives us a heightened appreciation of plucking as a potent geologic process (see figure 5.14). Evidence

for rapid breaching of natural lava dams in western Grand Canyon is noteworthy and is the subject of ongoing studies.[70]

Rapid Erosion at Glen Canyon Dam

Among the most instructive modern examples of rapid erosion of bedrock comes from Glen Canyon Dam, on the Colorado River, just above Grand Canyon.[71] Excessive snowfall, from the high country of the upper Colorado River basin in the late spring and early summer of 1983, caused excessive run-off that poured from all major reservoirs of the upper Colorado into Lake Powell at rates of up to 148,000 cubic feet per second. This rapid inflow threatened to fill Lake Powell and overflow Glen Canyon Dam. The emergency situation required engineers to risk damage to the spillway tunnel, which they knew would have to carry flows to nearly its design capacity. The maximum release of water from the dam during the emergency condition was 93,000 cubic feet per second.

In an effort to control the unanticipated flow rates, the power plant was run at full capacity, releasing 28,000 cubic feet per second through the turbines, but this was still not enough. The two outlet tubes were opened, each allowing an additional 17,000 cubic feet per second of water to drain from Lake Powell. This was still not enough to counteract the high rates of inflow from the Colorado River drainage network.

On June 15, 1983, the 40-foot-diameter left spillway tunnel was opened to drain from Lake Powell an additional 12,000 cubic feet per second. Four days later, the water flow from the spillway tunnel exit stopped "sweeping" (a rooster-tail shaped stream of water that indicates all is well), so the flow was raised to 17,000 cubic feet per second, and the "sweep" resumed. Then, on June 28, 1983, the flow was increased to 32,000 cubic feet per second. As the flow was raised to 32,000 cubic feet per second, "sweep" stopped abruptly, as large blocks of concrete and bedrock were hurled from the 40-foot-diameter tunnel. The water exiting the tunnel became red (the color of the surrounding sandstone), and noticeable ground vibrations (earthquakes) were felt by engineers. The spillway tunnel was immediately closed, so that damage could be evaluated.

The survey team discovered extensive cavitation damage in the spillway tunnel. The three-foot-thick, steel-reinforced concrete lining of the tunnel was penetrated by pits. At an elbow where the tunnel levels out, a hole 32 feet deep, 150 feet long, and 40 feet wide was cut through the lining into red sandstone bedrock. This enormous hole required 63,000 cubic feet of concrete to fill. It is shown in figure 5.24.

The speed of erosion in the Glen Canyon Dam spillway tunnel, on June 28, 1983, must have been very rapid. Most of the erosion occurred during the short period when the red color of water appeared and ground vibrations were generated. It is possible that cavitation was pulverizing concrete, steel, and sandstone at a rate in excess of 1,000 cubic feet per minute, during the peak period of erosion. This high rate of erosion is consistent with the amount of pulverized sandstone which would be needed to turn the water red. We can appreciate why engineers take very deliberate steps to avoid cavitation!

Summary

For more than one hundred years, geologists have attempted, in a very deliberate manner, to explain the erosion of Grand Canyon by uniformitarian agents. The elegant notion that the Colorado River eroded Grand Canyon slowly, during tens of millions of years, has been demonstrated repeatedly to be at odds with the empirical data. Most geologists familiar with the geology of northern Arizona, have abandoned the antecedent river theory. The less-rational explanation of Grand Canyon erosion by stream capture (enlargement of a precocious gully) involves an accident of incredible improbability. Both the antecedent-river and stream-capture theories have the extraordinarily difficult problem of disposing of the products of tens of millions of years of river erosion. Thus, evolutionary and uniformitarian theories have failed to explain the history of the erosion of Grand Canyon.

Geologists have freely admitted the problems with uniformitarian theories for the origin of Grand Canyon. Earle E. Spamer summarized the situation recently:

The greatest of Grand Canyon's enigmas is the problem of how it was made. This is the most volatile aspect of Grand Canyon geological studies. . . . Grand Canyon has held tight to her secrets of origin and age. Every approach to this problem has been cloaked in hypothesis, drawing upon the incomplete empirical evidence of stratigraphy, sedimentology, and radiometric dating.[72]

R. J. Rice provides his summary:

After a century of study, we seem, if anything, to be further than ever from a full comprehension of how the Grand Canyon has evolved.[73]

Here the printed words of geologist H. B. Baker are appropriate, ". . . the doctrine of uniformitarianism leads to poverty where riches are to be desired."[74]

The catastrophist concept is that Grand Canyon was eroded by flood drainage. Could Grand Canyon represent the eroded spillway from gigantic lakes whose dams have failed? That explanation continues to attract the attention of geologists. The breached dam theory is directly supported by evidence of sedimentary deposits from a lake to the east of the Kaibab Upwarp. Furthermore, mechanisms are known, by which floods are able to erode rapidly, even the most solid rock. Numerous landforms of the Colorado Plateau can be regarded as relics sculptured by catastrophic agents associated with rapid drainage of gigantic lakes in the post-Flood period. Today, these landforms endure, through the modern erosional epoch of much-reduced erosion, as monuments to catastrophe.

NOTES—Chapter 5

1. C. R. Longwell, "How Old is the Colorado River?" *American Journal of Science* 244 (1946): 817–835.

2. R. J. Rice, "The Canyon Conundrum" *Geographical Magazine* 55 (1983): 288–291.

3. D. L. Babenroth and A. N. Strahler, "Geomorphology and Structure of the East Kaibab Monocline, Arizona and Utah" *Geological Society of America Bulletin* 56 (1945): 107–150. H. E. Gregory and R. C. Moore, "The Kaiparowits Region, a Geographic and Geologic Reconnaissance of Parts of Utah and Arizona" *U.S. Geological Survey Professional Paper* 164 (1931): 1–161.

4. Ibid. Recently, W. E. Bowers ("The Canaan Peak, Pine Hollow and Wasatch Formations in the Table Cliff Region, Garfield County, Utah" *U.S. Geological*

Survey Bulletin 1331–B [1972]: 1–39) challenged the stratigraphic relationships at Canaan Peak. He suggested that the surface, called an unconformity at Canaan Peak is, instead, a fault surface. If the case for unconformity is weak, then the rim-gravel evidence should be used to evaluate the age of the Kaibab Upwarp.

5. D. P. Elston, R. A. Young, E. H. McKee, and M. L. Dennis, "Paleontology, Clast Ages, and Paleomagnetism of Upper Paleocene and Eocene Gravel and Limestone Deposits, Colorado Plateau and Transition Zone, Northern and Central Arizona," in D. P. Elston, G. H. Billingsley, and R. A. Young, eds., *Geology of Grand Canyon, Northern Arizona* (with Colorado River Guides) (Washington, American Geophysical Union, 1989), pp. 155–173.

6. Ibid.

7. J. W. Powell, "Exploration of the Colorado River of the West and its Tributaries," *Smithsonian Institution Annual Report*, 1875, 291 pp.

8. Ibid.

9. C. B. Hunt, "Cenozoic Geology of the Colorado Plateau," *U.S. Geological Survey Professional Paper* 279 (1956): 1–99.

10. Powell, "Exploration of the Colorado River . . . ," p. 198.

11. C. E. Dutton, *Report on the Geology of the High Plateaus of Utah* (Washington, U.S. Geological Survey, 1880), p. 16.

12. W. O. Smith and others, "Comprehensive Survey of Sedimentation in Lake Mead, 1948–1949," *U.S. Geological Survey Professional Paper* 295 (1960): 1–254. A considerable body of geologic literature has appeared recently, which argues that the average erosion rate calculated by Smith and others is very conservative. There appears to have been a dramatic and abrupt decrease in the sediment load of the Colorado River in the early 1940's. The decrease in sediment load may have ranged from 50 to 100 million tons per year. For a summary of the decreased-sediment-load observations, see S. A. Schumm, *To Interpret the Earth: Ten Ways to be Wrong* (Cambridge, Cambridge University Press, 1991), pp. 108–119.

13. T. H. van Andel and G. G. Shor, Jr., eds., *Marine Geology of the Gulf of California* (Tulsa, American Association of Petroleum Geologists, Memoir 3, 1964), 350 pp. P. Lonsdale, "Geology and Tectonic History of the Gulf of California," *in* E. L. Winterer, D. M. Hussong, and R. W. Decker, eds., *The Eastern Pacific Ocean and Hawaii* (Boulder, Colorado, Geological Society of America, The Geology of North America, vol. N, 1989) pp. 499–521.

14. Longwell, "How Old is the Colorado River?" pp. 831, 832, 823.

15. E. D. McKee, R. F. Wilson, W. J. Breed, and C. S. Breed, "Evolution of the Colorado River in Arizona" *Museum of Northern Arizona Bulletin* 44 (1967): 1–67.

16. E. Blackwelder, "Origin of the Colorado River," *Geological Society of America Bulletin* 45 (1934): 551–566.

17. Hunt, "Cenozoic Geology of the Colorado Plateau."

18. I. Lucchitta, "History of the Grand Canyon and of the Colorado River in Arizona," *in* J. P. Jenney and S. J. Reynolds, eds., *Geologic Evolution of Arizona* (Arizona Geological Society Digest 17, 1989), pp. 701–715.

19 D. P. Elston and R. A. Young, "Development of Cenozoic Landscape of Central and Northern Arizona: Cutting of Grand Canyon," *in* D. P. Elston, G. H. Billingsley, and R. A. Young, eds., *Geology of Grand Canyon, Northern Arizona (with Colorado River Guide)* (Washington, American Geophysical Union, 1989), pp. 145–153.

20. A. D. Howard and R. Dolan, "Geomorphology of the Colorado River in the Grand Canyon," *Journal of Geology* 89 (1981): 269–298.

21. P. Oetking, D. E. Feray, and H. B. Renfro, *Geological Highway Map of the Southern Rocky Mountain Region* (Tulsa, American Association of Petroleum Geologists, 1967), one sheet.

22. Ibid.

23. One of the few recent advocates of the ancestral river theory is E. M. P. Lovejoy, "The Muddy Creek Formation at Colorado River in Grand Wash: The Dilemma of the Immovable Object," *Arizona Geological Society Digest* 12 (1980): 177–192. Lovejoy defends the antecedent river theory by proposing that the Colorado River *did* flow through the Grand Wash area in Muddy Creek time, but, to our astonishment, left no sedimentary deposits. This opinion is *not* widely endorsed by geologists.

24. Rice, "The Canyon Conundrum."

25. A. N. Strahler, "Geomorphology and Structure of the West Kaibab Fault Zone and Kaibab Plateau, Arizona," *Geological Society of America Bulletin* 59 (1948): 513–540.

26. See discussion and diagrams in chapter 2.

27. Hunt, "Cenozoic Geology of the Colorado Plateau," p. 85.

28. W. N. Blair, "Gulf of California in Lake Mead Area of Arizona and Nevada During Late Miocene Time," *American Association of Petroleum Geologists Bulletin* 62 (1978): 1159–1170.

29. M. Shafiqullah, P. E. Damon, D. J. Lynch, S. J. Reynolds, W. A. Rehrig, and R. H. Raymond, "K-Ar Geochronology and Geologic History of Southwestern Arizona and Adjacent Areas," *Arizona Geological Society Digest* 12 (1980): 201–260.

30. R. E. Anderson, C. R. Longwell, R. L. Armstrong, and R. F. Marvin, "Significance of K-Ar Ages of Tertiary Rocks from the Lake Mead Region, Nevada-Arizona," *Geological Society of America Bulletin* 83 (1972): 273–288.

31. Shafiqullah and others, "K-Ar Geochronology. . . ."

32. I. Lucchitta and R. A. Young, "Structure and Geomorphic Character of Western Colorado Plateau in the Grand Canyon-Lake Mead Region," *in* J. D. Nations, C. M. Conway, and G. A. Swann, eds., *Geology of Central and Northern Arizona* (Geological Society of America, Rocky Mountain Section, Field Trip Guidebook, 1986), pp. 159–176.

33. P. E. Damon, M. Shafiqullah, and R. B. Scarborough, "Revised Chronology for Critical Stages in the Evolution of the Lower Colorado River," *Geological Society of America Abstracts with Programs* 10 (1978): 101,102.

34. R. B. Scarborough, *Chemistry of Late Cenozoic Air-Fall Ashes in Southeastern Arizona* (Tucson, University of Arizona, M. S. Thesis, 1975), 107 p. K-Ar ages for the pre-1980 period were recalculated, using new decay constants.

35. P. E. Damon, M. Shafiqullah, and J. S. Leventhal, "K-Ar Chronology for the San Francisco Volcanic Field and Rate of Erosion of the Little Colorado River," *in* T. N. V. Karlstrom and others, eds., *Geology of Northern Arizona, with Notes on Archaeology and Paleoclimate; Part I, Regional Studies* (Geological Society of America Rocky Mountain Section Meeting, Flagstaff, 1974), pp. 221–235.

36. E. E. Larson, W. C. Bradley, and M. Ozima, "Development of the Colorado River System in Northwestern Colorado During the Late Cenozoic," *in* J. E. Fassett, ed., *Canyonlands Country* (Four Corner Geological Society Guidebook, 8th Field Conference, 1975), p. 101.

37. C. S. Breed, "A Century of Conjecture on the Colorado River in Grand Canyon," *Geology and Natural History of the Grand Canyon Region* (Four Corners Geological Society Guidebook, 5th Field Conference, 1969), p. 66.

38. M. Collier, *An Introduction to Grand Canyon Geology* (Grand Canyon, AZ, Grand Canyon Natural History Association, 1980), p. 36.

39. I. Lucchitta, "Canyon Maker: A Geological History of the Colorado River," *Plateau* 59 (1988): 11.

40. The concept of rapid breaching of the Kaibab Upwarp by drainage from lakes has a long history. Geologic evidence of a large lake in northeastern Arizona ("Hopi Lake") was provided by Howel Williams ("Pliocene Volcanoes of the Navajo-Hopi Country," *Geological Society of America Bulletin* 47 [1936]: 111–172). Tectonic activity is thought to have interrupted the flow of the Colorado River creating a large lake behind the Kaibab Plateau followed by piping failure (G. C. Bowles, "Reinterpretation of Grand Canyon Geomorphology," *United States Geological Survey Professional Paper* 1100 [1978]: 72). Creationists were suggesting catastrophic drainage models in the 1960's and 1970's. One of the most noteworthy early creationist statements of the breached dam theory appeared in the writings of Clifford L. Burdick (*The Canyon of Canyons* [Caldwell, Idaho, Bible-Science Association, 1974], p. 27). Bernard E. Northrup proposed in 1968 that erosion of Grand Canyon was caused by release of trapped glacial melt waters in the post-Flood period centuries after Noah's Flood. Post-Flood ponding of water east of Grand Canyon behind a tectonic upwarp was suggested as the cause leading to cutting the Canyon by Steven A. Austin and John H. Whitmore (*Grand Canyon Field Study Tour Guidebook,* March 23–30, 1986 [Santee, California, Institute for Creation Research, 1986], p. 48). Edmond W. Holroyd, III, recognized that a lake bigger than one of the Great Lakes could be contained upstream of Grand Canyon if the Canyon was blocked approximately at the 5,600-foot elevation ("Missing Talus," *Creation Research Society Quarterly* 24 [1987]: 15,16). The breached dam theory was described in 1988 in a field guidebook (Steven A. Austin, *Grand Canyon Field Study Tour Guidebook,* April 9–16, 1988 [Santee, California, Institute for Creation Research, 1988], pp. 50–54). In 1989, Walter

T. Brown, Jr. in proposing the Hydroplate Theory, also proposed where a very large lake, at an elevation of 5700 feet, once occupied much of southeastern Utah and parts of Colorado, Arizona, and New Mexico, (*In the Beginning* [Phoenix, Arizona, Center for Scientific Creation, fifth edition, 1989], 58-83). Brown named it Grand Lake and wrote that it breached between what is now Vermilion Cliffs and Echo Cliffs. This, in turn, eroded the western bank of Hopi Lake. All the waters released eroded the Grand Canyon. Interesting field evidences for catastrophic drainage of lakes and dialog concerning the history of discussions is found in Edmond W. Holroyd, III ("Missing Talus on the Colorado Plateau," *Proceedings of the Second International Conference on Creationism,* 2 [1990]: 115–128). A summary of some of these theories was published by E. L. Williams, J. R. Meyer and G. W. Wolfrom ("Erosion of the Grand Canyon of the Colorado River: Part III—Review of the Possible Formation of Basin and Lakes on Colorado Plateau and Different Climatic Conditions in the Past," *Creation Research Society Quarterly* 29 [1992]: 18–24). Further comments were provided by Michael J. Oard. ("Comments on the Breached Dam Theory for the Formation of the Grand Canyon," *Creation Research Society Quarterly* 30 [1993]: 39–46).

41. The outline of the lakes was obtained by Edmond W. Holroyd, III, using a computer with data from an elevation database. Figure 5.8 is Steven Austin's replot of Holroyd's computer-generated map. The present topography of the Colorado Plateau could be made to contain the lake at slightly above 5,600 feet elevation assuming Grand Canyon was filled with an obstruction. The "pour point" behind the dam would be in southern Utah, east of the town of Kanab.

42. J. E. Allen, M. Burns, and S. C. Sargent, *Cataclysms on the Columbia* (Portland, Timber Pr., 1986), 211 pp.

43. V. R. Baker, "Large-Scale Erosional and Depositional Features of the Channeled Scabland," *in* V. R. Baker and D. Nummedal, eds., *The Channeled Scabland* (Washington, National Aeronautics and Space Administration, 1978), pp. 81–115.

44. S. A. Austin, "Rapid Erosion at Mount St. Helens," *Origins* 11 (1984): 90–98.

45. H. Williams, "Pliocene Volcanoes in the Navajo-Hopi Country," *Geological Society of America Bulletin* 47 (1936): 111–172.

46. J. D. Nations and J. J. Landye, "Cenozoic Plant and Animal Fossils of Arizona," *in* T. L. Smiley, et. al., eds., *Landscapes of Arizona: The Geological Story* (Lanham, Maryland, University Press of America, 1984) pp. 7–35, 428–479.

47. C. A. Repenning and J. H. Irwin, "Bidahochi Formation of Arizona and New Mexico," *American Association of Petroleum Geologists Bulletin* 38 (1954): 1821–1826. R. B. Scarborough, "Cenozoic Erosion and Sedimentation in Arizona," *Arizona Bureau of Geology and Mineral Technology, Open File Report* 85-3 (1984).

48. S. A. Schumm, M. P. Mosley, and W. E. Weaver, *Experimental Fluvial Geomorphology* (New York, John Wiley, 1987), 408 pp.

49. R. G. Shepherd, "Incised River Meanders: Evolution in Simulated Bedrock," *Science* 178 (1972): 409–411.

50. Allen and others, *Cataclysms on the Columbia*, p. 68.

51. A. D. Howard, "Groundwater Sapping Experiments and Modeling," *in* A. D. Howard, R. C. Kochel, and H. E. Holt, eds., *Sapping Features of the Colorado Plateau* (Washington, National Aeronautics and Space Administration, 1988), pp. 71–83.

52. M. H. Carr, "Formation of Martian Flood Features by Release of Water from Confined Aquifers," *Journal of Geophysical Research* 84 (1979): 2995–3007.

53. A. D. Howard and R. C. Kochel, "Introduction to Cuesta Landforms and Sapping Processes on the Colorado Plateau," *in* A. D. Howard, R. C. Kochel, and H. E. Holt, eds., *Sapping Features of the Colorado Plateau* (Washington, National Aeronautics and Space Administration, 1988), p. 47.

54. Ibid, p. 29.

55. For interesting discussion and observations of missing talus on the Colorado Plateau see Edmond W. Holroyd, III, "Missing Talus," *Creation Research Society Quarterly* 24 (1987): 15,16.

56. C. D. Winker, *Neogene Stratigraphy of the Fish Creek-Vallecito Section, Southern California: Implications for Early History of the Northern Gulf of California and Colorado Delta* (Tucson, University of Arizona, unpublished Ph.D. dissertation, 1987), 494 p.

57. Ibid., pp. 282–308.

58. Ibid., pp. 288.

59. A. Lambert and K. J. Hsü, "Non-annual Cycles of Varve-like Sedimentation in Walensee, Switzerland," *Sedimentology* 26 (1979): 453–461. R. J. Carson, C. F. McKhann, and M. H. Pizey, "The Touchet Beds of the Walla Walla Valley," *in* V. R. Baker and D. Nummedal, eds., *The Channeled Scabland* (Washington, D.C., National Aeronautics and Space Administration, 1978), pp. 173–177. D. J. W. Piper, "Turbidite Origin of some Laminated Mudstones," *Geology Magazine* 109 (1972): 115–126. G. A. Smith, "Missoula Flood Dynamics and Magnitudes Inferred from Sedimentology of Slack-Water Deposits on the Columbia Plateau, Washington," *Geological Society of America Bulletin* 105 (1993): 77-100.

60. J. E. Costa and R. L. Schuster, "The Formation and Failure of Natural Dams," *Geological Society of America Bulletin* 100 (1988): 1054–1068.

61. R. Scarborough, "Cenozoic Erosion and Sedimentation in Arizona," *in* J. P. Jenney and S. J. Reynolds, eds., *Geologic Evolution of Arizona* (Arizona Geological Society Digest 17, 1989), pp. 515–537.

62. The name "Canyonlands Lake" is introduced here for a lake which occupied the major portion of the extraordinary canyon country of southeastern Utah. The outline of the lake was first suggested by computer plotting by Edmond W. Holroyd, III ("Missing Talus," *Creation Research Society Quarterly* 24 [1987]: 15,16). Field evidences suggest Canyonlands Lake had an elevation above 5,800 feet in many areas. A lake with significantly different shoreline and lower elevation was suggested by Walter T. Brown, Jr. (*In the Beginning* [Phoenix, AZ, Center for Scientific Creation, fifth edition, 1989], p. 83). Brown used the name "Grand Lake" for his proposed lake in southeastern Utah. Grand Lake of Brown (1989) covered the La Sal Mountains, Abajo Mountains, and Aquarius Plateau, whereas Canyonlands Lake did not occupy these areas. Holroyd's plotting is superior to Brown's, and the name "Canyonlands Lake" is preferred.

63. Earth's largest modern lakes are:
      1st—Lake Baikal (5,000 cubic miles), Siberia
      2nd—Lake Tanganyika (4,500 cubic miles), Africa
      3rd—Lake Superior (3,000 cubic miles), North America
     The total volume of the Great Lakes of North America is almost 6,000 cubic miles.

64. V. R. Baker, "The Spokane Flood Controversy and the Martian Outflow Channels," *Science* 202 (1978): 1249–1256.

65. J H. Bretz, "The Grand Coulee," American Geographical Society Special Publication 15, (1932) 89 pp.

66. V. R. Baker, "Flood Erosion," *in* V. R. Baker, R. C. Kochel, and P. C. Patton, eds., *Flood Geomorphology* (New York, John Wiley, 1988), p. 89.

67. H. L. Barnes, "Cavitation as a Geological Agent," *American Journal of Science* 254 (1956): 493–505. For a recent summary of the physics of cavitation see F. R. Young, *Cavitation* (New York, McGraw-Hill, 1989), 418 p.

68. V. R. Baker, "Paleohydraulics and Hydrodynamics of Scabland Floods," *in* V. R. Baker and D. Nummedal, eds., *The Channeled Scabland* (Washington, National Aeronautics and Space Administration, 1978), pp. 59-79.

69. Ibid.

70. J. D. Rogers and M. R. Pyles, "Evidence of Catastrophic Erosional Events in the Grand Canyon," *Proceedings of the Second Conference on Scientific Research in the National Parks* 5 (1980): 392–454.

71. U. S. Department of Interior, Bureau of Reclamation, *Challenge at Glen Canyon Dam* (Salt Lake City, Film/Video, 1983), 27 minutes.

     For further discussion of the role of cavitation in erosion of rock, see E. W. Holroyd, III, "Some Simulations of the Possible Role of Cavitation in Catastrophic Floods," *Creation Research Society Quarterly* 27 (1990): 49–55.

72. E. E. Spamer, "The Development of Geological Studies in the Grand Canyon," *Tryonia* 17 (1989): 39.

73. Rice, "The Canyon Conundrum," p. 291.

74. H. B. Baker, "Uniformitarianism and Inductive Logic," *Pan-American Geologist* 69 (1938): 165.

Chapter 6

ARE GRAND CANYON ROCKS ONE BILLION YEARS OLD?

"What has been is remote and exceedingly mysterious.
Who can discover it?"
Ecclesiastes 7:24 (NIV)

Are Grand Canyon rocks one billion years old? Do radioisotope dating methods prove great ages for Grand Canyon rocks? Many people suppose that scientific data conclusively prove billions of years for rocks. Few people, however, have examined, critically, the methods of dating, and very few people understand the nature of the assumptions, which are foundational to these calculations of enormous geologic "ages."

The purpose of this chapter is to explain how "ages" of billions of years have been assigned to rocks. Specifically, this chapter explains how the "ages" contained in figure 6.8 were obtained for significant Grand Canyon rocks. This chapter begins with an elementary derivation of the equations and assumptions used to obtain "ages" by the most popular radioisotope dating techniques. Then, the methods are applied to Grand Canyon rocks. The material contained in this chapter is more technical than in other chapters. However, careful attention to this chapter, and use of high-school mathematics, prepares the reader to evaluate one of the most extraordinary problems in evolutionary theory.

For the reader who finds the mathematics of this chapter overly difficult, a review of figure 6.8 and the "Conclusion" statement of this chapter will provide a good summary of the problems with dating Grand Canyon rocks.

Assumptions of Radioisotope Dating

Measurement of time by radioactive decay of an element is analogous to measurement of time as sand grains fall through an hourglass. The hourglass shown in figure 6.1 has two chambers, from the uppermost of which grains fall into the lowermost at a constant rate. Basic mathematics can be used to show how the hourglass can tell time. The number of sand grains removed from the upper chamber after a set period of time has elapsed is:

$$P_r = P_o - P_t = k\,t \tag{1}$$

where P_r is the number of grains which have been removed from the upper chambers during the set period of time, P_o was the number of grains originally in the upper chamber, P_t is the number of grains remaining in the upper chamber after the set period of time, k is the number of grains which fall per unit time through the hourglass, and t is the time which has elapsed since the grains began to fall after the hourglass was inverted.

Measuring Time With an Hourglass

We can express the time which has elapsed in terms of the properties of the upper chamber of the hourglass and the rate of fall of the grains. This is accomplished by rearrangement of equation (1):

$$t = \frac{P_o - P_t}{k} \tag{2}$$

Now we have an equation for telling time with an hourglass.

Figure 6.1 *An hourglass can be used to measure elapsed time, and illustrates assumptions which are used in the radioisotope dating of rocks.*

We might suppose that all of the sand grains were originally in the upper chamber, and that P_o comprised all of the grains in the hourglass, but such does not need to be true. The hourglass could have been inverted, with a portion of the grains being already in the lower chamber. This shows us that we need to pay attention to the initial condition of the instrument, in order to measure elapsed time with equation (2).

Another equation can be written to describe the number of sand grains added to the lower chamber of the hourglass after a set period of time has elapsed:

$$D_a = D_t - D_o = k\,t \qquad (3)$$

where D_a is the number of grains which have been added to the lower chamber during the set period of time, D_t is the number of grains in the lower chamber after the set period of time, and D_o was the number of grains originally in the lower chamber. We can use equation (3) to express the time which has elapsed in terms of the contents of the lower chamber of the hourglass, and the rate of fall of the grains:

$$t = \frac{D_t - D_o}{k} \qquad (4)$$

Equations (2) and (4) give us elapsed time from the hourglass, provided we can observe the present number of grains in the chambers (P_t and D_t), provided we know the initial number of grains in the chambers (P_o and D_o), and provided we know the rate of fall of grains (k). There is little difficulty in determining the present number of grains now in the chambers (P_t and D_t). Furthermore, there is little problem in establishing the rate of grains flowing through the instrument (k), and we have reason to suppose the rate has been constant through time. However, when it comes to establishing the initial number of the grains in the chambers (P_o and D_o) when the hourglass was inverted, a problem may exist. No observer may have been present, and we may not be able to establish the initial number of grains. Because equations (2) and (4) depend on knowledge of initial conditions which may not be evident, we call these time equations "model-age" equations. They can be used to establish elapsed time, *if* we can assume the model of the initial conditions is true. In many respects, these "model-age" equations for the hourglass are similar to those used in radioisotope dating.

Measuring Time By Radioactive Decay

An important relationship can be obtained by manipulating equation (1) in the hourglass example. This relationship is:

$$P_t = P_o - k\,t \qquad (5)$$

The number of sand grains remaining in the upper chambers (P_t) is expressed in terms of the original number of grains (P_o), minus the number of grains which have been removed (kt). Equation (5) is defined, for all times, such that $0 \le t \le P_o/k$. For $t > P_o/k$, P_t is equal to zero, because all grains have fallen from the upper chamber.

A graph of equation (5) appears in figure 6.2a. Here, the number of grains remaining in the upper chamber is shown as a function of time. Notice that the graph shows a constant rate of decrease in the number of grains, from time zero to time P_o/k, then no remaining grains after time P_o/k. This agrees with our experiences with hourglasses.

Radioactive decay also has a graph similar to figure 6.2a. Observations have been made, repeatedly, on

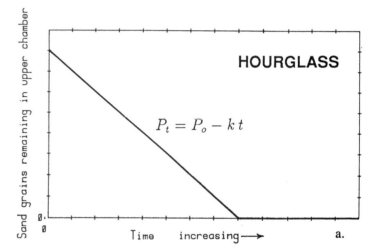

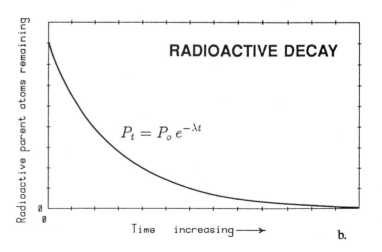

Figure 6.2 *Graphs showing the analogy between sand grains in the hourglass and the decay of radioactive parent atoms.*

Table 6.1 *Decay constants and half-lives for important radioactive isotopes. These are arranged from the slowest decaying isotope (samarium-147) to the fastest decaying isotope (carbon-14).*

Radioactive Parent	Stable Daughter(s)	Decay Constant (1/years)	Half-Life (years)
samarium - 147	neodymium - 143	6.54×10^{-12}	106 billion
rubidium - 87	strontium - 87	1.42×10^{-11}	48.8 billion
thorium - 232	lead - 208	4.9475×10^{-11}	14.01 billion
uranium - 238	lead - 206	1.55125×10^{-10}	4.47 billion
potassium - 40	argon - 40 (10.5%) calcium - 40 (89.5%)	5.543×10^{-10}	1.25 billion
uranium - 235	lead - 207	9.8485×10^{-10}	0.704 billion
carbon - 14	nitrogen - 14	1.21×10^{-4}	5,730

Data from Steiger and Jäger (1977) and Faure (1986).

radioactive decay of individual isotopes of radioactive elements. The amount of a radioactive parent isotope remaining as a function of time is shown in figure 6.2b. Notice that there is *not* a constant rate of decrease in the number of parent atoms, as with grains in the hourglass, but a steadily declining slope to the graph, as time increases. This describes what scientists call a "negative exponential curve."

The equation describing all radioactive decay is:

$$P_t = P_o e^{-\lambda t} \qquad (6)$$

where P_t is the number of atoms of the parent isotope presently in the rock, P_o is the number of atoms of parent isotope originally in the rock, e is the constant known as the natural base of logarithms (2.718...), λ is the decay constant for the parent isotope, and t is the "age"—the elapsed time in years since the rock formed. Equation (6) is so important, we call it the "radioactive decay equation."[1]

The decay constant (λ) deserves consideration. For the radioactive isotopes of geologic interest, it can be regarded as the probability that a given radioactive parent atom will decay during a one-year period of time. Measurements of radioactive decay have been made on large quantities of purified radioactive isotopes. The data have given good estimates of the probability that a given atom will decay during a one-year period of time. Furthermore, changes in the physical and chemical conditions of these samples have not significantly altered the probability of decay.[2] Therefore, λ is assumed to be a constant, irrespective of time, temperature, pressure, and other normal conditions. The decay constant (λ) is analogous to the rate of flow of sand grains in the hourglass illustration.

The value of λ is very small for many radioactive isotopes of geologic interest. Table 6.1 lists decay constants for important radioactive isotopes. Rubidium-87 (^{87}Rb) has a decay constant of 1.42×10^{-11} yr^{-1} and potassium-40 (^{40}K) has a decay constant of 5.543×10^{-10} yr^{-1}, according to recent laboratory studies.[3] The decay constant for carbon-14 (^{14}C) is 1.21×10^{-4} yr^{-1}, a much larger number.[4] Because the decay constant for ^{14}C is approximately ten million times larger than the decay constant for ^{87}Rb, a given atom of ^{14}C has nearly ten million times the probability of decaying during a one-year period, than a single atom of ^{87}Rb.

Sometimes the decay constant is expressed in terms of another constant, called "half-life," the theoretical period of time that would be required for radioactive decay to transform one half of an initial quantity of atoms of the parent isotope into the daughter isotope. The half-life can be calculated from:

$$T = \frac{\ln 2}{\lambda}$$

where T is the half-life and ln 2 is the natural logarithm of 2 (ln 2 = 0.6931...). The half-life of ^{87}Rb is 48.8 billion years, ^{40}K is 1.25 billion years, and ^{14}C is 5,730 years. The larger the value of T, the slower the radioactive decay. Half-lives for important radioactive isotopes are also listed in table 6.1.

The factor $e^{-\lambda t}$ of equation (6) deserves consideration. It is composed of the positive number e (2.718...), which is raised to the power $-\lambda t$. Because λ is a small positive number and t is a large positive number, the product of λ and t is also a positive number. Therefore, $-\lambda t$ is a negative number. The factor $e^{-\lambda t}$ is, therefore, composed of a positive number (e), which forms the base, and a negative number ($-\lambda t$), which forms the power. The important relationship derived from the property of a positive base raised to a negative power is that $0 < e^{-\lambda t} < 1$. Because all values of $e^{-\lambda t}$ lie between 0 and 1, we can regard its appearance, in equation (6), as giving the proportion of parent atoms remaining after a given time t.

Returning to equation (6), what is called the "radioactive decay equation," we notice that it can be manipulated to give

$$P_o = P_t e^{+\lambda t} \qquad (7)$$

Here, the original number of atoms of parent (P_o) can be calculated from the present number of parent atoms (P_t), if we know the decay constant of the parent (λ) and the age of the rock (t). This expression is useful for the derivations which follow.

An important principle of radioactive decay is the correspondence of parent to daughter. In most instances, the number of radioactive parent atoms which decay is equal to the number of daughter atoms produced. This principle is evident in the hourglass example: the number of sand grains removed from the upper chamber is equal

to the number added to the lower chamber. For most radioactive decay (as in the hourglass), we can write the following general equation:

$$P_r = D_a$$

where P_r is the number of atoms of parent removed and D_a is the number of atoms of daughter added. This equation can be rewritten from equations (1) and (3) as:

$$P_o - P_t = D_t - D_o \qquad (8)$$

where P_o is the number of atoms of the parent isotope initially in the rock, P_t is the number of atoms of the parent isotope presently in the rock, D_t is the number of atoms of the daughter isotope presently in the rock, and D_o is the number of atoms of the daughter isotope initially in the rock. Solving equation (8) for P_o gives:

$$P_o = D_t - D_o + P_t$$

which can be substituted into equation (7), giving:

$$D_t - D_o + P_t = P_t e^{\lambda t}$$

Simplifying yields:

$$\frac{D_t - D_o}{P_t} + 1 = e^{\lambda t} \qquad (9)$$

which can be rewritten in the form:

$$D_t = D_o + P_t (e^{\lambda t} - 1) \qquad (10)$$

This can be called the "general radioactive dating equation."[5] From equation (10), the specific equations used to estimate ages of rocks by radioactive methods can be derived. We will derive these equations, and illustrate the assumptions which must be made, if true ages of rocks are to be calculated.

The Model Age Equation

Equation (10) can be solved for time (t), to give an expression which is useful in estimating the ages of rocks. The easiest way to derive the equation is to begin with equation (9). If we take the natural logarithm of both sides of equation (9), we obtain:

$$\ln \left(e^{\lambda t} \right) = \ln \left(\frac{D_t - D_o}{P_t} + 1 \right)$$

which is equivalent to:

$$\lambda t \ln e = \ln \left(\frac{D_t - D_o}{P_t} + 1 \right)$$

Making use of the important property that the natural logarithm of e is exactly 1, we can solve for t. The resulting equation is:

$$t = \frac{1}{\lambda} \ln \left(\frac{D_t - D_o}{P_t} + 1 \right) \qquad (11)$$

which is the "general model-age equation."[6]

From equation (11) the "age" of a rock can be calculated, if we know the decay constant of the parent (λ), the number of atoms of daughter presently in the rock (D_t), the number of atoms of daughter originally in the rock (D_o), and the number of atoms of parent presently in the rock (P_t). The time calculated from equation (11) is called a "model age," because it requires that the number of atoms of daughter originally in the rock be known.[7] No analytical equipment can make such a measurement, and we must *assume* a model for the history of the rock which allows us to insert a value for D_o into equation (11).

Careful consideration of equation (11) allows us to list the assumptions that are made, if we are to assume that a "model age" represents the true age of a rock.

1. The number of atoms of daughter originally in the rock when it crystallized can be known (D_o can be known).

2. The number of atoms of daughter has not been altered, except by radioactive decay, since the rock crystallized (the rock remained closed to loss or gain of daughter since crystallization).

3. The number of atoms of parent has not been altered, except by radioactive decay, since the rock crystallized (the rock remained closed to loss or gain of parent since crystallization).

4. The decay constant of the parent is known accurately, and has not changed during the existence of the rock.

5. The abundances of parent and daughter have been determined accurately (laboratory measurements of P_t and D_t are accurate).

These assumptions require careful evaluation for each rock being dated, and impose certain restraints on the interpretation of resultant "model ages."

The "general model-age equation" can be used to derive specific equations, which estimate ages of rocks. For the decay of rubidium-87 (^{87}Rb) to strontium-87 (^{87}Sr) equation (11) becomes:

$$t = \frac{1}{1.42 \times 10^{-11}} \ln \left(\frac{^{87}Sr_t - ^{87}Sr_o}{^{87}Rb_t} + 1 \right) \qquad (12)$$

where $^{87}Sr_t$ is the number of atoms of ^{87}Sr presently in the rock, $^{87}Sr_o$ was the number of atoms of ^{87}Sr originally in the rock, and $^{87}Rb_t$ is the number of atoms of ^{87}Rb presently in the rock.[8]

The analytical equipment used to measure isotopes is more accurate in determining *ratios* of isotopes, than their absolute abundances. Therefore, ^{87}Sr, the isotope of strontium increased by radioactive decay of ^{87}Rb, is often shown relative to a reference isotope of strontium *not* increased by radioactive decay. Because of its abundance, ^{86}Sr is universally used as a reference isotope, and the analytical equipment measures the ratio of ^{87}Sr to ^{86}Sr. The measurement of the strontium isotope ratio is expressed as $(^{87}Sr/^{86}Sr)_t$ with the subscript t reminding us that it is today's ratio the machine is measuring. We are most interested in understanding how that ratio has changed from $(^{87}Sr/^{86}Sr)_o$, the original strontium isotope ratio possessed by the rock when it formed.

Making use of the fact that the abundance of ^{86}Sr should not change with time within a rock, we can transform equation (12) into a more useful expression for Rb-Sr model ages:

$$(13)$$

$$t = \frac{1}{1.42 \times 10^{-11}} \ln \left(\frac{\left(\frac{^{87}Sr}{^{86}Sr} \right)_t - \left(\frac{^{87}Sr}{^{86}Sr} \right)_o}{\left(\frac{^{87}Rb}{^{86}Sr} \right)_t} + 1 \right)$$

where $(^{87}Sr/^{86}Sr)_t$ is the present ratio of ^{87}Sr to ^{86}Sr in the rock, $(^{87}Sr/^{86}Sr)_o$ was the original ratio of ^{87}Sr to ^{86}Sr when the rock crystallized, and $(^{87}Rb/^{86}Sr)_t$ is the present ratio of ^{87}Rb to ^{86}Sr in the rock.[9]

For the decay of potassium-40 (^{40}K) to argon-40 (^{40}Ar) the development of the "model-age equation" is not as straightforward. First, ^{40}K decays to both argon *and* calcium, so equation (8) needs to be modified, as well as the derivations from it. Second, ^{40}Ar is a common atmospheric gas which can leak into minerals, making them appear older than their actual age. Conventional K-Ar model "ages" assume that a certain proportion of the ^{40}Ar in a rock is contamination, and, therefore, subtract a certain value of ^{40}Ar determined in the laboratory, in accordance with the ^{40}Ar to ^{36}Ar ratio of the present atmosphere.[10]

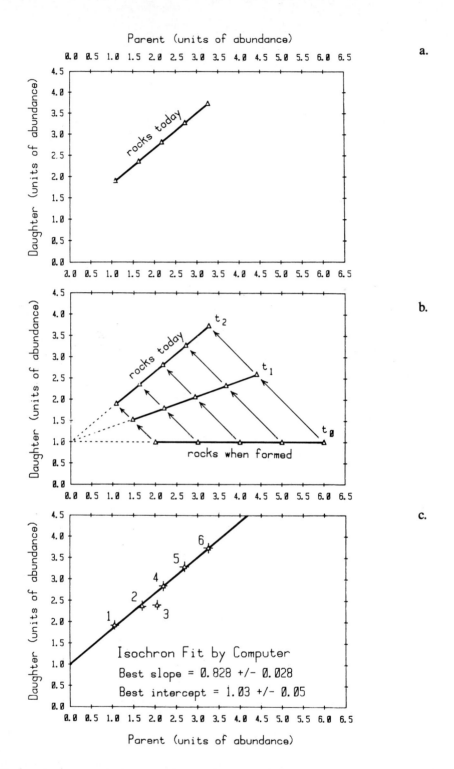

Figure 6.3 *The assumptions and methods of isochron dating are illustrated by diagrams depicting rocks of a hypothetical formation.*
a. *Study of five rocks of the formation indicates that their daughter-versus-parent compositions plot today as a linear array having positive slope.*
b. *The isochron model suggests that the five rocks, when they formed, all had the same abundance of daughter (1.0 "unit of abundance" in this case), but different abundances of parent. The compositions of the rocks today are assumed to have been derived by significant radioactive decay of parent and accumulation of daughter.*
c. *Six isotopic analyses of the rocks of the formation are plotted with error bars. A computer determines the "best-fit" line through the data points. The slope of the line can be used to estimate the "age" of these rocks. The greater the slope, the greater the "age."*

Also, it is convention to assume no ^{40}Ar was present in the rock when it initially formed.[11]

Careful laboratory studies indicate that 10.5% of ^{40}K atoms decay to ^{40}Ar atoms.[12] Thus, we can write the standard equation for K-Ar model "ages":

$$t = \frac{1}{5.543 \times 10^{-10}} \ln \left(\frac{^{40}Ar*}{0.105 \, ^{40}K} + 1 \right) \quad (14)$$

where $^{40}Ar*$ is number of atoms of radiogenic ^{40}Ar presently in the rock, after correction for ^{40}Ar contamination from the atmosphere.[13] The value ^{40}K is the present number of atoms of ^{40}K in the rock. Notice that the factor $^{40}Ar_o$, the initial ^{40}Ar incorporated into the rock as it formed, does not appear in the equation, because, as a matter of convention, it has been assumed to be zero.[14] We recognize that all of these assumptions need to be defended, if, indeed, "*model* ages" are to be accepted as *real* ages. We will return to this later.

The Isochron-Age Equation

Many geologists have recognized some of the shortcomings of the model-age method, and have proposed what is believed to be a superior dating method. Whereas the *model-age* method is based on a single isotopic analysis of a rock or mineral, the *isochron-age* method is based on multiple isotopic analyses of various rocks or minerals from an entire geologic unit. Multiple analyses, it is supposed, allow some of the more uncertain assumptions of the model-age method to be circumvented, and permit a higher degree of confidence in the resulting "age" estimate.

Here is how the isochron method works: If we select a number of rock samples from a single geologic unit, we should be able to claim that each rock formed at the same time, yet it is likely that each rock will differ in the amount of both daughter and parent isotope. We can construct a graph of the amount of daughter plotted against the amount of parent. Each rock sample would be represented as a distinct point on the graph. Figure 6.3a is such a hypothetical plot. Often these plots of daughter against parent form a linear array with strong linear correlation and positive slope as indicated in this figure. We notice from this plot that those samples of the geologic unit with larger amounts of parent, have corresponding larger amounts of daughter. Those samples with smaller amounts of parent, have corresponding smaller amounts of daughter.

This linear array plot might be interpreted as an effect produced by radioactive decay, because those samples having larger amounts of parent would, over time, accumulate larger amounts of daughter. Thus, an "age" interpretation of the linear array seems logical.

If we make the assumption that the linear array plot in this figure has been altered significantly by decay of parent and accumulation of daughter in each rock, where did each rock plot on the graph when the rocks formed? What did the plot look like *before* radioactive decay began?

Figure 6.3b is an "age" interpretation of the observed linear array data presented in figure 6.3a. We may assume that when the rocks formed, they had *different* amounts of parent but had the *same* amount of daughter. Such homogenization of the daughter might occur by a geological process which mixed the daughter, so that each rock in the geologic unit originally had the same abundance of daughter.

This figure shows the proposed composition of the rocks at the start. The original rocks are shown along a horizontal line labeled "rocks when formed." Each rock has 1.0 "unit of abundance" of daughter, but from 2.0-to-6.0 "units of abundance" of parent. For each "unit of abundance" of parent which decays, exactly one "unit of abundance" of daughter is produced. Therefore, the composition of each rock moved upward, and to the left, at a 45-degree angle along the arrows indicated from the original composition, as radioactive decay of parent occurred. Because more decay of parent would occur in those rocks with greater amounts of parent, *those* rocks would have greater deflection from the horizontal line.

An important consequence of the deflection of points, as a result of radioactive decay, is that the compositions of rocks after a set period of time also lie along a line. All points of "equal age" lie on the same line. Thus, this figure shows the five rocks at t_0, when they formed, along a horizontal line. At some later time, t_1, the rocks describe a sloping line after significant radioactive decay had occurred. Finally, this figure shows the five rocks at t_2, along another steeper line after even more decay had occurred. It is evident that the slope, or steepness of these lines through these rock samples *increases* as the "age" of the samples increase. Each of these lines of "equal age" is called an "isochron" (from Greek, *isos*, equal; and *chronos*, time).

Because the equations for all lines on an *x-y* plot have the familiar mathematical form:

$$y = b + mx,$$

we can write the equation for any isochron line in figure 6.3a. Instead of *x* and *y*, we use the analogous values P_t and D_t. Our equation for any isochron is:

$$D_t = D_o + m \, P_t \quad (15)$$

where D_t is the number of atoms of daughter isotope in any rock after time t has elapsed, D_o was the number of atoms of daughter isotope in the same rock originally, P_t is the number of atoms of parent isotope in the same rock after time t has elapsed, and m is the slope of the line ("rise" divided by "run") on the graph.

A very important relationship is suggested by comparing equations (15) and (10). Equation (15) has the *same form* as equation (10). Previously, equation (10) was derived as:

$$D_t = D_o + P_t (e^{\lambda t} - 1) \qquad (10)$$

which is the "general radioactive-dating equation." It is obvious, from comparison, that equation (15) becomes equation (10) when:

$$m = e^{\lambda t} - 1 \qquad (16)$$

Now we have derived the equation which gives the relationship between the "age" and the slope of a linear array plot.[15] Manipulating equation (16) and taking the natural logarithm of both sides, we obtain:

$$\ln (e^{\lambda t}) = \ln (m + 1)$$

which reduces to:

$$\lambda t \ln e = \ln (m + 1)$$

and, finally:

$$t = \frac{1}{\lambda} \ln (m + 1) \qquad (17)$$

This is the "general isochron-age equation" for most radioactive decay. The equation allows us to calculate an "isochron age" from any linear array plot, if we can establish the assumptions of the isochron method, especially the notion that $m = 0$ when the rocks formed.

Study of equation (17) shows that it does give plausible "ages" from slopes, if we make the isochron assumptions. Inserting a value of $m = 0$ into equation (17) does, indeed, give $t = 0$. Inserting any positive slope for m in equation (17), gives positive values for the "age" of a suite of rocks which might plot on the graph.

Attention needs to be directed at how the data points, on a linear-array plot of daughter versus parent are used to determine the "best-fit" isochron, and how the slope (m) is calculated. Figure 6.3c shows the isotopic analyses for parent and daughter for six rocks from the hypothetical geologic unit. Each of the six triangles in this figure represents one whole rock-isotope analysis. The laboratory equipment used to measure isotope abundances is not free from error, so the analytical uncertainties need to be shown as crosses underlying the triangles. The horizontal bars of the crosses represent the analytical error in determining the

actual amount of *parent* atoms, and the vertical bars depict the error in determining the amount of *daughter* atoms. The analytical errors are usually expressed as plus or minus one standard deviation (1σ) from a mean value. These errors are estimated, for the instrument making the measurements, by making numerous measurements on a single sample. For a single isotopic analysis, using our equipment, the true isotopic abundance should lie within the stated uncertainty range 68% of the time (errors expressed as one standard deviation). Although these errors are often small, they have significant application to the precision of radioisotope dates.

A computer program has been written to establish the "best-fit" line or "best-fit" isochron, through linear-array data.[16] A computer used the program to establish the "best-fit" line shown in this figure. Notice that five of the six uncertainty crosses touch the line established by the computer. Rock #3 lies significantly under the line. Why does Rock #3 fall significantly off the line? Is this due to analytical error in determining the abundance of isotopes? Or, did Rock #3 deviate from the original homogeneous mixture? These are all matters for interpretation which go into evaluating linear trends in data, and of the confidence we place in the isochron interpretation of that line.

Rock #3 demonstrates the value of obtaining multiple analyses from various rocks. Using a single sample for dating, we would not suspect that there was a problem, when Rock #3, or a rock like it, came to the laboratory.

The computer gives two outputs, when asked to fit a line to isotopic data: First, the computer estimates the slope (m) of the "best-fit" line, and the uncertainty value associated with that slope. Second, the computer estimates the "best-fit" line's intercept value (the abundance of daughter, if the abundance of parent is zero), and the uncertainty associated with the intercept. These two outputs uniquely define the line, or isochron.

In the hypothetical case shown in this figure, the computer gave the solution. The slope is $m = 0.828 \pm 0.028$, which can be inserted into equation (17), with an appropriate decay constant (λ), to estimate the "isochron age" of the suite of rocks. The intercept value estimated by the computer, is interpreted to be the initial abundance of daughter (D_o) in the suite of rocks when the suite of rocks formed, according to the assumptions of the isochron model. For the hypothetical case illustrated, the best intercept is $D_o = 1.03 \pm 0.05$ "units of abundance," which is assumed to be the abundance of daughter in each rock, when each rock formed. That is, when $m = 0$.

The data in this figure are shown as absolute abundances of daughter isotope versus parent isotope. In practice, however, the isochron method for estimating "age" is used most frequently with isotope ratios, rather than absolute abundances. This is practical, because the analytical equipment directly measures isotope *ratios*—not *absolute abundances* of isotopes. Therefore, parent-and-daughter isotopes usually are expressed as ratios relative to a reference isotope whose abundance is not affected by radioactive decay.

Careful consideration of equation (17) and the principles of isochron interpretation illustrated in this figure allows us to list the assumptions that are made, if we are to assume that the "isochron age" of a suite of rocks represents the true "age" of those rocks. Here are the assumptions:

1. Geologic evidence is sufficient to establish that the suite of rocks being analyzed is a "cogenetic unit." The term "cogenetic unit" implies that the time during which the suite of rocks formed is sufficiently short, compared to the true age of the rocks, to allow an "age" to be estimated.

2. All samples had uniformity, with respect to the daughter isotope, when the cogenetic unit formed. This means that over its whole area of occurrence, the geologic unit was sufficiently mixed, with respect to the daughter isotope, that $m = 0$ can be assumed to be the initial condition of the rocks.

3. Deviations from uniformity, with respect to the daughter isotope, has been caused within the suite of rocks, only by radioactive decay of parent. In other words, the rocks remained closed to loss or gain of daughter since the rocks formed.

4. The number of parent atoms has not been altered in the suite of rocks, by any geologic process, except radioactive decay. In other words, the rocks remained closed to loss or gain of parent since the rocks formed.

5. The decay constant (λ) of the parent is known accurately, and has not changed during the existence of the rocks.

6. The abundances of parent and daughter have been determined accurately (laboratory measurements of P_t and D_t are accurate).

An "isochron age" for a whole suite of rocks is considered, by most geologists, to be more reliable than a "model age" determined from a single rock sample. A "model age" requires that the initial number of daughter atoms (D_o) be known. *No analytical equipment can give this value.* The assumed value of D_o must be inserted into equation (11) in order to obtain the "model age." An "isochron age," however, requires no knowledge of the initial number of daughter atoms—only that there was uniformity, with respect to the abundance of daughter in all the rock samples. The isochron method can be used to estimate D_o, from the graphical plot of the intercept of the line. That value for D_o can be inserted into the "model-age equation," and gives a more reliable "model age." Here we see that the isochron-age technique strengthens, confirms, or even improves the model-age technique.

Confidence in the isochron method might appear to be increased by a number of internal checks to the reliability of the assumptions listed above. For example, we might be interested in determining the "isochron age" for a deeply buried basalt stratum (basalt cooled from an ancient lava flow). Because lava today issues from a local volcano, flows rapidly, and cools abruptly, the notion of a "cogenetic unit" (assumption #1) would appear to be verified. Also, lavas, which issue from a single volcano or series of volcanoes in a local area, might be supposed to have sufficient mixing to produce uniformity, with respect to the daughter (assumption #2). The fact that analyses of parent and daughter appear to form a linear-array plot, would seem to argue that geologic processes other than radioactive decay have not significantly changed the rocks, and support the notion that the rocks have remained closed (assumptions #3 and #4). If we obtain an analysis of a rock which appears to deviate from the isochron (i.e., rock #3 in figure 6.3c), we might suppose that such a rock was open to loss or gain of parent or daughter.

The elegance and simplicity of the isochron-age method are often praised by scientists. Davis A. Young speaks for many, as he expresses his confidence in isochron ages:

> *Not only can guesswork, even highly educated guesswork, regarding the initial Sr^{87} content of a sample be eliminated by the isochron method, but the results of this method have demonstrated just how well educated have been the guesses where guesswork is required by other radiometric methods. . . . From this it is rather obvious that geochronologists know what they are doing and have not been making wild guesses at the initial Sr^{87} contents of minerals simply to force prejudicially the age results into some preconceived uniformitarian scheme.* [17]

Evidence presented later in this chapter, however, significantly challenges the isochron assumptions which Davis Young and other geologists routinely endorse.

The "general isochron equation," equation (17), can be used to derive specific equations which estimate ages of suites of rocks. [18] For radioactive decay of ^{87}Rb to ^{87}Sr, equation (17) becomes:

$$t = \frac{1}{1.42 \times 10^{-11}} \ln(m + 1) \qquad (18)$$

and for radioactive decay of ^{40}K to ^{40}Ar, equation (17) becomes:

$$t = \frac{1}{5.543 \times 10^{-10}} \ln \left(\frac{m}{0.105} + 1 \right) \quad (19)$$

because only 10.5% of ^{40}K decays to ^{40}Ar. In both equations (18) and (19), the slope m is the "best-fit" line determined by the computer.

We recognize that the *isochron ages* derived by these equations can be *real ages*, only if we can verify the assumptions upon which the isochron method is based. We will use isotopic data from the Grand Canyon, in the next section of this chapter, to challenge the isochron assumptions.

"Ages" of Grand Canyon Rocks

Rocks of Grand Canyon provide data which can be used to test the reliability of the radioisotope-dating methods. However, not every rock of the Canyon gives accurate ages. Sandstone strata, for example, are made up of sand grains derived from older sources. Any attempt to date the sandstone strata would give the ages of the older sand sources—not the age of the stratum we desire. Because of the problem of inheritance of age, most sedimentary strata

of the Canyon are recognized as not being suitable for radioactive dating.

Three igneous formations of the Canyon have been considered prime candidates for radioisotope dating, and are shown in figure 6.4. The Cardenas Basalt occurs among the oldest strata, occurring in eastern Grand Canyon, within a tilted sequence of strata beneath 10,000 feet of other strata. Geologists have classified the Cardenas Basalt as Precambrian, because it lies well beneath what are believed to be the Cambrian strata. This formation is composed of basalt—an igneous rock which cooled rapidly from lava flows. Because crystallization occurred rapidly from molten material (in contrast with sedimentation of preexisting mineral grains), and because volcanoes are thought to erupt material which is well mixed, the Cardenas Basalt appears to satisfy the requirement of a "cogenetic" unit.

A second igneous formation also appears to be readily datable. This is the complex of diabase an intrusive equivalent to basalt, which forms dikes and sills beneath the Cardenas Basalt in the eastern Grand Canyon. Molten material forced its way upward into horizontal and vertical cracks in the Bass, Hakatai, Shinumo, and Dox formations, then cooled. The occurrences of diabase depicted in figure 6.4 would suggest that some of these dikes may have been the conduits through which molten material rose to the earth's surface to produce the Cardenas Basalt. The diabase and the basalt have similar compositions.

However, no diabase dike has been observed to connect to the Cardenas Basalt, so the geologic evidence does not prove that the two units formed at the same time, or that both belong to the same cogenetic unit.[19]

A third igneous formation appears to be easily datable. This is the Uinkaret Plateau basaltic rocks of western Grand Canyon, which also are shown in figure 6.4. These lava flows came from volcanoes on the Uinkaret Plateau north of the Colorado River. Some of the lava flowed over the north rim and cascaded into the Canyon, forming spectacular "frozen" lava falls. Several lava flows even reached the river, forming lava dams.[20] Although no Indian legends attribute them to recent eruptions, one early geologist remarked about the extraordinary freshness of lava: "It looks as fresh as any coulee of Vesuvius ejected twenty or thirty years ago."[21] These flows are obviously among the youngest formations of the Canyon and have been assigned to the Quaternary System. They are associated with older Tertiary lava flows, which have been identified widely in northern Arizona.

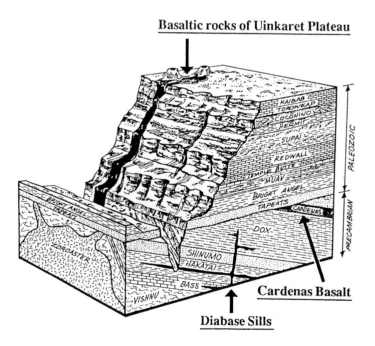

Basaltic rocks of Uinkaret Plateau

Cardenas Basalt

Diabase Sills

Figure 6.4 *Perspective diagram of Grand Canyon, showing the relationship of the Uinkaret Plateau basaltic lava flows (Quaternary) to the Cardenas Basalt and diabase sills (Precambrian).*

"Ages" of the Cardenas Basalt

Five published potassium-argon analyses for the Cardenas Basalt appear in table 6.2. This table contains values for

Table 6.2 *Potassium-Argon Data for Cardenas Basalt and Diabase Sills of Grand Canyon.*

Material dated Sample type Location Sample #	Data Source Code	K_2O (%)	^{40}K (mol/g)	$^{40}Ar*$ (mol/g)	$^{40}Ar*$ (%)	^{40}Ar (mol/g)	^{36}Ar (mol/g)	Model Age (millions of years with 1σ uncertainty)
Basalt flow Whole rock Basalt Canyon (no #)	FBM	2.40	5.95×10^{-8}	3.77×10^{-9}	96.6	3.90×10^{-9}	4.50×10^{-13}	853 ± 15
Basalt flow Whole rock Basalt Canyon b-8	MN	3.10	7.68×10^{-8}	4.63×10^{-9}	98	4.72×10^{-9}	3.20×10^{-13}	820 ± 20
Basalt flow Whole rock Basalt Canyon Tb-6	MN	3.33	8.25×10^{-8}	4.83×10^{-9}	95	5.08×10^{-9}	8.60×10^{-13}	800 ± 20
Basalt flow Whole rock Tanner Canyon b-4	MN	4.185	10.37×10^{-8}	5.98×10^{-9}	99	6.04×10^{-9}	2.04×10^{-13}	791 ± 20
Basalt flow Whole rock Palisades Creek (no #)	EM	2.089	5.18×10^{-8}	3.23×10^{-9}	98	3.30×10^{-9}	2.23×10^{-13}	843 ± 34
Diabase sill Pyroxene Hance Rapids (no #)	EM	0.303	0.751×10^{-8}	0.519×10^{-9}	64.4	0.806×10^{-9}	9.71×10^{-13}	914 ± 40
Diabase sill Plagioclase Tapeats Creek (no #)	EM	1.32	3.27×10^{-8}	2.39×10^{-9}	92.5	2.58×10^{-9}	6.56×10^{-13}	954 ± 30

Data Source Code: **FBM** = Ford, Breed and Mitchell, 1972, p. 225; **MN** = McKee and Noble, 1976, p. 1189; **EM** = Elston and McKee, 1982, p. 689.
Data on K_2O, $^{40}Ar*$ (moles/gram) and ^{40}Ar (%) are from above sources. Other values calculated.
Model ages calculated using new constants: $\lambda^{40}K = 5.543 \times 10^{-10}$ yr^{-1}, ^{40}K decays to ^{40}Ar = 0.1048, and moles ^{40}K per mole K = 1.167×10^{-4}.

^{40}K and $^{40}Ar*$ which can be inserted into equation (14) to yield K-Ar model ages.[22]

The first data published for the Cardenas Basalt, by Ford, Breed, and Mitchell,[23] in 1972, give an age of 853 ± 15 million years using the most recently accepted values for the decay constants. Four subsequent analyses of Cardenas Basalt published by McKee and Noble,[24] and by Elston and McKee,[25] yield "ages" of 820 ± 20, 800 ± 20, 791 ± 20, and 843 ± 34 million years. All five analyses would seem to limit the "age" of the Cardenas Basalt to somewhere between 780- and 880-million years. We would expect to be able to resolve the model age with more precision. Why do we have a one-hundred-million-year spread in "ages," when our equipment can estimate, presumably, ages to within ± 20 million years?

The data of table 6.2 can be used to make a linear-array plot of ^{40}Ar versus ^{40}K. This plot is shown as figure 6.5a. We notice immediately, a pronounced linear trend to the data in this figure. The five Cardenas Basalt analyses indicate the slope (*m*) of the "best-fit" line, as

0.0510 ± 0.0028, which, when inserted into equation (19), gives an "age" of 715 ± 33 million years.[26] The best intercept value is 0.83 ± 0.20 × 10^{-9} moles of ^{40}Ar per gram of rock. If we adopt an isochron model, we must require the linear array plot to have been derived from samples which all began with 0.83 × 10^{-9} moles of ^{40}Ar per gram of rock some 715 million years ago.

Reflection on the K-Ar method used thus far, allows us to recognize *two* types of dates with mutually contradictory assumptions. The "model ages" shown in table 6.2 were computed by using equation (14), which assumes *zero* initial ^{40}Ar, when the Cardenas Basalt cooled. The "isochron age," indicated by the line in figure 6.5a, assumes an initial *nonzero* common abundance of ^{40}Ar, when the lavas cooled. Only one of these assumptions could be correct! We also understand why the "model ages" are greater than the "isochron age."

More contradictory "ages" for the Cardenas Basalt are offered by evaluation of the Rb-Sr data shown in table 6.3. McKee and Noble[27] analyzed six basalt flows of the Cardenas Basalt from Basalt Canyon, in the eastern

Grand Canyon. A linear-array plot of their isotope ratio data is shown in figure 6.5b. The six samples shown as triangles, indicate the slope of the "best-fit" line, of 0.0154 ± 0.0010, which, when inserted into equation (18), gives an isochron "age" of 1.07 ± 0.07 billion years.[28] This Rb-Sr-isochron "age" is *much older* than the K-Ar-isochron "age" obtained from the same formation.

Model ages can be calculated from the isotopic ratios of basalt flows in table 6.3, using equation (13), *if* we have a value for the initial $^{87}Sr/^{86}Sr$ of the Cardenas Basalt when it cooled. Most geologists reviewing these data, would accept the isochron intercept value of 0.7065 ± 0.0015 from figure 6.5b. Using this value, we calculate six "model ages" for basalt flows shown in table 6.3. Concordance of these "model ages" with the Rb-Sr "isochron age" of 1.07 billion years is to be expected, because of the similarity between equations (13) and (18).

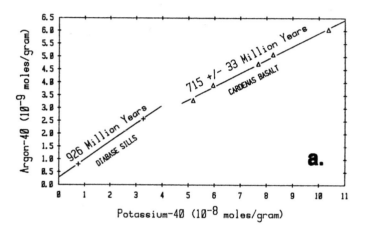

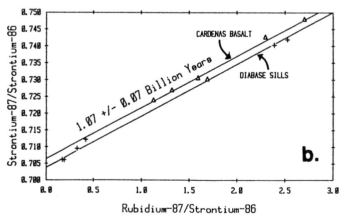

Figure 6.5 *Which linear array plot gives the true "age" of the Cardenas Basalt and diabase sills? Triangles indicate samples of Cardenas Basalt and pluses indicate samples of diabase sills. The K-Ar isochron "age" of the Cardenas Basalt is 715 ± 33 million years and is younger than the K-Ar isochron "age" of the diabase sills. The Rb-Sr isochron "age" of the Cardenas Basalt is 1.07 ± 0.07 billion years and is the same as the Rb-Sr isochron "age" of the diabase sills.*

"Ages" of Diabase Sills

The field geologic relationships of the diabase sills to the Cardenas Basalt (figure 6.4) suggested to early investigators that the diabase was approximately the same age as the lava flows. K-Ar model-age dates, however, suggested that the diabase was significantly *older* than the Cardenas Basalt. table 6.2 shows two K-Ar model "ages" for the diabase sills calculated by equation (14). These ages are 914 ± 40 and 954 ± 30 million years, significantly *older* than the five basalt-flow model "ages" also listed in this table, which average about 820 million years.

The isochron method would be expected to verify that the diabase sills are *older* than the Cardenas Basalt, and the K-Ar data appear to affirm this. The two diabase-sill samples plotted in figure 6.5a indicate a line of steeper slope than the line described by the five basalts in figure 6.5a. The slope of the line through the two diabase sills in figure 6.5a is 0.0704, which, when inserted into equation (19), gives an "age" of 926 million years. This "age" is significantly older than the K-Ar isochron "age" for the Cardenas Basalt, of 715 million years. The K-Ar isochron "age" of the diabase is also concordant with the two model "ages." Therefore, the K-Ar-dating methods assign greater "age" to the diabase, than the basalt.

Even more remarkable, is the isochron generated from the six Rb-Sr analyses of diabase shown in table 6.4. These six analyses of diabase are plotted as pluses in figure 6.5b, along with the Cardenas Basalt analyses. The diabase analyses allow us to establish the "best-fit" line with slope (*m*), of 0.0154 ± 0.0001. This slope is the *same* slope as determined for the Cardenas Basalt, and the isochron model would suggest the *same* "age" for the diabase and basalt flows. *This conclusion contradicts that based on the K-Ar methods.*

One significant difference exists between the diabase and the basalt: Figure 6.5b indicates that the diabase has a lower intercept value (initial $^{87}Sr/^{86}Sr$ value) than the lavas. The initial $^{87}Sr/^{86}Sr$ value is 0.7039 ± 0.0004 for the diabase. Substituting this value for the initial $^{87}Sr/^{86}Sr$ into equation (13), allows us to compute six Rb-Sr model "ages" for diabase, as shown in table 6.4. The Rb-Sr-diabase model "ages" do not give a coherent picture of "age." For the diabase sill intruded into the Hakatai Shale at Shinumo Creek, the model "ages" range over a 500-million-year interval, from 0.85 ± 0.17 to 1.37 ± 0.07 billion years. This "age" spread for a single igneous sill is geologically unreasonable, and causes us to question these model ages. Most geologists suppose rapid intrusion and cooling of sills. We might conclude that the Shinumo Creek sill was not thoroughly mixed in its initial strontium isotopes.

Table 6.3 *Rubidium-strontium Data for Cardenas Basalt of Grand Canyon.*

Material dated, Sample type, Location, Sample #	Rb (ppm)	Sr (ppm)	$^{87}Rb/^{86}Sr$	$^{87}Sr/^{86}Sr$	^{87}Rb (mol/g)	^{87}Sr (mol/g)	^{86}Sr (mol/g)	Model Age (billions of years with 1σ uncertainty)
Basalt flow Whole rock Basalt Canyon b-8	106	193	1.59	0.7307	3.45×10^{-7}	1.58×10^{-7}	2.17×10^{-7}	1.06 ± 0.07
Basalt flow Whole rock Basalt Canyon Tb-6	93.9	161	1.69	0.7303	3.06×10^{-7}	1.32×10^{-7}	1.81×10^{-7}	0.98 ± 0.06
Basalt flow Whole rock Basalt Canyon b-7	67.4	148	1.32	0.7271	2.20×10^{-7}	1.21×10^{-7}	1.66×10^{-7}	1.09 ± 0.08
Basalt flow Whole rock Basalt Canyon b-6	78.9	203	1.13	0.7241	2.57×10^{-7}	1.65×10^{-7}	2.28×10^{-7}	1.09 ± 0.10
Basalt flow Whole rock Basalt Canyon b-3a	108	116	2.70	0.7480	3.52×10^{-7}	0.97×10^{-7}	1.30×10^{-7}	1.07 ± 0.04
Basalt flow Whole rock Basalt Canyon b-3	85.4	108	2.30	0.7427	2.78×10^{-7}	0.90×10^{-7}	1.21×10^{-7}	1.10 ± 0.05

Data on Rb, Sr, and $^{87}Sr/^{86}Sr$ from McKee and Noble, 1976, p. 1189. Other isotopic values computed by method described by Faure, 1986, pp. 119, 120. Model ages computed using general model age equation assuming initial $^{87}Sr/^{86}Sr = 0.7065 \pm 0.0015$, the intercept value from the isochron. Constants used: λ $^{87}Rb = 1.42 \times 10^{-11}$ yr^{-1}, $^{85}Rb/^{87}Rb = 2.59265$.

"Ages" of Uinkaret Plateau Basalt

Lava flows on Uinkaret Plateau in the western Grand Canyon are among the youngest formations in the Canyon (see figure 6.4). The youngest potassium-argon model "age" yet published for a rock in Arizona (0.01 million years)[29] comes from Vulcan's Throne, a volcano on Uinkaret Plateau just north of the Colorado River. The mineral, olivine (known for its very low potassium content), from the same Vulcan's Throne basalt flow, was found to have an excessive amount of argon, and yields a K-Ar model "age" of 117 ± 3 million years.[30] This date is rejected by all geologists familiar with the volcano. Other Pleistocene basalt flows of western Grand Canyon give excessively old ages, with the cause of the old ages being attributed to "excess argon."[31] These excessively old ages are rarely reported in the geological literature. One of the basalt flows that spilled over the plateau and blocked the river gives a K-Ar model "age" of 1.2 ± 0.2 million years.[32] Basaltic rocks high on Uinkaret Plateau, give K-Ar model "ages" of 3.67,

2.63 and 3.60 million years.[33] Geologists regard Uinkaret-Plateau-volcanic rocks as Tertiary and Quaternary in age.

Because of the spread of model ages obtained for these Tertiary and Quaternary volcanics, it seems necessary to divide these rocks, to allow us to compare rocks which more faithfully represent the concept of a "cogenetic unit." Recent geologic mapping[34] allows us to recognize older and younger flows on Uinkaret Plateau, on the basis of strata sequence and filling of valleys. Furthermore, petrographic study of these lava flows allows *two* types of basaltic rocks to be distinguished: basanites and hawaiites.[35]

The first study of rubidium and strontium isotopes in basaltic rocks from Uinkaret Plateau was by Leeman,[36] who was attempting to understand the regional variation in strontium isotopes. Unfortunately, the analytical equipment used by Leeman only allowed the abundances of rubidium and strontium in these Grand Canyon rocks to be resolved to within plus or minus 10%. Today, it is standard procedure to use isotope-dilution technology, which is able to measure

Table 6.4 *Rubidium-strontium Data for Diabase Sills of Grand Canyon.*

Material dated Sample type Location Sample #	Rb (ppm)	Sr (ppm)	$^{87}Rb/^{86}Sr$	$^{87}Sr/^{86}Sr$	^{87}Rb (mol/g)	^{87}Sr (mol/g)	^{86}Sr (mol/g)	Model Age (billions of years with 1 σ uncertainty)
Diabase sill Whole rock Hance Rapids Tis-1	32.0	280	0.331	0.7096	1.04×10^{-7}	2.24×10^{-7}	3.15×10^{-7}	1.19 ± 0.09
Diabase sill Whole rock Shinumo Creek ba-6	76.8	93.3	2.39	0.7403	2.50×10^{-7}	0.78×10^{-7}	1.05×10^{-7}	1.06 ± 0.03
Diabase sill Whole rock Shinumo Creek ba-7	80.7	92.7	2.53	0.7419	2.63×10^{-7}	0.77×10^{-7}	1.04×10^{-7}	1.05 ± 0.02
Diabase sill Whole rock Shinumo Creek ba-8	24.5	l68.4	0.421	0.7122	0.798×10^{-7}	1.35×10^{-7}	1.89×10^{-7}	1.37 ± 0.07
Diabase sill Whole rock Shinumo Creek (ba-13)	31.5	502.7	0.181	0.7061	1.03×10^{-7}	4.00×10^{-7}	5.66×10^{-7}	0.85 ± 0.17
Diabase sill Whole rock Shinumo Creek (ba-16)	29.1	480.7	0.175	0.7062	0.948×10^{-7}	3.82×10^{-7}	5.41×10^{-7}	0.92 ± 0.18

Data on Rb, Sr, and $^{87}Sr/^{86}Sr$ from McKee and Noble, 1976, p. 1189 and Elston and McKee, 1982, p. 691. Other isotopic values computed by method described by Faure, 1986, pp. 119, 120. Model ages computed using general model age equation assuming initial $^{87}Sr/^{86}Sr$ = 0.7039 ± 0.0004, the intercept values from the isochron. Constants used: λ ^{87}Rb = 1.42×10^{-11} yr^{-1}, $^{85}Rb/^{87}Rb$ = 2.59265.

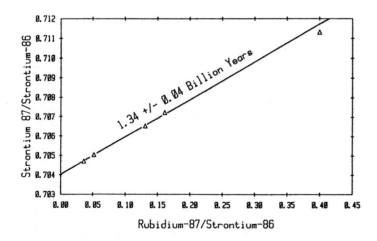

Figure 6.6 *Linear-array plot of rubidium and strontium isotope data for hawaiite lava flows from the Quaternary basaltic rocks of the Uinkaret Plateau in Western Grand Canyon. Excessively old "age" of 1.34 billion years is indicated by the computer fit line. Data from table 6.5.*

the abundances of rubidium and strontium to within plus or minus 1%.

In 1989, Dr. Steven Austin began a research project to interpret the rubidium and strontium isotopes in Uinkaret Plateau rocks, with high-precision, isotope-dilution-measurement technology.[37] Four obviously recent (Quaternary) lava flows of hawaiite composition were analyzed as whole rocks. From one of the whole rock samples, sodium plagioclase (a feldspar mineral) was separated. This mineral has a high rubidium to strontium ratio and high $^{87}Sr/^{86}Sr$. Table 6.5 shows the data and figure 6.6 is a plot of the $^{87}Sr/^{86}Sr$ versus $^{87}Rb/^{86}Sr$ data. The five data values form a linear-array plot with positive slope. The five values indicate the "best-fit" line with slope 0.0192 ± 0.0006. Substituting this slope into equation (18) gives an isochron "age" of 1.34 ± 0.04 billion years! This "age" is strongly discordant with the K-Ar "ages" for Uinkaret Plateau basalts (0.01 to 117 million years). Furthermore, the billion-year Rb-Sr-isochron "age" for these volcanic rocks is among the oldest age reported in a catalog of 1,688 "ages" for Arizona rocks.[38]

Table 6.5 *Rubidium-strontium Data for Uinkaret Plateau Basaltic Rocks (Quaternary) of Western Grand Canyon.*

Material dated Sample type Location Sample #	Rb (ppm)	Sr (ppm)	$^{87}Rb/^{86}Sr$	$^{87}Sr/^{86}Sr$ (with 1σ uncertainty)	^{87}Rb (mol/g)	^{87}Sr (mol/g)	^{86}Sr (mol/g)	Model Age (billions of years with 1σ uncertainty)
Hawaiite flow Whole rock Findlay Knoll QU - 1	9.37	745	0.0364	0.70470 (± 0.00001)	0.305×10^{-7}	5.91×10^{-7}	8.39×10^{-7}	1.32 ± 0.08
Hawaiite flow Whole rock Swapp Reservoir QU - 2	30.6	549	0.161	0.70722 (± 0.00001)	1.00×10^{-7}	4.37×10^{-7}	6.18×10^{-7}	1.39 ± 0.03
Hawaiite flow Whole rock Potato Valley QU - 5	11.4	634	0.0520	0.70504 (± 0.00001)	0.371×10^{-7}	5.03×10^{-7}	7.14×10^{-7}	1.38 ± 0.06
Hawaiite flow Whole rock Fredonia Road QU - 14	29.4	649	0.131	0.70652 (± 0.00001)	0.958×10^{-7}	5.16×10^{-7}	7.31×10^{-7}	1.34 ± 0.03
Hawaiite flow Sodic Plagioclase Fredonia Road QU - 14S	34.4	249	0.400	0.71131 (± 0.00013)	1.12×10^{-7}	1.99×10^{-7}	2.80×10^{-7}	1.27 ±0.04

Data from Steven A. Austin, who collected the samples and supervised their analysis. Model ages computed using general model age equation assuming initial $^{87}Sr/^{86}Sr = 0.70402 \pm 0.00004$, which is the intercept value of the isochron. Constants used: λ $^{87}Rb = 1.42 \times 10^{-11}$ yr^{-1}, $^{85}Rb/^{87}Rb = 2.59265$. Hawaiite is the hypersthene-normative basaltic rock. These data are from an ongoing study of Uinkaret Plateau basalts.

The intercept value of the line in figure 6.6 is 0.70402 ± 0.00004. This is the initial $^{87}Sr/^{86}Sr$ value for the isochron model—a value which can be inserted into equation (13) to compute the five Rb-Sr model "ages" shown in table 6.5. The concordance of these five model "ages" with the Rb-Sr-isochron "age" of 1.34 ± 0.04 billion years is to be expected, because of the similarity between equations (13) and (18).

The 1.34 ± 0.04-billion-years Rb-Sr-isochron "age" cannot be the true age for the Quaternary flows on the north rim of Grand Canyon. It is the oldest isochron "age" yet published for Grand Canyon rocks, but it represents the *youngest* lava flow in the Canyon. *The Rb-Sr isochron must be grossly in error!* These lava flows are among the most recent geological formations in Arizona, some of which even fill modern stream valleys.

Another isochron method for estimating the "age" of rocks employs lead isotopes. Lead-207 (^{207}Pb) is derived from decay of uranium-235 (^{235}U), and lead-206 (^{206}Pb) is derived from decay of uranium-238 (^{238}U). Because ^{235}U and ^{238}U have different decay constants, the ratios of

lead isotopes in a suite of uranium-bearing rocks changes with time. Instead of plotting daughter against parent, as in the normal isochron method, the two daughters can be plotted against each other. According to Faure,[39] a lead-lead isochron age can be calculated from a suite of rocks, if we can assume that they were a cogenetic unit, with all samples having the same lead isotope ratios initially.

The lead isotope compositions of Colorado Plateau volcanic rocks have been studied by Everson[40] and by Alibert, Michard, and Albarede.[41] All the volcanic rocks in these two studies are classified as late Cenozoic (late Tertiary and Quaternary), and come from the Colorado Plateau province of southern Utah, northern Arizona, and northwestern New Mexico. Fifty-five analyses are plotted in the $^{207}Pb/^{204}Pb$ versus $^{206}Pb/^{204}Pb$ array, in figure 6.7. Five of these points are basaltic rocks from the Uinkaret Plateau in the western Grand Canyon.

A strong linear trend of positive slope occurs in figure 6.7, indicating that these volcanic rocks may satisfy the assumption of a cogenetic unit. The "best-fit" line has the slope, 0.1748 ± 0.0049. According to the equation of the

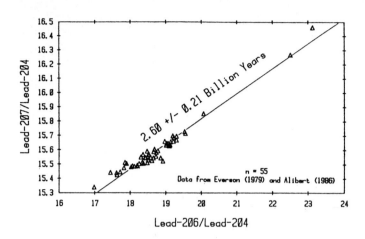

Figure 6.7 *Linear-array plot of lead isotope data from late Cenozoic volcanic rocks of the Colorado Plateau, including late Cenozoic volcanic rocks from Grand Canyon. The 2.6-billion-year isochron was determined by the computer for 55 analyses. Data from Everson (1979), and Alibert and others (1986).*

Pb-Pb isochron derived by Faure,[42] this slope is equivalent to an "age" of 2.60 ± 0.21 billion years. The fact that five rocks from Uinkaret Plateau lie along this line, argues that they are also this "age."

The Pb-Pb-isochron "age" of 2.6 billion years is older than any other reported in a recent catalog of radioactive isotope "ages" for Arizona rocks.[43] The fact that Uinkaret Plateau basaltic rocks overlie virtually all the Grand Canyon strata (see figure 6.4) must mean that these rocks, dated isotopically as the oldest, are among the *youngest* strata of Arizona. The Pb-Pb isochron cannot be reading the true age of these volcanic strata. There must be another explanation for these isotopic data.

Lead isotope ratios of Uinkaret Plateau basalts were studied recently by Austin.[44] Quaternary hawaiite flows, from a small area on Uinkaret Plateau, were reported to possess a linear variation in lead isotopes with strong positive slope. These new data follow the regional lead-isotope trend established by earlier investigators, and suggest an "age" of approximately three-billion years. These discoveries will, no doubt, promote further investigations of the isotope variations in these recent rocks.

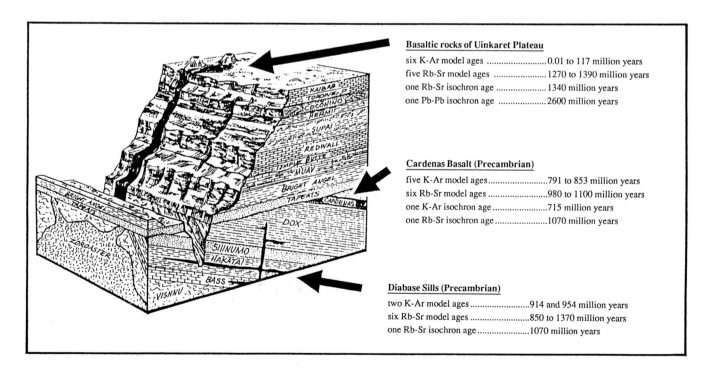

Figure 6.8 *Are Grand Canyon rocks one billion years old? Radioisotope dating methods give strongly discordant "ages." The lava flows at the rim of Grand Canyon, impose an incredible contradiction on radioisotope dating. The flows at the rim appear to be older than deeply buried lava flows. Data sources shown in text.*

Why Isochron Assumptions Must Be Challenged

Figure 6.8 summarizes the "ages" from the three important geologic units of Grand Canyon. For Uinkaret Plateau basaltic rocks, Cardenas Basalt, and diabase sills, no coherent picture of age emerges. Using our assumptions about radioactive dating, the analytical equipment should be able to resolve the "ages" of these rocks. However, *the various methods are usually strongly discordant!* K-Ar "ages" are frequently younger than Rb-Sr "ages" on the same rocks. One might suggest that loss of argon occurred as the gas diffused out of the rocks, making the K-Ar dates appear younger than the actual age.[45] Such reasoning would cause us to endorse Rb-Sr dates. However, we notice that the *oldest* Rb-Sr dates come from Uinkaret Plateau basaltic rocks, which are the *youngest* rocks in the Canyon. In fact, if we embrace the assumptions of radioisotope dating and the "ages" shown in figure 6.8, we might come to an extraordinary conclusion: The *youngest* rocks lie deeply buried within the Precambrian strata, and the *oldest* rocks lie on the surface, among Tertiary and Quaternary strata. Such a conclusion is, of course, geologically preposterous! *We must question the assumptions of radioactive dating, and ask whether an alternate explanation is possible for Grand Canyon rocks.*

The isochron-dating model is not the only explanation possible for the rocks of Grand Canyon. Rather than assuming that the datable lava flow cooled from molten rock having uniformity with respect to the daughter, we could assume nonuniformity of the daughter. In the case of the strontium in a lava flow, we might assume that the flow was not uniformly mixed, but that some samples had higher $^{87}Sr/^{86}Sr$ ratios than others. What if the strontium in the lava flow was *not* isotopically homogenized when the flow occurred? Could such a flow display the characteristics we normally would interpret to be an isochron suggesting great age?

The answer to these questions has been summarized by Gunter Faure.[46] According to Faure, the incomplete mixing of two magmas having different strontium isotope ratios produces a mixing diagram where all mixtures lie on a straight line on an $^{87}Sr/^{86}Sr$-versus-$^{87}Rb/^{86}Sr$ graph, *with the slope of the line having no identifiable time significance!* Such two-component *mixing diagrams* produce what Faure calls "fictitious isochrons."

Leeman considered the possibility that mixing could produce the dissimilar $^{87}Sr/^{86}Sr$ ratios he observed in the Uinkaret Plateau lava flows.[47] He suggested that molten rock could have been contaminated by crustal rocks having higher $^{87}Sr/^{86}Sr$, as the material ascended to the earth's surface. In Leeman's words, ". . . the data from a series of such contaminated lava rocks could produce a Rb/Sr—Sr^{87}/Sr^{86} mixing line that crudely resembles an isochron."[48]

Another geologic cause for these straight-line plots is offered by Dalrymple,[49] who recognizes that partial melting of old parent rock in the earth's mantle can create linear plots. If only five percent of a parent rock deep within the earth melts, and liquid is drawn off, that chemical composition can be significantly different, than if 10 percent of the parent rock melts. The variation in chemical compositions of melts occurs because different minerals of the parent rock melt at different temperatures. He states that if an "old" parent rock melts partially, it also can give off liquids of different *isotopic* compositions.

The partial-melting model for linear array plots is not difficult to understand. Certain minerals in the "old" parent rock, with high Rb/Sr, will have high $^{87}Sr/^{86}Sr$. Other types of minerals having low Rb/Sr, will have low $^{87}Sr/^{86}Sr$. As different liquids are drawn off of the source rock during different degrees of partial melting of its minerals, lavas will be produced having different $^{87}Sr/^{86}Sr$. Furthermore, the variation in $^{87}Sr/^{86}Sr$ will correlate positively with the Rb/Sr and $^{87}Rb/^{86}Sr$ of lavas produced.

A third geologic cause for these straight line plots is offered by Brooks, James, and Hart.[50] They document twenty-two examples of excessively old rubidium-strontium isochrons, and propose that such characteristics are inherited from the molten material's source at great depth in the earth. They propose that dissimilar $^{87}Sr/^{86}Sr$ ratios within various lava flows were acquired by major melting from the old magma source material, which also had dissimilar $^{87}Sr/^{86}Sr$ ratios deep in the earth. In other words, *lava flows look old not only at the time they cool, but from their deep source!* The straight-line plot, which would normally be interpreted as an isochron caused by time-dependent nuclear decay of ^{87}Rb within the rock, is explained, instead, by the geologic process of inheritance from heterogeneous source material. Thus, the "age" derived for the source material could be very much older than the true age, from cooling of the lava flow.

The conventional isochron model for isotopic variations within rocks has been challenged by new data and interpretations. Three alternatives to the isochron model have been offered:

1. Mixing of materials within the earth;

2. Partial melting of source materials within the earth; and

3. Inheritance of isotopic ratios from major melting of heterogeneous source material.

Of the three alternatives, the mixing-model for Uinkaret Plateau basalts has received the strongest criticism. Leeman, who was the first to promote contamination as a mechanism for the isotopic variations, has changed his mind. In his later explanation of Uinkaret Plateau basaltic rocks, Leeman[51] states, ". . . the compositional trends are not compatible with bulk crustal contamination, and a heterogeneous mantle source is a favored alternative." In fact, Leeman, in a number of his later papers, has become one of the primary advocates for inheritance of isotopic trends.

The partial-melting model also finds little support from studies of Uinkaret Plateau basalts. Alibert, Michard, and Albarede studied Cenozoic volcanic rocks of the southern Colorado Plateau, including Grand Canyon.[52] They specifically tested the partial-melting model, and discounted it as a primary cause of the isotopic variation in the rocks they studied. Austin[53] specifically tested the Uinkaret Plateau basalts, and used chemical and isotopic data to question the partial-melting model.

Evidence that a linear-array plot can be inherited, is provided by the lead-isotope study of volcanic rocks on the Colorado Plateau. The lead-isotope variation, shown in figure 6.7, would appear to reflect inheritance of the isotopic ratios from a deep-seated source. It would be difficult to imagine lead-isotope mixing or contamination processes which could operate so uniformly within numerous magma chambers throughout an area of several tens of thousands of square miles in Utah, Arizona, and New Mexico.

More evidence for inheritance of isotopic ratios comes from the study of diamonds. The argon-isotope ratios in ten diamond crystals from Cretaceous rocks of Zaire, form an excellent linear array, when plotted against potassium.[54] Figure 6.9 shows the data plotted. The sloping line indicates

an "age" of 6.04 ± 0.08 billion years. Such an "age" causes significant problems, for it is older than the "accepted age" of the earth. The scientists who did the study knew that the "accepted age" for the earth is 4.5 billion years. Therefore, they explained this as evidence that argon was trapped within the diamonds when they formed.[55] The data seem to require that, as each diamond crystallized, it incorporated variable amounts of ^{40}Ar, but at a constant $^{40}Ar/^{40}K$ ratio. The interpretation offered abrogates the isochron assumption.

The study of linear-array plots from important geologic formations remains in the forefront of research in isotope geology. It is evident that the isochron assumption is not needed, to interpret systematic isotopic variations within important geologic formations. Alternatives to the isochron model are being suggested and defended.[56] No doubt, future research will illuminate geologic processes by which these traits were acquired.

Conclusion

Estimating the "age" of a rock by radioisotope dating is analogous to telling time with an hourglass. In the case of the hourglass being used to tell elapsed time, we must know (1) the number of sand grains in the upper and lower chambers when the instrument was inverted, (2) that no sand grains have been added or removed from the instrument during the time period we are attempting to measure, and (3) that the rate of sand falling through the instrument has remained constant. In the case of radioactive isotopes being used to tell "age," we must know (1) the initial number or ratios of daughter isotope when the rock formed, (2) that parent-or- daughter isotopes have not been added to or removed from the rock since the rock formed, and (3) that the "decay constant" describing the radioactive decay of parent has, indeed, remained constant during the history of the rock.

These three assumptions of radioisotope dating find their application in two types of "age" estimates. The "model age" can be derived from a laboratory analysis of a single rock sample, if we make the assumption concerning the quantity or ratio of the daughter isotope when the rock formed. The "model age" of a rock is only as reliable as the "model" of the initial daughter isotope abundance we assume. No analytical equipment can confirm the initial condition we suggest as a model.

The "isochron age" can be derived from laboratory analyses of a suite of rocks, if we make the assumption that the rocks belong to the same well-mixed "cogenetic unit," where each rock had the same initial quantity or ratio of daughter isotope when the rocks formed. The *present* abundances, or ratios of parent and daughter in the suite of rocks are assumed to indicate the *initial* abundance,

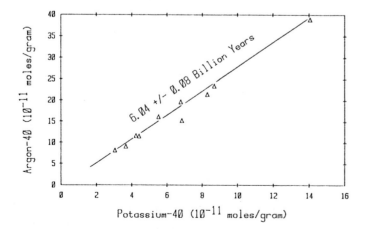

Figure 6.9 *Linear array plot of potassium and argon isotopic data for ten diamonds from Cretaceous kimberlite of Zaire. The "age" of six billion years, which is indicated by the computer fit line, is much older than the "accepted age" of the earth.*

or ratio of daughter common to the rocks. The degree of deviation of the daughter isotope from the assumed initial value, is believed to be a function of age. The isochron method assumes that a suite of rocks with great deviation from the initial condition, is very old. The "isochron-age" estimate for a suite of rocks, as the "model-age" estimate for a rock, assumes an initial condition which cannot be confirmed by laboratory analysis. For the "isochron age," the initial condition must be assumed, that the suite of rocks was sufficiently mixed, with respect to the daughter.

Do analyses of the radioactive isotopes of Grand Canyon rocks give reliable estimates of their ages? Are Grand Canyon lava flows really one billion years old? Careful study of the isotopic abundances of three important geologic units of Grand Canyon shows that *no* coherent picture of "age" emerges. Figure 6.8, the summary of the various "ages" obtained, shows that the various methods are strongly discordant. If we embrace the popular assumptions of radioisotope dating for Grand Canyon rocks, we can make a case for the *youngest* rocks being deeply buried within the Precambrian strata and the *oldest* rocks

being on the surface among the Quaternary strata. Such an interpretation is, of course, contrary to the fundamental superposition of Grand Canyon rocks worked out by geologists! The evidence for billion-year-old rocks in Grand Canyon remains very tenuous.

The problem with radioisotope dating methods lies not in the techniques used to determine the abundances of isotopes, but in the assumptions used to make the interpretation of great age. The isochron assumption regarding initial uniform mixing of the daughter must be challenged, if we are to understand Grand Canyon rocks. We must be prepared to acknowledge that rocks have inherited differing isotopic ratios, which might give them the appearance of great age. We recognize that geologic processes can, and did, contribute to the isotope ratios of rocks, which, in the evolutionary way of thinking, require a billion years of radioactive decay. The advocate of isochron assumptions is required to repair what appears to be a serious flaw in the billion-year "age" commonly assumed for Grand Canyon rocks. We might ask, "Has any Grand Canyon rock been successfully dated?"

NOTES—Chapter 6

1. Gunter Faure, *Principles of Isotope Geology* (New York, John Wiley, 2nd ed., 1986), pp. 38-70. The equation is developed by Faure using calculus. On page 39, he says: "It is the basic equation describing all radioactive decay processes."

2. For a discussion of perturbation in the surroundings of radioisotopes which have induced very small changes in decay constants, see Don B. DeYoung, "The Precision of Nuclear Decay Rates," *Creation Research Society Quarterly*, 13 (June 1976): 38–41.

3. R. H. Steiger and E. Jäger, "Subcommission on Geochronology: Convention on the Use of Decay Constants in Geo- and Cosmochronology," *Earth and Planetary Science Letters*, 36 (1977): 359–362. This work describes the "new" constants which slightly change and standardize "old" constants.

4. H. Godwin, "Half-life of Radiocarbon," *Nature*, 195 (1962): 984.

5. Faure, *Principles of Isotope Geology*, p. 40. He says, "This is the basic equation that is used to make age determinations of rocks and minerals based on the decay of a radioactive parent to a stable daughter."

6. Ibid., p. 42.

7. Ibid., p. 120

8. Ibid., p. 119

9. Ibid.

10. G. Brent Dalrymple and Marvin A. Lanphere, *Potassium-Argon Dating* (San Francisco, W. H. Freeman, 1969), p. 56.

11. Ibid., pp. 46-48.

12. Steiger and Jäger, "Subcommission on Geo-chronology. . . ."

13. Dalrymple and Lanphere, *Potassium-Argon Dating*, p. 49. The equation used by Dalrymple and Lanphere includes the "old" constants. Their equation has been updated to include the "new" constants.

14. Ibid., p. 121. For evidence that argon can be inherited and incorporated into crystals when they cool, see F. A. Podosek, et al., "Normal Potassium, Inherited Argon in Zaire Cubic Diamonds," *Nature*, 334 (August 18, 1988): 607–609.

15. Faure, *Principles of Isotope Geology*, p. 121.

16. The procedure for fitting a straight line to linear-array plots of isotope data has been described by Derek York, "Least Squares Fitting of a Straight Line with Correlated Errors," *Earth and Planetary Science Letters*, 5 (1969): 320–324. A computer program based on the method of York has been used to calculate the best-fit isochron. This program, with various modifications, has been circulating among dating laboratories. The Institute for Creation Research uses a version of this program written in Fortran, which is run on an MS-DOS, desktop computer.

17. Davis A. Young, *Creation and the Flood* (Grand Rapids, Baker Book House, 1977), p. 190.

18. Faure, *Principles of Isotope Geology*, pp. 73, 121.

19. P. W. Huntoon, G. H. Billingsley, W. J. Breed, J. W. Sears, T. D. Ford, M. D. Clark, R. S. Babcock, and E. H. Brown, *Geologic Map of the Eastern Part of the Grand Canyon National Park, Arizona* (Grand Canyon, Grand Canyon Natural History Association, scale 1:62,500, 1986).

20. E. D. Koons, "Geology of the Uinkaret Plateau, Northern Arizona," *Geological Society of America Bulletin*, 56 (Feb. 1945): 151–180.

21. C. E. Dutton, "The Tertiary History of the Grand Canyon District," *U. S. Geological Survey Monograph* 2 (1882): 111.

22. The value for $^{40}Ar*$ is calculated from the total ^{40}Ar measured. The amount of ^{36}Ar, the isotope of argon *not* derived by radioactive decay, is assumed to have been derived from atmospheric contamination. Because our atmosphere has 295 times more ^{40}Ar than ^{36}Ar, a quantity equal to 295 times the ^{36}Ar is assumed to be atmospheric ^{40}Ar. This atmospheric ^{40}Ar is subtracted from the total ^{40}Ar in the sample to give $^{40}Ar*$, the argon believed to have been derived by radioactive decay. Implicitly, the assumption has been made that there was no initial ^{40}Ar in the sample when it formed. If there was initial ^{40}Ar in the sample, it would show up in the value for $^{40}Ar*$, and the model age calculated would be excessively old.

23. T. D. Ford, W. J. Breed, and J. S. Mitchell, "Name and Age of the Upper Precambrian Basalts in the Eastern Grand Canyon," *Geological Society of America Bulletin*, 83 (Jan. 1972): 223–226.

24. E. H. McKee and D. C. Noble, "Age of the Cardenas Lavas, Grand Canyon, Arizona," *Geological Society of America Bulletin*, 87 (Aug. 1976): 1188–1190.

25. D. P. Elston and E. H. McKee, "Age and Correlation of the Late Proterozoic Grand Canyon Disturbance, Northern Arizona," *Geological Society of America Bulletin*, 93 (Aug. 1982): 681–699.

26. The computer program fits a straight line to linear array plots by a method described by Derek York, "Least Squares Fitting of a Straight Line with Correlated Errors," *Earth and Planetary Science Letters*, 5 (1969): 320–324. This computer program, with several modifications, is being used by various dating laboratories.

27. McKee and Noble, "Age of the Cardenas Lavas, Grand Canyon, Arizona."

28. McKee and Noble obtained an age of 1.09 ± 0.07 billion years, which used the "old" ^{87}Rb decay constants. The "new" constants give 1.07 ± 0.07 billion years.

29. S. J. Reynolds, F. P. Florence, J. W. Welty, M. S. Roddy, D. A. Currier, A. V. Anderson, and S. B. Keith, "Compilation of Radiometric Age Determinations in Arizona," *Arizona Bureau of Geology and Mineral Technology Bulletin*, 197 (1986): 1–258. The most recent volcano in Arizona is Sunset Crater, which erupted in 1064-1065 A.D., but yields a K-Ar model age of 0.23 million years. The standard explanation is that this model age is excessively old because the rocks contained argon when they cooled.

30. P. E. Damon and others, "Correlation and Chronology of the Ore Deposits and Volcanic Rocks," *U. S. Atomic Energy Commission Annual Report, No. C00-689-76*, (1967), 82 pp. Olivine is not considered a suitable mineral for K-Ar dating.

31. W. K. Hamblin, "Pleistocene Volcanic Rocks of the Western Grand Canyon, Arizona," *in* D. P. Elston, G. H. Billingsley and R. A. Young, eds., *Geology of Grand Canyon Northern Arizona (with Colorado River Guides)* (Washington, D. C., American Geophysical Union, 1989), pp. 190–204. Concerning the isotopic ages of basalt flows, Hamblin describes samples collected during 1972 and dated by G. B. Dalrymple. Hamblin says that four basalt flows gave "reliable dates," but notes that "many had excess argon" (page 199). The "ages" for those with "excess argon" are not reported in the publication. Steven Austin (unpublished data) tested for "excess argon" in Uinkaret Plateau basalts. A sample of Quaternary basalt was processed to isolate olivine and pyroxene, and these minerals separated were submitted for K-Ar analysis. These minerals had low potassium (0.55%) but had measurable argon (0.00022 ppm $^{40}Ar*$), yielding a K-Ar model age of 5.7 ± 1.5 million years. This model age is clearly much older than the stratigraphic position of this Quaternary basalt will allow, and significant "excess argon" must exist in this basalt.

32. E. D. McKee, W. K. Hamblin and P. E. Damon, "K-Ar Age of Lava Dam in Grand Canyon," *Geological Society of America Bulletin*, 79 (Jan. 1968): 133–136.

33. Reynolds and others, "Compilation of Radiometric Age Determinations in Arizona," pp. 14, 16.

34. W. K. Hamblin, "Late Cenozoic Volcanism in the Western Grand Canyon," *in* W. J. Breed and E. Roat, eds., *Geology of the Grand Canyon* (Flagstaff, Museum of Northern Arizona, 2nd ed., 1976), pp. 142-169. G. H. Billingsley, Jr. and P. W. Huntoon, *Geological Map of Vulcan's Throne and Vicinity, Western Grand Canyon, Arizona* (Grand Canyon, Grand Canyon Natural History Association, scale 1:48,000, 1983).

35. M. G. Best and W. H. Brimhall, "Late Cenozoic Alkalic Basaltic magmas in the Western Colorado Plateaus and the Basin and Range Transition Zone, U.S.A., and Their Bearing on Mantle Dynamics," *Geological Society of America Bulletin* 85 (Nov. 1974): 1677–1690.

36. W. P. Leeman, "Late Cenozoic Alkali-Rich Basalt from the Western Grand Canyon Area, Utah and Arizona: Isotopic Composition of Strontium," *Geological Society of America Bulletin*, 85 (Nov. 1974): 1691–1696.

37. In 1989, Dr. Austin began a five-year project to date Grand Canyon rocks using radioactive isotopes. The purpose of this project is to use the "most reliable" radioactive dating method with the most accurate analytical measurement technique, to establish the "ages" of various Grand Canyon rocks. Three specific objectives are:

a. To determine if the "most reliable" method of dating Grand Canyon rocks can uniquely distinguish the oldest rocks (deeply buried beneath strata) from the youngest rocks (exposed on the rim above other strata).

b. To test whether the "most reliable" method of dating can generate two or more concordant "ages" for the same rock, using different radioactive isotopes.

c. To investigate possible alternate explanations for abundances of isotopes in Grand Canyon rocks which are consistent with a creationist, young-earth model.

38. S. J. Reynolds and others, "Compilation of Radiometric Age Determinators in Arizona."

39. Faure, *Principles of Isotope Geology*, pp. 299, 300.

40. J. E. Everson, *Regional Variations in the Lead Isotopic Characteristics of Late Cenozoic Basalts from the Southwestern United States* (California Institute of Technology, Unpublished Ph.D. dissertation, 1979), 454 pp.

41. C. Alibert, A. Michard, and F. Albarede, "Isotope and Trace Element Geochemistry of Colorado Plateau Volcanics," *Geochimica et Cosmochimica Acta*, 50 (1986): 2735–2750.

42. Faure, *Principles of Isotope Geology*, p. 299.

43. Reynolds and others, "Compilation of Radiometric Age Determinations in Arizona." The oldest "age" listed in this catalog for an Arizona rock is 2.12 billion years (fission track method) for the Fort Defiance quartzite.

44. S. A. Austin, "Isotope and Trace Element Analysis of Hypersthene-normative Basalts from the Quaternary of Uinkaret Plateau, Western Grand Canyon, Arizona," *Geological Society of America Abstracts with Programs* 24 (1992): A261.

45. Elston and McKee, "Age and Correlation of the Late Proterozoic Grand Canyon Disturbance, Northern Arizona," p. 691. The authors believe that the anomalously young K-Ar ages are ". . . a consequence of argon-loss during a single episode of heating and cooling, an episode that resulted in partial to perhaps complete resetting of the Ar clock." A problem is that the basement granite, the diabase sills, and the Cardenas Basalt of Grand Canyon give three different K-Ar ages. It seems unlikely that one resetting event could produce different model ages *and* discordant isochrons.

46. Faure, *Principles of Isotope Geology*, pp. 145–147.

47. Leeman, "Late Cenozoic Alkali-Rich Basalt. . . ." p. 1693.

48. Ibid.

49. G. B. Dalrymple, "Some Comments and Observations on Steven Austin's Grand Canyon Dating Project," Unpublished manuscript, dated March 10, 1992, 8 pp.

50. C. Brooks, D. E. James, and S. R. Hart, "Ancient Lithosphere: Its Role in Young Continental Volcanism," *Science*, 193 (17 Sept. 1976): 1086–1094.

51. W. P. Leeman, "Tectonic and Magmatic Significance of Strontium Isotopic Variations in Cenozoic Volcanic Rocks from the Western United States," *Geological Society of America Bulletin*, 93 (June 1982): 493, 494.

52. Alibert, Michard, and Albarede, "Isotope and Trace Element Geochemistry of Colorado Plateau Volcanics," pp. 2739–2744.

53. Austin, "Isotope and Trace Element Analysis of Hypersthene-normative Basalts from the Quaternary of Uinkaret Plateau, Western Grand Canyon, Arizona."

54. S. Zashu, M. Ozima, and O. Nitoh, "K-Ar Isochron Dating of Zaire Cubic Diamonds," *Nature*, 323 (23 October 1986): 710–712. See also T. Akagi and A. Masuda, "Isotopic and Elemental Evidence for a Relationship Between Kimberlite and Zaire Cubic Diamonds," *Nature*, 334 (15 December 1988): 665-667. Akagi and Masuda give evidence that the diamonds come from Cretaceous kimberlite pipes.

55. F. A. Podosek, J. Pier, O. Nitoh, S. Zashu, and M. Ozima, "Normal Potassium, Inherited Argon in Zaire Cubic Diamonds," *Nature*, 334 (18 Aug. 1988): 607–609. This conclusion, that argon was inherited by the diamonds, was supported by Akagi and Masuda, (ibid.) who recognize "trapping of excess ^{40}Ar in the fluid would be the simplest explanation for the isochronlike relation."

56. For a critical evaluation of the assumptions of the isochron method, see Y. F. Zheng, "Influences of the Nature of the Initial Rb-Sr System on Isochron Validity," *Chemical Geology, Isotope Geoscience Section* 80 (1989): 1–16. On page 1, Zheng says: "The Rb-Sr isochron method has been one of the most important approaches in isotopic geochronology. But some of the basic assumptions of the method are being questioned at the present time."

Chapter 7

FOSSILS OF GRAND CANYON

"The world that then was, being overflowed with water, perished"
II Peter 3:6

Snapshots in Time

How did life begin? What were the earliest forms of life on Earth? When did our planet come to be populated with such diverse flora and fauna? Such questions will come naturally to those inquiring into the world around us. Just as someone curious about his family history might dig out an old box of photographs containing yellowed snapshots of his ancestors, paleontologists collect and study fossils, as they try to piece together the history of life. These fossils, "snapshots in time," can give us information about creatures once living, but which now are dead. Those photos at the bottom of the box of family snapshots could be considered older than those at the top. Similarly, those fossils found in lower strata represent organisms which died and were buried *before* those in the strata above. It is at this point, however, that evolutionists, working with a uniformitarian assumption, and creationists, working with a catastrophist framework, come to different conclusions.

According to the evolutionist, sediments were accumulated very slowly. During the lapse of ages, "simple" life forms evolved into "complex" life forms. Therefore, those creatures found fossilized lower in the strata are the ancestors of those found higher. In the same way, the evolutionist might interpret the family photographs in the box to have accumulated slowly. Each separate generation of the family is believed to have added it's own snapshots to the box. Thus, the box contains the records of successive generations of the family over the period of many tens of years.

The creationist supposes that most of the fossils represent traces of creatures that lived at the same time, and that some were simply trapped and buried before others, during the Flood of Noah's day. According to the creationist, there may be some fossils from both before and after the catastrophe, but most represent remains from that event. In the same way, the creationist might interpret the layers of family photographs in the box, as snapshots from a very unusual and large family reunion held at some distant time in the past. Hundreds of family members had their photographs taken at the reunion, and these snapshots were added to the box rather hurriedly, in the order in which they were taken. A few photographs in the box may be snapshots from *before and after* the family reunion, but the majority are from the family *at* the reunion. The major layers of photographs, therefore, represent a single generation of the family—not successive generations covering a long period of time.

The strata of the earth and their contained fossils provide data from which both evolutionists and creationists build their theories. Fossils give both evolutionists and creationists impressions of the creatures which have lived together, the conditions in which they lived and died, the circumstances which resulted in their burial, and their order of burial. Evolutionists believe the deepest strata contain the earliest life forms, from which the more complex plants and animals evolved. The lowest rocks, rich in multicellular fossils, are called "Cambrian" strata, and contain trilobites, brachiopods, and mollusks. If evolution occurred, we should be able to find the ancestors of these creatures fossilized in "Precambrian" strata buried beneath the Cambrian. It is understandable, that the Cambrian and Precambrian sedimentary strata have been searched for fossils, with great care. Grand Canyon strata are no exception.

Fossilization

What is a fossil? Though all fossils are evidences of past life, not all evidences of past life are fossils. The gravestones of our ancestors, the pyramids of Egypt, and Indian arrowheads are evidences of past life, but are not fossils. Items fashioned by humans of the past are considered archaeological artifacts, not fossils. The meat on your dinner plate, the seashells on the seashore, the footprints leading up to a dead animal are evidences of past life, but are not fossils. These are evidences of recent, not ancient, deaths. Evidences of recent deaths remain for a while, before the organic material is broken down by fungi and/or bacteria. Usually, only evidences of past life, which somehow have been preserved for an unusual period of time, are considered fossils.

What kinds of fossils are there? Fossils are either *trace* fossils, or *body* fossils. Trace fossils (also called *ichnofossils*) are evidences of the activity of organisms;

body fossils are evidences of the bodies of organisms. Body fossils, in which the organic material is preserved and chemically unchanged, are called unaltered fossils. On the other end of the spectrum, body fossils which preserve only the internal or external form of the organism and not any actual body parts, are called casts and molds. Trace fossils, unaltered original material, casts, and molds are formed when the sediments become rock. In other cases, pressure and heat can chemically transform the original organic material to either a carbon film or a coal. Finally, usually due to the motion of water through the sediment, organic material can be replaced by crystals of other substances, such as calcite ($CaCO_3$) or silica (SiO_2). These fossils are permineralized.

Among Grand Canyon fossils are both trace fossils and body fossils. Commonest in the Canyon, as in most places on Earth, are body fossils of the cast, mold, and permineralized types. As you examine the rocks of the Canyon, you may have the privilege of seeing examples of a wide variety of types of fossilization.

How old are fossils? Many people believe, having been so taught, that fossils must take a long time to form, and thus, must have been formed a very long time ago. If so, fossils are evidence of the earth's great age. For example, many who believe that the earth had an origin many thousands or millions of years before man, define a fossil as any evidence of an organism which lived in prehistory, or, more specifically, which lived more than about 10,000 years ago. The fact is, however, it is not at all easy to determine the age of a fossil. No person is able to hold a fossil and be able to determine directly how old it really is. Nor can any person tell whether it is older than written language. In point of fact, very few fossils have been dated at all.

In Grand Canyon, in particular, it is unlikely that any fossil (outside of an archaeological site) has ever been dated correctly. This is the subject of chapter 6. Claims of a particular fossil's "age," in the hundreds of thousands, millions, or billions of years, is based on the ages of the rocks in which it is found. These ages, in turn, are estimated by radioactive-decay products in rocks. Thus, we have no direct way to determine the "age" of any fossil taken from a rock in Grand Canyon. Because there is no direct means of dating fossils, the dating of rocks may be in serious error (see chapter 6 on the "age" of Grand Canyon rocks). It is reasonable to conjecture that fossils and rocks could have formed rapidly only *thousands* of years ago.

How fast do fossils form? Fossils could not have formed at all, unless some rather unusual events occurred. Decomposition and erosion are extremely efficient at destroying evidence of past life. Of the billions of human footprints made on beaches, both out of and within the water, none are known as trace fossils. To resist the effects of erosion, the sediment containing prints and trails must rapidly become somewhat solid, or trace fossils could never form. Of the millions of American bison killed in the last century, no fossils have been found. To avoid being eaten by carnivores and scavengers, and broken down by fungi and bacteria, a body must be placed in an environment where these decomposers cannot thrive. Yet, nearly everywhere you find oxygen, you'll find a carnivore, a scavenger, or, at the very least, decomposing fungi. Decomposing bacteria are found in the top few feet of soil, sand, and mud nearly everywhere on earth. Virtually, the only way for a body to avoid decomposition is to be buried quickly, completely, and deeply, thus sealing it from the decomposers. The commonness of body fossils throughout Grand Canyon argues that many, if not all, Grand Canyon rocks were deposited very quickly. The commonness of trace fossils throughout Grand Canyon means that many, if not all, sediments firmed up and, perhaps, turned into rock (i.e., lithified) rather rapidly. Thus, the fossils of Grand Canyon and the rocks in which they are found, were probably deposited and lithified very rapidly.

Earlier Fossils of Grand Canyon

Grand Canyon contains a thick sequence of Precambrian strata. Like similar deposits elsewhere in the world, its sediments have been explored, mapped, and studied. The various units here have been scoured by scientists for more than 100 years, in their search for fossils, and for any clues they might provide about ancient life forms. Except for a few remarkable instances, the search has not produced vast numbers of fossils. However, those fossils which have been discovered, are significant.

Stromatolites

Unusual, laminated structures, composed largely of calcium carbonate, are believed to have accumulated under the influence of sediment-binding, one-celled organisms, often called "blue-green algae." The structures created by these organisms are called "stromatolites." Various shapes, but often domal forms, characterize the fine (silty) detritus layers alternating with thin laminae of precipitated calcium carbonate. Stromatolites, then, are, in essence, modified bedding—bedding which has been modified by mats of one-celled organisms. Such structures are regarded as "fossils," because they are the products of organic growth. However, no specific organism, but, rather, an association of various organisms, is responsible for the sediment-binding and laminae precipitation. The *only* evidence of organic binding in most fossil stromatolites is the laminated structure. Rarely does microscopic examination reveal any trace of actual single-celled organisms.

In 1962, Logan, Rezak, and Ginsburg[1] proposed a classification system for stromatolitic structures. Understandably, they based their system on the shape of the structures they observed, rather than on the fossilized creatures responsible for the buildup. These classifications have been greatly aided by modern stromatolites in Shark Bay, Australia, which help us understand the fossilized forms. These scientists proposed that stromatolitic structures can be found in four basic forms: columnar, club-shaped, undulose, and spheroidal. There is also any number of combinations of these four types (see figure 7.1).

The identification and classification of stromatolites, however, is complicated, by the fact that numerous laminated structures are known to form *without* biological activity. Many precipitated materials (travertine, tufa, caliche, onyx, etc.) have laminated structures, some of which closely mimic stromatolites. Certain formations found in caves are strongly laminated and even domal in form, but were accumulated underground, in total darkness, where no algae can grow. Similarly, manganese nodules grow as laminated spheres on the deep ocean floor, in total darkness, without algae. Along the edge of the sea, laminated deposits of unusually varied forms accumulate by evaporation, particularly of splashing water. Furthermore, certain soil-forming processes produce laminated structures (duricrusts). These examples remind us that great care must be exercised in distinguishing true stromatolites from "stromatolite-like" structures.

In the Chuar Group of the Grand Canyon, stromatolites are reported to occur at three major levels: twice within the Galeros Formation and once in the Kwagunt Formation.[2] In the lowest occurrence, within the Jupiter Member of the Galeros, the structures are formed as wide, low domes, sometimes three feet across. The Carbon Canyon stromatolites, also in the Galeros, are more columnar and branched. In the Awatubi Member of the Kwagunt Formation, the stromatolites are tightly grouped, organically bound mounds called "bioherms," up to 12 feet in height and width. All three of these major horizons consist of stromatolites which are primarily dome-shaped. There appears to be little reason to doubt their organic origin.

A bed of stromatolites has been reported from the Comanche Point Member of the Dox Formation.[3] This bed ranges in thickness from six to twenty feet, and is composed primarily of laterally linked hemispheroids. The Bass Formation is reported to contain a few specimens.[4] These vary in form, from biscuit-shaped to mat-like to biohermic.

Understanding the single-celled organisms which formed stromatolites, has been greatly aided by modern examples of stromatolites forming in Shark Bay, Australia,

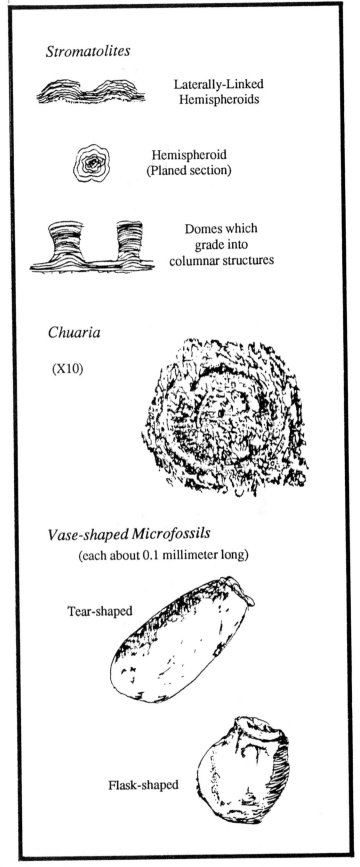

Stromatolites

Laterally-Linked Hemispheroids

Hemispheroid (Planed section)

Domes which grade into columnar structures

Chuaria

(X10)

Vase-shaped Microfossils
(each about 0.1 millimeter long)

Tear-shaped

Flask-shaped

Figure 7.1 *Precambrian fossils of Grand Canyon.*

and elsewhere. These primary organisms, involved with forming modern stromatolites, are photosynthetic, and usually blue-green in color. These creatures, therefore, are given the common name "blue-green algae," but are more properly called "cyanobacteria," or "cyanophytes."

Unlike the cells of our bodies and the cells of animals, plants, fungi, protists, and true algae, cyanobacteria cells do not have a true nucleus. This, and other characteristics of cyanobacteria, mean that careful biologists will call them cyanobacteria or cyanophytes—not blue-green algae. In fossils, of course, color is usually not preserved. Nor is it often possible to determine whether a cell-like fossil has a nucleus, or not. Modern cyanophytes come in one of two basic shapes: filamentous or coccoid. Filamentous forms contain rod-shaped cells set end-to-end inside an organic sheath. Coccoid forms look like tiny spheres—either isolated or connected as if they were beads on a string. Modern cyanophytes often live in association with other organisms. Some, for example, are found in symbiosis with fungi to make up lichens. A number of the modern filamentous cyanophytes are found complexly meshed together in the form of mats. In some forms, the cyanophyte mat encourages minerals to precipitate from the water and/or collect sand grains and other particles. For many of these mats, the particles and minerals protect the cyanophytes during unfavorable times, such as during low tide or the dry season, when the mats are exposed to drying out. Then, when times are more favorable, the cyanophytes grow between the grains of the protective layer and thrive again. Often these mats, with their alternating layers of particles, organic material, and cyanobacteria, will produce the very complexly layered structures we call stromatolites.

From where did the first bacterium come? The rocks of the earth do not tell us, for the oldest rocks which could tell us, already seem to have bacterial fossils in them. Origin-of-life experiments have not told us, for, even with a considerable amount of ingenuity and time, scientists have not been able to produce even a functioning DNA molecule, let alone a cell. Darwinism cannot tell us, because it tries to explain how life *changed,* not how it came to be. Although the theory of spontaneous generation ("abiogenesis") has been proposed to explain the origin of life, it also has failed to find an answer. The Second Law of Thermodynamics, which, briefly stated, says things tend to decay from the complex to the simple, seems to stand as an insurmountable obstacle for an unguided process to derive a complex DNA molecule. But of what value is DNA without a cell to contain it? Without the cell's ability to transcribe and translate the information of DNA into cellular materials, the information is useless. Many believe that life came into existence by an intelligent cause. The data provide a powerful argument for a Creator!

Chuaria

In 1899, C. D. Walcott reported the occurrence of Precambrian megascopic fossils in Grand Canyon.[5] He found small, circular imprints (see figure 7.1) in shales of the Awatubi Member of the Kwagunt Formation (Chuar Group). The fossils were aptly named *Chuaria circularis*, and, to date, similar remains have been discovered in Sweden, Iran, India, Siberia, Canada, France, and Australia. All of these occurrences have been in rocks formed supposedly 1,000 million to 570 million years ago, during what is known as the Upper Riphean time.[6] (The Precambrian/Cambrian boundary is usually estimated at 570 million years before the present.)

Early attempts at classification of *Chuaria* were very wide-ranging. *Chuaria* was suggested to be either a brachiopod; a gastropod; of inorganic origin; or algal, in nature.[7] Currently, the most widely accepted theory is that it was a very large, extinct, planktonic alga which, perhaps, went through an encysted stage.

Chuaria circularis specimens are disc-like fossils, ranging in size from 0.5 to 5 millimeters in diameter. Because they are never found atop one another, it is assumed that they were spheroidal in life. They have been discovered singly and in groups; they apparently came to rest washed together in random fashion. *Chuaria* is definitely organic, composed chiefly of carbon.

Plant Microfossils

In 1973, near the location of *Chuaria circularis* fossils, the presence of plant microfossils was reported.[8] In a distinct, cherty, limestone unit of the Walcott Member of the Kwagunt Formation, fossils were discovered at the periphery of pisoliths (spheroidal particles with concentrically laminated internal structure, ranging from 1 to 10 millimeters in diameter). These organisms were of two varieties: spheroidal and filamentous. The spheroids are probably related to the cyanophytes ("blue-green algae"), which form stromatolites. The tubular filaments, which are more numerous, are more difficult to classify. They might be similar to certain fungi or algae. Seemingly identical specimens have been collected in Greenland and Australia (also assigned to Precambrian sediments). No forms exactly like these have been found in the strata above the Precambrian.

Vase-shaped Microfossils

The cherty pisolite bed and carbonaceous shales of the Walcott Member of the Kwagunt Formation were the source of yet another type of fossil, as reported by Schopf, Ford, and Breed, in 1973.[9] They discovered vase-shaped, microscopic fossils in thin sections and in acid-resistant residues. These were classified as chitinozoans. Previously, all known chitinozoans had been found in rocks of Early Ordovician to Late Devonian age, sometimes having been used as index fossils. Their presence in Precambrian sediments is surprising.

The fossils in this locality were of two distinct forms: flask-shaped and tear-shaped (see figure 7.1). The "flask-shaped" variety average 91 microns in length, with a length-to-width ratio of 1.4:1, and are very similar to a genus of chitinozoans from the Ordovician and Silurian. The "tear-shaped" forms are longer, averaging 96 microns; their length-to-width ratio being 1.7:1.

If these microfossils of the Precambrian in Grand Canyon are assigned to the chitinozoans, then the possibility exists that they represent microscopic animals (protozoans or egg cases of metazoans)—the most common interpretation of chitinozoans. However, until an undeniable protozoan is discovered in the Precambrian, it is presumptuous to assume that these "mystery fossils" will fill major gaps in the fossil record between unicellular autotrophs (primary producers, e.g., "blue-green algae") and multicellular heterotrophs (primary consumers).

Recently, the whole notion that the vase-shaped microfossils of the Canyon represent chitinozoans has been challenged. Bonnie Bloeser[10] interpreted these fossils as the encystment stage of an unidentified alga. The case appears to be strong. If this is true, these fossils cannot be the first animals on Earth, and the supposed evolutionary ancestry of animals remains speculative.

Pollen

Pollen and spores possess a coating of *sporopollenin*, an extremely durable substance, which is found in fossil form, in many sedimentary rocks. Sporopollenin is virtually inert in hydrofluoric acid, whereas silicate minerals of sedimentary rocks dissolve quickly in the acid. Using this property of resistance of spores and pollen to strong acids, researchers have been able to isolate fossil spores and pollen from rocks, and have been able to identify the types of plants which produced them.

In 1966, C. L. Burdick published a controversial paper,[11] claiming that pollen of vascular plants had been isolated from the Hakatai Shale (Precambrian) of the Unkar Group of the Canyon. The pollen Burdick isolated is from pine, juniper, and Mormon tea, all plants which grow today in Grand Canyon. Naturally, there was concern that his samples of Hakatai Shale had been contaminated somehow by modern pollen, either having been carried by wind from trees in the vicinity and infiltrated into the rock, or by having been added unintentionally, during the laboratory-isolation procedure itself.

Other researchers have tried to duplicate Burdick's work: Arthur V. Chadwick[12] collected fifty samples of Hakatai Shale from the same locations as Burdick had earlier, paying close attention to possible sources of contamination. Shale was sealed at the outcrop in special containers, and later in the lab these samples were washed, using filtered water, and were trimmed with a rock saw to remove external surfaces which had been in contact with a crack or with the air. The shale was processed in filtered solutions; glassware was scrupulously clean, and the air of the laboratory was filtered and maintained at positive pressure to avoid contamination. Special techniques were also employed to prevent accidental loss of material during processing. Chadwick found no authentic pollen in the fifty samples of Hakatai Shale. The inability to repeat Burdick's work with fifty samples at his collection sites indicated to Chadwick that Burdick had *not* collected authentic Precambrian pollen, he had collected contamination.

Work by G. F. Howe, E. L. Williams, G. T. Matzko, and W. E. Lammerts[13] appears to confirm Burdick's earlier work. Two out of ten preparations of Hakatai Shale were observed to contain pollen. Pollen from pine was identified in the two preparations, which came from either one or two rock samples of Hakatai Shale. Less care was taken than by Chadwick to avoid contamination, but the procedure appears adequate. The sample, or samples with pollen, were collected by chipping into three inches of solid, "unweathered" shale.

One legitimate explanation for the occurrence of pine pollen in Hakatai Shale is that the pollen has infiltrated from the modern atmosphere into pores within the rock. Pollen is microscopic, and could have migrated into the rock between mineral grains, during more than a thousand years of recent exposure at the surface. Are Howe, Williams, Matzko, and Lammerts confident that such small objects as pollen grains did not infiltrate into the shale along fractures and between mineral grains after the rock was lithified? They are confident, but not certain.

The possibility of pollen in Precambrian rocks, no doubt, will remain controversial among creationists, and the concept is likely to find little favor among evolutionists. Evolutionists usually assume that vascular plants did not evolve until after the Cambrian. However, evidences of higher plants have been reported elsewhere from "Cambrian," or from strata beneath the "Cambrian." Fossils of vascular plants have been documented in strata conformably overlain by early Cambrian strata in the Salt Range in Punjab, India, and in the Middle Cambrian of eastern Siberia.[14]

Jellyfish

At various times in the past, claims as to the discovery of complex metazoan fossils from Precambrian rocks have been made. In 1951, Van Gundy[15] reported a fossil jellyfish in a silty sandstone of the Nankoweap Formation in eastern Grand Canyon. However, it has since been suggested that the structure was inorganic, formed by "compaction of fine sands deposited . . . over a small gas blister."[16]

Other "jellyfish" claims were made by R. M. Alf, in 1959[16]—these from the Bass Limestone, but Cloud felt they were impressions made by falling raindrops,[17] whereas Seilacher[18] thought they had formed around crystals while lithification occurred. There is some debate as to the actual cause of these structures, but, at this point, the existence of jellyfish imprints seems unlikely.

Later Fossils
of Grand Canyon

A variety of both invertebrate and vertebrate fossils has been found in Grand Canyon strata above the Precambrian. Some of these are shown in figure 7.2. Especially interesting are the attempts to relate these fossils to the sparse record of the underlying Precambrian. Paleontologists also want to understand the diversity of Grand Canyon fossils, so that a model of the ancient ocean floor can be constructed (see figure 7.3).

Plants

Plant material is relatively fragile, and requires rapid burial for the best preservation. This is especially true for leaves and stems. Having few hard parts, plants are best preserved in a matrix of very fine-grained sediment. Because they are land-derived, they are more often found in shale layers than they are in limestone layers. The Bright Angel Shale contains a segmented alga. Also, fern and gymnosperm are common in the Hermit Formation.

An alga composed of tear-drop-shaped segments, 3 to 5 millimeters long per segment, can be found on many green-shale bedding planes of the Bright Angel Shale.[19] A hand-sized piece of green shale can reveal the algae as having crossed cleavages, and thus has formed a multi-branched structure of up to two dozen segments. Cyanophytes ("blue-green algae") are also reported from the Supai.[20]

The Supai Group shales contain specimens of the horsetail rush *Calamites*.[21] Near the top of the Supai, and throughout the red Hermit Formation above it, are found fern-like foliage (thought to belong to seed ferns) and stems of conifers.[22] In the Hermit Formation, excellent specimens of these plants can be seen in the Cedar Ridge area on the South Kaibab Trail, and at the head of Hermit Canyon on the Hermit Trail.

Ichnofossils

Indirect traces of life, such as trackways, burrows, and resting sites, compose the group of cast fossils known as *ichnofossils*. They include trilobite trackways of the Tapeats, Bright Angel, and Muav formations, the worm burrows of the Bright Angel Shale, and vertebrate trackways common in the Supai Group, Hermit Formation, and Coconino Sandstone. Trackways might be expected to be less abundant than shell fossils, because a shell can be washed from place to place and still be preserved. But a track made in soft sediment must be buried and preserved where it was made. Once buried, the trackway is still unlikely to be preserved. Any eroding current could easily destroy a trackway, and biological activity within the sediment by burrowing organisms or rooted plants, could obliterate it. Because special conditions seem necessary to preserve ichnofossils, we are surprised to find them common, worldwide.

The generalized name "worm trails" is given to a variety of ridge and groove patterns, as well as to tubes of infilled mud which resemble feces trails of giant, mud-burrowing worms. Many of these may represent feeding trails of a variety of marine organisms; some, undoubtedly, were worms, but others may have been mollusks, brachiopods, or crustacea. Other trails may represent escape burrows, formed as animals burrowed out of sediment which was being rapidly deposited.

Sponges

Although sponges are multicellular, aquatic organisms, they are not regarded as metazoans. They have only a few types of cells, and these resemble those of the protozoans. There is no real organization of cells into tissues, and there is no central nervous system. In many ways, sponges appear to be between protozoans and metazoans in their level of organization. Thus, they can be regarded as among the simplest animals.

Sponges can be recognized by calcareous, or siliceous, needle-like rods (spicules), or by insoluble fibrous protein (spongin) which are combined as a framework to form the internal skeleton of the creature. This internal skeleton forms the support structure vital for feeding and respiration. Fossils of numerous types of sponges have been identified chiefly by the organization of their rigid and easily fossilized internal skeletons.

If evolutionary theory is correct, these simplest multicellular animals should leave an excellent fossil record, especially in the lowest marine strata. Siliceous and calcareous spicules should be easy to fossilize, and the ancestry of sponges should be particularly apparent in

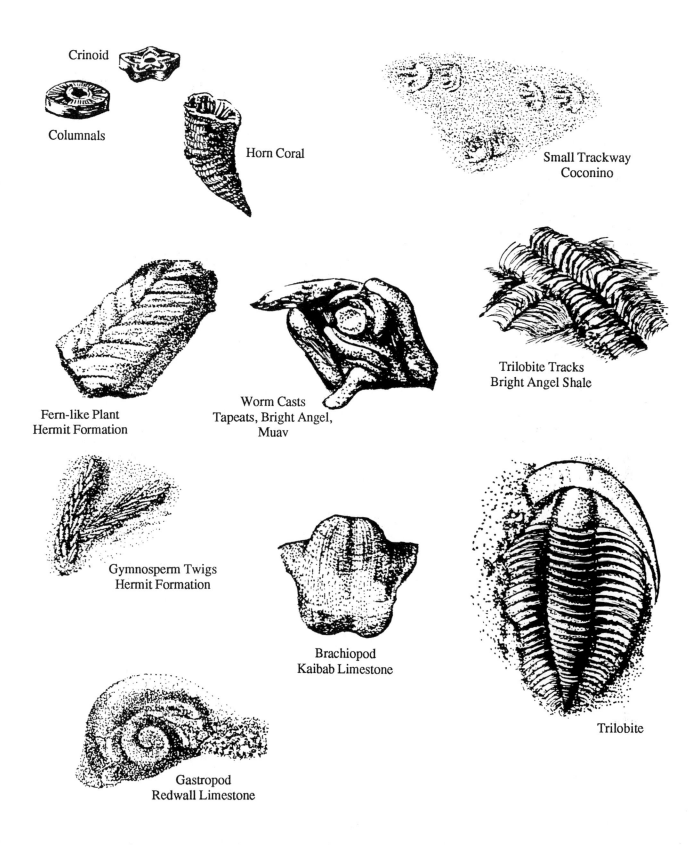

Crinoid

Columnals

Horn Coral

Small Trackway
Coconino

Fern-like Plant
Hermit Formation

Worm Casts
Tapeats, Bright Angel,
Muav

Trilobite Tracks
Bright Angel Shale

Gymnosperm Twigs
Hermit Formation

Brachiopod
Kaibab Limestone

Trilobite

Gastropod
Redwall Limestone

Figure 7.2 *Common fossils of Grand Canyon. (Drawings by Walter Barnhart.)*

Figure 7.3 *Reconstruction of pre-Flood ocean floor suggested by Paleozoic fossils. (1) Crinoids, (2) Jellyfish, (3) Sponges, (4) Starfish, (5) Trilobites, (6) Nautiloid, (7) Clam, (8) Brachiopods, (9) Sea urchins, (10) Segmented worms, (11) Snails, (12) Coral, (13) Fish. The assortment of different body plans is similar to modern oceans.*

the lower Grand Canyon marine strata. Do we find fossils of sponges in the *lowest* Grand Canyon strata? No evidence of sponges has been found in Precambrian strata of the Canyon, and the fossil record of sponges from Cambrian and Devonian strata is strongly disputed. Unusual six-rayed structures have been described from the Bright Angel Shale[23] and Muav Limestone.[24] These have been assigned to *Chancelloria,* a genus originally believed by Walcott to be a sponge (Phylum Porifera). Recent researchers,[25] however, have challenged the assignment to sponges, claiming that *Chancelloria* belongs to a separate phylum. Isolated spicules from sponges have been found in the Redwall Limestone,[26] but the fossil record there has not been used to argue for the complete body of a sponge.

Our study of Grand Canyon sponges leads to a remarkable conclusion. Sponges, the most primitive of animals in their construction, are found in the highest strata of the Canyon! The one most common to be found there is *Actinocoelia meandrina,* and is identified only in the Kaibab Limestone (Permian) at the rim.[27] Chert nodules in the limestone often contain evidence of this sponge. It is so distinctive of the Kaibab Limestone, that any isolated boulder found lower in the canyon which contains the sponge, can be assumed to have rolled down from the Kaibab. Elsewhere in the world, sponges are found in strata as low as in the Middle Cambrian.[28] Their apparent absence in the lower Grand Canyon strata, after diligent search, remains a mystery.

Foraminifera

Unicellular organisms which secrete a single (sometimes chambered) shell of calcium carbonate, are assigned to the Phylum Foraminifera. These are very small marine planktonic and benthonic protists which live in the modern oceans, and are found as fossils. We might consider these organisms, as are the sponges, to be among the most primitive living things. Do we find their fossils in the Precambrian strata of Grand Canyon? No! Foraminifera have not been found in the Precambrian, Cambrian, or Devonian strata of the Canyon. They have been reported in the Redwall Limestone, Supai Group, and Kaibab Limestone. Again, as with the sponges, we find the simpler forms at the top of the stratigraphic succession. Elsewhere in the world, Foraminifera are found in Cambrian strata. Their apparent absence in Lower Grand Canyon, as in the case of sponges, remains a mystery which is not explained by current evolutionary theory.

Corals

Corals, a subgroup of the soft-bodied coelenterates (Phylum Cnidaria), come in many varieties in Grand Canyon. A common, dome-shaped, tabulate coral,

Syringopora, is often seen in the Redwall Limestone at specific horizons. Some of these specimens may give the impression of a growing reef; however, they are frequently only broken slabs, and we might assume that a long period of time was required to accumulate a bed with coral slabs in growth position. But, it is important to note, that were corals to be moved by water, they would have a high probability of landing in an upright position. Orientation during deposition would be caused by the differential density of the coral. They are more dense at the bottom, and less dense at the top. Many of these corals obviously have been disturbed and are not in growth position. Large, organically bound frameworks have not been found, so these assemblages of coral differ markedly from modern reefs.

Branching corals are also common in Grand Canyon, but they are found higher in the Kaibab Limestone. There they appear as broken fragments mixed with echinoid spines and broken pieces of brachiopods.

The solitary rugosa, or horn coral, is another Redwall coral.[29] Ranging from 2 to 4 centimeters in height, these horn corals managed to stand on the apexical, or pointed, end. They do not, however, occur attached to solid substrata. Individual specimens embedded in the hard limestone are often exposed in cross section, so identification of corals is best made on examination of the internal septa, which radiate in toward the center in characteristic patterns for individual species.[30]

Bryozoans

Modern bryozoans are marine animals which seem to resemble the hydroids of the coelenterates superficially, when, in fact, their internal organization is much more specialized. The most easily recognized characteristic is their one-way digestive tract, with mouth, esophagus, stomach, intestine, and anus.[31] Living bryozoans generally occur as encrusting layers on other marine organisms, but fossil forms often constructed an elaborate, high-form structure, which appears distinctively in the fossil record. The most common fossil forms are various open lattice works, or screens of calcareous skeletons, which provide internal structure for the soft-bodied creatures. The structure of the lattice is useful for identification.

Because of the fragile nature of the lattice, most bryozoans found in Grand Canyon are broken fragments which have been found in formations above the Muav.

Brachiopods

There are about 250 species of brachiopods living today, but many thousands more are found in the fossil record. Because all living brachiopods are marine organisms, and fossil brachiopods are usually associated with life now restricted to ocean environments, it is thought that *all* brachiopods were marine organisms.

Brachiopods have two calcium carbonate or calcium phosphate shells, and look similar to clams. They do, however, differ rather markedly from clams, in several ways: First of all, the shells of clams are applied to the *sides* of the clam body, usually making it impossible to divide a given shell into two equal halves (with the exception of scallops and some unusual fossil forms), but, at the same time, usually making each shell a mirror image of the other (with the exception of oysters and some unique fossil forms). The shells of brachiopods, on the other hand, are applied to the *top* and *bottom* of the brachiopod body, making the two sides of a given shell mirror images of one another, and thus preventing each shell from being the mirror image of the other. Another difference is that the brachiopod breathes and eats by filtering water through an organ called a lophophore, which fills most of the space within the shell. It has a nervous system, digestive system, simple excretory system, and reproductive system, and it also has a number of very powerful muscles for opening and closing the shell, and for burrowing and imbedding itself in sediment. Once again, the complexity of brachiopods and the lack of ancestral forms in the fossil record seem to argue for their *creation*, rather than for their *evolution*.

Brachiopods are very diverse in shape. The smooth-surfaced, thumb-nail-sized *Lingula* is found from Bright Angel Shale[32] (Cambrian) all the way up through the Kaibab Limestone (Permian), and there are living species today.[33] The large, heavily spined and ribbed *Penicularis* (common genus of productid) is also found in the Toroweap and Kaibab formations. The division between these formations was made by the presence or absence of another pair of brachiopods.

Brachiopods are some of the most common fossils worldwide, as is true in Grand Canyon, as well. Specimens of many different groups can be found almost anywhere in the Canyon.

Mollusks

Molluska is a large phylum which includes both living and fossil forms as diverse as the clam (*pelecypoda*), snail (*gastropoda*), and squid (*cephalopoda*). Fossils of all three of these major divisions of the mollusks are found side by side with the brachiopods. The pelecypods (clams) and gastropods (snails) show the greatest diversity only higher in the strata column, while the diversity of the cephalopods (represented by the nautiloids) is best seen in the lower strata. The difference in locations would suggest different ecological niches, not descent from a common ancestor, because the nautiloids are by far the most complex of the three.

In Grand Canyon, clams and snails are fossilized in great variety, but often as casts, rather than the actual shell. Brachiopods, however, are more often found as fossilized shell material. The poorer preservation of mollusks may be due to the fact that their shells were more susceptible to mineral solution than were the brachiopods. Mollusk shells are often preserved as the matrix for chert nodules.

The cephalopods, which include the living octopuses, squids, and cuttlefishes, have an important and diverse fossil group known as the nautiloids. The nautiloids possessed external shells of conical form which were straight, curved, or coiled. Excellent examples of the coiled nautiloids from the Redwall Limestone are on display at the Yavapai Museum in Grand Canyon Village. Straight-shelled nautiloids occur in the Redwall Limestone in Nautiloid Canyon, off Marble Canyon[34] at the eastern end of the Canyon, and in Elves Canyon,[35] towards the western end.

The Nautiloid Canyon specimens are up to 20 inches in length and as much as 6 inches in diameter, making them some of the largest found in the western United States. These from Nautiloid Canyon do not appear to have fallen to the bottom with random orientations of their cigar-shaped shells; instead, the long axes of numerous shells appear to be aligned in a dominant direction, suggesting that a strong current was in force as they were being embedded in fine-grained lime mud.[36]

Echinoderms

The echinoderms are a diverse group of marine animals whose name means "spiny skin." This group contains the living starfish, sea urchins, sand dollars, and sea cucumbers. They are further identified by their five-point radial symmetry. It is extremely rare to find the whole organism fossilized. Almost always, decomposition and abrasion broke the organism apart before it was fossilized. An example of echinoderm fossilization is spines seen on eroded surfaces of Kaibab Limestone. Individual spines may be from a few millimeters to six centimeters long. Discerning the species of a particular spine would be an exceedingly difficult task, so, the fossils are usually referred to their general class.

The most common echinoderm fossil represented in Grand Canyon is the crinoid, a very important fossil group worldwide. Living crinoids in today's oceans are reduced greatly in their diversity and importance. They resemble a feathery starfish on the top of a long stem, which floats above a holdfast attached to the substrate. In fossil forms (figure 7.4), the body was held to the bottom by a root or holdfast, and was supported above the bottom on a stalk by a series of ring-shaped columnals or disks stacked in the form of a column. On top of the stalk was the crown, composed of a head and arms. The main portion of the head was contained within the many plates of the calyx, and food was generally grabbed from the water by means of brachioles, or arms. The body was supported and moved by increasing and decreasing water pressure in a complex set of water canals and tubes, called a water vascular system.

Crinoid columnals (disks) are the most frequently encountered fossils. They have made a vivid impression on mankind, seem to have been among the first fossils observed, and have excited the imagination of observers down through the years. These "star-stones" have been collected by medieval metaphysicists, American Indians, and twentieth-century picnickers. The disks were strung by central plains Indians for their "wampum."

Study of modern crinoids reveals that the head of the organism is subject to almost immediate disintegration upon death. It is easy to understand why crinoid fossils are so often dispersed fragments. However, crinoid heads are known as complete fossils, in rare instances. One example is from the Redwall Limestone on the Hermit Trail in the central Grand Canyon, where many crinoid heads occur in a matrix of broken and sorted crinoid columnals. Rapid burial by an ocean current is indicated, because the same water that sorted the columnals also must have buried the crinoid heads before decomposition. Complete crinoid heads also have been found in the Bright Angel Shale.

Elsewhere in the Redwall Limestone, large bodies of crinoid columnal limestone occur. These are often recrystallized, but still are easily identifiable. The columnals are typically sorted by size, with all of the disks of the same size comprising an individual bed. In different areas of the Redwall the columnals are very different in size. In some places all of the columnals are 1.0 centimeter and over, while in other areas, all are under 0.5 centimeters. Again, water currents, sediment transportation, and rapid burial are implied. Crinoids are not limited to the Redwall; scattered columnals can be found in the limestones of the Supai Group and in the Toroweap and Kaibab formations.

Arthropods

The largest and most diverse group of animals is the arthropods. This includes all of the insects, spiders, and crustacea (crabs and lobsters). In the fossil record, this group also includes the trilobites.

Fossil insects are represented in Grand Canyon by wings and wing fragments. The most impressive find is a single wing over 10 centimeters long, thought to belong to a giant member of the fly family (diptera). It was found with seed fern foliage in the Hermit Formation near the Hermit Trail.[37] Together, these fossils give the impression of a lush tropical environment.

Trilobites compose a very large and diverse group of extinct arthropods found as fossils worldwide. They occur among the earliest fossils of the Cambrian, and are indeed the lowermost multicellular fossil with hard parts found in the Canyon. Typical examples are *Alokistocare*, an eyeless, two-to-four-centimeter species, and *Glossopleura*, five to seven centimeters long, with small eyes pointing outward. Both are found in the Cambrian Bright Angel Shale. Trackways and resting sites considered to have been made by trilobites have been found in the Tapeats, Bright Angel, and Muav formations. The Kaibab Limestone contains *Ditomopyge*, a four-to-six-centimeter trilobite with large and pronounced eyes.[38]

A review of the anatomy of trilobites reveals that they are, perhaps, the most complex of all invertebrate creatures. The reconstruction in figure 7.5 is based on some rather remarkable fossils found in British Columbia, which have preserved both the hard and the soft parts of the organism.

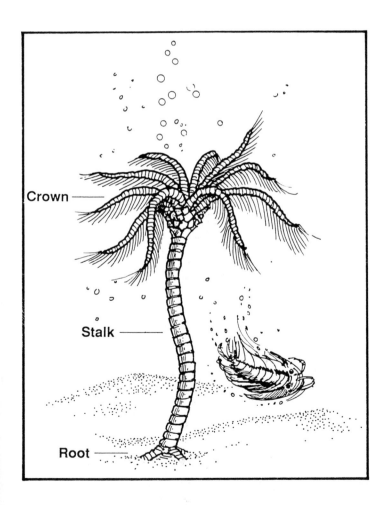

Figure 7.4 *The crinoid is the most abundant fossil representative of the echinoderms. A trilobite is shown swimming to the right of the stalk of the crinoid.*

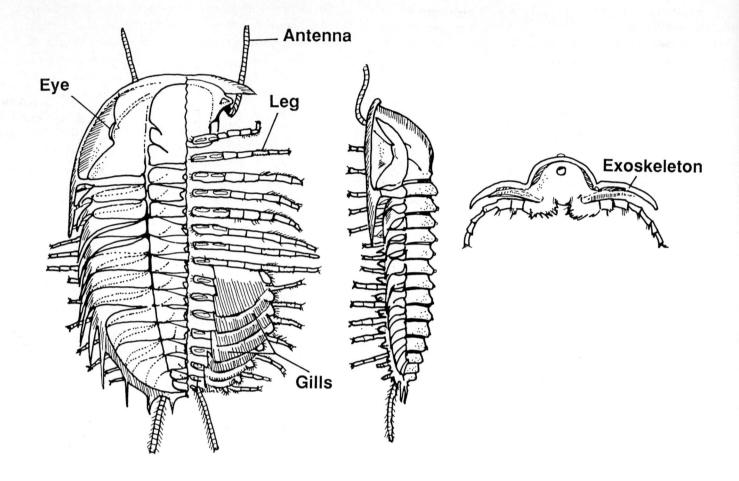

Figure 7.5 *The amazing anatomy of the trilobite. The dorsal view (left) is shown with the right side of the exoskeleton removed to show legs and gills. The lateral view (center) shows the left side of the trilobite. The cross-sectional view (right) cuts across the thorax. Trilobites had a segmented body, with head, thorax, and abdomen, all of which was covered with a chitinous exoskeleton. The exoskeleton implies that trilobites grew by periodic molting—a very complex process. The jointed legs and other appendages require that the animal had complex musculature, whereas the compound eyes and antennae imply a complex nervous system. Bristles which covered appendages were used for swimming and respiration, indicating that trilobites must have had a heart-and-blood circulatory system. Although evolution theory proposes that trilobites were among the first multicellular organisms with hard parts to evolve, in no way can trilobites be regarded as "simple," or "primitive." (The drawing shows* **Olenoides serratus** *from the Burgess Shale, British Columbia, after drawings by H. B. Whittington.)*

Trilobites are thought to have been marine creatures, because their fossils are commonly found with the remains of creatures living in oceans today. Furthermore, they appear to have had a set of gills associated with every leg. A trilobite is usually evidenced as a fossil by its shell, which was a calcium carbonate and chitin secretion onto the back of the animal. The shell is usually divisible into three sections—the head shield, or cephalon; a series of segments making up the thorax; and the tail shield, or pygidium. Each shell shield is made up of a raised central ridge, or spine, and a wide flange on each side. These three lobes have given the animal its name (*tri-* for three; *-lobite* for the lobes). Fossils provide us with evidence that the trilobite occasionally molted its skeleton as it grew, a

complex process used by many species of crabs and lobsters today. Because it had jointed legs and antennae, the trilobite is classified with lobsters, crabs, scorpions, spiders, and insects in the animal Phylum Arthropoda. The legs require the animal to have had complex muscle systems. Because of their similarity to modern arthropods, trilobites are thought to have had a circulatory system, including a heart. They also had a very complex nervous system, as indicated by antennae, which probably had a sensory function, and the presence of eyes on many species.

Aside from man's own inventions, some scientists believe that the aggregate (schizochroal) eyes of some trilobites were the most sophisticated optical systems ever utilized by any organism.[39] The schizochroal eye (figure

7.6) is first of all a compound eye—that is, it is made up of more than a single lens. Because each lens of the compound eye "sees" through only a very narrow window, the compound eye has been determined to be ideally suited to detect motion (thus the difficulty of sneaking up on a fly). Each individual lens of an insect eye, however, does not produce a clear image. The insect thus sees a rather fuzzy composite image. In contrast, each one of the lenses of the trilobite's schizochroal eye is specially designed to correct for spherical aberration, thus allowing each lens to construct a clear image. It is presumed, then, that schizochroal eyes were not only ideally suited for motion detection, but also for clear vision. Furthermore, some schizochroal eyes provided the trilobite with a zone of overlapped vision, thus allowing for depth perception, as well. Some such eyes even allowed for vision in virtually all directions—up, down, forwards, backwards, sideways, etc., at the same time!

The elegant physical design of trilobite eyes employ Fermat's principle, Abbe's sine law, Snell's laws of refraction, and compensates for the optics of birefringent crystals. Thus, trilobites could see an undistorted image under water. Imagine being able to see with undistorted vision in all directions, being able to determine distance in part of that range, while, at the same time, having the optimum sensor for motion detection. Such a vision system would have all the evidences of being constructed by an exceedingly brilliant designer!

The trilobite's extraordinary complexity presents a dilemma for evolutionists. Such a creature would not be the type which evolutionists would predict as stemming from the lowest strata containing multicellular animals with hard parts. Most evolutionists would have supposed that something resembling a sponge would be first. But the trilobite is among the Cambrian strata deep in Grand Canyon. Furthermore, if evolution were true, we would expect such a complex creature to have documentable ancestral fossils showing how that complexity arose. Such fossils have not been found. Instead, the amazing complexity of trilobites, and their abrupt appearance in Cambrian strata, argue for design and fiat creation.

Fish

At least two evidences of fish are found in the Grand Canyon region. Fish teeth are found in the Kaibab, and even one shark's tooth has been reported.[40] Of special interest are placoderm plates which are occasionally found in the Temple Butte Limestone outside of Grand Canyon near Flagstaff.[41] Placoderms, now extinct, were fish with plates rather than scales covering their head region. No bones of fish have been reported in Grand Canyon rocks.

a.

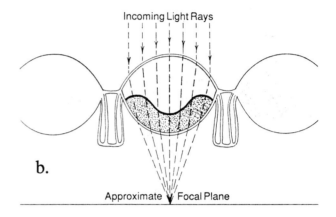

b.

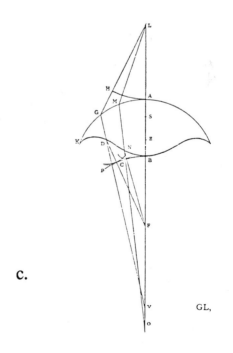

c.

Figure 7.6 *The eyes of the trilobite. (a) Shown here is the compound structure of schizochroal eyes. (b) Each lens is composed of two crystalline materials (calcite and chitin) which are mated along a curved boundary to allow the lens to correct for spherical aberration. (c) Aspherical aplanatic lens designed by Huygens (Traité de la Lumière, 1690). Note that Huygens' 1690 design employs the same curved boundary as the trilobite eye!*

Nonskeletal Fossils of Vertebrates

Of the land vertebrates, no bone or actual physical portion of the animals has been discovered in any of the strata within Grand Canyon. The only evidence we may have of vertebrates are their trackways.[42]

Vertebrate trackways have been studied for many years from the Supai, Hermit, and Coconino Sandstones.[43,44,45] Footprints were left as very distinct impressions in the mud or sand by clawed feet of wide-bodied, quadrupedal vertebrates.

Gilmore, in his intensive study of footprints in these layers, listed the number of genera from the Supai as three, and from the Hermit as seven. He described each genus as being quite distinct from the others, but with multiple specimens from varied locations of several of the genera.

Whether the tracks were made by amphibians or reptiles is a matter currently in dispute. Many of the trails were produced by feet pushing outward, much as a salamander would waddle today. Footprints vary considerably, from less than one centimeter (typical of a 10-to-15-centimeter salamander) up to 10 centimeters across (suggesting a four-footed animal of one meter length, in the size range of ichthyostegids). A tail drag is found with some of the trackways, which might suggest an animal of amphibian origin. In at least the upper portion of the Supai, the trailways are generally headed up slope on bedding planes which have their dip to the south. The up slope trails and the southerly dip of cross beds are also characteristic of the trackways in the Coconino Sandstone.[46]

An argument for reptilian origin of the trackways has been their occurrence in the Coconino Sandstone. The classical uniformitarian view has been that the Coconino Sandstone accumulated as enormous desert sand dunes. Because amphibians have gilled, aquatic larvae, they would be at a disadvantage in a well-drained, sandy desert. Therefore, the Coconino footprints have been generally described as reptilian,[47] even though G. F. Matthew originally referred to them as "batrachian" (amphibian) and "definitely not reptilian."[48] Since the earliest work on these trackways, some 22 species have been identified from the Coconino Sandstone. Most workers now suggest that these fossils could be equally well defined as either amphibian or reptilian.

Dr. Leonard Brand, of Loma Linda University, conducted original research with amphibians in his laboratory on sand simulating the Coconino Sandstone.[49] Trackways were impressed on dry sand, dampened sand, and fully submerged sand. He found that the trackways made under water most closely resembled the best footprints found in the Coconino Sandstone, in the detail of both toe and pad impressions. The collection of data would seem to carry some weight in disputing the desert-sand-dune model for the Coconino Sandstone. Instead, the data appear to indicate that the Coconino Sandstone was deposited as sand waves, by south-flowing water currents. That subject is explored in detail in chapter 3. The animals are supposed to have been resting, or walking on the bottom on the sheltered, down-current side of the submerged sand dune.

It appears that more trackways in Grand Canyon await discovery and description. One recent discovery of regularly spaced depressions in the top of the Tapeats Sandstone may represent three or more quadruped trackways, with more than 20 individual prints.[50] The pattern of pace and stride is different from vertebrate trackways in sandstones found higher in the Canyon. Nevertheless, evidence of quadrupeds in the Middle Cambrian would be a serious blow to evolutionary theory, which supposes that these animals appeared much later. While body fossils of vertebrates are not known from Cambrian strata, bony plates from fishes are reported in Upper Cambrian strata of northeastern Wyoming.[51]

Other problematic trackways have been described and pictured by McKee[52] and Gilmore[53] from the Esplanade Sandstone (uppermost Supai Group). These tracks have anterior ends with semi-oval forms, and posterior ends with extremities elongated backward. The rounded, or oval ends all point in a common direction, the tracks appear in narrowly spaced pairs, and each track is remarkably uniform in shape. All these characteristics suggest that the trackways were made by large, four-footed animals, which had legs positioned *under* their bodies. Gilmore[54] comments that the impressions have "superficial resemblance to tracks made by horses' hoofs," and remarked that the Supai Indians "regarded them as tracks made by a band of horses." That such a trackway could be made by a quadrupedal terrestrial mammal (e.g., a horse) is contrary to conventional evolutionary theory, which has such animals evolving much later. These mystery tracks, no doubt, invite further study.

Significance of Grand Canyon Fossils

What can we learn from the fossils in the Grand Canyon? We can find them; we can observe them; but, if all we learn from them is their names, then we have imposed on them the organization of our system but have not let them speak to us. But, on the other hand, if we can ask each of them the questions and take from them the small portion of the answer each supplies, letting their names merely serve as reference guides, they then can reveal to us some of the history that lies buried in these rocks.

How Were the Strata Laid Down?

Each sedimentary formation of Grand Canyon bears evidence of deposition by water. The only formation in dispute is the Coconino Sandstone, which has been supposed by some to have accumulated by wind. Yet, even the Coconino can be interpreted in terms of water deposition.

What kind of water formed Grand Canyon strata? Were these strata accumulated in calm and placid seas? Or were many strata deposited by rapid and catastrophic flood action? These questions were addressed in chapter 3. Studying fossils helps us piece together a good interpretation of the nature of the process which resulted in the accumulation of the strata. In the Redwall Limestone we find large nautiloids which appear to have been buried by strong currents bringing in lime mud. Also in the Redwall Limestone, are crinoid heads which are embedded in a matrix of sorted crinoid columnals, which indicate strong current and rapid burial. Add to these observations and interpretations the geologist's concept that significant thicknesses of sandstones and limestones accumulated as submarine sand waves in deep flowing water, and a catastrophist view of sedimentation is the most logical.[55]

Some of the Precambrian strata of the Canyon have the appearance of being more normal ocean floor. In the Galeros and Kwagunt formations of the Chuar Group (Precambrian) in the eastern Grand Canyon, large stromatolites form domes which may have formed *in situ*. These strata may represent the pre-Flood ocean floor that was not moved, eroded, or redeposited during the Flood.

Did Life Slowly Evolve?

Does the fossil record in Grand Canyon and elsewhere show evidence of slow, evolutionary process? For each fossil considered, the species, genus, family, order, class, phylum, and kingdom appear abruptly in the rocks of the Canyon. This means that whenever one type of organism is found, there is never found preceding it, a series of intermediates between that organism and any other. Each type of organism appears in the rocks as being fully formed. This pattern of abrupt appearance is a feature of the entire fossil record everywhere on earth.

Another feature of the worldwide fossil record is stasis: Every species in the fossil record shows no substantive change from its deepest occurrence to its shallowest occurrence. This, on top of the nearly simultaneous abrupt appearance of a large number of different animal types in the earliest Cambrian rocks (the Cambrian Explosion), argues for the sudden, independent origin of different animal types, rather than for a common evolutionary ancestor.

Do we find the ancestors of the Cambrian fossils in Precambrian strata of Grand Canyon? Indisputable, multicellular animals have not been found in Precambrian strata of the Canyon. Plausible, ancestral forms for Grand Canyon fossils have not been found in any Precambrian strata anywhere in the world. Where are the ancestors

required by organic evolution for the trilobite, brachiopod, worm, mollusk, coral, and crinoid? These ancestors may exist in the minds of evolutionists, but they have not been found in the fossil record.

A Great Progression?

Do fossils of Grand Canyon show an ordered progression that could be predicted by evolutionary theory? A popular book on Grand Canyon says:

> *In the ascending formations are found fossils of ascending forms of life—trilobites (primitive crablike animals), fish, the tracks of amphibians and reptiles. . . .*[56]

Many people think fossils appear in the rocks in the same order that evolutionists claim they should occur. Although it is possible to find a series of fossils in the Canyon and elsewhere to be in the order of evolution, the pervasive pattern is contrary. Sponges, foraminifera, and corals, which are thought to precede trilobites in evolution, are first found in the Canyon *above* the first trilobites. Brachiopods, which are thought by many to be evolutionary descendants of bryozoa, are found *below* the first bryozoa, both in the Canyon and worldwide. Finally, recent studies have placed the trilobites as the most evolutionarily advanced of the arthropods, yet they are the first arthropods to be found, both in the Canyon and elsewhere in the world. It is not clear whether the order of appearance of organisms in Grand Canyon, or anywhere on Earth, for that matter, is necessarily any different than a random order which a flood might produce.[57]

Diversity and Disparity

Biologists often use the word *diversity* to describe the number of species within a distinct taxonomic group. Among the insects (Phylum Arthropoda, Class Insecta) there are more species than are found in all the other living animals and plants combined. It is likely that over *one million species* of insects exist today. We can contrast insects with brachiopods, because within the brachiopods (Phylum Brachiopoda), only 250 species are living today. We speak of *low diversity* among living brachiopods, but *high diversity* among the insects.

Diversity can be contrasted with disparity. Whereas *diversity* concerns the varieties *within* a basic body plan, *disparity* concerns the differences *between* basic body plans. The higher taxonomic categories (phyla and classes) can be understood to express disparity. The Arthropoda (including Class Insecta) and the Brachiopoda, for example, manifest very different body plans. *They* illustrate disparity. We can speak quantitatively about *disparity*, by noting the number of *phyla* that exist at a particular time; we can

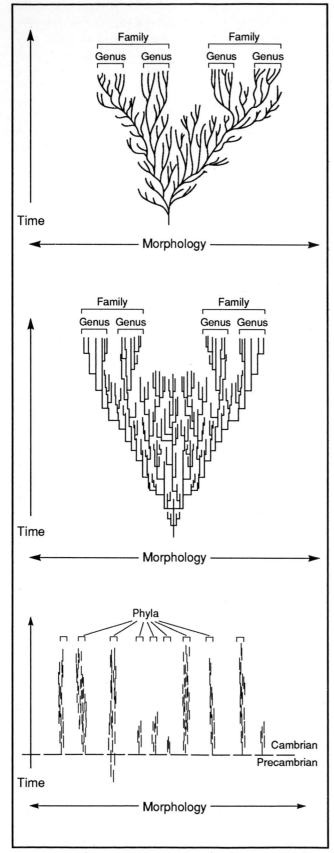

Figure 7.7 *Patterns of diversity and disparity through time: (a) suggested by Darwinian gradualism, (b) suggested by punctuated equilibrium theory, and (c) suggested by the fossil record. (Drawn by Arthur L. Battson, III.)*

speak quantitatively about *diversity*, by noting the number of *species* that exist within a particular group at a particular time.

Evolutionary theory makes predictions concerning diversity and disparity which can be tested against the fossil record. This is shown in figure 7.7. Evolution predicts the general branching patterns which should unfold through the history of life. Both major theories of evolution popular today (Darwinian Gradualism and Punctuated Equilibrium) predict that, as speciation events occur, clusters of species will form new genera, which eventually cluster to form new families. As increasing diversity takes place over time, new orders, classes, and, ultimately, new phyla should appear. In short, *diversity should precede disparity*. The origin of the higher taxa and their novel body plans (*disparity*) should be the result of the gradually increasing *diversity* of the lower taxa. The pattern of geological succession predicted by evolution is from bottom to top: species to genera; genera to families; families to orders; orders to classes; classes to phyla.

The dominant pattern of geological succession, as evidenced by the fossils, especially those of Grand Canyon, is in contradiction to evolutionary theory. *Disparity precedes diversity!* The initial appearance of virtually all phyla occurs with very low species diversity. This is shown diagramatically in figure 7.7 (bottom diagram). The origin of the major body plans is not shown by fossils with increasing diversity among the lower taxa. Rather, the pervasive pattern is top to bottom, contrary to Darwinian theory. As paleontologists Douglas Erwin, James Valentine, and John Sepkoski describe the situation:

> *The fossil record suggests that the major pulse of diversification of phyla occurs before that of classes, classes before that of orders, and orders before families. This is not to say that each higher taxon originated before species (each phylum, class, or order contained at least one species, genus, family, etc. upon appearance), but the higher taxa do not seem to have diverged through an accumulation of lower taxa.[58]*

Darwin admitted that the fossil evidence is the "most obvious and gravest objection which can be urged against my theory." At the time, he was only concerned over the lack of transitional forms in the fossil record. Today, not only do we have fewer transitional forms than Darwin had in his day,[59] but scientists are beginning to recognize that the order of appearance is backwards. It would seem that the "family tree" of life gets *wider* toward its base!

This evidence further substantiates the fact that microevolution cannot be extrapolated to account for major evolutionary change. It appears that the living world is in a state of decay, rather than in a metamorphosis of evolutionary progression. As a result, animals have become, and continue to become extinct.

A Creationist View of Fossil Disparity

The disparity between groups of fossils found in Grand Canyon allows us to organize our thoughts into a creationist interpretation. Rather than suppose common ancestry for these early organisms, we can propose that the major body plans were separate and distinct from the very beginning. We can propose that living things appeared abruptly, that they were fully formed *when* they appeared, and that modern organisms were derived from these types.

Figure 7.8 shows how a creationist might interpret fossil disparity. The top of figure 7.8 illustrates present disparity of some living things we see today. We notice that modern organisms can be classified into broad categories called phyla (Arthropoda, Brachiopoda, Molluska, etc.) which are very distinct from each other morphologically. These individual phyla can be divided further into classes, orders, families, genera, and species. The bottom of figure 7.8 shows some of the Cambrian fossil species which have been identified. These particular species are represented by dots. Using the same principles of classification as for modern organisms, we can assign these Cambrian fossil species to the same phyla we have today. In fact, our observations of Cambrian fossils allow us to circumscribe the same phylum divisions around these ancient organisms as we can the modern ones.

Some interesting conclusions can be drawn from consideration of figure 7.8. We can state that the branches of the "family tree" of life do not appear to diverge from a common ancestor in the early strata. Instead, the similar morphological distances of both Cambrian and present seem to argue that a process of phylum-level *stasis* has operated during the history of life. This type of analysis leads to extraordinary conclusions. Clams have always been clams; brachiopods have always been brachiopods; fish have always been fish.

Three generalizations come to our attention from the study of Grand Canyon fossils: First, we see evidence that living things appeared abruptly on the earth without leaving evidence of primitive ancestors. Second, we see disparity from the start between the important categories of organisms suggesting that the "family tree" of life is as wide at its base as it is at its top. Third, we conclude that the major categories of organisms have persisted without significant modification.

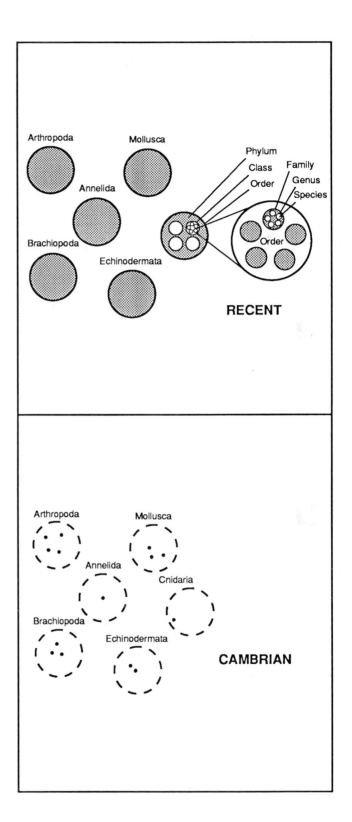

Figure 7.8 *The morphological distances between modern species are compared to the morphological distances between Cambrian species. Stasis, not organic evolution, is indicated by the study of Cambrian fossils and modern species. (Drawn by Arthur L. Battson III.)*

Our three generalizations find support in Scripture: The observation of abrupt appearance of life is implied by the Biblical statement that God "spake, and it was done" (Psalm 33:9). The notion that significant disparity in body plan existed from the start is consistent with the statement, ". . . how manifold are thy works! In wisdom hast thou made them all" (Psalm 104:24). The understanding that stasis is indicated by fossils is concordant with God's command that each living thing reproduce "after his kind" (Genesis 1:11,12,21,24,25).

Why Trackways Without Body Fossils?

Numerous vertebrate trackways have been described in Grand Canyon strata, but no vertebrate-body fossils of these trackmakers have been reported in Grand Canyon. This observation would seem to be at odds with the uniformitarian view of Grand Canyon strata. If the strata represent many geologic ages, we would expect the highest probability of vertebrate body fossils in the strata deposited during the life and death of these vertebrates. Those strata containing trackways should contain the corresponding body fossils.

Leonard Brand[60] surveyed the geologic literature, and documented the worldwide tendency for body fossils of amphibians and reptiles to occur in strata *above* their trackways. A flood model was suggested by Brand to explain these data. He proposed that the trackways were made in actively forming sediments, and that they were buried and preserved immediately after they were made. The animals continued to live, and escaped burial in the same layers as their footprints. If an animal died, its bloated body would tend to float. A dead animal would, therefore, be carried away, and have a higher probability of being fossilized in strata above its footprints.

Could body fossils of four-footed animals producing trackways in the Supai, Hermit, and Coconino formations be found in strata which once overlaid the Kaibab Limestone in Grand Canyon? The Moenkopi and Chinle formations have been eroded almost completely from the Canyon, so we cannot prove that the body fossils were there. Elsewhere, however, the Moenkopi and Chinle formations *do* contain four-footed-animal-body fossils.[61]

God's Judgment and Mercy

The original creation, a remnant of which we see in the fossil record, was one of much greater variety and complexity than the present remnant of that creation available for study today. A significant number of plants and animals we see fossilized in Grand Canyon are now extinct. All of the trilobites are gone; most of the brachiopods, nautiloids, crinoids, and giant insects are gone; the seed ferns are gone; most of the amphibians and reptiles that left trackways are gone. The varieties of many of these groups that are left today are the smaller and less robust representatives. The fossils show us that God looked on the corruption of the earth and His holiness demanded judgment—a purging of the corruption. The layers of rock represent a giant graveyard; the fossils, a silent testimony to the end result of sin.

God, however, did not totally destroy that original creation, but provided a way that the purified creation could be preserved. Today, plants, animals, and man find their homes in the very earth God judged. Man continues to marvel at the monument God has left. Grand Canyon is a testimony of our Lord's mercy. He is "long-suffering to us-ward, not willing that any should perish, but that all should come to repentance" (II Peter 3:9). He has promised to create "new heavens and a new earth, wherein dwelleth righteousness" (II Peter 3:13).

NOTES—Chapter 7

1. B. W. Logan, R. Rezak, and R. N. Ginsburg, "Classification and Environmental Significance of Algal Stromatolites," *Journal of Geology*, 72 (1964): 68,69.

2. T. D. Ford and W. J. Breed, "Late Precambrian Chuar Group, Grand Canyon, Arizona," *Geological Society of America Bulletin*, 84 (Apr. 1973): 1243–1260.

3. G. M. Stevenson and S. S. Beus, "Stratigraphy and Depositional Setting of the Upper Precambrian Dox Formation in Grand Canyon," *Geological Society of America Bulletin*, 93 (Feb. 1982): 163–173.

4. R. O. Dalton, Jr., *Stratigraphy of the Bass Formation*, (Unpublished master's thesis, Northern Arizona University, Flagstaff, 1972), 40 pp.

5. C. D. Walcott, "Precambrian Fossiliferous Formations," *Geological Society of America Bulletin*, 10 (1899): 199–244.

6. T. D. Ford and W. J. Breed, "The Problematical Precambrian Fossil *Chuaria*," *Paleontology*, 16 (1973): 535–550.

7. T. D. Ford and W. J. Breed, "The Younger Precambrian Fossils of the Grand Canyon," in W. J. Breed and E. Roat, eds., *Geology of the Grand Canyon* (Flagstaff, Museum of Northern Arizona, 2nd ed., 1976), pp. 34–36.

8. B. Bloeser, J. W. Schopf, R. J. Horodyski, and W. J. Breed, "Chitinozoans from the Late Precambrian Chuar

Group of the Grand Canyon, Arizona," *Science*, 195 (1977): 676–679.

9. J. W. Schopf, T. D. Ford, and W. J. Breed, "Microorganisms from the Late Precambrian of the Grand Canyon, Arizona," *Science*, 179 (1973): 1319–1321.

10. B. Bloeser, "*Melanocyrillium*, a New Genus of Structurally Complex Late Proterozoic Microfossils from the Kwagunt Formation (Chuar Group), Grand Canyon, Arizona," *Journal of Paleontology* 59 (1985): 741–765.

11. C. L. Burdick, "Microflora of the Grand Canyon," *Creation Research Society Quarterly*, 3 (1966): 38–50.

12. Arthur V. Chadwick, "Precambrian Pollen in the Grand Canyon—A Re-examination," *Origins*, 8 (1981): 7–12.

13. G. F. Howe, E. L. Williams, G. T. Matzko, and W. E. Lammerts, "CRS Studies on Precambrian Pollen, Part III: A Pollen Analysis of Hakatai Shale and Other Grand Canyon Rocks," *Creation Research Society Quarterly*, 24 (Mar. 1988): 173–182.

14. B. Sahni, "Age of Saline Series of the Salt Range of the Punjab," *Nature* 153 (1944): 462,463. J. Coates, H. Crookshank, E. R. Gee, P. K. Gosh, E. Lehner, and E. S. Pinfold, "Age of the Saline Series in the Punjab Salt Range," *Nature* 155 (1945): 266,267. S. Leclercq, "Evidence of Vascular Plants in the Cambrian," *Evolution*, 10 (1956): 109–114.

15. C. E. Van Gundy, "Nankoweap Group of the Grand Canyon Algonkian of Arizona," *Geological Society of America Bulletin*, 62 (Aug. 1951): 957,958.

16. R. M. Alf, "Possible Fossils from the Early Proterozoic Bass Formation, Grand Canyon, Arizona," *Plateau*, 31 (1959): 60–63.

17. P. Cloud, "Pseudofossils: A Plea for Caution," *Geology*, 1 (Nov. 1973): 123.

18. A. Seilacher, "Der Beginn des Kambriums als Biologische Wende," *Neues Jahrbuch fur Geology und Palaeontology*, 103 (1956): 155–180.

19. Observation by Walter Barnhart: algae are often not completely described by geologists when the strata contain invertebrate fossils.

20. Edwin D. McKee, "The Supai Group of Grand Canyon," *U. S. Geological Survey Professional Paper* 1173 (1982): 179.

21. W. J. Breed and B. T. Foster, "Paleozoic Fossils of Grand Canyon," in W. J. Breed and E. Roat, *Geology of the Grand Canyon*, (Flagstaff, Museum of Northern Arizona, 2nd ed., 1976), p. 70.

22. McKee, "The Supai Group of Grand Canyon," pp. 179–182.

23. D. K. Elliott, "*Chancelloria*, an Enigmatic Fossil from the Bright Angel Shale (Cambrian) of Grand Canyon, Arizona," *Journal of the Arizona-Nevada Academy of Science*, 21 (1987): 67-72.

24. E. D. McKee and C. E. Resser, "Cambrian History of the Grand Canyon Region," *Carnegie Institute of Washington Publication*, 563 (1945): 185.

25. J. K. Rigby, "Some Observations on Occurrences of Cambrian *Porifera* in Western North America and Their Evolution," *in* R. A. Robinson and A. J. Rowell, eds., *Paleontology and Depositional Environments: Cambrian of Western North America* (Provo, Utah, Brigham Young University, Geological Studies, vol. 23, 1976), pp. 51–60. See also D. K. Elliott, op. cit.

26. E. D. McKee and R. G. Gutschick, *History of the Redwall Limestone in Northern Arizona* (Boulder, Colorado, Geological Society of America, Memoir 114, 1969), pp. 33, 113.

27. R. L. Hopkins, "Kaibab Formation," *in* S. S. Beus and M. Morales, eds., *Grand Canyon Geology* (New York, Oxford University Press, 1990), p. 239.

28. E. N. K. Clarkson, *Invertebrate Paleontology and Evolution* (Boston, Allen & Unwin, 2nd ed., 1986), p. 70.

29. Breed and Foster, "Paleozoic Fossils of Grand Canyon," p. 68.

30. Septa are small, interior dividing walls deposited by the coral, and seem to be genetically determined.

31. R. C. Moore, C. G. Lalicker and A. G. Fischer, *Invertebrate Fossils* (New York, McGraw-Hill, 1952), 766 pp.

32. McKee and Resser, *Cambrian History of the Grand Canyon Region*, pp. 189–191.

33. Brachiopods virtually identical to Cambrian species are harvested today as a food source in Japan. Cambrian and Ordovician *Lingula* have been arbitrarily named *Lingulella*, because preservation is often of low quality, and because those systematists with an evolutionary perspective are convinced that a genus cannot exist unchanged for half a billion years.

34. W. J. Breed, "The Discovery of Orthocone Nautiloids in the Redwall Limestone, Marble Canyon, Arizona," *Geology and Natural History of the Grand Canyon Region* (Durango, Colorado, Four Corners Geological Society, 1969), p. 134.

35. Observation by Walter Barnhart, June 1988.

36. Observations made by Steven A. Austin in April 1989 and April 1991 at Nautiloid Canyon. See the discussion of nautiloid fossils in chapter 3.

37. C. W. Gilmore, *Fossil Footprints from the Grand Canyon* (Washington, D.C., Smithsonian Miscellaneous Collection, v. 80, no. 3, 1927), p. 1.

38. Breed and Foster, "Paleozoic Fossils of Grand Canyon," p. 74.

39. R. Levi-Setti, *Trilobites: A Photographic Atlas* (Chicago, University of Chicago Press, 1975), pp. 23–45.

40. J. S. Shelton, *Geology Illustrated* (San Francisco, W. H. Freeman & Co., 1966), p. 284.

41. Ibid, p. 275.

42. Charles Schuchert, "On the Carboniferous of the Grand Canyon of Arizona," *American Journal of Science*, 45 (1918): 347.

43. R. S. Lull, "Fossil Footprints from the Grand Canyon of the Colorado," *American Journal of Science*, 45 (1918): 337–346.

44. Gilmore, *Fossil Footprints from the Grand Canyon*, pp. 1–78.

45. McKee, "The Supai Group of the Grand Canyon," p. 91–96.

46. Gilmore, *Fossil Footprints from the Grand Canyon*, p. 9. The generalization concerning the trackways is attributed to L. F. Noble, an early geologist who investigated Grand Canyon.

47. Lull, "Fossil Footprints from the Grand Canyon of the Colorado."

48. Ibid, p. 346.

49. Leonard Brand, "Field and Laboratory Studies on the Coconino Sandstone (Permian) Vertebrate Footprints and Their Paleoecological Implications," *Palaeogeography, Palaeoclimatology, Palaeoecology*, 28 (1979): 25–38.

50. Research in progress by Walter Barnhart.

51. J. E. Repetski, "A Fish from the Upper Cambrian of North America," *Science*, 200 (1978): 529–531.

52. McKee, "The Supai Group of Grand Canyon," pp. 93–96, 100.

53. C. W. Gilmore, *Fossil Footprints from the Grand Canyon* (Washington, D.C., Smithsonian Miscellaneous Collection, v. 77, no. 9, 1926), pp. 37–39.

54. Ibid, p. 37.

55. Evidences of rapid sedimentation are presented in chapter 3. There, models of uniformitarian and catastrophist sedimentation of Grand Canyon strata are contrasted.

56. R. Wallace, et al., *The Grand Canyon* (New York, Time-Life Books, 1972), p. 68.

57. K. P. Wise, "Ecological Zonation and the First Appearances of Higher Taxa," unpublished manuscript, 1989.

58. D. Erwin, J. Valentine, and J. Sepkoski, "A Comparative Study of Diversification Events," *Evolution* 41 (1988): 1183.

59. D. M. Raup, "Conflicts Between Darwinism and Paleontology," *Field Museum of Natural History Bulletin* 50 (1979): 22.

60. Leonard Brand and James Florence, "Stratigraphic Distribution of Vertebrate Fossil Footprints Compared with Body Fossils," *Origins*, 9 (1982): 67–74.

61. C. S. Breed and W. J. Breed, *Investigations in the Triassic Chinle Formation* (Flagstaff, Museum of Northern Arizona, Bulletin No. 47, 1972), 103 pp.

Chapter 8

BIOLOGY OF GRAND CANYON

"Bring forth with thee every living thing that is with thee, of all flesh,
both of fowl, and of cattle, and of every creeping thing that creepeth upon the earth;
that they may breed abundantly in the earth, and be fruitful, and multiply upon the earth"

Genesis 8:17

Design

An Intelligent Cause

It has been pointed out recently by Dr. Charles Thaxton that we use the "principle of uniform experience" to conclude that there is an intelligent cause for life.[1] The principle is illustrated perhaps, best, when we observe the heads of U.S. Presidents at Mount Rushmore, in South Dakota. Even though we did not see the construction process, we conclude from our experience that these stones were carved by workmen following a blueprint, or plan, which was devised in the mind of an architect. We recognize intelligence at Mount Rushmore, because of the *symmetry* of the form of the stone, the overall *interdependence* of the forms to compose the entire surface, and the obvious *purpose* revealed by the sculpture. We reject the notion that the shapes of these rocks are the product of wind-and-water erosion.

Likewise, according to the "principle of uniform experience," we infer that order and complexity in a living organism was programmed by a genetic code which was devised by an intelligent cause. Our experience tells us that it takes an intelligent agent to generate information, a code, or a message. We never see functional complexity come from disorder, by chance. Figure 8.1 illustrates the chain of logic.

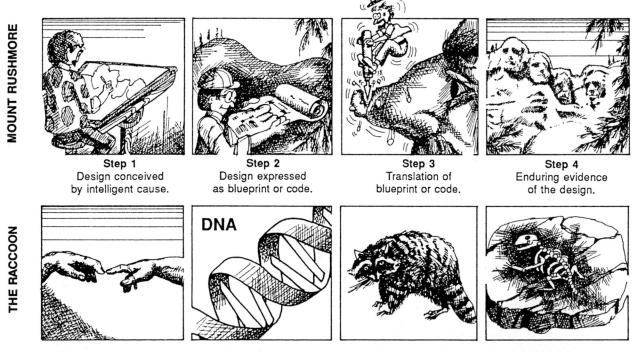

MOUNT RUSHMORE			
Step 1 Design conceived by intelligent cause.	**Step 2** Design expressed as blueprint or code.	**Step 3** Translation of blueprint or code.	**Step 4** Enduring evidence of the design.

THE RACCOON

DNA

Figure 8.1 *How to use logic to infer an intelligent cause. Our understanding of the steps leading to the sculpture of the faces of U.S. Presidents at Mount Rushmore (top illustrations) is analogous to our understanding of the origin of the fossil skeleton in a rock (bottom illustrations). We see the faces at Mount Rushmore and infer sculpture by workmen following a designer's plan. Similarly, we see the fossil skeleton and infer the raccoon built by a genetic code that was devised by an intelligent cause. These illustrations apply the "principle of uniform experience."*

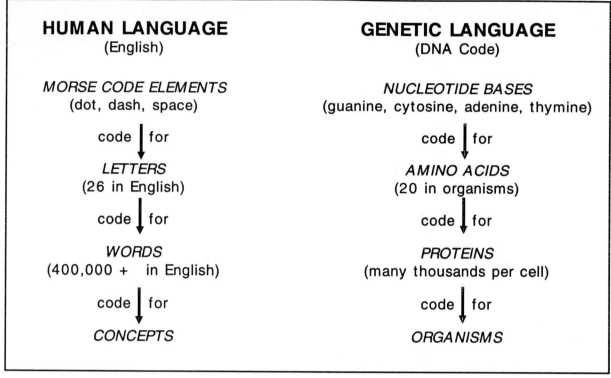

Figure 8.2 *The analogy between human language and genetic language. The similarity is great enough to conclude that an intelligent cause was necessary for the origin of the DNA code. (Drawn by Kurt P. Wise.)*

The greatest biochemical discovery of the twentieth century was the unraveling of the chemical structure of chromosomes. The language of genetics is founded on four nucleotide bases (guanine, cytosine, adenine, and thymine), which are linked to form a complex molecule called deoxyribonucleic acid (DNA). The sequence of bases in DNA is actually a code for amino acids, the building blocks for proteins—the basic components of living organisms.

A remarkable analogy exists between *human* language and *genetic* language. This is shown in figure 8.2. By international human agreement, the elements of the Morse Code (dot, dash, and space) are used by intelligent humans to code for letters. Similarly, the elements of the biochemical code (the four nucleotide bases) were organized by an intelligent cause to code for amino acids. Ultimately, the letters that humans use, as delineated by Morse Code, are assembled to form words for the purpose of communicating concepts. In the same way, amino acids that this intelligent cause uses, as delineated by the genetic code, are assembled to form proteins for the purpose of producing living organisms.

The similarity between the two codes is great enough to make a general conclusion by our "principle of uniform experience"—there must be an *intelligent cause* for both. Intelligent humans devised the Morse Code in a fashion similar to how an intelligent cause devised the genetic code. We note that human intelligence is external to the Morse Code, and we stipulate that the intelligent cause is external to the genetic code. Thus, the intelligence is not latent

within these codes themselves, as the pantheist might assume. The intelligence is *outside* these codes. The sequence of dots and dashes in the Morse Code has no meaning, unless words and language exist external to the code; the sequence of bases in DNA has no meaning without both amino acids and the machinery external to the code to build proteins for living organisms.

Not only is the intelligence *external* to the genetic code, but the intelligence must have *incredible sophistication*. It can be concluded that, because man is just beginning to understand DNA structure, the origin of life is due to a cause with greater intelligence and manipulative ability than man. Yet, even this is still an insufficient picture of the nature of this cause. The DNA molecule is only a small part of the complexity of the simplest cell. Without the ability to reproduce itself, the DNA would eventually succumb to destruction. The process of replication, therefore, is essential to life. Without transcription and translation of DNA into cellular materials, the information is useless. Thus, transcription and translation are necessary to life, as well. Upon consideration of these and the many more complexities of even the simplest cell, it becomes clear that the origin of the cell must be assigned to a cause with incredible intelligence and manipulative ability. Compared to the functional complexity of the simplest cell, all of man's most noteworthy technological achievements are primitive.

The discovery of the unique design and functional complexity of living organisms has caused many to doubt that life came into being by a random combination of chemicals. Two evolutionists, R. Augros and G. Stanciu, ask:

> *What cause is responsible for the origin of the genetic code and directs it to produce animal and plant species? It cannot be matter because of itself matter has no inclination to these forms, any more than it has to the form Poseidon or to the form of a microchip or any other artifact. There must be a cause apart from matter that is able to shape and direct matter. . . . For the same reasons there must be a mind that directs and shapes matter in organic forms. . . . This artist is God, and nature is God's handiwork.* [2]

The Designer's Genius

Rene Descartes is the 17th-century philosopher and mathematician usually blamed for the current view in biology that living organisms are simply biochemical machines. While we can overlook Descartes' ignorance of the facts of biology, it is hard to wink at this same lack of knowledge so prevalent in most modern aspects of evolutionary teaching. No more than the hands of a watch make the various gears and springs with their precise dimensions and ratios, neither do the chemicals of a living organism produce the essence of life. The parts exist for the other parts, but not *because* of the other parts. A watch*maker* is responsible for the fit and form, the plan and purpose—the *design*. So, too, there is a Grand Designer for living organisms.

And what a design! Living things differ from machines in many significant ways. As we reflect upon the following differences between living organisms and machines, we can appreciate the genius involved in the creation of the living world. Furthermore, we can understand why the most brilliant scientists and engineers involved in the present technological explosion have not been able to duplicate these incredible characteristics in even the most sophisticated machines.

1. No machine rebuilds and repairs its own parts. Living things constantly renew their cells and tissues. Bacteria cells, for example, are replaced every 20 minutes!

2. Machines *never* grow from eggs; they are always assembled from the *outside*. Machines contain all the necessary parts when they begin working—or else they simply don't work! Organisms, however, develop from some type of egg, or potential growth unit, and are assembled from the *inside*! Furthermore, living organisms *mature* (even teenagers, thank goodness). That is, their cells not only increase in *number* (they grow), but also increase in *variety*. A human being starts as a single cell, but that single cell increases to the 100 trillion cells that make up the mature human body. And from that one cell comes the hundreds of different kinds of cells—liver, brain, muscle, etc.—all assembled within the body itself, and all assembled in the right place.

3. Living organisms can produce similar organisms within themselves, but without destroying themselves. Factories produce; living organisms *re*produce. The parent-survivability aspect disqualifies viruses as living organisms, since the parent virus must be disassembled and used as a template in reproducing more viruses.

4. Machine parts are interchangeable and not unique to that kind of machine—tires that are used on a car can be used on an airplane, tractor, or three-wheeler, with little or no compromise in function or design. However, parts of a living organism are unique to that organism. Human liver cells, human muscle cells, or human DNA, can be recognized as *human* and distinguished from lower-animal liver cells, lower-animal muscle cells, and lower-animal DNA.

5. Living things have the ability to convert external materials into themselves! No matter how much bacon you eat, you will never turn into a pig (in spite of what some folks say). Vegetarians do not become vegetables; they convert vegetables into their own unique biochemicals.

6. Unlike machines, living organisms can completely disassemble some organs and reassemble them again when needed. The placenta of pregnancy is discarded after the first pregnancy only to reappear at the time of the second. Organelles are small microscopic parts inside the cell. Many of these disappear from the cell only to be reproduced at a time when the cell again needs them.

7. Unlike machines, living organisms cannot be turned off completely and then restarted to resume normal function. Nor can all the parts be disassembled and then reassembled as in a machine. Such a practice kills an organism but not a machine (surgeon take heed!).

These are just a few of the characteristics that separate living things from machines. Oparin said:

> *The actual principles of construction of any machine now in existence reflect the*

character of the person who made it, his intellectual and technological level, his aims, and his methods of solving the problems in front of him.[3]

If, as Oparin suggests, machines reflect the genius of the designer, what level of genius do living organisms indicate regarding their Designer? Logic and a more complete knowledge of biology demand an answer consistent with the Scripture's statement:

For the invisible things of him from the creation of the world are clearly seen, being understood by the things that are made, even His eternal power and Godhead; so that they are without excuse (Romans 1:20).

Cooperation

Another myth that still permeates biology teaching is the concept that all living organisms are involved in a life-and-death, "dog-eat-dog," struggle for existence. Darwin popularized this concept of a "free-for-all" conflict between plants and animals competing for food, water, territory, and shelter. This concept of nature hardly fits with what the Bible describes—an intelligent, loving Creator God who created all living things to co-exist in peace and harmony until man's rebellion and the consequent curse. Even in a fallen world, one would expect to see evidence of the original "goodness" (Genesis 1:4,10,12,18,21,25), if not the original "very goodness," of Genesis 1:31.

But what does the evidence show? Because, as Darwin proposed, the driving force of evolution is this struggle for survival, we must either find this struggle or seriously question the evolutionary concept which predicts it. Numerous excellent studies that have been made over the last 50 years have shown conclusively that *cooperation*, not *competition*, is the rule of nature. Entomologist P. S. Messenger states, "Actual competition is difficult to see in nature."[4] Daniel Simberloff says, "It is rare to see two animals, particularly animals of different species, tugging at the same piece of meat."[5] Another group states, "Instances of direct mutual harm between species are not known to us."[6] The story is much the same for plants. Frits Went, a plant physiologist, reports:

There is no violent struggle between plants, no warlike mutual killing, but a harmonious development on a share-and-share basis. The cooperative principle is stronger than the competitive one.[7]

Among *desert* plants, we might suppose the struggle for survival to be most evident, because the life of each

plant depends directly on obtaining a sufficient quantity of water. Went writes:

In the desert, where want and hunger for water are the normal burden of all plants, we find no fierce competition for existence, with the strong crowding out the weak. On the contrary, the available possessions—space, light, water and food—are shared and shared alike by all. If there is not enough for all to grow tall and strong, then all remain smaller. This factual picture is very different from the time-honored notion that nature's way is cut-throat competition among individuals.[8]

Observations reveal that the struggle for survival, which, supposedly, drives evolution, is a *myth*—an illusion of our age taught as though it were fact.

Why cooperation? What purpose could it serve in an intelligent Creator's plan? By decreasing competition to a minimum, the various areas of the earth would be able to support a much greater diversity of plants and animals than if they were competing in a winner-take-all struggle. A team effort, where all members cooperate, consistently produces a better result than when the one superstar hogs the ball. Herein lies the secret to refilling the entire earth after the Flood with a great diversity of plants and animals in a very short amount of time. Again, God proves to be a Designer of immeasurable genius.

Cooperation, as evidenced by lack of competition is accomplished in several ways in the living world:

1. Size of food is a limiting factor. Most animals are limited as to the size of their prey (men, especially fishermen, are exceptions). Animals must select prey of suitable size to overpower, yet large enough to supply ample nutrition for the amount of energy needed for life.

2. Space is another limiting factor. Robert MacArthur did an extensive study on five species of warblers, all of which inhabit the same spruce trees and eat the same bud worms. In spite of sharing the same food and tree, the five species occupy different areas of the same tree with only slight overlap of territory and never invade a neighboring territory. "Peaceful coexistence, not struggle, is the rule,"[9] he concludes.

3. Time is another factor that reduces competition. In nature, there is a day shift and a night shift, which allows a greater variety of organisms to occupy the same space. Some animals will actually limit their hunting activity to only a few hours and

then voluntarily relinquish it to the "next shift," whether they have been successful or not.

4. Finally, animals very rarely, if ever, fight to the death over food, territory, or mates. Realizing that discretion is more important to survival, one fighter retreats before any real injury results, and, in fact, animals show a reluctance to inflict serious injury to an opponent which is not intended to be a meal. Even in capturing prey, animals use the least amount of force necessary.

Having looked at *passive* cooperation achieved by means of avoiding competition, what about *active* cooperation between organisms? Do living organisms of different species join forces and work together in a way that benefits each other? Despite Darwin's statements to the contrary, active cooperation is the *rule*, not the *exception* in nature. And, because the hallmark of any good scientific idea is how well it can make predictions that will later be proven by observations, we can only conclude that Darwin's concept of evolution is poor science.

Visitors to the desert of the southwestern United States can observe one of the most imposing of plants, the yucca (see figure 8.3). This plant is composed of a rosette of stiff, sword-shaped leaves at the base and clusters of white, waxy flowers on a stem. Less well-known is the alliance of the yucca plant to the yucca moth (*Tegeticula*), a relationship indicating remarkable mutualism and cooperation.[10] The flower of the yucca can be fertilized by no other insect, and the larva of the moth has no other source of food. The female moth gathers pollen from one yucca flower with special mouth parts constructed for the job, flies to another yucca flower, and inserts the pollen mass into the opening where four or five eggs are laid. Larvae of the moth eat about half of the 200 seeds produced. In this way, the plant benefits from seeds produced by the fertilization, and the moth larvae benefit from the surplus food supply.

A classic example of cooperation is one between the various types of cleaner fish or cleaner shrimp and the normally aggressive fish they "clean." Large predator fish line up, wait their turn, and then allow the tiny fish (or shrimp) to swim in and out of mouth and gills in order to pick them clean of the pieces of food debris that collect in the larger fish. Why don't these larger fish eat the small cleaners? Why don't the larger predator fish push the smaller ones out of line? Evolution's insistence on the theory of struggle for survival would never be able to rationalize such behavior.

Even in the area of protection and shelter, we find evidence of cooperation. Up to 12 species of marine animals may live in the mud burrow of the sea worm, *Urechis cauop*, also known as "the innkeeper." These visitors all reside together, none consuming the other, but, instead,

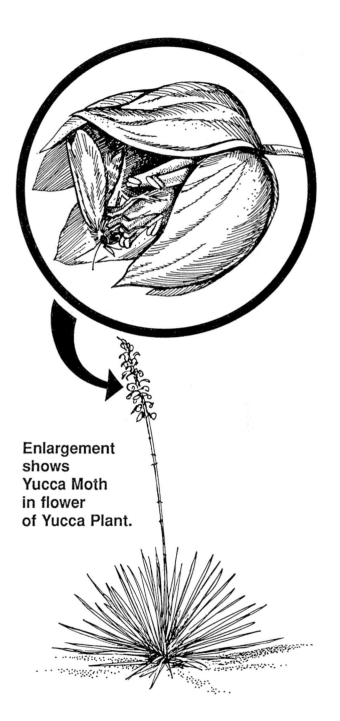

Enlargement shows Yucca Moth in flower of Yucca Plant.

Figure 8.3 *The relationship between the yucca plant and the yucca moth reveals remarkable cooperation. The flower of the yucca can be fertilized by no other insect, and the larva of the moth has no other source of food.*

surviving by simply eating the leftovers the sea worm does not consume.

Peace With the World

Darwin also proposed a fierce struggle between all organisms and their environment. Wind and water, heat and cold—all aspects of the natural environment are bitter enemies of living organisms that struggle to survive not only against each other, but also against the very world in which they live—a literal "world war." This was Darwin's concept of the world around him, one in which life itself had a bare foothold, teetering on the brink of destruction. Unfortunately, while many evolutionists now realize Darwin's knowledge was incomplete, modern text-writers doggedly broadcast their seeds of inaccurate and false dogma in the fertile soil of our young peoples' minds.

If Darwin's concept of organisms scratching out a living in a harsh environment is true, no place should depict this better than in areas where conditions are extreme—either the hot, arid conditions of the desert or the cold of the arctic. However, even in these extreme environments, we find plants and animals functioning, surviving, and even flourishing. One such animal, the kangaroo rat, lives and thrives in the dry desert regions of the western United States (see figure 8.4). The scarcity of rainfall should seriously challenge this animal's ability to survive, because no living organism can live without water. However, this animal completely avoids the necessity of drinking water by obtaining its water supply in a different way. It is able to use the water its own body produces when it metabolizes food. The byproducts of this metabolizing are carbon dioxide and water. The kangaroo rat is able to conserve this water, thereby completely avoiding the need to drink. In addition, this remarkable animal uses several methods of water conservation to minimize its loss: the creature is nocturnal, sweats little, and has extremely efficient kidneys. Great engineering, therefore, eliminates any struggle and turns adversity into advantage.

Perhaps one of the most interesting examples of temperature control is found in the jackrabbit (see figure 8.4). These large, floppy-eared rabbits inhabit not only the deserts of the southwest, but also large reaches of midwestern prairie. At one time it was supposed that the large ears were used to enhance their hearing ability, but it has been found that their ears perform a far more important function. Laboratory investigations on heat-stressed jackrabbits have indicated that the blood *leaving* the ear is significantly cooler than the blood *entering* the ear. During heat stress, a jackrabbit can increase ear blood flow to very high levels through expanded blood vessels. The research indicates that the large, nearly bare ears serve as efficient heat radiators! Thus, even in mid-day heat, this animal may

Ord Kangaroo Rat

Black-tailed Jackrabbit

Figure 8.4 *Grand Canyon animals provide evidence that animals do not fight their environment but work with it or around it. The kangaroo rat never needs to drink water because it gets water from metabolism of food. The jackrabbit is accustomed to hot conditions because its nearly bare ears serve as very efficient heat radiators.*

sit in the shade of a bush with its ears crect, and radiate sufficient heat toward the cool portion of the sky (away from the sun) to prevent it from reaching uncomfortable temperatures. Studies on a number of large mammals possessing permanent horns with high blood circulation, have shown that these structures also are useful for heat regulation.

There are a number of mechanisms used by plants to help them adapt to the dry conditions of the desert. Some flowers succeed by sheer opportunism, only germinating, flowering, and seeding every ten years or so when the conditions are right. Went writes:

> *Probably their most remarkable feature is that they are perfectly normal plants, with no special adaptations to withstand drought. Yet they are not found outside the desert areas. The reason lies in the peculiar cautiousness of their seeds. In dry years the seeds lie dormant. This itself is not at all amazing; what is remarkable is that they refuse to germinate even after a rain unless the rainfall is at least half an inch, and preferably an inch or two.* [11]

In fact, if living organisms are designed by a Perfect Engineer, they should reflect not only the best possible solution to various problems presented by the environment, but also utilize the most *efficient* solutions—those expending the least amount of energy and materials while producing the exact degree of performance required by the organism, and, at the same time, with little or no waste. After all, it would be inefficient and wasteful for humans to have a kidney as efficient as the kidney found in the kangaroo rat. This would be neither economical nor reflect optimal engineering. Nature operates more intelligently, *not* more rigorously.

Economy and Efficiency

If living organisms present the best solution to various design problems, then we would predict that solutions which human engineers have already discovered should also be represented in nature. And that is exactly what we find! Unfortunately, sometimes engineers and scientists look too late.

The first large steel-hulled ocean-going vessel was a ship named *The Great Eastern*. Despite the fact that it was powered by a screw propeller, paddle wheels, and auxiliary sails, it was too inefficient to be profitable. Engineers had designed and constructed it with little or no knowledge of the laws of physics which govern objects moving through water (a fitting testimony to the type of product which results from random chance and ignorance). The end product was a vessel that moved so much water it was too slow to be efficient. Before the next ship was constructed, however, much research and experimentation was done, during which it was discovered that a vessel whose width-to-length ratio is around 0.25 will require the least amount of effort to propel it through water. Having determined this, the engineers then began to study the fastest-swimming marine animals to equate their ratio of body width to length. And, just as would be expected, the fastest swimmers have ratios of between 0.23 and 0.26, just as if an intelligent designer had fashioned them specifically for speed!

Sometimes scientists find solutions to problems only by consulting the Master Engineer. Aircraft engineers sought for several years for the solution to the problem involving the tremendous air turbulence that develops over jet aircraft wings on landing and takeoff. After many failed attempts to correct this dangerous problem, they discovered that birds of prey dive at tremendous speeds onto rapidly running prey with pin point accuracy with no loss of stability, and, obviously, with no turbulence. But how? The answer was so simple, so efficient, and so economical as to be almost ludicrous. Birds have *one single feather*, the alula, which, upon takeoff and landing, protrudes slightly from the leading edge of the wing. This one feather effectively eliminates turbulence. The engineers utilized this concept, thus solving the problem.

Among the most interesting birds at Grand Canyon are the woodpeckers. The common flicker (*Colaptes auratus*) and hairy woodpecker (*Picoides villosus*) are residents of the forests of both rims of the Canyon. Their familiar hammerings can be heard among the other sounds of nature, as they probe for insects or drill a nesting place. These birds, as with all woodpeckers, are a marvel of economy and efficiency. The common flicker is shown in figure 8.5.

Analysis of high-speed photography at UCLA shows that a woodpecker can slam its beak into a tree trunk at a speed of over 20 feet per second and experience an enormous deceleration on the order of 1,000 G. This occurs during a peck lasting less than one thousandth of a second! Researchers, investigating why woodpeckers don't experience severe headaches, found a number of features which protect the woodpecker's brain. The brain is very light and is tightly packed into a case of tough spongy bone. They discovered that the precise head-on trajectory of the bird's peck protects the brain from tissue-tearing, shearing forces. There are opposing muscles which appear to have a shock-absorbing effect and are coordinated by the neck muscles becoming tense at the point of impact. They also discovered that the bird blinks as the peck is delivered. This not only protects the eye from wood chips, but keeps the eye within its socket during sharp and repeated decelerations. Researchers have employed the engineering designs of these remarkable creatures in the manufacturing of modern safety helmets.

For the woodpecker, drilling holes is only the first step in obtaining the insect food which lies within a tree. He uses his long flexible tongue to penetrate deep into the galleries that wood-boring insects occupy. As figure 8.6 shows, this tongue is actually part of the hyoid apparatus—tissue stiffened with flexible bone which is

Figure 8.5 *The common flicker, a resident on the north and south rims of Grand Canyon, is widespread in distribution across North America. Like other woodpeckers, it is a marvel of economy and efficiency. The special grasping feet and stiff tail feathers serve to position the bird effectively. The neck, head, and beak are designed to deliver the brain-jarring peck. After the woodpecker pecks, the amazing tongue (figure 8.6) is able to penetrate deeply within the tree to extract insects.*

wrapped around the skull of the bird. The hyoid bones are fastened in the bird's right nostril, split into two segments, wrap around the skull under the sheath of skin, pass on both sides of the neck bones, and join to the base of the tongue beneath the lower jaw. When this apparatus is contracted by a sheath of muscles around the head of the bird, the snake-like tongue is protruded an unusually great distance. Can any more ingenious structure be devised for housing and extending this lengthy, elastic, and sticky tongue? How could such a structure evolve from a normal bird's tongue?

Again we see an example of how the Master Engineer has not solved just the most difficult problems, but has done so using the least amount of materials with the least possible effort, to get the *best* possible results. Could random chance achieve what the most educated engineers in the world could not? If so, why waste time and money sending doctors to medical school; just let them guess!

We can only agree with the apostle Paul (Romans 1:20) that the creation gives more than abundant testimony to the existence of God; so much so, that anyone who fails to admit it is without excuse. David was more candid in his

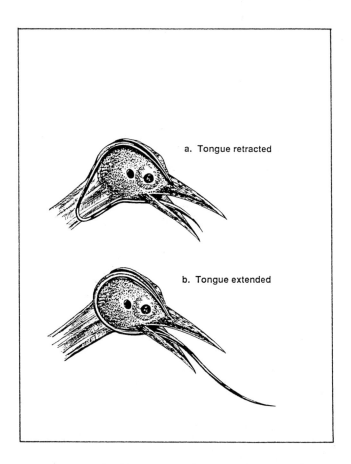

a. Tongue retracted

b. Tongue extended

Figure 8.6 *The amazing tongue of the woodpecker. The skin and feathers from the head of the flicker have been removed to show the tongue in retracted and extended positions. The tongue is attached to the hyoid apparatus, tissue stiffened by bones which are wrapped around the bird's head.*

summation of such resistance to the truth, calling such a skeptic and unbeliever a "fool" (Psalm 14:1)! Creation scientists will continue to point to the truth of a loving Creator God who wants us to know Him personally through His Son, Jesus Christ. It is this same Jesus who has *defeated* death—the enemy of all living organisms—through *His* death, burial, and resurrection. Our Lord offers in exchange not just life—mortal life; abundant life—but *eternal life.*

> *All things were made by Him; and without Him was not any thing made that was made. In Him was life; and the life was the light of men. . . . He was in the world, and the world was made by Him, and the world knew Him not. . . . But as many as received Him, to them gave He power to become the sons of God, even to them that believe on His name (John 1:3,4,10,12).*

Life in the Desert

Visitors to Grand Canyon, expecially those who visit the Canyon's lower elevations, have ample opportunity to observe characteristics of one of the great deserts of the world. The North American desert is the fifth largest, encompassing approximately one-half million square miles of dry, hot, and often desolate country. The North American desert is often subdivided into the four areas, as shown in figure 8.7. The Great Basin, lying in the rain shadow of the Sierra Nevada on the west and the Rockies on the east, covers all of Nevada and parts of adjacent states to the east and north. The Mojave Desert lies between Los Angeles and Las Vegas. The Sonoran Desert covers southeastern California, southern Arizona, and much of northwestern Mexico. The Chihuahuan Desert extends from south central New Mexico to the heart of old Mexico.

While human beings may be scarce in most parts of the desert (large cities like Phoenix, Tucson, Las Vegas and Salt Lake City are obvious exceptions), plants and animals are not. It is tempting to think of many parts of the desert as being devoid of life. Nothing could be farther from the truth. Anyone who has ever witnessed a desert "bloom," which results from a favorable conjunction of season, moisture, and temperature, will testify to the riotous profusion of flowers—of colors and blossoms which can coat the desert floor. Even the animals, which at first glance seem absent, are present in large numbers. The careful observer will note delicate telltale signs in the sand which temporarily record the movements of small mammals, insects, or even an occasional reptile.

How is it possible for living systems, all of which depend on water-based chemical reactions at moderate temperatures, to exist and even flourish in the desert where lack of water and lethal temperatures are characteristic?

What features do desert organisms have that allow them to live comfortably in a harsh environment?

Desert Plants

Most plants are composed of at least 80% water. Thus, desert plants can only survive if they can obtain and conserve significant quantities of this vital substance. Some desert plants avoid the problem altogether, by growing only in riparian (stream bank) environments, or close to other areas where long tap roots can usually reach the water table. Trees such as the tamarisk, cottonwood, and sycamore are representatives of this type, and may often be seen growing along the Colorado River, both in southern Arizona and in the Grand Canyon itself. A number of intermittent streams north of Phoenix support an adequate water table, and green trails across the arid desert here often reveal the otherwise hidden presence of ground water.

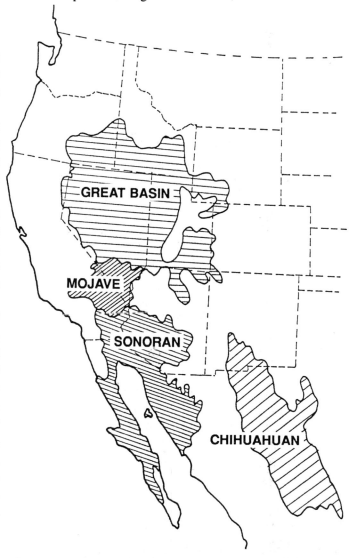

Figure 8.7 *Four subdivisions of the North American desert. The lower elevations in Grand Canyon represent an inclined access corridor between the Great Basin and Sonoran/Mojave deserts.*

There is another way of avoiding arid conditions: many seeds exist in what might be called suspended animation. During this time, before germination, the living germ cells inside the seed can exist without external water. When adequate soil moisture is present, these seeds rapidly germinate, and in a matter of a few days, put forth roots, stems, leaves, and flowers. Pollination occurs, and new seeds are produced before soil moisture plummets to lethal levels. As drought conditions ensue, the parent plant dies, but the seeds, now fully mature, survive until germination is triggered by another rain shower. These plants, called ephemerals, appear only occasionally on what otherwise may appear to be a totally barren desert area.

The presence of moisture is not the only signal for germination for some plants which grow along dry washes. These intermittent streams may be totally dry for all but a few days a year. However, during sudden rainstorms, they are often the scenes of violent but short-lived flooding. Seeds shed along and in such streams are subject to considerable abrasion by rocks and gravel during the flooding. The tough seed coat is scarred or broken, providing the stimulus for rapid germination in the now moist stream bed. Germination in seeds of the ironwood, palo verde, and smoke trees is controlled in this fashion.

Many plants of the desert are extremely drought tolerant and may be able to resist severe desiccation by a number of means. Some have a reduced leaf-surface area through which evaporation might occur. In these, the green chlorophyll needed for photosynthesis is found extensively in the stems. Others may be able to curl the leaf into a roll to avoid direct sunlight exposure. Some may turn the leaf sideways so that only the edge is directly facing the hot sun. Also, the leaves of many desert plants have a thick waxy covering which slows evaporation.

While water is scarce in the desert at most times, there are occasional rains. Some desert plants take advantage of this by quickly absorbing and storing large quantities of water. Perhaps the best example of this is the stately saguaro cactus, which may be seen spreading its giant arms throughout southern and central Arizona. A mature specimen may exceed 50 feet in height and weigh over ten tons. Over 80% of this weight may be water. The saguaro is equipped internally with fleshy cells which can rapidly take up water. The trunk of the cactus has vertical, accordion-like pleats which allow the trunk to expand as water is drawn in through an extensive root system. This stored water is sufficient to keep the saguaro alive through many months of drought.

Some plants meet arid conditions by giving up. Selective die-back of older branches and leaves slows evaporation, reduces the need for water in photosynthesis, and preserves precious water resources. The wide-spread creosote bush is perhaps the most hardy of all desert bushes, surviving in areas where temperatures often exceed 120°F and where rainless periods are often more than a year in length. It uses a combination of features including selective die-back, drought tolerance, and an extensive root system, thus allowing it to be almost the sole inhabitant of the driest desert areas.

Desert Animals

The botanist studying plants has a significant advantage over the zoologist who studies animals. The botanist simply walks up to the plant and begins the study, while the zoologist first has to catch his little critters. But it is precisely this ability to hide and be secretive which allows many small mammals to survive in the desert. It is also this habit of secretiveness which gives the desert its deceptive appearance of lack of animals. Driving the back roads of the desert at night will often reveal just how heavily populated the country really is.

The surface of the desert and the air next to it may become incredibly hot in direct sunlight. Desert nights, because of low humidity and lack of cloud cover, may become very cool—even in places such as Death Valley. However, the temperature a few feet below the surface, in the den of a desert rodent, may remain a comfortable temperature throughout the 24-hour cycle. It should not be surprising, then, to find such small mammals tucked away in the cool subsoil below the blistering-hot surface. Most small desert mammals are nocturnal; that is, they are active primarily at night. Even their mid-day forays are marked by rapid returns to their relatively cool den, before body temperatures can rise to uncomfortable levels. This kind of temperature control is called behavioral thermoregulation. Other types of behavioral thermoregulation which may be practiced by a wide variety of desert animals include shade resting, orientation parallel to the sun's rays to reduce heat exposure, and migration out of arid regions during drought season.

Many animals, like some plants, although living in the desert, do not face a lack of water because they live in or around riparian environments, oases, or man-made lakes. Others may subsist almost exclusively on succulent plants, or insects. An example of a complex ecological association is presented by a large number of fruit-fly species. The fruit fly, long a favorite subject of study of the laboratory geneticist, is found throughout the warmer parts of the world, and many species are confined to the North American Desert. Here, unique species of fruit flies eat select species of yeast which are found in the rotting parts of particular cactus species. The fruit flies, themselves, would rapidly desiccate in the dry, hot desert air, but find shade, water, and food in the rotting parts of the cacti.

One way to exist in a dry environment is to carefully conserve water resources. The kangaroo rat, for example,

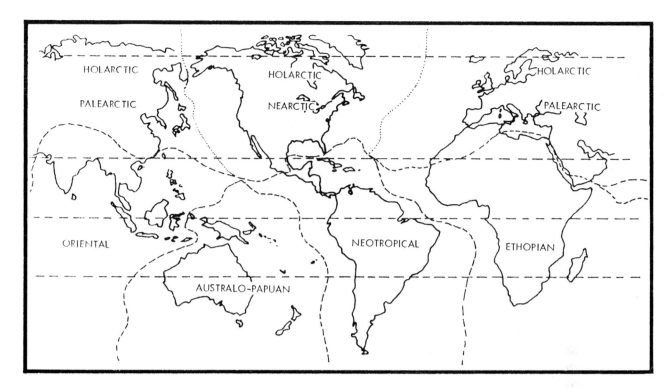

Figure 8.8 *Zoological regions of the world.*

probably never takes a drink in its entire life time. In captivity, it lives nicely on just barley seeds. Carbon dioxide, water, and energy-release are the results of the combustion of fuel. As oxygen combines with carbohydrates, carbon dioxide is formed from the burning of the carbon atom, and water is formed from leftover hydrogen atoms. In like manner, the metabolism which powers living animals produces carbon dioxide, water, and energy-release. This metabolic water, if conserved, is sufficient to meet the needs of many small rodents. These rodents retreat to burrows during high temperature, thus keeping evaporation to a minimum. They have very efficient kidneys, which produce a urine relatively low in water concentration, and they produce very dry feces. Their ability to exist on metabolic water (probably along with licking up some dew) means that they have no need for drinking water.

Some foods—seeds, in particular—are especially good at allowing the formation of metabolic water and, strange as it may seem, they are abundant in the desert. Parts of the North American desert have been found to contain from 5,000,000 upwards to 100,000,000 seeds per acre. One kangaroo rat was found to have over 900 seeds tucked away in his cheek pouches. Caching of seeds appears to be a compulsive habit of many arid-country rodents. In deserts characterized by continually shifting sand and dunes, some insect species live their entire lives under the sand, existing solely on organic matter, including seeds which have blown in and been covered.

Bigger mammals, such as big-horn sheep and burros, which may be encountered within Grand Canyon itself, are sufficiently mobile to gain access to water, at least every few days, but they do have a problem with the heat. While we normally think of hair in animals as a means of protection from the cold, it also provides protection from direct radiation from the sun. The fur or hair of an animal acts as an insulator, slowing heat flow in either direction. These animals, along with camels in the Old World deserts, have the ability to withstand a considerable rise in temperature. This stored heat is then given up at night as the animal cools down.

Distribution of Organisms

Visitors to Grand Canyon quickly recognize the distinct bands of vegetation that are arranged vertically along the descending trails into the inner gorge. For example, the north and south rims in the vicinity of the Visitor Center are characterized by a rich ponderosa pine forest which successively gives way to a pinyon pine-juniper community which extends from the rim down to the top of the Redwall Limestone. Next, a blackbrush community starts at the base of the Redwall and spreads out across the Bright Angel Shale of the Tonto Plateau to its junction with the Tapeats Sandstone. The inner gorge produces talus that supports a variety of desert scrub plants such as sagebrush (upper river), creosote bush (lower river), or saltbush (alkaline soils). Immediately adjacent to the river and extending up tributary streams, there is a riparian community with

/////	TUNDRA
::::	CONIFEROUS FOREST
/	DESERT
\\\	GRASSLANDS
≡	TEMPERATE DECIDUOUS FOREST
////	TROPICAL RAIN FOREST
▓	SAVANNA

Figure 8.9 *Vegetative biomes of North America.*

cottonwood, tamarisk, grasses, and forbs. Such vertical zonation resembles the horizontal floral changes that are seen with changes of latitude from the tropics to the arctic or even other vertical changes in climbing mountains such as Mt. Humphreys near Flagstaff, about 50 miles to the south.

From where did these plants come, and what determines their distribution? The answer to these questions is found in the study of zoogeography and geographical ecology. Large-scale groupings of organisms have been globally placed into five regions, as shown in figure 8.8. These are the Australo-Papuan, Neotropical, Ethiopian, Oriental, and Holarctic. These approximately follow the distribution of the continents. Grand Canyon lies within the Holarctic region and displays examples of coniferous forest, pinyon pine, interior chaparral, desert sage, creosote, and, lastly, riparian woodland.

Two approaches to the classification of biotic distributions were used historically: faunistic systems and ecological systems. The former systems were further developed by different authors into faunal areas, life zones, biotic provinces, or faunal elements according to climatic and physiographic emphases during the 130-year period between 1823 and 1953.

Schouw in 1823 first subdivided North America into geographic units for plants. Allen followed this example using temperature and humidity to separate faunal areas in 1892. In the North, temperature was the primary factor for separating groups, whereas, in the South, humidity became important.

C. Hart Merriam presented a life-zone system between 1890 and 1910. He believed that animal life had dispersed from two great centers: one in the far north (Boreal) and the other in the southwest (Sonoran). These groups could be distinguished primarily by temperature preference.

In 1889, Merriam studied the composition of these communities in Arizona, especially at the San Francisco Peaks and at Grand Canyon along the Old Hance Trail. He drew some generalizations about the life zones, comparing them to the flora that exist in latitudinal bands from the tropics to the arctic. From these bands, he arrived at the six zones (essentially elevational belts) which characterize much of the literature about the Canyon:

Zone	Climate	Plant Community
Arctic-Alpine	Frigid moist	Tundra-like plants
Hudsonian	Cold moist	Spruce-fir on the north rim
Canadian	Warm dry	
Transition	Semiarid	Ponderosa pine
Upper Sonoran	Arid	Pinyon-juniper/blackbrush/ sagebrush
Lower Sonoran	Arid	Creosote bush

Merriam tried to extend this classification system to other regions of North America, but, because there are many exceptions, the scheme became just another generalization about biota.

Biotic provinces were the next concept to receive attention in the period 1911–1943. Kendeigh described a biotic province as a continuous geographic area that possesses a fauna distinguishable at the species and subspecies level from fauna of adjacent areas. The boundaries correlate with topographical barriers.

Quite a different way of thinking about faunal aggregates is to approach the problem from the history and dispersal route of individual members or "elements" of an existing community. Frequently, the species of organisms living together may have come from very different centers of origin. These studies took place between 1930 and 1950.

The modern method used widely to characterize distribution of organisms emphasizes environmental and community dynamics. The biome is the major biotic complex of communities of an area which is recognized by a particular life form and dominant plant species. It includes both transition stages (seres) as well as the stable terminal stage (climax). Nine terrestrial biomes are recognized: temperate deciduous forest, coniferous forest, woodland, chaparral, tundra, grassland, desert, tropical savanna, and tropical forest. The seven most widespread biomes in North America are shown in figure 8.9.

Grand Canyon itself serves as an inclined access corridor between the lower Sonoran hot desert and the higher Great Basin cool desert. Mojave Desert (Sonoran type) species extend along the canyon slopes as far as mile 39 below Lees Ferry. Above this point, Great Basin Desert plants take over. In like manner, riverine species can migrate up or down the riverway according to mobility. Evidence of this was seen after Glen Canyon Dam was completed, causing a change in flows (smaller magnitudes) and temperature regimes (much colder), not to mention sediment loads (dramatic decrease). Tamarisk, an exotic tree, has gained a foothold along the stabilized riverbanks since 1963. On the other hand, several endemic, warm-water fish species have been eliminated, as a result of the cold-water discharge from Lake Powell.

Limiting Physical Factors

Within the Grand Canyon region of Arizona, temperature and moisture are the principal limiting factors for organisms. Because the Canyon, for most of its length, runs east to west, incident solar radiation is pretty much the same except where north- and south-facing slopes provide differences in exposure to direct sunlight. These differences can cause local plant groupings unlike the general populations in that vicinity. Thus, just beneath the south rim, near the trail head at Bright Angel, in sheltered troughs, are Douglas fir stands, while, above them, on the rim, are pinyon-juniper

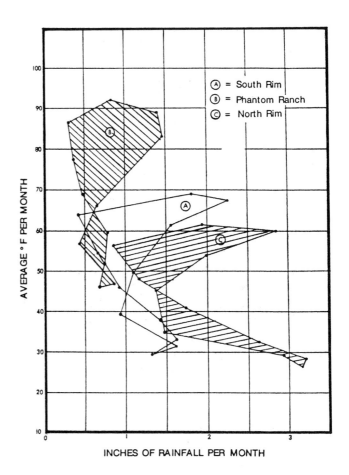

Ⓐ = South Rim
Ⓑ = Phantom Ranch
Ⓒ = North Rim

AVERAGE °F PER MONTH

INCHES OF RAINFALL PER MONTH

Figure 8.10 *Average monthly temperature and precipitation at three stations in Grand Canyon. Temperature and precipitation plotted from table 8.1 show the differences among the three stations.*

Table 8.1 *Grand Canyon National Park temperatures and precipitation (Fahrenheit and inches).*

	South Rim		Inner Gorge		North Rim	
	Temp.	Precip.	Temp.	Precip.	Temp.	Precip.
January	29.5	1.32	46	0.68	26.5	3.17
February	33	1.55	52	0.75	28.5	3.22
March	38	1.38	59.5	0.79	32.5	2.63
April	46	0.93	69	0.47	41	1.73
May	54.5	0.66	77.5	0.36	48	1.17
June	64	0.42	86.5	0.30	56.5	0.86
July	69	1.81	92	0.84	61.5	1.93
August	67.5	2.25	89	1.40	60	2.85
September	61.5	1.56	83	0.97	54	1.99
October	49.5	1.10	66	0.65	45	1.38
November	39.5	0.94	57	0.43	35	1.48
December	31.5	1.62	47	0.87	30	2.83
TOTAL		**15.54**		**8.51**		**25.24**

woodlands. The usually more elevated fir can find cool and moist conditions in the shade comparable to those on the north rim.

Temperature varies with elevation, so there is a dramatic difference between rim-and-gorge temperatures (a drop of about 5,000 feet) at any particular time, which ranges up to 30°F. Not only are average daily, monthly, and seasonal temperatures important, but day-night cycles of warming and cooling control activities of plants and animals. A common hiking experience is to start warmly dressed at the rim in the morning and have to dress down to shorts and a short-sleeved shirt by noon at the river. Campers in the canyon also frequently experience warm rising winds during the day and cool descending winds in the evening, not unlike coastal land and sea breezes.

Because the medium of living processes is essentially water, most terrestrial organisms are faced with either obtaining or conserving water as a daily chore, which arrives from rain, snow, hail, frost, dew, or fog; departing by runoff, percolation, evaporation, or being bound in some form as ice, snow, or organic matter. *Plants* use *transpiration of water* to facilitate circulation of

metabolites, and *animals* use *evaporation* to regulate temperature.

The difference between the amount of moisture in the air (humidity) and the amount of moisture the air could hold under the prevailing circumstances is called saturation deficit.[12] Life is affected by both of these variables in the suppression or acceleration of moisture losses. Tropical plants exist in humid environments, while desert plants experience dry air. The amount of humidity also modulates sudden changes in temperature due to the heat-absorbing characteristics of water. In Grand Canyon, wide ranges in daily temperatures (20°–50°F) are experienced because of the low humidity and frequent lack of cloud cover.[13]

Plants have been classified by their high-to-low water requirements into hydrophytes, mesophytes and xerophytes,[14] and they use moisture in both soil and air for metabolism. The seasonal and geographical distribution of water in precipitation plays an important role in climate, and exerts control over the types of organisms that may exist. When hot temperatures and dry seasons coincide, then a desert can be expected; hot moist seasons support

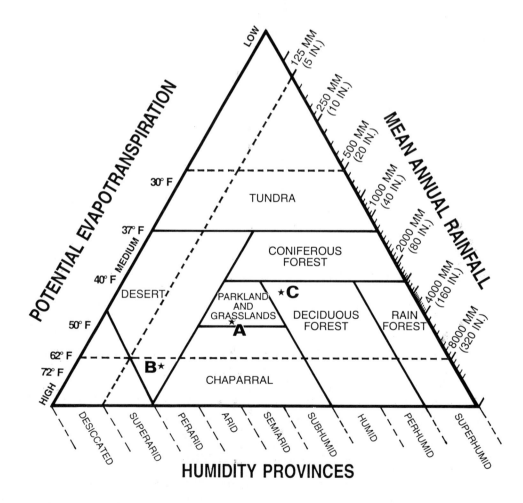

Figure 8.11 *Holdridge diagram for temperature, humidity, and rainfall regions with data for the south-rim (A), Phantom Ranch (B), and the north-rim (C) stations.*

rain forests. Amounts of rainfall in temperate latitudes can be used to predict life forms.

Rainfall (inches/year)	Life Group
0 – 10	Desert
10 – 30	Grassland or Open Woodland
30 – 50	Dry Forest
50+	Wet Forest

Table 8.1 shows temperature and precipitation data for three stations in Grand Canyon. If we plot the temperature-moisture climographs for these three stations (see figure 8.10), we can visualize the microclimates of the three locations. At Grand Canyon Village on the south rim, the monthly rainfall averages about one inch per month, with a total yearly rainfall of 15.5 inches. Two wet periods are seen in the late summer and winter. A modest average yearly range of 40°F (29–69°F) is experienced at this juncture. The north rim shows more rainfall (average 25.2 inches), colder temperatures (26–61°F), and more pronounced rainy seasons. In the gorge at Phantom Ranch, the average annual rainfall is only 8.5 inches, with an emphasis on summer rains. The much warmer temperature range is an impressive 46°F (46–92°F).

Holdridge, in 1947, prepared a system of climatic classification that is a triangular plot of mean annual temperature, mean-annual rainfall, and humidity conditions.[15] Latitudinal and additional overlays are shown to indicate how geographical features would fit into the scheme. The three data points from Grand Canyon field stations have been spotted in figure 8.11 to show how well they fit the predicted biome. The Phantom Ranch data (point B) would imply a desert location which is exactly what is experienced along the adjacent talus slopes. However, due to the Bright Angel Creek, Phantom Ranch itself is a rich tree, brush, and emergent-stream community typical of riparian corridors.

The south rim station (A) lies in a mixed parkland of pinyon pine, ponderosa pine, Gambel oak, and some grasses. The north rim station (C) lies in a transition forest of ponderosa pine, Gambel oak, and New Mexico locust. Although points A and C on the system don't give the refined descriptors, they can be seen to lie in the upper sectors of grassland and deciduous forest, respectively, where transition conditions would be expected.

Life Zone Communities

The following discussion of plant and animal groupings that can be seen by hiking into Grand Canyon is intended to be only superficial, in order to whet the appetite of the novice hiker to examine the living components of this grand location. Many field guides are available to identify the flowers, trees, shrubs, mammals, birds, and reptiles. A good field guide takes the budding naturalist one step farther into knowing the community inhabitants. A summary of the plant communities is shown in figure 8.12, with later figures summarizing each community.

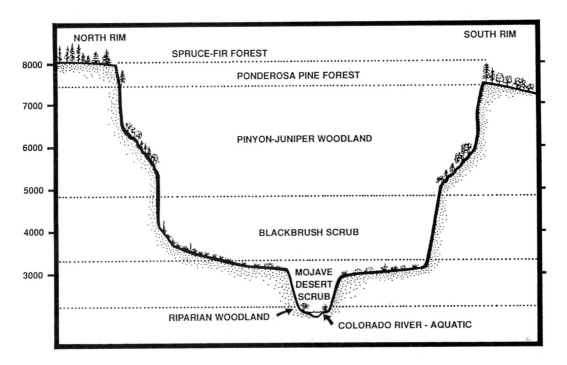

Figure 8.12 *Plant communities of Grand Canyon. Temperature and moisture are the principal limiting factors for organisms.*

Behavior of the community members starts to take on significance when the roles of the players unfold. Seeing this drama requires alert attention to the scenes that appear before the visitor. We only catch a glimpse of what the annual happenings are when we visit for a few short days. But the images we capture as we watch the living cast make us appreciate, all the more, the handiwork of our great Creator God. Now let us examine some of the creatures we might see during our visit.

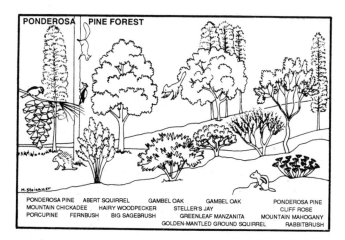

Figure 8.13 *Ponderosa pine forest community.*

Ponderosa Pine Forest

At the south rim near the Bright Angel trail head (elevation 6,960 feet), the plant community might be considered Transition Zone. Here, the ponderosa pine (*Pinus ponderosa*), or western yellow pine, is quite abundant. It can be distinguished by its long (5–11 inches) needles, which come in bundles of three, when compared to the pinyon pine, whose shorter needles (2 inches) come in bundles of two. The large size of the ponderosa and the shape and size of its cones distinguish it from the pinyon pine.

Common associates of the ponderosa pine are the New Mexico locust (*Robinia neomexicana*) and Gambel oak (*Quercus gambelii*), which are found on dry hillsides and slopes. Both are used for browse by deer, whereas quail and squirrels use the seeds of the locust. Other shrubs found in this zone are the cliff rose (*Cowania mexicana*) and Apache plume (*Fallugia paradoxa*), both members of the rose family.

Rodents of this rim community are the tassel-eared Abert squirrel (*Sciurus aberti*) and the golden-mantled ground squirrel (*Spermophilus lateralis*). Abert squirrels utilize the ponderosa bark, cones, and terminal buds as a source of food. While the Abert squirrel spends considerable time building its nest in the pines, the ground squirrel spends its time on the forest floor, usually digging burrows

near rocks and logs. This ground squirrel eats insects, nuts, seeds, and berries.

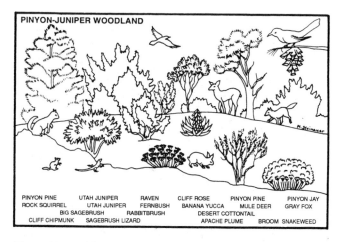

Figure 8.14 *Pinyon-juniper woodland community.*

Pinyon-juniper Woodland

The next zone, which overlaps the rim community and extends down to 4,000 feet elevation, is that of the pinyon-juniper woodland. In addition to the pinyon pine (*Pinus edulis*), the codominant plant species is the Utah juniper (*Juniperus osteosperma*). These two species are the most abundant trees in the Southwest. The juniper has scale-like leaves, a single trunk, and intermediate size (15 feet). It inhabits dry, rocky places.

Smaller shrubs associated with this community are rabbitbrush, big sagebrush, banana yucca, Utah serviceberry, cliff rose, and Apache plume. Rabbitbrush (*Chrysothamus nauseosus*) is a one-to-seven-feet tall evergreen, much branched with erect stems, and found on dry slopes. Big sagebrush (*Artemisia tridentata*) grows up to four feet tall and is usually aromatic. Utah serviceberry (*Amelanchier utahensis*) can be shrubby to six feet, or treelike, up to fifteen feet. The leaves are alderlike; the fruit is blueberrylike, and edible. It is a deciduous shrub found on protected dry slopes and rocky hillsides. Banana yucca (*Yucca baccata*) is found on dry slopes all the way down to Tonto Plateau. The fruit is fleshy and bananalike. A small moth visits the flowers by night to pollinate the self-sterile flowers by laying its eggs in the blossoms. Birds eat the fruit covering, and rodents take the seeds.

Common animals in this zone are the pinyon mouse, rock squirrel, gray fox, mule deer, and pinyon jay. The rock squirrel (*Spermophilus variegatus*) is much larger than other Grand Canyon ground squirrels and is found in rocky areas, where it is active during the daytime. It is a common beggar along the upper parts of the Bright Angel Trail. Its den is an elaborate tunnel system beneath boulders or thick bushes. It lives on cactus, yucca, agave fruit, and juniper berries.

The pinyon mouse (*Peromyscus truei*) is found in bushy and rocky places. It has very large ears, a bicolored tail, and feeds on seeds and nuts.

The most common fox in western America is the gray fox (*Urocyon cinereoargenteus*), a small animal weighing between seven and ten pounds. It is active either day or night and often can be seen trotting briskly among the shrubs and rocky places, and it even climbs trees. Mice, rats, rabbits, game birds, frogs, and domestic fruit are its primary diet.

Usually recognized by its large ears and black-tipped tail, the mule deer (*Odocoileus hemionus*) is a large animal with the bucks weighing up to as much as 400 pounds. It is commonly seen near the rims in small bands and is active at sundown and sunup. It is not unusual to see the deer moving out from Indian Gardens where they have been resting during the day, to feed out on Tonto Plateau during the early evening, on leaves, buds, and tender shoots of green plants. Because mule deer drink regularly, they are always found within a few miles of water.

The pinyon jay (*Gymnorhinus cyanocephalus*) has a uniform blue-gray color and is often found in flocks. Being gregarious, it even nests in colonies among the pinyon and other pines. It prefers pinyon nuts for its food, but will feed on grasshoppers and other insects.

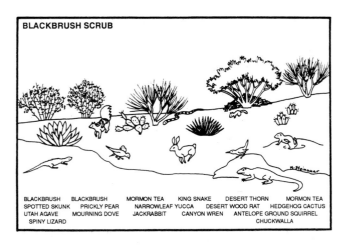

Figure 8.15 *Blackbrush scrub community.*

Blackbrush Scrub

From below the Redwall Limestone down to the Tonto Plateau is found the blackbrush (*Coleogyne ramosissima*) scrub zone. It is commonly found on heavy soil with underlying hardpan. The branches are tangled and often spine-tipped with the leaves having rolled-up margins. It is a dense, low-growing, desert shrub that is

named for the dark gray of the twigs, which turn blackish as they mature. It is found on dry slopes below 5,000 feet, between the creosote-bush zone and pinyon-juniper woodland.

Mormon tea (*Ephedra viridis*) is a shrubby conifer that ranges from the rim to the canyon bottom. Its stems are bright green, with leaves that are small and scalelike at the stem joints and is found on dry, rocky slopes and canyon walls. Another shrub of about six feet in height is the desert thorn (*Lycium pallidum*), whose branches are spiny and sometimes downy. It is found on dry rocky hills and mesas. The fruit, which looks like small cherry tomatoes, is bitter, but edible. Livestock, birds, and other animals use it for food and for retreats or roosts.

Utah agave, or century plant (*Agave utahensis*), a shrub with rigid, fleshy, daggerlike leaves which are up to 15 inches long, is found in scrub woodland from the rim to the canyon bottom and can be distinguished from the yucca, which has fiber strands along the leaf margins, by its terminal spine and spiny edges. It blooms only once, after 15 to 25 years, and then dies, often leaving behind a distinctive 15 to 30 foot flower stock. It forms large colonies in washes and on dry, rocky slopes below 5,000 feet. The seeds can be ground into flour.

On dry mesas and slopes between 2,700–7,500 feet, the narrowleaf yucca (*Yucca angustissima*) is found. It is usually stemless but may, on occasion, have a short stem that lies on the ground. Its fruits were eaten raw or roasted, or were dried for winter meats by the Indians.

Beavertail cactus (*Opuntia basilaris*) is found on the plateau and in the gorge. The gray to purplish pads are flattened (three to six inches long) and spineless, as is its egg-shaped fruit, and the areas where spines are normally found, do have small bristles in reddish tufts.

Grizzly bear cactus (*Opuntia erinacea*) is also found on Tonto Plateau but is densely spined.

Animals common to this zone are the antelope ground squirrel, Desert Wood rat, spotted skunk, jackrabbit, canyon wren, chuckwalla, and common king snake. White-tailed antelope ground squirrels (*Ammospermophilus leucurus*) are pale brown in color, with white stripes on each side of their backs. The tail curls over the back when the animal runs. It can be distinguished from chipmunks of higher elevations by the absence of cheek stripes. It is very active during the day.

A collection of sticks and woody debris among rocks may signal the presence of the desert wood rat (*Neotoma cinerea*). It has a bushy, squirrel-like tail and is nocturnal. Another night forager is the spotted skunk (*Spilogale putorius*). It is smaller than the regular striped skunk and finds shelter in rock heaps or in the burrows of other animals. Crickets, small rodents, birds, carrion, eggs, and some plant materials make up its diet.

The jackrabbit (*Lepus californicus*) is really a hare. Its young are born with fur, eyes open, and ready to move. It lives in the open and rests in "forms" under shrubs, not in burrows or holes. It runs with its ears held flat and with the tail tucked between its haunches. Grass and most vegetable matter, even cactus, are its food.

Among the cliffs and rock crevices, the canyon wren (*Catherpes mexicanus*) finds its home. Its white throat and breast and brown belly distinguish it from other wrens, all of which have a slightly down-curved beak and faint tail banding. It searches for insects near streams, in rock crevices.

The chuckwalla (*Sauromalus obesus*) is common in riparian and scrub communities, where it rests in crevices and is very difficult to dislodge because of its behavior of inflating its lungs to fill the crevice space. It can be recognized easily by its large size and loose folds of skin on the sides of its body. This lizard is herbivorous and feeds upon several desert plants such as the creosote bush, the burroweed, and the indigo bush. Another reptile, the common king snake (*Lampropeltis getulus*), is also found in riparian, scrub, and woodland communities among the rocks and brush. It usually grows to a size of five feet and catches its prey by seizing and constricting it with its body coils. It can even catch rattlesnakes, because it is immune to snake venom. It is active by day and at dusk.

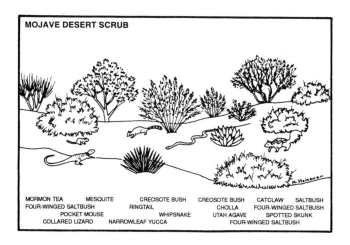

Figure 8.16 *Mojave desert scrub community.*

Mojave Desert Scrub

In the inner gorge below 4,000 feet is a community that is dominated by the four-winged saltbush. Important associates not mentioned above are mesquite, catclaw, ringtail, pocket mouse, collared lizard, and the whipsnake. Four-winged saltbush (*Atriplex canescens*) is common from the rim to

the gorge and often inhabits saline soils. It is a shrub about two feet tall that is gray to white in color. The four-winged bract seed pod is characteristic of the plant. It is used as forage by cattle, sheep, and goats in winter. Deer, pronghorn, and rabbits also use it for food, and its seeds are eaten by several kinds of birds.

Mesquite (*Prosopis juliflora*) is found in the gorge and side canyons, as well as along riparian sandy bottoms. It is a shrub up to 20 feet tall, with straight thorns in pairs at the leaf axils. Its leaves have two stems bearing numerous slender leaflets. The fruiting body is a peapod that comes from a catkin. Catclaw (*Acacia greggii*), another member of the pea family, looks a lot like mesquite. It, too, is a riparian shrub that forms thickets along river streams and dry washes. Branches with recurved spines bear leaves that are bipinnate as above. It is a food source for many species.

The ringtail (*Bassariscus astutus*) is a member of the raccoon family and has a similar, black-and-white, ringed tail. It feeds on white-footed mice, wood rats, sparrows, and manzanita berries. It is nocturnal and holes up in oaks, small caves, or spaces in rock piles. Historically, some have been made into pets and nicknamed "miners' cat."

One of the smallest rodents found in the Canyon is the pocket mouse (*Perognathus intermedius*). This nocturnal mammal inhabits rocky places along the canyon and is characterized by naked soles on its hind feet and by its fur-lined cheek pouches. It is a seed eater, and solitary, in habit, spending its days in burrows, and foraging at night. It hops on its long hind feet, using its tail for balance.

Western collared lizards (*Crotophytus collaris*), as the name implies, have a black-and-white collar and rounded tail. They frequent rocky slopes and canyons, rather than open sand and are frequently seen basking in the sun on large rocks.

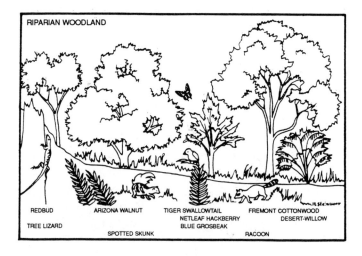

Figure 8.17 *Riparian woodland community.*

Common along stream beds, the whipsnake (*Masticophis taeniatus*) hunts among the rocks, trees and shrubs.

Riparian Woodland

The dominant plants along the banks of the Colorado River and its tributary streams and springs are the tamarisk and Fremont cottonwood. Important associates are the willows and redbud. Animals found here are raccoon, ringtail, spotted skunk, mallard, spotted sandpiper, Lucy's warbler, blue grosbeak, red-spotted toad, and the tree lizard. Only a few representatives will be discussed.

Tamarisk, or salt cedar (*Tamarix pentandra*), has scalelike foliage that appears feathery and drooping. The branchlets are deciduous in the winter. It is a water-seeking plant with an extensive root system along water courses. In the Imperial Valley of California, it is used as a windbreak along some agricultural fields. The Fremont cottonwood (*Populus fremontii*) is a willow-family member that grows quite tall (40–90 feet) and has bright green leaves which are almost triangular in shape. The seeds bear very cottony hairs that give it the name. Rotted cavities in the trunks are used by raccoons. In Indian Gardens, these stately trees and the creek bring shade and a peaceful rustle to tired campers.

A striking sight for the hiker along Bright Angel Trail is the redbud (*Cercis occidentalis*) in full bloom about Easter time. The pink-to-red-purple flowers blossom before the leaves are fully out, giving a bouquet appearance against the black branches and stems. This small tree is found near seeps and springs.

Grizzled gray with black mask and tail rings describes the winsome raccoon (*Procyon lotor*). This nocturnal visitor is found mostly near water and feeds on rodents, rabbits, birds, frogs, insects, etc.

The mallard (*Anas platyrhynchos*) is another riparian visitor that prefers open waters. The male duck has a green head, white collar, and blue wing patch. It is a surface feeder, but may "tip up" to reach some plants.

Another shorebird of interest is the spotted sand piper (*Actitis macularia*). It is a fairly common summer resident along the river. Its teetering behavior is interspersed between short runs. On taking to flight, it makes an arc over the water to some distant shore. It feeds on small aquatic animals and insects. It does not flock, but is rather solitary or in pairs.

The red-spotted toad (*Bufo punctatus*) is olive-green to gray-brown with numerous red warts. It is most active at twilight, breeds in pools and streams, and rests in rock crevices. Hikers at Indian Gardens have great fun spotlighting the various frogs and toads near and in the creek after dark.

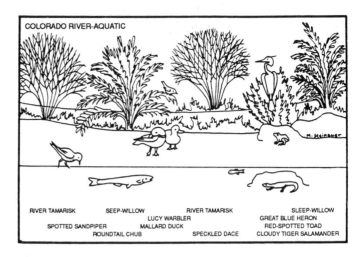

Figure 8.18 *Colorado River-aquatic community.*

Colorado River—Aquatic

Flowing swiftly through the gorge after leaving Lake Powell and on its way to Lake Mead, the river drops 2,200 feet in about 280 miles. It has a large number of fishes and abundant aquatic life within its reach. Three native species—the Colorado squawfish, humpback chub, and bonytail chub—are considered to be endangered species. More than a dozen exotic species have been introduced, such as trout, catfish, carp, and several species of minnows. Rainbow trout, brook trout, sunfish, salmon, and largemouth bass are also present.

Historically, eight species of native freshwater and marine fish were common to the lower river: the desert pupfish, humpback chub, humpback sucker, flannel-mouth sucker, Colorado squawfish, bonytail, ten-pounder, and striped mullet. Today, the variety of fish has increased, primarily as a result of introduction of numerous exotic game and forage fishes which include: black crappie; red-ear sunfish; bluegill; green sunfish; channel and flathead catfish; black, brown, and yellow bullhead; largemouth and smallmouth bass; striped bass; carp; mosquitofish; threadfin shad; golden and red shiner; goldfish; white bass; warmouth; two species of molly; and at least three different species of tilapia. These introductions have severely altered the predator-prey relationships within the lower river to the detriment of the native fish, many of which have either been eliminated from the lower river or have been reduced to such low population levels that continued survival is questionable.

The native fish fauna displayed some of the most bizarre body shapes found among aquatic vertebrates. Much has been written as to how the original habitat must have "selected" these body shapes for survival, yet laboratory studies of flow-and-behavior patterns of these species have not supported one another.

Today, a majority of the native fish which were originally common to the lower basin are listed as endangered, threatened, or extinct by federal and state agencies. In some locations, adult populations are reproductively extinct due to the introduction of exotic predatory fishes.

Research Studies

The following is a review of three research studies conducted in Grand Canyon which are especially pertinent to the creation-evolution dialog. The first two of these studies, the Kaibab Deer and the environmental impact of the Glen Canyon Dam, illustrate substantial changes in biota, yet do not offer the slightest evidence for evolution. The third study, on the other hand, which concerns the fascinating distribution among varieties of the tassel-eared squirrel, has been suggested as evidence for evolution, yet, upon closer examination, fits very well into a creationist model.

In these studies, one is unprepared for the dramatic shifts in populations that were brought on by such trivial disturbances, and that is the point. It is instructive to note that all of our scientific observations establish, not the evolution of new creatures to occupy the disturbed habitats, but instead, the recruitment of taxa from the outside. Some species become extinct, but very few, if any, genera can be shown to have evolved and taken over disturbed or open life zones. Is there a mechanism by which evolution occurred? Our pragmatic science indicates that adaptation is not sufficient, presently, to lead to evolution. The survivors in each example that follows have not become new species.

On the other hand, species that have existed in these habitats continue to occupy them generation after generation. They show every evidence of being substantially unchanged over recorded time, and, hence, demonstrate *stasis* or *conservation*. Although it is difficult to demonstrate the formation of new taxa, it is easy to document the extinction of species associated with the Canyon. This, then, supports the decay principle, in agreement with what can be seen in both the fossil and current records.

Impact of Glen Canyon Dam on Organisms

The Colorado River originates in the headwaters of the Rocky Mountains of north-central Colorado. The Green River, which empties into the mainstream Colorado River in southeastern Utah, originates in southwestern Wyoming. Together, these two rivers are the principal source for water flowing throughout the basin. A single molecule of water travels a total of 1,700 miles from its Green River origins

until it reaches the Gulf of California. During this entire journey, elevation drops over two miles.

This once large, turbid, and warm river system flowed unrestricted for the entire 1,700 miles, through five states. Steamboats once navigated parts of the river carrying supplies to various military outposts along the shores. Today, the river has been divided into an upper and lower basin for purposes of water management. Lees Ferry, Arizona, approximately 15 miles below Glen Canyon Dam (Lake Powell) is the official dividing point for the upper and lower basins. The once-wild river is today regulated by a series of dams constructed after the early 1900's. These dams have changed the seasonally raging torrent into a series of placid reservoirs, connected by a riverway that is smaller, colder, and less turbid than its predecessor. In addition, this change has altered the fish population structure in both basins as well as brought about a fish fauna change in the Lower Basin.

In 1956, the Bureau of Reclamation started construction on the Glen Canyon Dam. By 1980, the 180-mile-long Lake Powell was filled, and the basic character of the Colorado River was substantially changed. Now the flows of water and the quality are considerably different than they were before the dam. Discharge from the hydroelectric plant is regulated by energy demand and legislation. The primary justification for damming the river in the first place was that it would give several western states a means to comply with the terms of the 1922 Colorado River Compact (an agreement between seven states located in the river drainage which split 15,000,000 acre feet of water equally between the upper and lower compact states for industrial and public use). The water is clear and cold, compared with the predam warm and turbid conditions.

Three limiting factors for lotic (flowing-water) ecosystems are fluctuations in water volume, variation in sediment transport, and range in water temperatures. Fall and winter low flows and spring and summer floods characterized the predam regimen. Now, a daily cycle of discharges gives the river a tidal fluctuation. Sediments, deposited in the impoundment, leave the cold, clear discharge water as a suitable habitat for algae growth. Instead of the average 170 million tons of sediment being carried along, the load has been reduced to 20 million tons annually. Consequently, instead of sandy beach building along the shores, there is a tendency toward continued erosion. Temperature ranges have narrowed from 40°–51°F. This is because the 200-foot-deep penstocks take lake water from well below the zone of surface heating and mixing. That deep, cold-water layer is called the lake's hypolimnon.

Since the early 1900's, the native fish population has declined because of two interrelated causes. The first cause was the construction of dams throughout the basin, which caused severe alteration in historic water-flow patterns. These dams regulated the once warm, turbid, high-seasonal flows to an almost continuous reduced flow of cold, clear water. This loss of seasonal-flow pattern reduced adult-fish access to suitable spawning grounds, and all but eliminated necessary warm-fish nursery areas. Habitat requirements for many of these native fishes have been lost or so severely altered they may never be re-established.

The second major cause for the demise of native fishes was the introduction of exotic fish species. This was directly tied to the altered habitat, resulting from dam construction. The new habitat characteristics were thought to be "ideal" for experimental introduction of many different species. Some of these exotic species that were introduced, however, were predatory species, and all needed a good source of forage fish. Unfortunately, the native fish served as this initial source of forage. As the number of predators in the lower basin increased, reproductive success for all species began to collapse. The predators ate not only the native fish, but also their own young. Several reservoirs, today, contain populations of older adult native fish, as well as older adult exotics. The younger-age classes are all but gone, because so many predators are eating just about anything smaller than themselves.

Today, large areas within the lower basin contain drastically altered fish habitat. Much of this altered habitat cannot be restored to its initial condition, and should be considered a total loss for natural propagation of native fishes. However, these areas can be used for maintaining various exotic fish populations.

Within the lower basin, there are a few areas of pristine headwaters where a limited native-fish population still survives. These areas can, and should be set aside, as natural areas for native fish populations and should manage to prevent further exotic introductions. These areas enhance the continued survival of the historic native fauna.

Once the scouring action of the predam flood waters was eliminated in 1963, the verdant belt of streamside vegetation became established. In contrast to the river ecosystem, which is quite simple now, the riparian communities before the dam were quite diverse, with perennial vegetation becoming established on the beaches and shores up to the old high-water mark. Above that mark, the mesquite, catclaw acacia, and Apache plume are still entrenched. Many trees and shrubs are *phreatophytes*, plants whose roots reach the water table. Tamarisk, or salt-cedar, is among the most conspicuous of the phreatophytes, which was introduced into the Southwest from the Mediterranean area before 1900. Since the plants became established, animals have followed and rapidly increased in numbers. Where previously there had been bare ground, rodents, reptiles, amphibians, and small birds now abound in a developing streamside forest. Now, with floods all but gone and food abundant, even beavers are enjoying a made-to-order habitat.

Thus, the presence of the dam has changed the river's quality, quantity, and behavior. These factors, in turn, have led to new biotic communities in and along the river. In addition, man's use of the river has been multiplied in energy production, angler days, and white-water rafters. For the moment, the dam's operating schedule supports these uses, but all that could change, if the power production is shifted to erratic peak-load releases.

Thus, construction of the Glen Canyon Dam has been a catastrophe to certain aquatic and riparian species—both plants and animals which were found in the watershed below the dam. In theory such an environmental crisis might initiate evolutionary events which create new species. However, existing species found in the surrounding habitats fill in the gaps left by species that become extinct or unable to survive in the new conditions. Both extinction (a form of decay) and recruitment (without speciation) are evidences for creation.

Management of Kaibab Deer

Rasmussen[16] made an extensive study of the five biotic communities of the Kaibab Plateau between 1929 and 1931. One important contribution was to estimate the changes in size of the mule deer herd from 1905 to 1938 and to correlate the dramatic fluctuation in numbers to the management practices of the Grand Canyon National Game Preserve, created in 1906 by President Theodore Roosevelt.

The story of the population change as interpreted at the present time is: With the creation of the game preserve, the killing of deer was prohibited. At the same time there was a marked decrease in numbers of domestic sheep, grazed in the area. From 1906 to 1923, government hunters were employed in killing predatory mammals. Total removal (1906 to 1939 inclusive) has been 816 mountain lions, 30 wolves, 7,388 coyotes, and 863 bobcats. . . . This resulted in extermination of wolves and definite reduction in other species. The decrease in competition for forage, the check in natural enemies, and the prevention of killing by man caused an increase in the deer herd. . . [from] 4,000 of 1906. . . [to] 100,000 in 1924. The peak was reached, the range depleted, and the deer population started downhill. There were deaths by the thousands from malnutrition and related causes. The herd has continued to decrease slowly until an estimated 10,000 were present in 1939.[17]

This event is frequently treated as the type example of an eruptive fluctuation that is checked by the depletion of the food. Caughley[18] reviewed the history of this example and concluded that the data on population numbers, as well as correlation to causative factors, were hard to confirm. Nevertheless, he studied the growth-and-decline characteristics of another ungulate in New Zealand, and determined that, indeed, eruptions are "a response to a change in conditions of life, and that the eruption is terminated by modification of habitat by the animals themselves."[19]

Environmental catastrophes frequently upset the balance of animal and plant associations which invariably revert to an earlier stage of development. In an evolutionary picture, such upsets affect the succession of associations, and, could in theory, lead to speciation and in turn evolution. On the other hand the disruption of the mule deer association did not lead to any known evolutionary progression, but rather reestablished a similar mix of preexisting species. Such conservation of species would be predicted in a creation explanation.

Studies of Tassel-Eared Squirrels

Grand Canyon of the Colorado River is of interest to creationists, not only because of its geological features, but also because it represents one of the world's sharpest barriers

Figure 8.19 *Comparison of coloration for Kaibab squirrel and the Abert squirrel. Except for its nearly pure-black belly and its white tail, the Kaibab squirrel (left) is indistinguishable from the Abert squirrel (right). Do these squirrels provide an example of evolution in action?*

to the movement of many land animals. Here, the Colorado River separates the Kaibab Plateau on the north from the Coconino Plateau on the south, by one of the largest canyons on earth. Throughout many of the scattered, high-altitude ponderosa pine (yellow pine) forests of the southwest, one may hear the incessant chatter of the tassel-eared squirrel (*Sciurus aberti*). Because of specific needs for the cones and terminal buds of the ponderosa as a food source, these squirrels, like the forest they inhabit, are characterized by a "patchy" distribution.

In northern Arizona, Grand Canyon acts as a barrier separating two populations of these squirrels. These are shown in figure 8.19. The white-tailed population north of the Canyon (Kaibab squirrel) is confined to the Kaibab Plateau, an area 60 miles long and 35 miles wide, ranging from 8,000 to about 9,200 feet in elevation. The population south of Grand Canyon (Abert squirrel) is found not only in higher areas of the Coconino Plateau, but also in an arc southward into central Arizona, eastward into New Mexico, and northward into the Colorado Rockies. There are also several isolated populations in Mexico.

Because of differences in color between the two populations separated by the Canyon, evolutionists have used this feature as ". . . a classical example of the role of geographical isolation in evolution."[20] Creationists, however, have found reason to believe that the squirrel's distribution and limited color differences are much more consistent with limited change within the populations and provide indirect evidence for a recent origin for the Canyon itself.[21] Animal distribution within Grand Canyon continues to be an important part of creationist studies.[22] The biology and biogeography of tassel-eared squirrels will be surveyed here.

Abert and Kaibab Varieties

In general, the main color features of the typical Abert squirrel (see figure 8.19) include a dark-colored tail, white belly, and a steel gray body. A rufous-brown spot of variable size is found on the back. In particular, the tail is gray on the dorsal side across most of its width and nearly to the tip. The lateral edges are white. The belly tends to be nearly pure white in most specimens, with the color extending to about the edge of the dorsal side.

The Kaibab squirrel is considered to be the most handsome of all squirrels. The flash of its white tail in the green foliage of the ponderosa pine trees belies its presence, as it jumps from limb to limb, or attempts concealment by flattening itself against the top of a high branch. More careful examination of the typical Kaibab squirrel reveals the white tail is streaked with a central line of dark hairs. Except for the nearly pure-black belly and the white tail, the Kaibab is indistinguishable from the Abert squirrel.

Two Varieties/One Population?

The animals studied by Dr. John Meyer[23] were all specimens found in the research collection of Grand Canyon National Park. Most of the animals were obtained from road kills within the park itself. Thus, the two groups of specimens may not represent the full range of variations possessed by the tassel-eared squirrel in Northern Arizona.

White coloration in most populations of Abert squirrels is quite variable throughout most isolated populations. Those specimens found within Grand Canyon National Park tend to be relatively uniform in tail coloration. Tails of the Kaibab squirrels, however, range from almost pure white to nearly as black as those of the Abert. In the 94 museum specimens examined, considerably more abdominal color variation was seen in the Aberts than in the Kaibabs. Abert abdominal coloration was almost pure white in most specimens, but nearly pure black in others. Kaibab squirrel abdominal colors varied from pure black to the presence of a significant number of white hairs seen along the mid-ventral region. In no case, however, did the light color approach that seen on a typical Abert. Nevertheless, the similarities between certain Aberts and Kaibabs are striking.

This is illustrated by Hall's reference to some of the squirrels on the north rim as "Abert-like Kaibabs."[24]

During the examination of the Abert specimens in the Grand Canyon National Park Study Collection, Dr. John Meyer noted a drawer of animals marked "Kaibab-like Aberts." Whereas the average color characteristics for Kaibabs and Aberts show significant differences, it is possible to pick "outliers" in each population that are very similar in coat color. Thus, the "Kaibab-like Aberts" on the south rim show very close resemblances to the "Abert-like Kaibabs" on the north rim. Dr. John Meyer[25] concluded that the south rim Aberts and the north rim Kaibabs form, for all practical purposes, one continuous population. One is left to wonder how long Grand Canyon has been in existence.

A Barrier to Migration

The two rims of the Canyon, although located only a short distance apart and characterized by similar plant and animal populations, present strikingly different climatological environments for the two squirrel populations. Even more striking is the difference in weather between the floor of the Canyon at Phantom Ranch and either rim. The extent of these differences in precipitation and temperature are displayed in figure 8.20. These data indicate dramatic

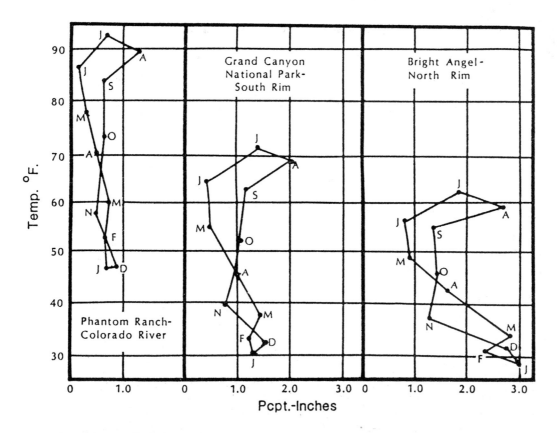

Figure 8.20 *Climatic diagrams relating monthly precipitation to temperature for weather stations located within Grand Canyon at Phantom Ranch and on both adjacent rims. Each point represents data averaged over several decades for the indicated month.*

differences in weather patterns across the width of Grand Canyon. Experienced Grand Canyon hikers know it is quite possible to start an early morning descent from the south rim in mid-winter surrounded by a howling snowstorm, only to meet upward-bound hikers who report moderate temperatures, sunshine, and no precipitation at the bottom of the Canyon. Thus, any small terrestrial mammal accustomed to the high, cool woodlands which attempts to traverse the Canyon, would find itself in a hostile environment at the bottom.

Recency of Barrier

Of major interest in evaluating the isolation of Kaibab squirrels on the north rim is the time factor involved. It is clear, from an examination of the literature, that the evolutionary explanation for the history of the Colorado River in the vicinity of Grand Canyon has not crystallized, and seems unlikely to do so for the foreseeable future. Hunt refers to this as ". . . the grand problem of the Colorado, the age of the Grand Canyon."[26] This problem appears to arise in large part because of the unquestioning acceptance of certain widely divergent, radiometrically inferred dates associated with various parts of the Grand Canyon area. Some evolutionary investigators believe the lower end of the Canyon is about 10 million years of age, while others suggest it may be around 2.6 million years. On the other hand, estimates of the age of the upper part of the Canyon range from seven million upwards to 40 million years. This divergence in dating for upper-and-lower Canyon areas has led to a number of interesting controversies, with highly imaginative and improbable scenarios for canyon formation. Chapter 4 should be consulted for details.

Given the differences of opinion regarding the process of formation of Grand Canyon and the dates assigned to the dissection of the Coconino-Kaibab Plateau by the Colorado River, we are left in a bit of a quandary in trying to arrive at an evolutionarily accepted date for the isolation of the two populations. Surely, however, no evolutionist could argue that two million years is too long a time, so we will arbitrarily choose this as an absolute minimum for significant isolation of the two populations. In view of this postulated minimum time span of separation, it is instructive to look at the forces of evolutionary change which should be working on the squirrels.

Testing the Stability of a Population

Most discussions of the supposed process of evolution center on exceptions to the restrictions necessary for the "Hardy-Weinberg equilibrium population." Volpe (an evolutionist) suggests "An understanding of the Hardy-Weinberg equilibrium provides a basis for recognizing the forces that permit evolutionary change."[27] In view of the importance attached to the Hardy-Weinberg concept by evolutionists, it is instructive to consider this idea, the conditions under which it fails to apply, the implications of this failure, and, finally, how the whole concept relates to the Kaibab squirrel situation.

Simply stated, the Hardy-Weinberg equilibrium population is just a group of interbreeding animals which are not changing from one generation to the next. Such a group of animals would be considered to have a fixed or static gene frequency across time. Because one definition of evolution (actually microevolution to be more exact) is the change in gene frequency from one generation to the next, a Hardy-Weinberg equilibrium population would be viewed as a non-evolving population. Howe and Davis note the significance of the Hardy-Weinberg equilibrium population to evolutionary theory, when they state:

> *The evolutionist uses this stable base from which to launch an argument for change within gene pools. He asserts that the assumptions listed are important precisely because they are impossible to attain in actual populations. For this reason he views the Hardy-Weinberg equations as describing a hypothetical null set or 'non-evolving' population to which real populations may be compared.*[28]

Is the Kaibab Squirrel Population at Equilibrium?

The extent to which the Kaibab squirrels violate the tight restrictions of the Hardy-Weinberg model should give us some insight into the rate at which the population is changing across time. Thus, if the population conforms to all of the restrictions, we should expect a stable gene pool, even across immense expanses of time. On the other hand, if any of the restrictions are violated, we should expect to see progressive changes roughly correlated with the time involved and the degree of restriction violation. Therefore, let us now consider the available information relating to each of the restrictions given by Stansfield in his widely used text entitled *The Science of Evolution.*[29]

1. *Population is composed of a very large number of sexually reproducing diploid individuals (theoretically infinitely large).* National Forest Service personnel have derived a number of population estimates for the Kaibab squirrel, based on various sources. Apparently, for the last several decades, their numbers have averaged somewhere around 20,000, but with considerable yearly

fluctuations. Thus, the population is clearly not infinitely large.

2. *Mating is completely at random.* Given the extent of the Kaibab Platcau and the limited range of an individual squirrel, mating must be much more likely with members of the population in the vicinity, than with those located at some distance. On a higher level of resolution, the squirrels are not even distributed evenly at the local level, for they apparently prefer some ponderosa pine trees to others, based on the highly variable content of turpentine-related chemicals in the sap. Thus, with an erratic distribution pattern throughout the Kaibab Plateau, mating cannot be completely at random.

3. *Alternative genes are adaptively neutral, i.e., there is no selection.* This must hold for all genes within the gene pool. Stansfield[30] questions if any characteristic can be adaptively neutral. Other evolutionists assert that, even if some characteristics were adaptively neutral, it would be impossible to recognize them or their effects. Furthermore, when one compares the different climates faced by the Kaibab and Abert squirrels, it would appear that a number of genes which should be beneficial for one environment would be less than optimal for the other.

4. *The population is closed.* At the present time, this restriction does appear to hold rather firmly because of the unique geographical isolation of the Kaibab Plateau. On the other hand, if one holds a uniformitarian approach to the origin of Grand Canyon rather than a catastrophic origin, one must assume a rather gradual development of the Canyon, which, in its earlier years, would have provided, at best, a partial barrier to the movements of squirrels. Thus, while this restriction now holds rather tightly, it apparently did not always do so.

5. *Mutation is disallowed.* The rare albino form of the Kaibab squirrel is likely the result of a single mutation. Since mutations are considered random changes in genetic material, it can hardly be denied that all parts of the gene pool are subject to this process.

6–7. *Generation overlap does not exist, and all members of the population are of equivalent reproductive age.* The Kaibab squirrel population is composed of animals of all different ages up to a maximum of about 9 years. Thus, this restriction cannot hold.

8. *Production of egg-and-sperm cells is completely normal for all individuals.* It is generally held that sex-cell production always has the possibility for

abnormal production in all sexually reproducing organisms. This restriction, therefore, cannot be valid.

9–10. *Gene frequencies are identical in males and females, and parents make equal contributions to the heredity of offspring.* Not only is this restriction unlikely in any population of sexually reproducing organisms, the presence of sex chromosomes necessarily leads to a violation of these restrictions. This is clear, since the male chromosome is much smaller than the female, thus necessitating an unequal contribution to the offspring.

Of the ten restrictions needed to ensure an unchanging gene pool across generations, at least eight of them clearly fail the test of credibility and supporting data. One (closed population) must have been violated in the early isolation of the population, if the evolutionary scenario is correct. The probability for the eighth restriction (production of egg and sperm cells being completely normal) is vanishingly minute. Thus, it is obvious that the Kaibab squirrels could not possibly have remained genetically stable during their existence; i.e., by the standard definition, they should be "evolving," and doing so at a rather rapid rate.[31] If this is the case, we must ask an important question: Why is it that the differences between Kaibab and Abert squirrels are so minor?

A Proposed Model

How, then, does one account for the Abert-Kaibab complex from a recent-creationist perspective? To attempt an answer to this question, we present a model which is plausible, and which incorporates the objective data in hand. The model encompasses the following features of the tassel-eared squirrel situation in the southwest.

1. High degree of variability in Abert coat color;
2. Presence of Abert squirrels on the south rim and the distinctively (though not uniformly) colored Kaibab squirrels on the north rim;
3. Presence of Kaibab-like Aberts on the south rim;
4. Presence of Abert-like Kaibabs on the north rim;
5. The Grand Canyon as a highly effective isolating mechanism throughout most of its existence.

The proposed model is displayed in figure 8.21. It is suggested that the original colonizing squirrels, being short on predators and long on available habitat, rapidly established themselves in the cool, relatively moist, high-altitude ponderosa pine forests in northern Arizona and other similar areas of the southwest. Increasing temperatures and decreasing moisture began to take their toll on the lower-altitude ponderosa pines. Local populations

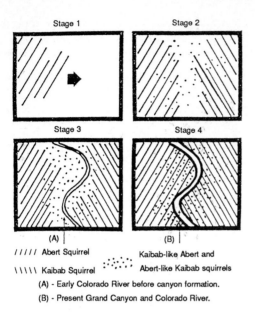

///// Abert Squirrel	Kaibab-like Abert and
\\\\\ Kaibab Squirrel	Abert-like Kaibab squirrels

(A) - Early Colorado River before canyon formation.

(B) - Present Grand Canyon and Colorado River.

Figure 8.21 *Proposed model for the origin of the Kaibab-Abert squirrel complex in the Grand Canyon region. (1) Migration of the Abert squirrel into northern Arizona. (2) Establishment of local sub-populations. (3) Origin of the Colorado River. (4) Development of Grand Canyon as an effective isolation barrier. Similar pattern exists today.*

of Abert squirrels were cut off from their neighbors by the disappearing pine forests of the valleys. Thus, higher-altitude ponderosa pine forests became isolated islands of vegetation, providing an imprisoned habitat for local populations of Abert squirrels. One of the ponderosa pine forest islands that *did* contain the Abert squirrel was found in northern Arizona. Here, small numbers of early immigrants made disproportionate contributions to the gene pools of following generations (Founder Principle), and natural calamities (forest fires, severe weather, predation) arbitrarily altered gene frequencies in small populations (genetic drift). An occasional mutation, although almost inevitably harmful, further altered local gene pools. By this time, stage 2 of figure 8.21 had been reached.

Sciurus aberti aberti flourished on the south, while *Sciurus aberti kaibabensis* thrived to the north. In between was a hybrid population exhibiting varying degrees of coat color characteristic of their parent stock. There was still no Grand Canyon with an established river dividing the populations, but then, by some type of rapid event, the cleavage of the Canyon was established through the

center of the mixed intermediate forms of the squirrel (stage 3). As the Canyon was created through northern Arizona, it provided a highly efficient barrier, keeping the two squirrel populations from sharing gene pools, and, thus, establishing the populations in essentially the pattern seen today (stage 4).

The Non-Evolution of the Tassel-Eared Squirrel

If any group of animals was ever going to undergo significant degrees of evolution from parent stock and, thus, obtain resultant speciation, surely the Kaibab squirrel would be one of the more likely candidates. Supposedly isolated from their neighbors for hundreds of thousands of generations over a period of at least two million years, and significantly violating almost every restriction of the Hardy-Weinberg equilibrium, these organisms, even by creationist standards, should have undergone significant and detectable changes. In reality, all they show are moderate variances, primarily in two coat-color characteristics for part of the population. However, the squirrel is known to have highly variable coat color throughout its range, anyway. Therefore, even the differences displayed appear to be easily accounted for by several mutations and a slight change in gene frequencies in a relatively short period of time—well within the perspective of recent creation.

The failure of any population to meet the restrictions of the Hardy-Weinberg equilibrium appears to be well founded, thus allowing for production of variation within species. This leaves us with the problem of time. How much time has been allotted for violations of the Hardy-Weinberg equilibrium situation? Perhaps the most logical answer for this, and, indeed, for the entire study of geographical isolation of the Kaibab squirrels, is *that time has been the limiting factor.*

The above, therefore, provides indirect evidence, not only for time limitation of the biology of northern Arizona, but also for the actual formation of the Canyon itself. If we are correct in our interpretation of the existing data regarding the tassel-eared squirrel of northern Arizona, we have no other choice than to assign a recent origin to Grand Canyon and its role as an isolating mechanism for the Kaibab squirrel.

NOTES—Chapter 8

1. C. B. Thaxton, "In Pursuit of Intelligent Causes: Some Historical Background," (unpublished paper presented to *Sources of Information Content in DNA, an Interdisciplinary Conference*, Tacoma, Washington, 1988), 24 pp. Thaxton has developed the "uniform-experience" argument of philosopher David Hume: "Since therefore the effects resemble each other, we are led to infer . . . that the causes also resemble; and that the Author of Nature is somewhat similar to the mind of man . . ." (*Dialogues Concerning Natural Religion*, p. 30). William Paley, later, more forcefully used the principle to argue for an intelligent cause. For a recent defense of the biological evidence and reasons for intelligent cause, see P. Davis, D. H. Kenyon, and C. B. Thaxton, *Of Pandas and People: The Central Question of Biological Origins* (Dallas, Texas, Haughton Publishing Co., 1989).

2. R. Augros and G. Stanciu, *The New Biology*, (Boston, New Science Library, 1987), p. 191.

3. A. I. Oparin, "The Nature of Life," *in* R. Blackburn, ed., *Interrelations: The Biological and Physical Sciences* (Chicago, Scott, Foresman, 1966), p. 200.

4. P. S. Messenger, "Biotic Interactions," *Encyclopaedia Britannica: Macropaedia* (15th ed.), vol. 2, p. 1048.

5. Daniel Simberloff, "The Great God of Competition," *The Sciences* 24 (July–August 1984): 20.

6. W. C. Allee, A. Emerson, O. Park, T. Park, and K. Schmidt, *Principles of Animal Ecology* (Philadelphia, Saunders, 1959), p. 699.

7. F. W. Went, *The Plants* (New York, Time-Life, 1963), p. 168.

8. F. W. Went, "The Ecology of Desert Plants," *Scientific American* 192 (April 1955): 74.

9. R. MacArthur, "Population Ecology of Some Warblers of Northeastern Coniferous Forests," *Ecology* 39 (October 1958): 617.

10. W. Linsenmaier, *Insects of the World* (New York, McGraw-Hill, 1972), p. 228.

11. Went, "The Ecology of Desert Plants," p. 71.

12. A. S. Pearse, *Animal Ecology* (New York, McGraw-Hill, 1939), p. 75.

13. S. Aitchison, *A Naturalist's Guide to Hiking the Grand Canyon* (Englewood Cliffs, New Jersey, Prentice-Hall, 1985), p. 16.

14. E. P. Odum, *Fundamentals of Ecology* (Philadelphia, Saunders, 1971), p. 365.

15. L. R. Holdridge, "Determination of World Plant Formations from Simple Climatic Data," *Science*, 105 (1947): 367, 368.

16. D. I. Rasmussen, "Biotic Communities of the Kaibab Plateau, Arizona," *Ecological Monographs* 11 (1941): 229–275.

17. Ibid.

18. G. Caughley, "Eruption of Ungulate Populations, with Emphasis on Himalayan Thar in New Zealand," *Ecology* 51 (1970): 53–72.

19. Ibid.

20. J. G. Hall, "White Tails and Yellow Pines," *National Parks Magazine*, 41 (1967): 9–12.

21. J. R. Meyer, "Origin of the Kaibab Squirrel," *Creation Research Society Quarterly* 22 (1985): 68–78.

22. J. R. Meyer, "The Biological Isolation of Shiva Temple," *Creation Research Society Quarterly* 24 (1988): 165–172.

23. Meyer, "Origin of the Kaibab Squirrel."

24. J. G. Hall, "The Kaibab Squirrel in the Grand Canyon National Park," *Report to the National Park Service* (Mimeographed, 1967).

25. Meyer, "Origin of the Kaibab Squirrel."

26. C. B. Hunt, *Natural Regions of the United States and Canada* (San Francisco, W. H. Freeman, 1974), pp. 425–458.

27. E. P. Volpe, *Understanding Evolution* (Dubuque, Iowa, W. C. Brown, 1982), p. 61.

28. G. F. Howe and P. W. Davis, "Natural Selection Reexamined," *Creation Research Society Quarterly* 8 (1971): 30–43.

29. W. D. Stansfield, *The Science of Evolution* (New York, MacMillan, 1977), pp. 295,296.

30. Ibid.

31. Meyer, "Origin of the Kaibab Squirrel."

Chapter 9

THE ATMOSPHERE ABOVE GRAND CANYON

"The heavens declare the glory of God;
and the firmament sheweth His handywork"
Psalm 19:1

The Night Sky

After sunset, Grand Canyon continues to offer a grand vista—only now, not of itself, but of the sky above. Arizona is renowned for its clear, dry air, and astronomers have long taken advantage of it. Flagstaff, near the south rim of Grand Canyon, is something of an astronomical center, with three observatories located there. On clear, moonless nights at the Canyon rim, the visibility can be nearly as good as anywhere on Earth. Even when conditions are not ideal—for example, during a full moon, or the observer is at the bottom of the Canyon—more stars will probably be seen than are ever visible from large cities.

The locations of stars in the sky change with the seasons, with the hour of observation, and with the observer's latitude. Figure 9.1 locates constellations in the springtime sky during early evening hours. These charts are drawn for April at 9:00 p.m., from the Canyon at 36° N latitude, and may also be used for the midnight sky of February or the early morning sky of December. To use these charts, face in one of the four compass directions, and select the appropriate chart. The horizon is represented by the horizontal line at the bottom. The point directly overhead (the zenith) is represented by the highest point above the horizon.

Many people, upon first observing the night sky, will immediately recognize two constellations: High in the northern springtime sky, nearly overhead and upside down, is the Big Dipper (actually the tail of "Ursa Major," or "Great Bear"). The two end stars of the bowl are the "pointer stars," so called because a line run through them passes close to Polaris, the North Star. Polaris is nearly aligned with the earth's axis of rotation, and, therefore, seems to stand still as the night hours pass. All the other stars appear to rotate around Polaris, and this has served as a valuable navigational aid for centuries. Ironically, since the Big Dipper and Polaris together number eight fairly bright stars, people who can pick them out through city lights often have trouble with a truly dark sky, where many more stars are visible.

The other well-known constellation many will recognize is Orion, the "mighty hunter." Low in the western sky, just after sunset, the dominant constellation of winter is making a final appearance before retiring for the summer. It is in battle dress, fighting off, to its left, Taurus the Bull, readily identifiable by the "V" that marks its head and horns. A little farther to its left (your right) reside the Pleiades, part of Taurus, a delicate, wistful cluster of stars also mentioned twice, along with Orion, in the two references in Job. Its beauty can be appreciated even through common binoculars or a small telescope. It is one of the very few groupings of stars visible with the naked eye that is actually bound together. Constellations, as such, are not physically bound together, but consist simply of stars that happen to be in our same line of sight. Directly above Orion is Gemini, the "Twins," marked by the prominent stars Castor and Pollux. The apostle Paul sailed to Rome on a ship named after them.

Return to the Big Dipper now, and, using the handle this time, "Make an arc to Arcturus." That is, extend its arc counter clockwise about the length of the Dipper, to one of the brightest stars in the sky. Arcturus, too, is mentioned in Scripture (Job 9:9; 38:32). In fact, Arcturus, the Pleiades, Orion, and constellations of the Zodiac, such as Taurus and Gemini, are all used by Job as examples of God's order and power. ("Zodiac" is the proper astronomical term for the constellations the sun seems to move through in the year. The name was borrowed by astrologers for their own superstitious practices.)

Canst thou bind the sweet influences of
Pleiades,
or loose the bands of Orion?
Canst thou bring forth Mazzaroth
(probably, Zodiac) in his season?
or canst thou guide Arcturus with his
sons?
Knowest thou the ordinances of heaven?
(Job 38:31–33).

182

Grand Canyon: Monument to Catastrophe

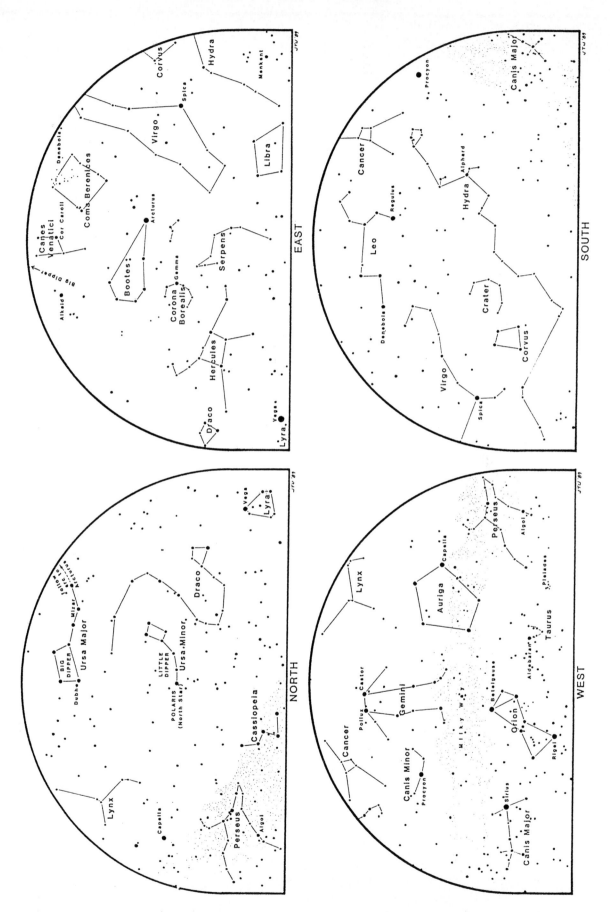

Figure 9.1 *Locations of stars and constellations in the springtime, early evening sky at Grand Canyon.*
(Drawn for April 1 at 9:00 p.m.)

Just to Orion's right (your left) you should be able to see the faint, wispy band of the Milky Way, our own galaxy, which is shaped something like a thin disk. Our planet is located about two-thirds of the way out from the center, in one of the spiral arms (see figure 9.2). All that we can see with the naked eye (except for the faint Andromeda Nebula) belongs to our galaxy, and when we look perpendicular to the plane of the disk, we see nearby stars, with nothing else beyond. When we look parallel to the plane of the disk, however, we see nearby stars, and then many more stars much further away. It is these many stars far away that merge into one another to form what we call the "Milky Way." When you look in Orion's direction you are looking out toward the edge of the galaxy, so the Milky Way is relatively faint. But, if you rise up early on a spring morning at Grand Canyon and gaze at the brighter Milky Way of the southern sky, you will be looking toward the center of the galaxy, the actual center of which is located beyond the constellations Sagittarius and Scorpius (see figure 9.2). The dark spots, or "holes," that give it an uneven appearance, are large dust clouds that block light from stars behind them. Even small binoculars will resolve the Milky Way into a myriad of "tiny" stars, each of them, on average, the size of our sun!

The heavens declare the glory of God;
and the firmament sheweth His handiwork.
Day unto day uttereth speech,
and night unto night sheweth knowledge
(Psalm 19:1,2).

The Composition of Our Atmosphere

The earth's atmosphere is composed of four important gases, the most abundant being nitrogen (N_2), which comprises about 78%. Oxygen gas (O_2) is the second most common ingredient, being present at 21%. Argon gas (Ar) is third, at slightly less than 1%. Fourth, in much lower abundance, is carbon dioxide (CO_2), present at 0.03%. Also present is a variable amount of water vapor (H_2O).

These gases can be divided into two main categories: inert and reactive. Argon is inert and nitrogen is also very

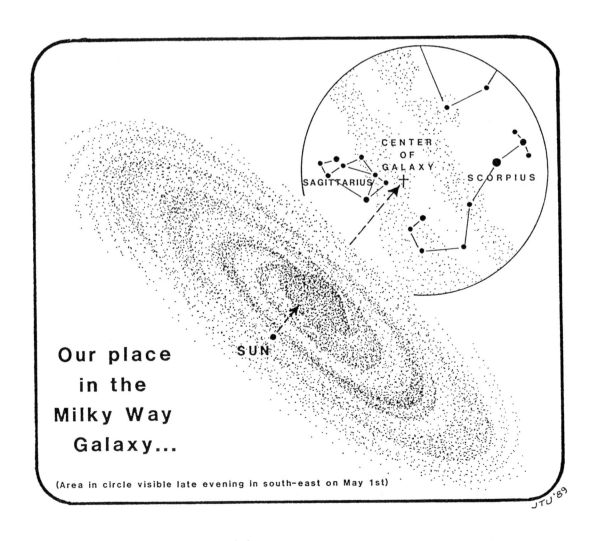

Our place in the Milky Way Galaxy...

SUN

CENTER OF GALAXY

SAGITTARIUS

SCORPIUS

(Area in circle visible late evening in south-east on May 1st)

JTU '89

Figure 9.2 *Diagram for locating the sun's place within the Milky Way Galaxy.*

inactive. These enter into very few chemical reactions. It is, indeed, fortunate that nitrogen gas does not readily combine with oxygen; otherwise, we could have an ocean full of nitric acid!

Oxygen is the most common reactive gas in our atmosphere. The presence of abundant oxygen is the feature which most distinguishes our atmosphere, for oxygen in more than trace amounts has not been discovered in the atmosphere of any other planet.

Unlike nitrogen, oxygen readily enters into reactions with other gases, with organic compounds, and with rocks, and the present level seems to be optimum. If we had more oxygen, combustion would occur more energetically. Rocks and metals would weather faster, and life could be adversely affected. If oxygen were less abundant, respiration would be more difficult, and we would have a decreased quantity of ozone gas (O_3) in the upper atmosphere, which shields the earth's surface and living things from deadly ultraviolet rays.

Carbon dioxide is also a reactive gas which forms an essential part of our atmosphere. This gas is required by plants, serves to effectively trap the sun's radiation, and mixes with water to form an acid which dissolves rocks to add important nutrients to the ocean. Without a constant supply of carbon from the atmosphere, life on Earth would be impossible.

Important as carbon dioxide is to the present earth and life, it comprises only 0.03% of our atmosphere! This minute amount, however, seems to be near the optimum value. If we had less carbon dioxide, the total mass of terrestrial and marine plants would decrease, providing less food for animals; the ocean would contain less bicarbonate, becoming more acidic; and the climate would become colder due to the increased transparency of the atmosphere to heat. While an *increase* in atmospheric carbon dioxide would cause plants to flourish (a beneficial circumstance for the farmer), there would be some unfortunate side effects. For example, a fivefold increase in carbon dioxide pressure (the optimum level for organic productivity) would, alone, cause the average world surface temperature to be a few tens of degrees Fahrenheit warmer!

Water vapor (H_2O) in trace amounts is also a component of our atmosphere. Just as with carbon dioxide, water vapor absorbs the sun's heat radiation and serves to raise the temperature of the lower atmosphere, where, today, most of the water vapor occurs. Clouds, which condense from the atmosphere's water vapor, serve as signposts of the weather. Rain produced by clouds is an essential element of the earth's water cycle. A permanent reserve of *liquid* water, a very unlikely occurrence in space, is known to exist only on our planet.

The uniqueness of our atmosphere can be appreciated by considering our two nearest neighbors in space: Venus

has an atmosphere composed largely of carbon dioxide, but at one hundred times the pressure of our atmosphere, and with a surface temperature of 880°F (470°C); Mars also has an atmosphere of essentially pure carbon dioxide, but with only one-one hundredth the pressure of our atmosphere. Very turbulent winds occur on Mars, and the night temperature drops to as low as -99°F (-73°C). Creationists recognize that God has expressed His intelligence and design in making our atmosphere.

How the Sun Heats Our Atmosphere

Radiation

The earth is almost a sphere. The diameter across the equator is only 0.3% longer than the diameter from the North Pole to the South Pole, and usually, we can ignore the difference. Because of this, the average angle between sunlight and the ground changes from latitude to latitude. In figure 9.3, it is noon at places on the earth's surface designated by A, B, and C; these points are receiving the maximum intensity of sunlight they will receive on this day. The stations on the right, D, E, and F, are receiving no sunlight at all; they are experiencing local midnight. But, do A, B, and C get the same amount of light and solar energy? At point A, the sun is overhead, and the light intensity is great; at C, the rays of the sun just graze the surface, and the amount of light received is very small. This figure is drawn for March 21 or September 23—times at which the equator gets most of the light at local noon and the poles receive the least. This distribution of the sun's energy is true only for March 21 and September 23. At other times, other latitudes may get more radiation than

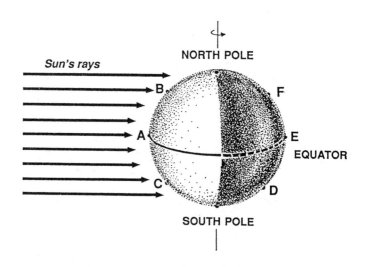

Figure 9.3 *Angles of the sun's rays at positions on Earth.*

the equator. Over the year, however, the *equator* gets the *most radiation*, and the *poles* the *least*. This simple difference is the basic cause of large-scale atmospheric motions, and, therefore, of the traveling weather systems that course our planet.

The reason the motion of the atmosphere is linked to these temperature differences can be explained through an analogy of the heating in a room. We know, by the drift of smoke across a room, or the rustling of curtains, or the feel of a faint draft on our faces, that radiators produce weak circulations of air in a closed room. The air in contact with the hot surfaces of the radiator is heated, expands, and rises, and cooler air moves in to replace it. The cause of this very small-scale wind circulation is differential heating, which means that one portion of air in the room is heated more than another, thereby producing temperature and pressure differences that lead to acceleration of the air and the production of winds. On a much larger scale, the complicated circulations of the atmosphere also owe their existence to differential heating, where the sun is the radiator and the entire atmosphere is the room.

So far, we have not explored the role of terrestrial radiation. The temperature of the atmosphere near the ground depends on a balance between energy *gained* and energy *lost*. These two components of the radiation are illustrated in figure 9.4, which shows how the mean-annual-radiation budget changes with latitude. Obviously, the tropics get much more solar radiation than do the poles. (The radiation level at the poles does not drop to zero because, during its summer, each pole receives quite a bit of radiation.)

The outgoing terrestrial radiation does not show nearly as much variation with latitude as does the incoming solar radiation. The hotter an object, the more radiation it emits, and, indeed, the tropical regions of the earth are emitting more radiation than the polar regions. The difference is not very pronounced, however, because most of the long-wave radiation that escapes to space is emitted by the atmosphere, rather than by the ground. At the levels in the atmosphere from which the radiation can escape out to space, there is not a pronounced change in temperature with latitude.

There is a striking discrepancy between the two curves of figure 9.4. The tropics receive more radiative energy than they lose, whereas the poles lose more than they gain. If radiation were the only means of transporting heat, the situation could not remain long as it is; the tropics would warm in response to all the excess energy received, and the poles would cool even further. Clearly, there must be some mechanism other than radiation to transport energy from the tropics where there is a surplus, to the high latitudes where there is a deficit. This transport of heat is accomplished by both the winds in the atmosphere and the

currents in the oceans. In the atmosphere, the major transport occurs in cyclones and anticyclones. These circulatory-wind systems act as giant eddies in global circulation, mixing cold, dry air from the polar regions with warm, moist air from the tropics. In the portion of these eddies in which the winds are blowing poleward, the air is warm and moist. On the other side of the circulation, where the winds are blowing equatorward, the air is cool and dry. Therefore, even though there is little net flow of air poleward or equatorward, there is a systematic transfer of heat and moisture from low-to-high latitudes.

Seasons

Even those who have not traveled extensively know that the temperature variation between the tropics and the poles is not as extreme in summer as in winter. Traveling cyclonic storms that give us much of our weather is one of the important mechanisms for transporting surplus energy from the tropics to the polar regions. These storms are not as severe in summer as in winter. This points to the decreased temperature variation with latitude in the summer. Thus, if we know why the latitudinal variation of temperature changes with the season, we have a basis for understanding the seasonal variation of storms.

The seasons are caused primarily by the motion of the earth around the sun and the tilt of the earth's axis of rotation. To begin with, the earth revolves around the sun in an ellipse (nearly a circle), as illustrated in figure 9.5. Here, the ellipse is exaggerated to emphasize the characteristics of an elliptical orbit. The sun is at a focus of the ellipse, so both the maximum and minimum distances between the earth and sun occur when the earth is located on the major axis. Minimum distance, perihelion (Greek for near the sun), occurs around January 3; maximum distance, aphelion (Greek for away from the sun), occurs about six months later. The obvious result of this difference

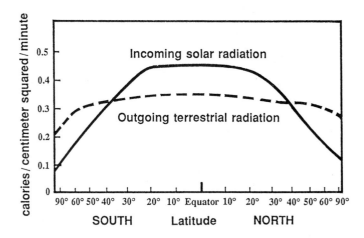

Figure 9.4 *The amount of incoming and outgoing radiation depends on latitude.*

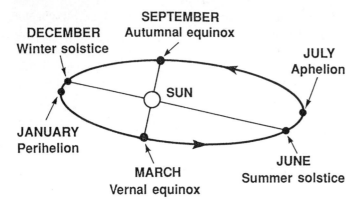

Figure 9.5 *The earth's changing position relative to the sun throughout the year.*

in distance is that July should be colder than January. Yet it is not—at least for people in the Northern Hemisphere. So the changing distance between the earth and sun cannot be the main reason for seasonal change. For many purposes, we can minimize this difference in distances—it is only about 3.5%. Considering that the intensity of radiation varies as the inverse square of the distance from the source, the entire earth gets about 7% more radiation from the sun in January than in July. However, if we are to make accurate calculations, we should take this difference into account. For example, if summer in the Northern Hemisphere occurred at perihelion, the summer would be hotter. Also, in that case, winter would be at aphelion, and winters would be colder. Therefore, seasons in the Northern Hemisphere would be more severe than they are at present.

In figure 9.5, we note another consequence of the elliptical shape of the earth's orbit: The distance the earth has to travel from the beginning of spring (March 21) to the beginning of autumn (September 23) is longer than the distance from the beginning of fall to the beginning of spring. Not only that, but Johannes Kepler showed long ago that the earth travels more slowly when its distance from the sun is greater than when its distance is less. Therefore, in the Northern Hemisphere, the total length of spring and summer is substantially longer (about a week) than it is in fall and winter. If you do not believe this, count the number of days from March 21 to September 23 and compare it with the number of days between September 23 and March 21. In the past, this difference in the length of the seasons has been as much as a month, so, we in the Northern Hemisphere have nice long springs and summers. We must remember, though, that the seasons are reversed in the Southern Hemisphere, which, therefore, has relatively short springs and summers.

Now we come to the real reason for the difference between seasons: The plane of the earth's equator is not parallel to the plane of the earth's orbit. Instead, there is an angle between the plane of the equator and the plane of the earth's orbit (also called the ecliptic). This angle, which

has the impressive name "obliquity of the ecliptic," is 23.5°.

As the earth revolves around the sun, its axis points in the same direction in space. Figure 9.5 shows the earth in four positions: on March 21, June 22, September 23, and December 22. On June 22, the Northern Hemisphere is directed toward the sun. The North Pole is in sunlight all day, and the South Pole is shaded all day. In the Southern Hemisphere, days are short, and the sun is never far from the horizon. Therefore, all points in the Northern Hemisphere get more sunlight on June 22 than the corresponding points in the Southern Hemisphere. This date is called the summer solstice, or "sun-stand-still." The sun "stands still," in the sense that it ceases its daily northward migration in the noon sky, hesitates, and then heads back toward the southern sky.

Why the Sky Is Blue

Have you ever asked yourself why the sky is blue, why clouds are white, and why sunsets are red? The explanation lies in the selective scattering of different wavelengths of light by various-sized particles in the atmosphere. Electromagnetic radiation is composed of wavelengths from very short waves (gamma rays) to very long waves (radio waves). Near the middle of the electromagnetic spectrum are the wavelengths we experience as light (0.4–0.7 micron). The short wavelengths of light are blue; the longer wavelengths are red. When light from the sun intersects our atmosphere, some wavelengths are scattered laterally by molecules of gas. Because of their small size, oxygen and nitrogen molecules scatter blue light effectively, but allow the remainder of the light to travel to the earth's surface relatively unimpeded. The blue light is then reflected by other oxygen and nitrogen molecules to our eyes from the entire sky, making the sky appear blue.

If the gas in our atmosphere were composed of larger molecules, it would probably be a different color. For instance, on Mars, where the atmosphere is composed of carbon dioxide, the sky would appear red, because carbon dioxide molecules are larger and more likely to scatter red light. On the moon, where there is practically no atmosphere, the sky appears black, because there is no scattering.

Our sky appears reddish in the morning and evenings, because the light from the sun must travel greater distances through the atmosphere to reach our eyes along a path tangent to the earth's surface. When light travels greater distances through the atmosphere, more of the *red* light is scattered in addition to the *blue*. More dust and water vapor are also present near the ground, which is more effective in scattering red light. The presence of clouds in the evening sky enhances the beauty of the scene, by reflecting the red light from various shapes.

In general, when direct light from the sun is reflected by clouds, there is little selective scattering of light into different wavelengths, because cloud particles are so much larger than gas molecules. These large cloud droplets or ice crystals scatter and reflect light equally at all wavelengths, producing white clouds against a blue sky. Such beauty is evidence of God's goodness. Only a loving Creator would make provision of food for our souls as well as food for our bodies.

Summary

We have seen in this section so far that the difference in incoming-and-outgoing radiation between the poles and the equator causes climate-and-weather patterns over the surface of the earth. We have found that the different quantities of radiation received as the earth orbits the sun with a fixed axis oriented in space causes the seasons. We have further explained why the sky is blue, why clouds are white, and why sunsets are red. Next, we are going to focus on the movement of air over the globe, called the "general circulation," and how it is related to differential heating, caused by radiation effects.

General Circulation of Our Atmosphere

Pressure-and-temperature variations result in two kinds of motion in our atmosphere: (1) the movement of air in ascending-and-descending currents (vertical motions) and (2) the horizontal flow of air known as "wind." We will deal mostly with the horizontal flow of air, and treat the movement of air in ascending-and-descending currents only briefly.

It is difficult to distinguish between cause and effect of wind, pressure, and temperature because of their close interrelationship. Actually, wind affects the very thing that causes it, in a never-ending struggle to obtain equilibrium—just as the ocean tends to maintain a constant level. Wind occurs because there are horizontal-pressure differences in the atmosphere. But horizontal-pressure differences are primarily the result of uneven temperature distribution. On the other hand, wind very definitely affects both the horizontal and vertical distribution of temperature. It also is the main mechanism through which the mass (weight) of the atmosphere is redistributed, thus causing the pressure to change. As the transportation agency for water vapor, wind has an important effect on the formation of fogs and clouds and on the production of precipitation. The term "circulation" used in this discussion refers simply to the movement of air relative to the earth's surface.

Because our atmosphere is fixed to the earth by gravity and rotates with the earth, there would be no circulation if some force or forces did not upset the atmosphere's equilibrium. Also, the pressure exerted by the weight of the atmosphere would be the same over the entire earth (assuming a common-reference level such as sea level). But sea-level pressure does vary considerably, both with time and location. Pressure tends to be lower than standard in some areas and higher than standard in others. Areas where pressure tends to be relatively high or relatively low, change with the season. In India, for example, a low-pressure area forms over the hot land during the summer months, but disappears and reforms over the warmer ocean when the land cools in winter. Balloons and automobile tires burst when over inflated, because pressure tends to equalize itself. Air moves from the broken balloon or automobile tire to the area surrounding it. In other words, the air moves from an area of high pressure to an area of lower pressure. But why is the pressure of the atmosphere higher in one place than another? The low-pressure area in India, in summer, is evidence that these differences in pressure are closely related to differences in the amount of heat.

The sun heats the earth's surface unevenly. The most direct rays of the sun strike the earth in the vicinity of the equator, thus heating equatorial regions much more than it does the polar regions. In addition, equatorial regions re-radiate to space less heat than is received from the sun, while the reverse is true at the poles. Yet, the equatorial regions do not continue to get hotter and hotter, nor do the polar regions get colder. The only plausible explanation is that heat is transferred from one latitude to another by the actual transport of air.

A popular method of illustrating what is often regarded as the basic cause of air movement is presented in figure

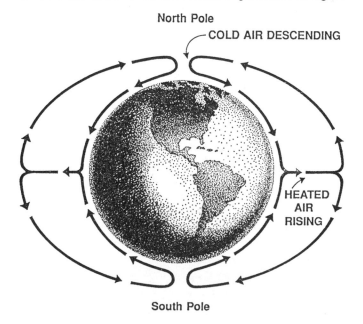

Figure 9.6 *Theoretical air movement if the earth did not rotate.*

9.6. Here is theorized what the atmosphere's circulation would be if the earth did not rotate and had a uniform surface. As the air near the equator is heated, it becomes less dense. The heated air rises and flows away, resulting in lower atmospheric pressure than that in the surrounding area, where the air is more dense because of its cooler temperature. Thus, the air from the north and south moves toward the equatorial low-pressure belt (the equatorial trough), forcing the warm air upward. The cooler air, in turn, becomes warm, is forced to rise, travels aloft toward the poles, and returns along the earth's surface to the equator in a never-ending process.

Accepting the fact that the earth does rotate and its surface is not uniform, let's examine the more important ways in which the simple circulation pattern in figure 9.6 is modified.

Coriolis Force

The rotation of the earth brings about an apparent force on the atmosphere which deflects the wind along its direction of travel toward the right in the Northern Hemisphere, and toward the left in the Southern Hemisphere. This deflective force, called the "Coriolis Force," can be illustrated as follows: Start rotating the turntable on a phonograph record player; then, with the use of a ruler and a piece of chalk, quickly draw a "straight" line from the center to the outside edge of the rotating turntable. To the person drawing the line, the chalk traveled in a straight line. If the turntable is then stopped, it can be seen that the line drawn on it is not straight, but is curved, as indicated in figure 9.7.

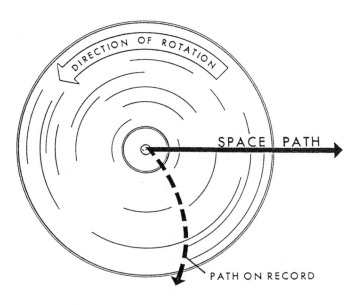

Figure 9.7 *Deflective force due to rotation of a horizontal plane.*

Similarly, air moving a considerable distance over the earth is deflected, because of the spinning of the earth on its axis. In fact, any free-moving body is deflected as it moves over the earth. Viewed from some point in space, the free-moving body would appear to follow a straight line. To one stationed on Earth, however, its path would appear to be a curve. Hence the "force" is only apparent, but the deflection is real, as far as we on Earth are concerned.

With the discussion limited to the Northern Hemisphere, the Coriolis Force may be applied to a simplified pattern of circulation: As the air is forced to rise and moves northward from the equator, it is deflected toward the east; by the time it has traveled about a third of the distance to the pole, it is no longer moving northward, but eastward. This causes the air to pile up in the so-called "horse latitudes" (around 30° north latitude), and produces a high pressure area. Air moving southward out of the horse latitudes is deflected toward the west, producing the northeast trade winds. Wind direction is always stated as the direction from which the wind is blowing.

In the polar regions, a similar process is in operation, with the southward-moving polar air being deflected toward the west to become an east wind. Air is forced northward from the high pressure area near 30° N. latitude and is deflected toward the east to become a west wind, thereby producing the so-called "prevailing westerlies" of the middle latitudes. When this air meets the colder polar air, it moves up over the colder air, producing an accumulation of air in the upper latitudes. The cold polar air, as a result, is forced to break out spasmodically in waves which surge toward the equator, reducing the accumulated pressure. This is called a "polar outbreak," or "cold wave." The boundary zone where the wedge of cold polar air and the warmer air of the prevailing westerlies come into contact is called the "polar front."

Pressure Gradient Force

As previously indicated, air tends to flow from high pressure to low pressure. This flow would be direct, if this were the only force operating. Wind speed increases as the pressure gradient (change of pressure with distance) increases. Spacing of isobars on surface-weather charts and contours on constant-pressure charts, therefore, gives a rough indication of wind speeds. When they are close together, the pressure gradient is strong, and wind speeds are high.

The deflection of air as a result of the Coriolis Force tends to counterbalance the horizontal pressure gradient force. There is a tendency, therefore, for air to flow parallel to the isobars and contours, rather than directly from high pressure to low pressure. Assume that straight parallel isobars are running in a west-east direction with low pressure to the north. The pressure gradient force starts the air moving northward from high to low pressure, but, at the same time, the Coriolis Force begins to push the air particles to the right of their path, or toward the east. When the air is blowing parallel to the straight isobars, the Coriolis Force is balanced by the pressure-gradient force.

Friction

Friction tends to retard the air movement. Since the Coriolis Force varies with the speed of the wind, a reduction in the wind speed by friction means a reduction in the Coriolis Force, which results in a momentary disruption of the balance. When the new balance, including friction, is reached, the air blows at an angle across the isobars from high pressure to low pressure. This angle varies from 10° over the oceans to as much as 45° or more over rugged terrain. Frictional effects on the air are greatest near the ground, but the effects are also carried aloft by ascending currents. Surface friction is effective in slowing down the wind as far up as to about 1,500 to 2,000 feet above the ground. Above this level, the effect of friction may be considered negligible, for all practical purposes. Therefore, air about 2,000 feet or more above the ground tends to flow parallel to the isobars.

Centrifugal Force

Isobars and contours are curved around pressure systems. This curvature creates centrifugal force on the movement of air, causing a tendency for the air to flow outward from the center of these systems. The effect of this force is to increase the speed of wind in high-pressure areas and decrease it in low-pressure areas. Other forces in operation, however, usually more than compensate for this effect, since the wind near high-pressure centers is usually light and the wind near low-pressure centers is typically strong. The strength of the centrifugal force increases with wind speed and decreases as the radius of curvature increases.

Vertical Air Motions and Temperature Distributions

Air tends to move horizontally because the atmosphere is normally stable, and pressure forces direct the air to move in a horizontal direction. However, while moving horizontally, the air also may be moving upward slightly, if it is in a low-pressure region, and downward slightly, if in a high-pressure region. When air ascends, it expands and becomes cooler, thereby enabling it to hold less water in vapor form. When air descends, it is compressed and becomes warmer, thereby increasing its capacity to hold water vapor. Consequently, rising air near low-pressure regions is cloudy, and descending air near high-pressure regions is clear. Air near fronts or clouds can experience rapid vertical motions, but these are limited to small areas.

When hiking Grand Canyon, one quickly becomes aware of the vertical temperature distribution in the atmosphere. When near the rim of the Canyon (7,000 feet) in the spring, the average temperature at night is about 30°F, at the bottom of the Canyon (2,000 feet) the average night-time temperature is about 60°F. During the day, the average temperature at the rim is about 60°F and at the bottom, about 90°F. This is an average difference of about 30°F between the top and bottom of the Canyon, or about 6° per every 1,000 feet. Why does this temperature distribution occur, and why doesn't all the warm air at the bottom of the Canyon rise to the rim?

Before we attempt to explain this phenomenon, let us say that this effect is common to the entire atmosphere in the lowest 30,000 feet or so. Why are the mountains cooler than the lower elevations? Because the air is cooler at higher altitudes. When we fly in modern jet aircraft at 40,000 feet, the captain will frequently announce that the temperature outside the cabin window is -40°F or so. One will frequently see ice form on the window or the wings of the aircraft at these altitudes. Only during unusual conditions will the air temperature increase with altitude. When it does, we call this an inversion. Under these conditions, the air is extremely stable, no clouds form, and the winds are very light. In the Los Angeles basin, smog becomes trapped under inversions, and an alert may be called.

Now, the reason the temperature in the atmosphere normally decreases with elevation is because of a principle called hydrostatic equilibrium. A parcel of air at a given level in the atmosphere has a density or weight determined by the pressure and temperature at that level. If the parcel of air is displaced upward a small amount, its temperature will decrease slightly because it has expanded as the pressure decreases. If the temperature of the parcel of air at its new level is colder than the surrounding air, it will be denser, or heavier, and will sink back to its original level. This condition is known as "stable air." If, on the other hand, the temperature of the parcel of air at its new location is warmer than the surrounding air, it will be less dense, or lighter, and will continue to rise. This condition is known as "unstable air."

The distinction between "stable air" and "unstable air" occurs when the variation of temperature with elevation exceeds a value of about 6°F per 1,000 feet. If a parcel of dry air is lifted 1,000 feet, it will be cooler by about 6°F. When the atmosphere is colder than a 6°F difference at the new level, the parcel will be warmer than the surrounding air, and become "unstable." This leads to vertical air motions, the formation of clouds, and precipitation. Most of the time, the atmosphere has a temperature distribution close to that of dry air which is lifted vertically. This condition is caused by the atmosphere continually adjusting to small-scale air motions, radiation effects, and pressure effects. Thus, the temperature at the bottom of the Canyon is typically about 30°F warmer than that at the rim, although on some days it could be somewhat different. Consequently, warm air at the bottom of the Canyon will not rise to the rim, because the air is "stable."

Other Effects

In the discussion of the general circulation, the earth thus far has been considered as a uniform, smooth globe. This circulation is complicated considerably by the irregular distribution of oceans and continents, the relative effectiveness of different surfaces in transferring heat to the atmosphere, irregular terrain, the daily variation in temperature, the seasonal changes, and many other factors. These factors, together with the distribution of solar radiation and the rotation of the earth, lead to the establishment of semipermanent regions of high and low pressure, which control the general atmospheric movements in their particular regions. These semipermanent highs and lows are important to our basic understanding of the atmosphere's circulation. Of far greater significance, however, are the moving lows (migrating cyclones) and highs (migrating anticyclones) which are associated with the rapid changes in weather so characteristic of the middle latitudes.

Cyclones and Anticyclones

Persons living in the temperate zone and farther north know that their weather is changing almost constantly with the alternate passage of cyclones (low-pressure systems) and anti-cyclones (high-pressure systems). These migrating systems, on the average, move from west to east with the prevailing westerly winds. They are accompanied by wind shifts, and, with some exceptions, large and rapid changes in temperature, and broad moving areas of precipitation. Migrating cyclones and anticyclones furnish the most important means through which heat is exchanged between high and low latitudes.

Cyclones are usually a few hundred miles in diameter. Anticyclones are generally larger and often more elongated—the longer axis extending for 2,000 miles or more, in some cases. In the Northern Hemisphere, air flows counterclockwise around cyclones (low-pressure systems) and clockwise around anticyclones (high-pressure systems), and a person with his back to the wind has low pressure on his left. The opposite is true in the Southern Hemisphere, where the air flow around cyclones is clockwise, the flow around anticyclones is counterclockwise, and a person with his back to the wind has high pressure on his left.

Wind speeds tend to be considerably greater in cyclones than in anticyclones, but there are notable exceptions, especially in some geographical areas. For example, polar outbreaks are accompanied by rapidly rising pressure and strong winds.

Summary

We have now described how the general circulation of the earth operates, vertical air motions, and temperature distributions. We have further described local wind effects, such as cyclones and anticyclones. But one important element is still missing: In addition to radiation, temperature, pressure, and wind, we daily experience the occurrence of clouds and precipitation distributed over the surface of the earth. The next section will describe types of clouds and how they are formed.

Clouds

Clouds are weather signposts in the sky. They indicate what the atmosphere is doing—giving visible evidence of the atmosphere's motions, water content, and degree of stability. In this sense, clouds are a friend to pilots and others who wish to determine what the weather is likely to be over the next 24–72-hour period. Knowledge of principal cloud types can help in visualizing expected weather conditions and knowledge of cloud formations assist in recognizing potential weather hazards when flying.

Clouds are composed of minute liquid water droplets and/or ice crystals, depending on the temperatures within them. When their temperature is between the freezing point (32°F or 0°C) and 5°F (-15°C), they are composed largely of supercooled water droplets, but usually have some ice crystals. At temperatures below 5°F (-15°C), clouds usually are composed entirely of ice crystals. However, super-cooled droplets sometimes exist at temperatures as low as -40°F (-40°C).

Cloud particles average about one-thousandth of an inch in diameter, but are clustered together sufficiently to make them visible. They must grow enormously in order for precipitation to be produced. The average raindrop contains about one million times the water of that in a cloud droplet. Condensation nuclei, such as dust and products of combustion, compose the centers of cloud particles. These water-absorbent impurities must be present for cloud droplets or ice crystals to form when the air becomes saturated. Clouds differ from fog only in that they do not reduce the horizontal visibility beneath them. In other words, fog is a cloud which lies at the earth's surface.

The forms, species, and varieties of clouds are numerous enough to fill a large book with illustrations and descriptions of each type. These many kinds of clouds are, however, internationally recognized. A detailed description of each type is available in the International Cloud Atlas, a publication of the World

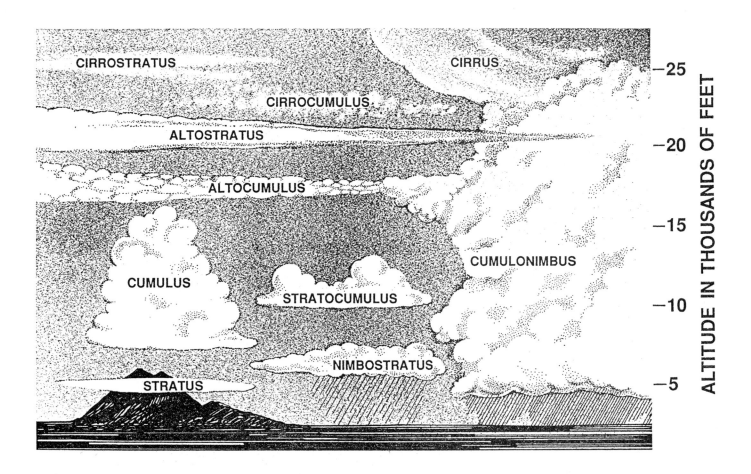

Figure 9.8 *The names given to clouds are descriptive of their shapes and altitudes.*

Meteorological Organization (WMO). For the purpose of identification, we need to be concerned only with the more basic cloud types shown in figure 9.8. These cloud types may be divided into four "families:" high clouds, middle clouds, low clouds, and clouds with extensive vertical development. Within the high-, middle-, and low-cloud families, there are generally two main subdivisions: (1) clouds formed when localized vertical currents carry moist air upward to the condensation level, and (2) clouds formed when whole layers of air are cooled until condensation takes place. The clouds in the first subdivision have a lumpy, or billowy appearance, and are called "cumulus type," meaning "accumulation," or "heap." Those in the second subdivision lie mostly in horizontal layers, or sheets, and, because of their appearance, are called "stratus type," meaning "spread out." In addition to these subdivisions, the word "nimbus," which means "rain cloud," is added to the names of clouds that normally produce precipitation. Thus, a horizontal cloud from which rain is falling is called "nimbostratus"; a heavy and swelling cumulus that has grown into a thunderstorm is referred to as a "cumulonimbus." Clouds that are broken into fragments

are usually identified by adding the suffix "fractus" to the classification name. For example, fragmentary cumulus clouds are referred to as "cumulus fractus."

Clouds form when water vapor condenses into visible droplets. Although on rare occasions the dew-point temperature increases to the air temperature, the usual cause of condensation is cooling of the air to its dew-point temperature. When the dew point and air temperature become the same, the air is saturated (relative humidity of 100%), and further cooling produces condensation. The cooling can take place (1) in localized vertical air currents produced by heating from below, or (2) through forced ascension of whole layers of air.

When clouds form, the degree of stability of the air helps determine what type they will be. Cumuliform clouds, because of associated vertical air currents, invariably have some degree of turbulence within them. Since there is little or no vertical motion within horizontal cloud layers, little, if any, turbulence is experienced within them.

When air is forced to ascend, the structure of any clouds which form depends almost entirely on the air's stability prior to the ascension. For example, very stable air being forced to ascend a mountain slope will remain sufficiently stable to prevent appreciable vertical development, and clouds will be layerlike, with little or no turbulence. If the air which is forced upward is initially unstable, however, the mountain slope will, itself, increase the tendency for vertical development, and cumuliform clouds may grow considerably.

Sometimes horizontal layers of clouds will change partly to cumuliform clouds, as a result of heating from below. Forced ascension of an entire layer produces similar conditions, if the air is conditionally unstable. This transition in cloud formation can sometimes be noted when flying over a relatively smooth cloud deck, with cumulus-like clouds beginning to project upward. Sometimes these projections appear as only random puffs, but, at other times, they form in groups, or in lines. Lines of cumuliform clouds, projecting upward out of a horizontal cloud deck, sometimes indicate a frontal zone (the boundary between warm and cold air masses). A similar cloud pattern often occurs at a coastline, the result of a temperature difference between the land and water. Mountain ranges, properly oriented relative to the flow of air, will produce lines of cumuliform clouds within what is otherwise a horizontal cloud layer.

Clouds produce two major effects: (1) they form precipitation; and (2) they block radiation to the earth's surface. If the cloud is at temperatures warmer than 32°F (0°C), rain or drizzle will occur. If colder than 32°F (0°C), snow, sleet, or hail may occur. The rate and amount of precipitation will depend on the depth of cloud, the intensity of upward vertical motions, and the length of time a cloud exists over a given location. Clouds reflect radiation very effectively from the top. Pictures taken from space show clouds to be brilliantly white in the daytime, indicating high reflectivities.

Summary

These discussions regarding radiation, general circulation, and clouds pertain to the atmosphere as we know it today. The basic principles we have described likely would have been operating also in the atmosphere before the Flood. However, from the account given early in Genesis, the conditions may have been significantly different. It appears that a vapor canopy may have been present above, or on top of the atmosphere; the temperatures could have been tropical over the entire globe, and no rain or rainbows could have been present. The next section will describe the conditions which may have existed between the eras of Adam and Noah.

The Sky Has Fallen

The worldwide Flood recounted in Genesis has no parallel in today's world. Yet, few serious attempts have been made to explore the meteorology of the Flood and the

atmosphere of the antediluvian world. Several advances have recently been made, however, in developing atmospheric models and comparing model predictions with observations. These attempts to understand what the atmosphere (firmament) was like before and during the Flood help us realize that, indeed, "the sky has fallen."

Models

One method used to explore geophysical events is to construct a model of the event and then to correlate these observations with predicted effects of the model. For example, Fultz[1] has built a physical model of the earth's global circulation in a so-called dishpan experiment that enabled him to simulate motions we observe in today's atmosphere. Whitcomb and Morris[2] have developed an elementary, conceptual model of the vapor canopy theory which Dillow[3] has expanded significantly. Dillow[4] has made other important strides forward, by attempting to quantify many of the results. He has developed mathematical models of portions of the vapor canopy and compared the results with related observations in the geological record.

The conceptual vapor-canopy model developed by Dillow specifies that the earth was surrounded by a vapor canopy before the Flood of Noah. This pre-Flood atmosphere contained the equivalent of about 40 feet of water in the form of a canopy resting on top of the current atmosphere. The canopy condensed suddenly during the first 40-day period of Noah's Flood, causing the downpour of rain.

Given such a conceptual model, at least three predictions can be compared with appropriate observations to help confirm or refute the model:

1. An extensive greenhouse effect would have existed prior to the Flood;

2. Physical processes would have been different, and plant and animal life would have been affected by the increased atmospheric pressure under the vapor canopy;

3. Temperatures in the polar regions would have decreased rapidly and permanently, as a result of the precipitation of the canopy.

Greenhouse Effect

The greenhouse effect gets its name from the observation that the air inside a greenhouse is warmer than the air outside, because heat is trapped by the glass windows. Shortwave radiation from the sun travels relatively unimpeded through the glass, but longwave radiation, returning from the plants and earth inside the greenhouse, cannot be transmitted easily back through the glass. Consequently, the heat is trapped, and the temperature in the greenhouse rises. A similar effect occurs in our atmosphere today. If it were not for this effect the surface of the earth would be like the moon, which gets extremely hot during the day and extremely cold at night.

Prior to the Flood, the greenhouse effect would have been amplified greatly. An amplified-greenhouse effect not only would have caused the atmosphere to be warmer, but would have tended to create a uniform temperature distribution from equator to poles. In addition, it is likely that the temperature in the canopy would have been greater than that near the surface of the earth. In the pre-Flood atmosphere, if one were to have gone to the mountains (assuming there were mountains prior to the Flood), he would have found that the temperature increased, rather than decreased, as he got higher. Such a condition is called an inversion, as was discussed on page 189. We know that such conditions lead to pollution episodes around large cities today, because under an inversion, the air is very stable and the winds are very light to non-existent. In the pre-Flood atmosphere, the inversion would have been very strong and the pole-to-equator temperature difference would have been very small, resulting in light winds, no storms, and no rain! The entire earth, including the poles, would have been much warmer than it is today.

There is abundant evidence that the polar regions were much warmer at one time. A fallen 90-foot fruit tree with ripe fruit and green leaves still on its branches has been found in the frozen ground of the New Siberian Islands. The only tree vegetation that grows there now is the one-inch-high willow. Palm-tree fossils have been found in early Tertiary strata in Alaska, large fossil leaves of tropical plants have been found in Permian sandstone 250 miles from the South pole, and crocodiles were once prolific in New Jersey and in England. It is estimated that the mean sea-level air temperatures at the poles was 45°F (7°C) during the Cretaceous Period. Today, the temperature there is -4°F (-20°C).

The evidence of warm polar regions is so extensive that the theory of continental drift was developed by evolutionary geologists to help explain how tropical fossil material can be accounted for at the poles. The vapor canopy theory, on the other hand, explicitly predicts tropical vegetation at the poles, without the need for refinements to the theory.

Increased Atmospheric Pressure

Pressure is the weight pressing on a surface per unit area. Pressure decreases, the higher one goes in the atmosphere, because there is less mass of gas stacked above. Prior to the Flood, when the vapor canopy was resting on top of the ancient atmosphere, its additional weight, according to Dillow, approximately would have doubled the surface pressure we experience today.

There are several features in the geologic record which might be explained by greater atmospheric pressure at some time in the past. One of the puzzles of natural history is the gigantic flying reptile called the pteranodon. This creature had a wingspan of up to 20 feet. Many authors have questioned how such an animal could launch itself into the air from flat ground. The minimum speed for the pteranodon to achieve flight has been computed to be more than 15 miles per hour, in today's atmosphere. Because the pteranodon could not run, this meant that a wind of more than 15 miles per hour would have had to occur before the reptile could have become airborne. Pilots know, however, that it is easier to take off at lower altitudes, where the pressure is greater. If the atmospheric pressure prior to the Flood were twice what it is today, it would have been much easier and would have required much lighter winds for the pteranodon to take flight. Calculations show that it would have required a wind of just over 10 miles per hour for the pteranodon to get airborne in the pre-Flood atmosphere.

Even more intriguing is the recent discovery of the pterosaur—a variation of the pteranodon. The Texas pterosaur is estimated to have had a wingspan of over 50 feet, but the minimum flight speed in today's atmosphere would have been just over 25 miles per hour.

Did a pterosaur flap its wings to initiate and maintain flight? If it did, this reptile's power requirements likely would have exceeded modern birds. How could a pterosaur maintain flight for an extended time in today's atmosphere? In the pre-Flood atmosphere, with its greater pressure, however, it is likely the pteranodon and pterosaur would have had an easier time. In either environment, however, the biomechanics of these reptiles is near the margin of their ability to fly. This may explain why they are extinct today. After the canopy collapsed, the atmospheric conditions were no longer suitable to accommodate this type of creature.

Another illustration of the possible effects of greater atmospheric pressure before the Flood is the presence of gigantism in the fossil record. Enormous dinosaurs, weighing over 40 tons; insects with 25-inch wingspans; and giant shell creatures, spiders, and other invertebrates once lived on the earth, but not today. Is it possible that the greater pressure in the pre-Flood atmosphere helped supply more oxygen to the biomass of these animals, allowing them to live longer, healthier lives, and grow larger?

Evidences that higher oxygen pressures are beneficial to biological systems was discovered recently in the aquanaut program. One of the aquanauts reported that a severe cut on his hand healed completely within 24 hours while submerged in a diving bell at a pressure of ten atmospheres. It was theorized that the higher pressure forced more oxygen into the tissue surrounding the wound and healed it at a faster rate. Based on this observation, experiments in hyperbaric surgery were started, with excellent results. Greater atmosphere pressure has been found to result in relief from some effects of aging and the cure of some diseases. It is not hard to believe that such an effect could be related in some way to gigantism and the longevity of life evident before the Flood.

In a Master's thesis at the Institute for Creation Research, David Rush[5] has found that the quantity of water vapor might have been limited, in the vapor canopy, by the high surface temperatures produced by the enhanced greenhouse effect. The effect of clouds was not treated by Rush, but it is likely that the pre-Flood atmosphere was not as extreme as that proposed by Dillow.[4] Further research on this subject is currently being conducted at ICR.

Rapid Post-Flood Ice Age

The ice caps today on Greenland and Antarctica would not have existed during the more tropical climate that characterized the pre-Flood earth. We also must consider the evidences from erratic boulders and moraines of gravel and sand. These indicate that great continental glaciers existed on North America, Europe, and Asia. The geologic evidence is even very strong that valley glaciers existed in headwaters of the Colorado River drainage basin. Could such evidences for an "ice age" be explained as rapid, post-Flood phenomena following the collapse of the vapor canopy?

Creationists have found that the Biblical data do produce a climate model which leads to a scientifically sound explanation for continental glaciation.[6] Two requirements are necessary for an "ice age:" (1) global cooling, and (2) substantially increased moisture in the atmosphere. The rapid climatic cooling following the Flood provides a likely catastrophic mechanism meeting the first requirement. The left-over heat generated by the various volcanic and tectonic processes of the Flood would increase evaporation from the ocean. The extra heat of the ocean, therefore, satisfies the second requirement. Both requirements would occur simultaneously in the post-Flood earth. Indeed, it is difficult to imagine that the Flood *could not* generate an "ice age."

Cooling of the post-Flood atmosphere would be a consequence of the loss of the canopy, thus causing the atmosphere to trap less of the sun's heat. Also, large amounts of volcanic aerosols would remain in the atmosphere following the Flood, generating a large temperature drop over land, by reflecting much solar radiation back to space. Volcanic aerosols appear to have been replenished in the atmosphere for hundreds of years following the Flood, because of high post-Flood volcanism, which is indicated in Pleistocene sediments.

The moisture needed for the "ice age" would be provided by strong evaporation from a much warmer ocean immediately following the Flood—the consequence of a warmer pre-Flood climate and the release of hot subterranean water during the eruption of "all the fountains of the great deep" (Genesis 7:11).

A conceptual model[7] of how the "ice age" may have occurred is shown as figure 9.9. This figure depicts the global atmospheric circulation following the Flood, as the oceans cooled and polar ice caps formed and then receded. The major assumption of the model is the uniform ocean temperature from top to bottom and from equator to pole immediately following the Flood. As the polar regions cooled, large quantities of water vapor were evaporated from the warm oceans and deposited over cold polar regions. Precipitation rates would have been enormous initially, slowing to that observed today.

We know that evaporation over the ocean is proportional to the temperature difference between the ocean and the atmosphere, the dryness of the air, its instability, and the speed of wind. Indirectly, evaporation is proportional to sea-surface temperature. An 18°F (10°C)-air-sea temperature difference, with a relative humidity of 50%, will evaporate seven times more water at a sea-surface temperature of 86°F (30°C) than it will at 32°F (0°C). As to the warm ocean immediately after the Flood, the areas of greatest evaporation would be at higher latitudes and off the east coast of Northern Hemisphere continents. Focusing on northeast North America, the combination of cool land and warm ocean would cause the high-level winds and main storm tracks to parallel the east coast. Storm after storm would develop near the eastern shoreline, similar to modern-day Northeasters, but with much more moisture, that would drop frequent heavy snow over the continent. In this way, glaciers could form. Once a snow cover was established, more solar radiation would be reflected back to space, reinforcing the cooling over land.

The ice sheet would continue to grow as long as the large supply of moisture was available, depending upon the warmth of the ocean. The time to reach maximum ice volume would be determined by the cooling time of the ocean. Michael Oard, a meteorologist with the U.S. Weather Bureau, estimated that it would take about 500 years to reach maximum ice volume, assuming plausible, post-Flood, atmospheric, and oceanic conditions.[8] Even more startling is the melting time that would be required once the oceans had cooled. He estimates that approximately

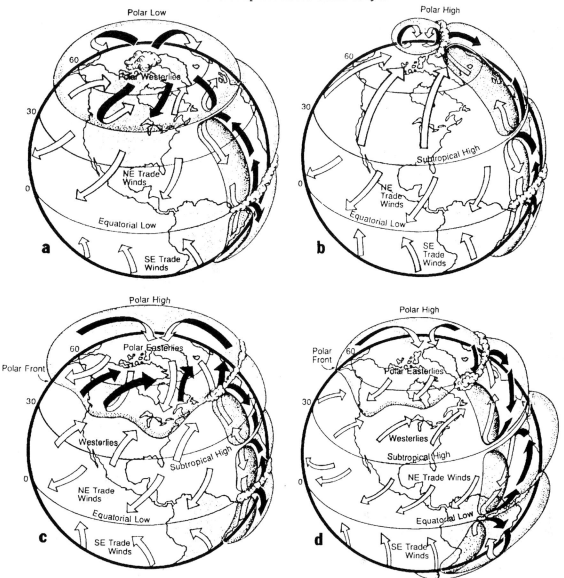

Figure 9.9 *Global atmospheric circulation patterns after the Flood: (a) immediately after Flood; (b) within 100 years; (c) at maximum extent of ice sheet; (d) today.*

100 years would be required for the meltings of major continental glaciers.

An interesting consequence of this model for a rapid post-Flood ice age would have been relatively mild temperatures, especially in coastal areas, because of the oceanic heat source and warm oceanic air mass. In coastal areas, even at high latitudes, it appears that man, animals, and plants were able to disperse from the Ark and populate great areas of the earth. When the ice sheet was at maximum volume, sea level would have been hundreds of feet lower, allowing animals and people to travel over land bridges between Asia and Australia, and between Asia and North America. This appears to have occurred about the time of the Tower of Babel. The mild-but-rapid ice-age model could

also account for the large numbers of well-fed mammoths in Siberia, many of which became frozen in surface-soil layers.[9]

Conclusions

Models for the pre-Flood canopy and post-Flood ice age are bound to create discussion and controversy. At the same time, however, they will increase the interest and enthusiasm of specialists in the atmospheric sciences and concerning the canopy theory. More quantification of such mathematical models is desirable and their conclusions will greatly enhance our understanding of the Flood and the antecedent atmosphere. The final result will produce even greater confidence in the Word of God.

NOTES—Chapter 9

1. D. Fultz, "A preliminary report on experiments with thermally produced lateral mixing in a rotating hemispherical shell of liquid," *Journal of Meteorology*, 6 (1949): 17–33.

2. J. C. Whitcomb, and H. M. Morris, *The Genesis Flood*, (Philadelphia, Presbyterian & Reformed Publishing Company, 1961), pp. 250–258.

3. J. C. Dillow, *The Waters Above* (Chicago, Moody Press, 1981), 479 pp.

4. J. C. Dillow, "The Vertical Temperature Structure of the Pre-Flood Vapor Canopy," *Creation Research Society Quarterly* 20 (1983): 7–14.

5. D. E. Rush, *Radiative Equilibrium Temperature Profiles Under a Vapor Canopy* (Santee, California, Institute for Creation Research, unpublished M.S. thesis, 1990), 140 pp.

6. M. J. Oard, *An Ice Age Caused by the Genesis Flood* (El Cajon, California, Institute for Creation Research, 1990), 243 pp. Creationists will find much in this book which is of value to understanding the relationship of the Flood to the Ice Age. The data of the Bible allow a climate model to be produced which leads to a scientifically sound explanation for continental glaciation.

7. L. Vardiman, *Ice Cores and the Age of the Earth* (El Cajon, California, Institute for Creation Research, 1993, 85 pp.

8. M. J. Oard, "An Ice Age Within the Biblical Time Frame," *Proceedings of the First International Conference on Creationism* 2 (1986): 157–166.

9. H. G. Coffin, *Origin by Design* (Hagerstown, Maryland, Review and Herald Publishing Association, 1983), pp. 256–267.

Chapter 10

EARLY PEOPLES OF THE SOUTHWEST

"And hath made of one blood all nations of men to dwell
on all the face of the earth; . . . that they should seek the Lord. . . ."
Acts 17:26,27

The Early Peoples

To come to the Southwest is to venture into a harsh land rich in Indian history and prehistory. The Southwest abounds with more archaeological national parks and monuments than does any other part of the United States. Man has roamed, hunted, cultivated, and settled the plateaus, canyons, and valleys of this arid land for over four thousand years. While Jesus taught the multitudes and walked along the shores of Galilee in Palestine, other men had already come across the Bering Strait into North America and had begun to populate the Southwest.

Early Cultures

Figure 10.1 shows three main cultures that began to flourish at this early date: the Anasazi (Navajo for "ancient ones"), the Hohokam (Pima for "those who have gone"), and the

Figure 10.1 *A large part of the modern Native Americans of the Southwest come from three main cultures: the Anasazi, the Hohokam, and the Mogollon.*

Mogollon (for the range of mountains in central Arizona where their cultural remains are found).[1]

The Anasazi were a prehistoric group of people who lived in the northern Southwest from approximately 700 A.D. to 1300 A.D. Before that time, they were referred to as Basket Makers (100 B.C. to 700 A.D.) because of the beautiful baskets and sandals they wove. After approximately 700 A.D., they began to build spectacular apartment complexes called pueblos. Mesa Verde (Colorado), Chaco Canyon (New Mexico), and Kayenta (Arizona), represent the height of their civilization. Today the Hopi, Zuni, and Pueblo Indians are their descendants. The Hohokam settled in the southern deserts of Arizona, where they developed canals and advanced systems of irrigation, cremated their dead, and traded extensively with Mexican cultures. Casa Grande National Monument, south of Phoenix, is an example of the ancient Hohokam culture. The present day Pima and Papago Indians are most likely their descendants. Much less is known about the Mogollon culture, which developed in southern New Mexico and Arizona, because their tradition was less advanced than the other two, and it seems the Mogollon absorbed traits from both the Anasazi and Hohokam cultures. The Rio Grande Pueblos, Acoma, Hopi, and Zuni are their present-day descendants.

For about 1,300 years these cultures traded with one another, farmed, made baskets and pottery, and developed complex social and religious centers. Then, by 1250 A.D., they began to disappear. Archaeologists are not sure of the exact reason for this mass abandonment of dwellings throughout the entire Southwest, but several explanations have been given: adverse climatic change, overpopulation and famine, a deterioration of the social and religious structure, severe erosion, disease, and raids by other Indian tribes. Whatever the cause, they left behind their centuries of civilization well preserved by a dry climate.

Figure 10.2 shows the traditional interpretation of the history of the Anasazi, Hohokam, and Mogollon peoples. The illustration shows the primary periods of growth and expansion, followed by periods of decline and disintegration.

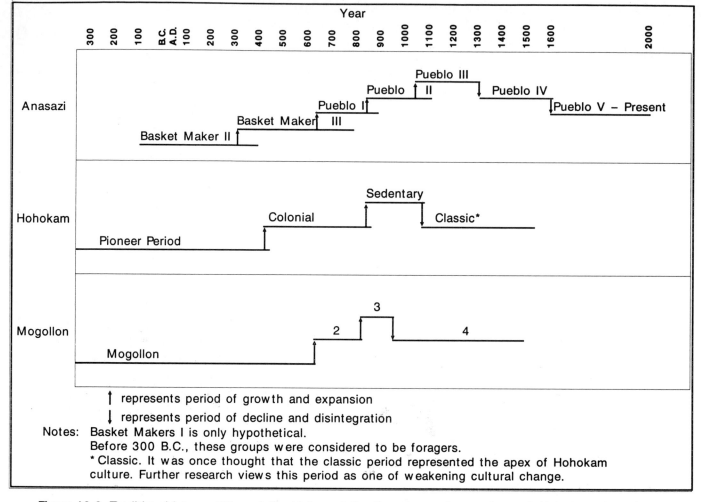

Figure 10.2 *Traditional interpretation of the history of Southwestern cultures: Anasazi, Hohokam, Mogollon.*

As we drive through portions of the northern Southwest, we mainly concern ourselves with the culture of that region—the Anasazi, better known as the Basket Makers and Pueblo peoples. As Psalm 77:5,6 states, "I have considered the days of old, the years of ancient times . . . and my spirit made diligent search." We will now look at their physical traits, clothing, food subsistence and resources, architecture, arts and crafts, and religious beliefs.

The Anasazi

In uncovering skeletal remains in Anasazi ruins, physical anthropologists have concluded that the "ancient ones" were somewhat shorter than are Americans today. The average life span of an Anasazi was 34 to 40 years. Due to their diet of cornmeal, ground by stone, sand from the grinding stones (figure 10.3) wore down their teeth. It was not unusual for individuals to have lost most of their teeth by 20 years of age. Abscesses and diseases in the bones of the jaw and skull became so painful that often the person could no longer eat and eventually died from starvation. When an individual died, the body was usually flexed and buried with funerary offerings in a cave, beneath the floor of a house, or in the village refuse mound. Excavating a refuse mound, by the way, reveals much about the lifestyles and resources of any people.

Though some authors depict the early inhabitants and their life-styles as romantic and picturesque, in reality, their lives were filled with great toil, high infant mortality, sickness, disease, and death at an early age, and were usually reduced to a struggle for survival.

Clothing

The Anasazi were masters at utilizing natural resources for clothing and food. From yucca and buffalo grass, they stripped fibers and wove their beautiful sandals and baskets. The early Anasazi are, in fact, also called "Basket Makers," because of the many baskets found in their caves and rock shelters (figure 10.4). Loincloths were made from native cotton and grasses. Between 700 and 900 A.D., cotton began to be domesticated, and the true loom took precedence over finger-weaving.[2] Figure 10.5 illustrates the craft of finger-weaving. During the cold months they fashioned blankets made of domesticated turkey feathers and rabbit fur. Shell and coral beads and pendants, traded with people

a.

b.

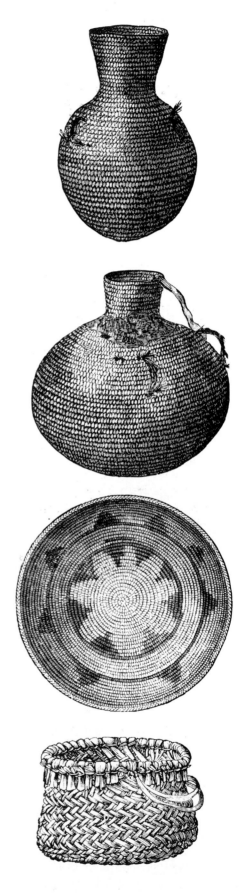

Figure 10.3 *Grinding stones (from J. W. Powell, "Canyons of the Colorado").*

a. *Grinding stones in a Hopi house.*

b. *An ancient Pueblo metate. Not shown here is the mano—the rock used to grind corn on the metate.*

Figure 10.4 *Basketry (from J. W. Powell, "Canyons of the Colorado").*

Figure 10.5 *Finger-weaving, here performed by a Navajo man (from J. W. Powell, "Canyons of the Colorado").*

from the Gulf of California and Mexico, were worn, along with turquoise and bone beads, which were fashioned locally.

Diet

Hunting, gathering, and dry land farming were all part of the everyday life of the early people of the Colorado Plateau. At first, they used spear points hafted to throwing sticks, called atlatls, then later developed the bow and arrow. Mule deer, rabbit, big horn sheep, elk, and small fowl added to their diet of pinyon nuts, cactus fruit, and other wild seeds and plants. Corn, beans, and squash, introduced from Mexico, were cultivated in terraced fields, arroyo bottoms, and natural depressions.

Architecture

One of the most important contributions the Anasazi made to the prehistory of the Southwest was their development in architecture.[3] On the Colorado Plateau, it is necessary that the people construct warm and dry dwellings. During

the height of Anasazi culture, they developed what would be considered America's first apartment buildings.[4] Their multi-storied, flat-roofed buildings, sometimes constructed on cliff walls, still astound archaeologists who study them today (figure 10.6). Most of the buildings were constructed of stone, with an adobe mixture that doubled as mortar and interior plaster. They had few windows and doorways, probably to preserve heat and keep dust out. Most were south-facing to maximize the sun's rays (figure 10.7).

Pottery

Basketry, pottery, woven goods, jewelry, pictographs, and petroglyphs give evidence of their artistic abilities. In the early days of the Anasazi, before they settled more into a sedentary agricultural life, baskets were commonly used. Due to the availability of grasses and yucca (as previously mentioned on page 192), the art of basketry was highly developed. Then, as they began to cultivate crops and remain in an area for a longer period of time, sources of clay were located, and pottery was made. Pottery technique was acquired from the Mogollon, who, during one later phase of their development, crafted exquisite pieces of black-on-white pottery known as Mimbres. At first, the Anasazi had a simple gray ware, but as expertise increased, they made black-on-red, black-on-orange, and other combinations. In addition, they constructed intricate geometric designs (figure 10.8).

Religion

Most anthropologists agree that religion influenced a major portion of Indian culture. However, their prevailing view of religion is that it has been created in the mind of man by atheistic evolution. They also dismiss any possible supernatural influences on any civilization at any time as figments of man's imagination.

The Anasazi were a very religious people, as evidenced by the many kivas (semi-subterranean ceremonial structures found in Pueblo villages). These religious centers were associated with the religious symbolisms found in petroglyphs and pictographs, designs in pottery and jewelry, fetishes, effigies, and burial techniques (figures 10.9 and 10.10). All these indicate great preoccupation with the supernatural. From the artifacts gathered and a study of their present-day descendants (the Hopi, Zuni, and Rio Grande Pueblos), the Anasazi were most likely animists. Animists believe that all things around them, the plants and animals, the wind, rocks, and rivers, are like themselves. They have life, consciousness, and indwelling spirits. Numerous rituals and ceremonies, including dances, were devised to appease these spirits, thus ensuring good health, harvest, hunting, etc.

Figure 10.6 *Wupatki Pueblo, a three-story structure called "Tall House," was abandoned by the Anasazi before 1250 A.D. This pueblo-type construction may represent America's oldest apartment house. (Photo by Hannah Rush.)*

Figure 10.7 *Pueblo architecture consisted of flat-topped roofs and small windows (from J. W. Powell, "The Hopi Villages").*

Figure 10.8 *Ancient pottery from the village named Tusayan (from J. W. Powell, "Canyons of the Colorado").*

Figure 10.9 *Fetishes. These charms are regarded as possessing consciousness, volition, supernatural qualities, or magical powers (from J. W. Powell, "Canyons of the Colorado").*

Modern tribes today still perform these same dances and ceremonies at designated times throughout the year. In fact, their way of life revolves around belief in the supernatural. However, in discerning the power source for the mystical, and even miraculous events that often occur in their ceremonies and in their lives, one must be careful in attributing them to God. Just because an event or happening is supernatural does not mean that it necessarily comes from God.

The Bible says there are two doors that, if opened, lead into the realm of the supernatural. One is through Jesus Christ; the other through the demonic power of Satan. Jesus said, "I am the door; by me if any man enter in, he shall be saved and shall go in and out and find pasture" (John 10:9). Jesus also said, "Verily, Verily, I say unto you, He that entereth not by the door into the sheepfold, but climbeth up some other way, the same is a thief and a robber" (John 10:1). Jesus referred to the work of Satan and his activities: "The thief cometh not, but for to steal, and to kill, and to destroy: I am come that they might have life, and that they might have it more abundantly" (John 10:10).

According to traditional Judaeo-Christian teachings in the Mosaic Law, idolatry is one door that opens to the hidden powers of darkness (Psalm 106:34–43; I Corinthians

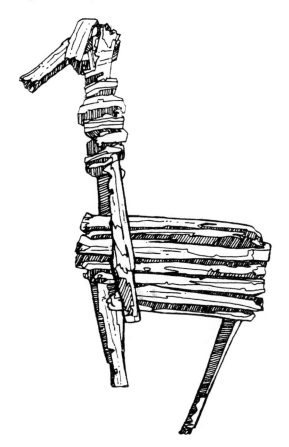

Figure 10.10 *Split-twig figurine found in a cave of Grand Canyon. These are the earliest evidences of man in Grand Canyon.*

10:20). When a person worships, sacrifices to, or venerates any object (fetish) or person other than Jesus Christ, he either knowingly or unknowingly contacts these demonic spiritual powers. When a person enters into this type of alliance, he may be able to manipulate these supernatural powers for a time, but, if he continues, he eventually becomes entangled and enslaved. Fear becomes the overwhelming spirit that pervades such a life.

There are many warnings in both the Old and the New Testament concerning specific occultic practices. In fact, the very first commandment given by God states:

> *I am the LORD thy God, which have brought thee out of the land of Egypt, out of the house of bondage. Thou shalt have no other gods before me. Thou shalt not make unto thee any graven image, or any likeness of any thing that is in heaven above, or that is in the earth beneath, or that is in the water under the earth. Thou shalt not bow down thyself to them, nor serve them: for I the LORD thy God am a jealous God, visiting the iniquity of the fathers upon the children unto the third and fourth generation of them that hate me; And shewing mercy unto thousands of them that love me, and keep my commandments" (Exodus 20:2–6).*

Other specific occultic practices are listed in Deuteronomy 18:10–14:

> *There shall not be found among you any one that maketh his son or his daughter to pass through the fire, or that useth divination, or an observer of times, or an enchanger, or a witch, Or a charmer, or a consulter with familiar spirits, or a wizard, or a necromancer. For all that do these things are an abomination unto the LORD: and because of these abominations the LORD thy God doth drive them out from before thee. Thou shalt be perfect with the LORD thy God. For these nations, which thou shalt possess, hearkened unto observers of times, and unto diviners: but as for thee, the LORD thy God hath not suffered thee so to do.*

How, then, did man become so confused and so attracted to counterfeit spiritual practices? In the beginning, it was not so. Noah was their ancestor, and they had the truth. "These are the three sons of Noah: and of them was the whole earth overspread" (Genesis 9:19). Beginning at Babel and continuing throughout the long years of migration across Asia to North America, they lost the truth about God. As Romans 1:21–25 states:

Because that, when they knew God, they glorified Him not as God, neither were thankful; but became vain in their imaginations, and their foolish heart was darkened. Professing themselves to be wise, they became fools. And changed the glory of the uncorruptible God into an image made like to corruptible man, and to birds, and fourfooted beasts, and creeping things. Wherefore God also gave them up to uncleanness through the lusts of their own hearts, to dishonour their own bodies between themselves: Who changed the truth of God into a lie, and worshipped and served the creature more than the Creator, who is blessed for ever. Amen.

Man's disobedience and rebellion against God has been universal through all cultures. However, God had a plan that included all of us, no matter what race, language, or culture, if only we would turn away from our own desires and old habits and seek the one true God and Savior of all mankind. ". . . For thou wast slain, and hast redeemed us to God by thy blood out of every kindred, and tongue, and people, and nation" (Revelation 5:9).

The Archaeology of Grand Canyon

The Grand Canyon has been known to man for at least 4,000 years. Ancestors of the Native American Indians were the first to discover and explore this huge and awesome chasm.

The earliest evidence of human use comes from split-twig animal figurines (figure 10.10) found in remote caves in the Redwall Limestone of the Canyon.[5] Because these figurines were not found in direct association with other cultural material, but appear to be carefully cached, archaeologists strongly believe that the people who made them were so called "magicians." These tiny wooden animals, representing mountain sheep, deer, and prong-horned antelope—some with spears protruding from them—suggest that the early inhabitants ritualistically offered these animals to ensure a successful hunt. After the people of the Split-Twig complex left the Canyon, it appears not to have been used again by man for several hundred years.

Then the Kayenta Anasazi, one of the major subdivisions of the Pueblo culture, entered the inner canyon from the east at about 700 A.D. They settled some areas of the Canyon bottom, where permanent sources of water could be found, such as Kwagunt, Nankoweap, Unkar Delta, and Bright Angel. These sites were located mostly along fertile deltas and on terraces just above the river. With the use of check dams and agricultural rock terraces to trap the water, the Anasazi were able to cultivate corn, beans, and squash. They also gathered rice grass, seeds, mesquite pods, and various other plants—all of which were stored in granaries.[6] Also around 700 A.D., or shortly before, the southwestern end of the Canyon was entered by a hunting-and-gathering group called the Cohonina. Some anthropologists believe that the present-day Havasupai Indians, who inhabit Havasu Canyon, are possibly descended from the Cohonina.

Population continued to grow between 1000 and 1150 A.D., until over 500 sites dotted the Canyon and its rims. These Pueblos, however, never did match the size or the magnificence of the Pueblo centers to the east, such as Betatakin, Chaco Canyon, or Mesa Verde.[7]

Between 1150 and 1200 A.D., Grand Canyon was almost totally abandoned by the Anasazi, with possibly only the Havasupai continuing to live in Havasu Canyon. The small ruin on the South Rim, called Tusayan, most likely represents the last inhabited site in the area.[8] It is thought that a regional drought might have caused the migration out of the Canyon, or perhaps it was increased population pressures that resulted in a decrease of foods available. Whatever the case, the Anasazi moved to more

Figure 10.11 *The Powell Expedition (1869) was the first to explore the inner canyon and document archaeological material (from J. W. Powell, "The Canyons of the Colorado").*

permanent water sources, approximately 100 miles to the east.

The modern-day Hopi Indians living on the Hopi Mesas most likely represent the descendants of Grand Canyon Anasazi. Today, the Hopi still use the Tanner Trail to take pilgrimages to ceremonial salt deposits in the Canyon of the Little Colorado. They also use the Grandview Trail to Horseshoe Mesa to collect blue copper, used in making paints. To the Hopi, Grand Canyon is considered a sacred place, in that it is believed to be a giant sipapu, an opening where both animals and humans emerge from the underworld, and from where the dead return.[9]

In 1540, white men first viewed the splendors of Grand Canyon. Captain Don García López de' Cárdenas and a small number of Spanish soldiers were sent by Coronado to locate a "great river" to the west. They were led to the Canyon's southern edge by the Hopi. After trying unsuccessfully to descend into the Canyon for several days, they returned with the Hopi guides to their pueblos.[10]

Grand Canyon was left to the Native Americans for the next two centuries, until 1776, when two Franciscan priests, desiring to bring Christianity to them, actually descended into the Canyon from opposite directions. Father Garcés was the first European to enter the southwestern area of the Canyon, descending the long trail to the Havasupai village. A few months later, Father Silvestre Vélez de Escalante descended into the northeastern end. Then, in 1869, John Wesley Powell was the first to explore the inner canyon and record archaeological material (figure 10.11).[11]

After Powell's exploration of the Canyon, miners began to enter the Canyon in the 1880s, using Indian trails. Prospectors sank shafts, carried in heavy mining equipment on the backs of mules, and even built cable crossings over the river. They discovered copper, asbestos, uranium, lead, and other minerals, but most of the mines played out, and the miners left the area. Claims on mineral rights, however, still exist within the Canyon, and mining interest continues.

Today, the Canyon is mostly uninhabited, except for the Havasupai—"people of the blue-green water"—who live in Havasu Canyon. While all others have left this rugged land of sharp contrasts and incredible relief, the Havasupai continue to farm and profit from tourism.

According to Havasupai beliefs and legends, the Canyon was formed as water rushed off the earth, which at that time was covered with water.

As the waters of the world dried and flowed away, the face of the earth cracked, and was worn full of deep canyons. One of these

canyons was very narrow and filled with rattlesnakes. This was the canyon of the Havasupai.[12]

Another account of their flood legend says:

The people put a small girl in a log with the ends blocked with pitch. She had with her food, water, birds, and animals. Two men told her she would be going up and down in the water and that they would all be drowned. She should remember the San Francisco Peaks so she could find it [sic] if she came back to earth in another place. She was to get water from a spring on top of the peaks. The water covered all the earth and drowned all the people.[13]

As one continues on with this account, however, one sees immediately that much in the way of fantasy and magic, obscenity and lewdness is added, so caution needs to be taken in drawing too much from their mythology.

It is generally recognized by ethnographers that a large number of North American Indian tribes possess a variety of deluge stories. As one examines different cultures, many record the account of a worldwide flood having been caused by their own disobedience to their god or gods. From a Biblical perspective, as the tribes dispersed farther and farther from the Middle East (Tower of Babel), their stories were altered, distorted, exaggerated, and colored by the different peoples. By the time these tribes reached North America, much had changed in their accounts, but the general theme of a flood remained.

Perhaps the most comprehensive survey compiled on the Indian tribes of North America was that commissioned by Congress in 1847. The work took a decade, and filled many volumes. One of the results of the survey states:

There is one particular in which the tribes identify themselves with the general traditions of mankind. It is in relation to a general deluge, by which the races of men were destroyed. The event itself is variously related by an Algonquin, an Iroquois, a Cherokee, a Muscogee, or a Chickasaw; but all coincide in the statement that there was a general cataclysm, and that a few persons were saved.[14]

In summary, it appears that the remembrance of Noah's Flood has survived better among American Indians than at American universities.

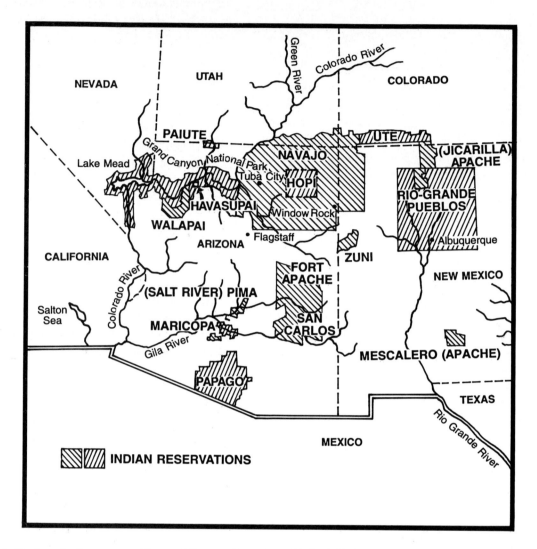

Figure 10.12 *Modern Indian reservations of the southwestern United States.*

Present-Day Southwest Indian Peoples

The locations of Southwest Indian tribes are shown in figure 10.12. Six tribes are described here:

Navajo—The largest Indian tribe in the United States. They migrated from northwest Canada between 1200 and 1400 A.D. to settle in the Southwest. The Navajo plagued the Pueblo Indians with raiding parties for many years. In 1864, the U.S. government commissioned Kit Carson to subdue the Navajo, which he did, in a four-year campaign. The decisive blow came when he located and successfully attacked their seemingly impregnable canyon fortress in Canyon de Chelly (Arizona). Their will to resist was broken, and scattered bands surrendered one by one at Ft. Defiance, Arizona. From here, they were forced across most of New

Mexico to Ft. Sumner, an infamous march remembered as the "Long Walk." Many died along the way. After a final peace treaty was signed with the rest of the nation in 1868, they were returned to their land, where they still herd sheep and goats. They are well known for their silverwork and woven rugs.

Havasupai—A very small tribe living mostly in Supai Village in Havasu Canyon, a tributary to the Grand Canyon. They farm and raise cattle.

Hopi—They live in the center of the Navajo reservation. Descended from the Anasazi, they have been the most resistant to modern influences. *Oraibi*, one of the Hopi villages, is said to be one of the oldest continuously occupied towns in the United States (see figure 10.13). The mother is the center of the household and much of the religious and social life revolves around her. Hopi women are excellent

Figure 10.13 *Oraibi, a Hopi village, showing terraced pueblo with entrance to a kiva in the foreground (from J.W. Powell, "The Canyons of the Colorado").*

basket weavers, the Hopi men carve *Kachina* dolls. Much emphasis is placed on ceremonies, the most well known being the Hopi Snake Dance.

Zuni—Also descendants of the Anasazi, they live near Gallup, New Mexico. They like to farm, but are famous for their pottery and exquisite turquoise inlay work. Their best-known dance is the Shalako dance, performed in November or December.

Paiute—Later arrivals to the southwest (1200 A.D.) who were probably raiders of the pueblos, as were the Navajo. Today, they live along the western Utah-Arizona border.

Pima and Papago—Descendants of the Hohokam, they live in southern Arizona. The Pima ("river people") are farmers who also gather cactus fruit, wild plants, and seeds. Papago ("desert people") are also farmers and gatherers, and are renowned for their remarkable baskets.

How to Locate an Archaeological Site

Have you ever been hiking along a trail in the backcountry and wondered if perhaps the early pioneers or Native Americans ever walked this very trail many years ago? Many of the trails used today originated as game trails, which were trodden by the natives to pursue animals for food. These game animals knew where water was, they knew the easiest routes up and over the mountains, and they found ways down into the deep canyons. By following these wild animals, the Native Americans and early

explorers not only found food, but water and often shelter, as well. They later used these same trails as trade routes to contact other tribes for exchange of food, goods, and cultural items.

If the trail you are using has designated campsites, very often they are located on top of Native American campsites. But what will tell you if it is an archaeological site? Look for flakes, points, pottery shards, surface structures, unusually shaped or smooth stones, smoothed depressions in bedrock outcroppings, and petroglyphs and pictographs on boulders and cliff faces. Examine any naturally protected areas such as caves, overhangs, natural windbreaks, and edges of stands of trees for archaeological materials. Level, or flat terraces, near or above water sources, are good areas to explore. If you're walking through an arroyo or stream bed, examine the cut banks for burned clusters of rock, ash, charcoal, bones, flakes, points, etc. Topographic maps are useful in locating water sources and possible sites. Also, aerial photographs are of valuable assistance, if you are venturing into arid land. Unusual surface features can be easily observed in aerial photographs that might be otherwise overlooked on the ground.

Recently, one of the backpacking groups from an Institute for Creation Research tour in Grand Canyon discovered a previously unrecorded Anasazi site. The discovery of various Anasazi materials occurred while the group of hikers was exploring a side canyon. Pottery, basketry, masonry walls, and a burial site were observed. The cultural material was not disturbed. Upon returning to the rim, the group leader immediately notified the proper National Park officials and gave the location and description of all the artifacts. The National Park archaeologist took appropriate actions to preserve the site.

The Antiquities Act of 1906 was the law passed to preserve and protect natural resources on government lands. This law applies to archaeological sites, and states that vandalism or theft of artifacts from a site is considered a crime. A fine of up to $500, or imprisonment of 90 days, or both, could be placed upon a person who excavates, removes, or destroys any historic or prehistoric ruin, or any object of antiquity. This federal law protects archaeological sites on public land. Private land is not covered. A majority of the states have enacted similar laws aimed at protecting sites on state-owned land. Remember, it is a serious offense to remove any object having historic or prehistoric value from public lands. If you do discover an archaeological site, it is best to contact the appropriate government officials and give them the location and general description of the site.

NOTES—Chapter 10

1.   D. Butcher, *Exploring Our Prehistoric Indian Ruins* (Washington, D.C., National Parks Association, 1950) p. 10.

2.   R. H. Lister and F. C. Lister, *Those Who Came Before*, (Tucson, Arizona, University of Arizona Press, 1983) p. 32.

3.   Ibid., p. 29.

4.   D. Butcher, *Exploring Our Prehistoric Indian Ruins* (Washington, D.C., National Parks Association, 1950) p. 11.

5.   J. D. Hughes, *In the House of Stone and Light* (Grand Canyon, Arizona, Grand Canyon Natural History Association, 1978) p. 9.

6.   L. Stevens, *The Colorado River in the Grand Canyon* (Flagstaff, Arizona, Red Lake Books, 3rd ed., 1987) p. 20.

7.   J. D. Hughes, *In the House of Stone and Light,* p. 11.

8.   Ibid.

9.   D. W. Schwartz, "A Historical Analysis and Synthesis of Grand Canyon Archaeology," *American Antiquity*, 31 (1966): 476,477.

10. Ibid., p. 470.

11. J. W. Powell, *Canyons of the Colorado* (New York, Flood & Vincent, 1895) 400 p.

12. F. H. Cushing, "The Nation of the Willows," *Atlantic Monthly*, 50 (1882): 558.

13. C. L. Smithson and R. C. Euler, "Havasupai Religion and Mythology," *Anthropological Papers, Department of Anthropology, University of Utah*, 68 (1964): 33.

14. H. R. Schoolcraft, *History of the Indian Tribes of the United States,* (Philadelphia, J. B. Lippincott and Co., vol. 6, 1857) p. 571.

Figure 10.14 *Land of Standing Rock (from J. W. Powell, "The Canyons of the Colorado").*

Grand Canyon: Monument to Catastrophe

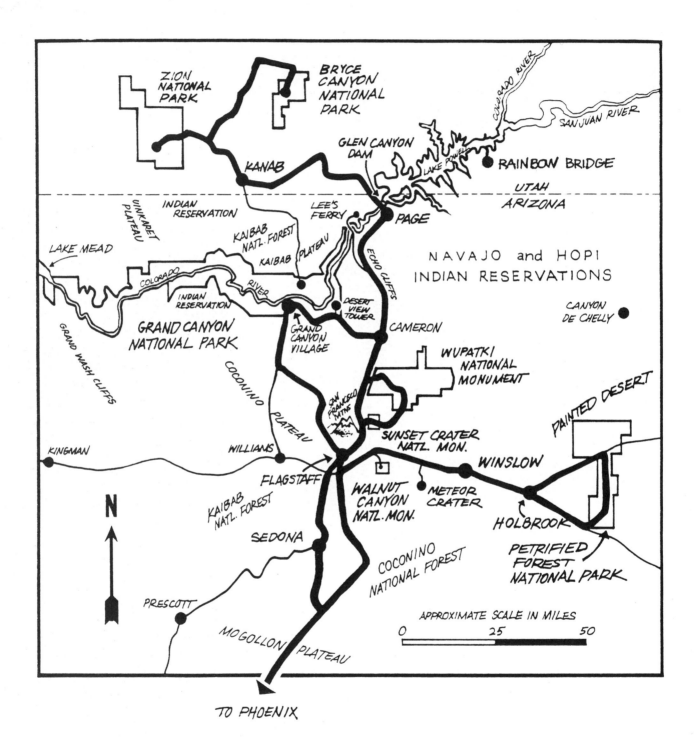

Figure 11.1 Location map for the "things to see and do" in northern Arizona and southern Utah. These places are described in the following chapter.

Chapter 11

THINGS TO SEE AND DO

"Speak to the earth and it shall teach thee"
Job 12:8

Northern Arizona and southern Utah boast more natural parks and monuments than any similar size area in the world. This is for good reason: The arid climate has faithfully preserved a wide variety of archaeological treasures, the rugged terrain exposes impressive geologic structures and formations, and the variety of elevations provides the habitat for diverse plants and animals. Plan your trip well; take as much time as possible; allow yourself to see as much as you can.

The Institute for Creation Research has been leading tours of northern Arizona and southern Utah since 1980. These yearly activities have occurred in April, and have featured tours by bus, hiking and camping in the Canyon, mule rides into the Canyon, and motorized raft trips on the Colorado River. This chapter describes many of the points of interest visited by these tours (see figure 11.1). Also included in this chapter is information about activities which require advanced planning (overnight camping, mule rides, raft trips, etc.) should you choose to take your own trip. Appendix C contains mailing addresses and phone numbers for information and reservations.

As you plan your visit to Grand Canyon, you should keep weather and climate in mind. The Colorado Plateau is an arid continental region with variable temperatures and sometimes harsh storms. The best seasons to visit Grand Canyon are in the spring and fall when temperatures are intermediate and rainfall the lowest. Summer on the south rim at 7,000 feet elevation is warm (maximum of about 84°F), while along the Colorado River corridor, at 2,400 feet elevation, it is very hot (high temperatures may exceed 115°F in July). Late summer in Grand Canyon usually brings much-needed rains and cloudy afternoons. That may be refreshing to hikers who usually are on the trail only in the early or late hours of a summer day. Pacific winter storms usually begin in November. From December through March, there is usually snow accumulation on the south rim. In general, it is best to be prepared for unexpected weather conditions.

Grand Canyon National Park

Grand Canyon Village and the South Rim

The main stop for most visitors to the Canyon is Grand Canyon Village (see figure 11.2). Located on the south rim at an elevation of 6,860 feet, it provides the most accessible overlook of Earth's most amazing erosional wonder. Here you can find all the conveniences of home: market, post office, hotels, trailer park, campground, clinic, airport, restaurants, etc. Unlike the more rustic settlement on the north rim, the south rim stays open all year.

There is also the option of staying overnight at the small city of Tusayan, located seven miles south of the Village, just outside the park. At Tusayan is Grand Canyon Airport where short overflights of the Canyon can be arranged. These are a popular way to see the Canyon.

While at the Village, you will want to see the Visitor Center as well as the geological museum at Yavapai Point. These contain interpretive displays and literature. A good way to gain an easy introduction to Grand Canyon is to take East Rim Drive and West Rim Drive from Grand Canyon Village. Many people affirm that the best sunset observations of Grand Canyon are from Hopi Point, just west of the Village. Two famous trails (Bright Angel and South Kaibab) begin at Grand Canyon Village.

The North Rim

The north and south rims of the Canyon are only ten miles apart as the crow flies (see figure 11.3). However, by road, the two rims are 215 miles (five-hour drive) apart. For those traveling to Grand Canyon from the north, it may be more convenient to visit the north rim. However, it should be remembered that because of greater snowfall, the facilities at the north rim remain closed from mid-October to mid-May.

The north rim averages 1,000 feet higher elevation than the south rim, where the cooler and wetter condition allow a spruce-fir forest to grow. The more arid condition of the south rim promotes growth of a pine-juniper forest.

From Grand Canyon Lodge on the north rim, you can drive to Cape Royal and Point Imperial. These overlooks allow you a most extraordinary vista of eastern Grand Canyon and the Painted Desert, to the east.

Travel Below the Rim

For those who desire to go below the rim into the Canyon, there are only two options: hiking or by mule. The "world's most famous footpath" (the Bright Angel Trail) begins at Grand Canyon Village on the south rim and descends into Garden Creek Canyon (along the Bright Angel Fault) to Indian Garden Campground and the Colorado River (see figures 11.2 and 11.3). There are frequent water stops along the trail. The suspension bridge crossing the river

allows access to Bright Angel Campground and Phantom Ranch. Overnight mule riders can stay at the ranch.

If spectacular vistas are your interest, you might hike the South Kaibab Trail (see figures 11.2 and 11.3). The trailhead is near Yaki Point just east of Grand Canyon Village. This trail descends on a ridge into the Canyon and also crosses the Colorado River. No water sources are available, however, until the river. This is one of the steepest trails into the Canyon, but it is superbly constructed.

Numerous backcountry trails also enter the Canyon and allow hiking and primitive camping. One of the most popular of these is the Grandview Trail (lower right of figure 11.3). The trailhead is at Grandview Point about ten miles east of Grand Canyon Village. The well-constructed trail was built for mining activity by John Hance almost

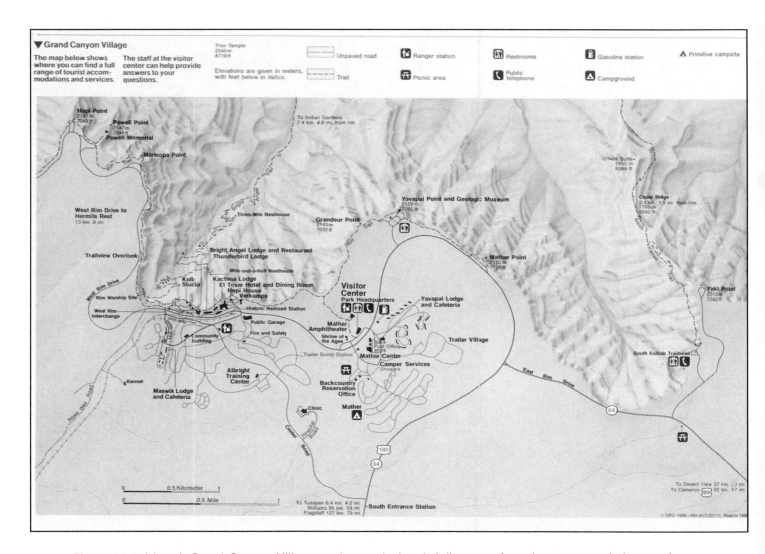

Figure 11.2 (above) *Grand Canyon Village at the south rim. A full range of tourist accommodations and services is available at the village. The Bright Angel Trail and the South Kaibab Trail begin at Grand Canyon Village.*

Figure 11.3 (right) *North rim to south rim in Grand Canyon National Park. This map shows a more expanded area, including the area north and east of Grand Canyon Village. Grandview Point is in the lower right, with the north rim at the top.*

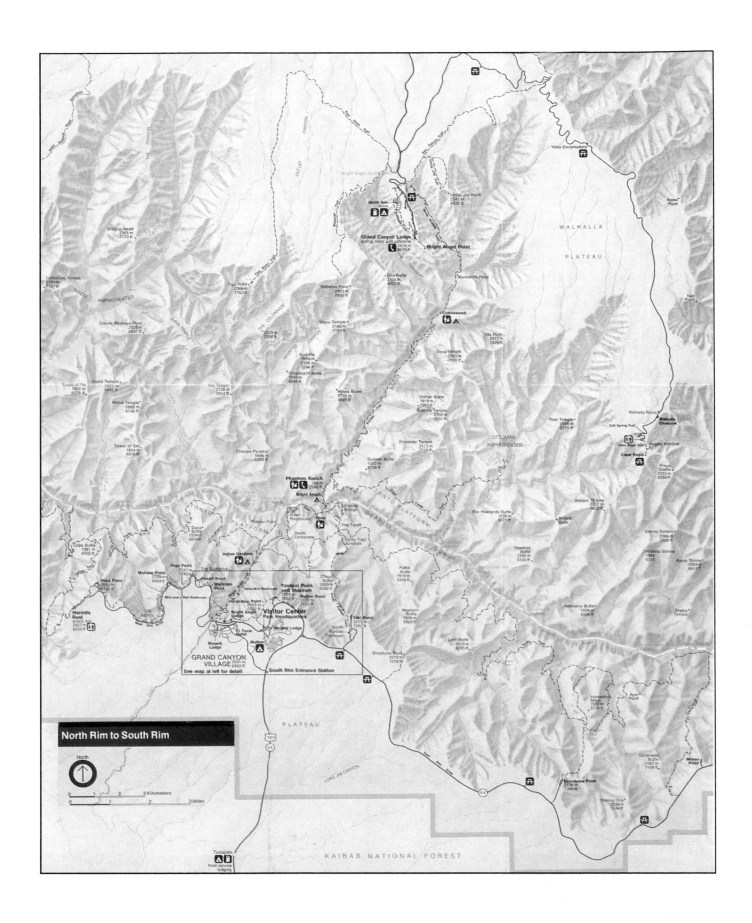

100 years ago. Tourism, however, proved more profitable. The Grandview Trail descends into a canyon and crosses Horseshoe Mesa, a major promontory thrusting northward into the Canyon. From Horseshoe Mesa you have access to Cottonwood Creek and Hance Creek—two excellent areas for primitive camping. The trail from Hance Creek to the Colorado River traverses excellent exposures of tilted Precambrian strata.

Day hikes below the rim do *not* require a permit. However, if you intend to camp overnight, you should obtain a permit through the mail by writing to the Backcountry Reservations Office. To ride mules into the Canyon you need a reservation from Grand Canyon National Park Lodges. Trail information is available through the Backcountry Reservations Office. Mailing addresses and telephone numbers are found in appendix C. Topographic maps of the trail areas from the south rim are found in appendix B.

Seeing the Canyon From the River

Twenty licensed companies offer float trips on the Colorado River where you can see the Canyon by motorized rafts, oar-powered rafts, or dories. Most of the trips launch at Lees Ferry, just below Glen Canyon Dam. Trips vary in length from 89 miles (minimum of three days), to over 200 miles (up to three weeks). Reservations need to be made with raft operators, and a list of the companies can be obtained from Grand Canyon National Park. The Institute for Creation Research offers guided, creationist, raft trips through Grand Canyon in April of each year, as was stated at the beginning of this chapter. The mailing address for more information on river trips is found in appendix C of this book.

Tusayan Pueblo

Grand Canyon National Park contains approximately 500 prehistoric Indian ruins. Most of them are hidden in remote parts of the Canyon and are so inaccessible, they are seldom seen by visitors. The majority of the sites are relatively small, but have yielded valuable artifactual materials.

Tusayan Pueblo, an Indian site on East Rim Drive, three miles west of Desert View Tower, is an Anasazi settlement built about 1185 A.D. It was inhabited by about 20 people for approximately 25 years. The estimated time of habitation was determined by the amount of refuse left at the site, patterns of wear on manos and metates, and the different styles of pottery made during this time. The pueblo has about 15 rooms, with about half used for living—the rest for storage. Ladders were positioned through the smoke holes atop the flat roofs and served as doorways. Most daily activity was conducted outdoors, where the Anasazi farmed, collected wild plants, hunted, and made pottery and other essentials. To supplement the meager natural rainfall, they built check dams to trap runoff water, which made agriculture possible. These dams can still be seen to the northeast of the pueblo.

Figure 11.4 *The Colorado River in the extreme eastern Grand Canyon. Rafters from an Institute for Creation Research raft trip are returning from the Indian granaries at Nankoweap (base of cliff at right) to their rafts (on the river in lower center).*

Desert View Tower

Desert View is the most popular eastern vantage point in Grand Canyon. The stone-block tower stands as a prominent landmark on the south rim allowing spectacular vistas of the Canyon to the north and an overlook of the Painted Desert to the east. Desert View provides one of the best places to review the geology of Grand Canyon and Painted Desert.

Beginning at the bottom of the Canyon is one of the world's finest examples of an angular unconformity, "The Great Unconformity," where the lowermost Precambrian strata are uptilted and overlain by the relatively horizontal sequence of Tapeats Sandstone, Bright Angel Shale, etc. The rock layers are stacked like a layer cake up to the Kaibab Limestone upon which the tower stands. Because all of the bedded rock north of Desert View must have been deposited originally as sediment horizontally (or nearly so), then we must infer that later earth movements have taken place where these strata are uptilted or bent. Two excellent examples of such movement can be seen from Desert View: the East Kaibab Monocline and the uptilted beds beneath the Great Unconformity. Might the Great Unconformity mark the onset of Noah's Flood?

As one looks to the east, a step-like terrain, called "The Grand Staircase," rises to the top of Black Mesa. This area comprises the Painted Desert. These exposures contain remnants of strata that lie above the Kaibab Limestone and probably covered the area of the present Canyon prior to uplift and erosion. Rock layers, such as the Chinle Formation, which contains the great logs of the "Petrified Forest" and the Morrison Formation, with its world-famous dinosaur skeletons, are found east of Desert View. In fact, if a well were drilled through Black Mesa, a "layercake" of some 8,000 feet in thickness would be penetrated, including a strata sequence very similar to that exposed in the Canyon, before the Great Unconformity would be penetrated. You might ask, "Which of the rock strata near Desert View may be interpreted as the closing stages of the Great Flood?" We look to the upper layers east of Desert View, such as those exposed on Black Mesa, for evidence.

Northeastern Arizona

Wupatki National Monument

> *"Come, behold the works of the LORD, what desolations He hath made in the earth"* (Psalm 46:8).

As you enter this very desolate region of Northern Arizona, you ask yourself just how people could have survived and even thrived in this land, yet they did! Between 1100 and 1225 A.D., the Wupatki area was a cultural melting pot with a population of around 4,000. This was an important Anasazi settlement.

Before the eruption of Sunset Crater (10 miles south of Wupatki) in 1064 and 1065, the population was scattered and small. The people lived, then, in pit houses. They hunted, gathered, and farmed. They are known as the "Sinagua" people, from the Spanish for "without water." Perhaps, earthquakes and the opening of fissures in the vicinity provided sufficient warning, for they apparently gathered their belongings and fled. The eruption covered 800 square miles with ash, which provided a rich mulch and reduced evaporation from the soil. The Indians then moved back into the area to farm and build what are now the pueblos.

Wupatki Pueblo, called "Tall House" because of its three-story units, may be North America's oldest apartment building. It contains some 100 rooms, a large kiva, and a ball court. The uncovering of the ball court in 1965 gave clear evidence of the influence from the Hohokam, and Mexico to the south. The ball court, an open-air structure where players propelled a rubber ball around a court, originated in Mesoamerica. The game, at various times, was played over a wide area of the Americas, and, here at Wupatki, reached its northern-most limit. Also, such trade items as copper bells, shells, and macaws indicate contact with the Hohokam and, possibly, Chaco Canyon in New Mexico.

Examples of fine architecture and decorative walls can be seen at Wupatki. The area was abandoned by 1250 A.D., shortly before the Great Drought of 1276–1297.

Sunset Crater National Monument

Sunset Crater is Arizona's most recent volcano. One of 400 or so cinder-cone volcanoes that dot this small region in the shadow of San Francisco Peaks, Sunset Crater reminds us that great amounts of geologic work have been accomplished in the past at rates that can only be described as catastrophic. Although quite different from the San Francisco Peaks, which represent the remains of a much larger "composite-cone" (Mount St. Helens type) volcano, all of the volcanoes in this area rest on fossil-bearing flood strata, and so must have formed subsequent to the Genesis Flood. Perhaps the onset of volcanism was related to the same crustal disturbances responsible for the East Kaibab Monocline.

The sunset tints of red and yellow which give the crater its name, are caused by oxidation of the freshly cooled volcanic rocks by hot, steaming gases that continued to emerge as volcanic activity ceased. Iron oxides, gypsum, and sulfur are some of the minerals found in the area. Tree-ring dating and historical accounts confirm the volcano's eruption to have been in historic times—about the same time William the Conqueror set out for England, in 1065 A.D.

Although history records that Sunset Crater formed 900 years ago, potassium-argon dating of the rock gave an excessively old age. Two samples of the lava flow yielded "ages" of 210,000 and 230,000 years! The explanation offered by S. J. Reynolds and others (*Arizona Bureau of Geology and Mineral Technology Bulletin 197*) is that argon gas was retained in the rocks as they cooled. Because argon-40 would normally be considered to have formed by radioactive decay of potassium-40, these rocks appear excessively old.

A 40-minute hike across one of the frozen lava flows gives the visitor an impression of the magnitude of volcanic power. Sometime following the lava flows, the volcano belched out great volumes of cinder, which are pieces of once molten lava which congealed as they made contact with air, and fell, literally as a shower of rocks over an area of 120 square miles. Sunset Crater is made from a loose pile of such cinders that is too unstable upon which to build. This is why there are no roads to the top.

Walnut Canyon National Monument

The ruins of approximately 200 small cliff dwellings can be found in the eroded walls of the Toroweap Formation, where this Toroweap is dominated by sandstone. Walnut Canyon was named for the stand of Arizona walnut trees found in the bottom of the Canyon. The people who inhabited these apartment houses were the Sinagua who came to this area around 700 A.D., and, at first, lived on top of the Canyon in pit houses. Because they had a permanent water supply and an abundance of game and fuel from the nearby forests, life in the Canyon was made easier. Besides hunting and gathering, they also grew crops such as corn, beans, and squash. They were skilled in making pottery and basketry, and reached their zenith of cultural development around 1200 A.D. About 1250 A.D., this canyon was abandoned, for unknown reasons, and left untouched for several hundred years.

In the 1880's, the Smithsonian Institution collected some artifacts and mapped the area. However, shortly after the cliff dwellings were discovered, people came to pot-hunt and disturbed the ruins. Much destruction took place until 1933, when the ruins were put under the protection of the National Park Service.

Meteor Crater

There is an immediate and obvious difference between this type of crater and Sunset Crater, yet both represent enormous amounts of geologic work performed in very short order. Meteor Crater, probably the finest example of such a structure on Earth, formed from the prehistoric impact and subsequent explosion of a meteor estimated to have been 80–100 feet in diameter, weighing over 60,000 tons, and traveling at perhaps 40,000 miles per hour. After penetrating some distance into the earth, the meteorite exploded, throwing thousands of molten fragments as far as five miles away. The Kaibab Limestone and Coconino

Figure 11.5 *Meteor Crater, Arizona.*

Sandstone are upturned at the lip of the crater from the force of the explosion. Because the fragments are of almost pure, elemental iron, the meteor is not without economic value, and the underground drilling by Mr. Barringer makes a very interesting episode in history. Despite the warnings of evolutionary geologists (i.e., anti-catastrophist) and numerous failed drilling attempts, the main fragment was found buried beneath more than 1,350 feet of sedimentary rock, or well over twice the depth of the present crater! Curiously, ballistics experiments liken this crater to the pockmark left by a rifle fired into soft mud.

Meteor Crater is 4,200 feet wide, 570 feet deep, and could accommodate two dozen Rose Bowls seating 2.5 million people. The crater was excavated by an explosion equivalent to 1.7 million tons of TNT. The plateau on which this crater is located is 5,000 feet above sea level.

The straightforward interpretation that a large, high-velocity impact excavated Meteor Crater, came to be accepted only after the most skeptical resistance by the geological establishment. For 35 years, it was attributed by the best geologists to volcanic processes.

The anti-catastrophist bias goes back to classical Greek times. Aristotle, the Greek scientist who died in 322 B.C., correctly accepted shooting stars as atmospheric phenomena, but denied that they were caused by rocks from space. "How could earthly things fall from heaven?" he reasoned. Heaven, he stated, only contains heavenly things. He classed "meteors" with rainbows, halos, and auroras. If anybody had seen a large stone fall from the sky, Aristotle maintained that the wind had picked up the rock and moved it.

During the Renaissance, the notion that anything could fall from space was dismissed as preposterous by scientists. In 1790, the Académie Francaise, then the world's foremost scientific organization, was so convinced of the absurdity of stones observed by common people to have fallen from space, they implored museums everywhere to discard their long-treasured meteorites. That same year a shower of meteorites fell in southwestern France, following which, the Académie, after receiving rock samples and more than 300 descriptions from eyewitnesses, asserted the event to be a "physically impossible phenomenon." The Académie was convinced, in Normandy during 1803, by the thunderous pelting of 2,000 stony meteorites.

By 1820, the evidence for meteorites being from outer space was truly overwhelming, and such rocks could fall even in France without embarrassing scientists. Still, scientists did not fully acknowledge the implications. That Meteor Crater in Arizona was caused by the collision of an 80-foot-diameter rock, moving at 40,000 miles per hour, was denied for 35 years by the most prestigious scientists, even though meteorites had been collected for years around the structure. It was not until 1929, after a half-million-

dollar drilling project, that what seemed obvious was proven by the recovery of meteorites from beneath the structure. Even today, geologists are reluctant to accept that collisions with asteroids, in excess of seven miles in diameter, have produced enormous craters in the earth, because to accept such events would revive the unorthodox and supposedly spurned doctrine of catastrophism.

For thousands of years, non-scientists have held high regard for, and even attached religious significance to, rocks fallen from the sky. A Hittite king, Mursilis II, described how a great ball of fire from heaven destroyed his enemy, the King of Ephesus. This meteorite at Ephesus was later carved into an image of the goddess Diana (see Acts 19:35). Even today, Muslims pray by turning to the sacred stone at Mecca, which is almost certainly a meteorite. According to Hopi Indian legend, a god descended from the clouds, making his temple abode at Meteor Crater, Arizona.

The writers of the Bible affirm the reality of the phenomenon of stones falling from the sky. Scripture describes "a great hail out of heaven, every stone about the weight of a talent [about 100 pounds]" (Revelation 16:21), and the fall of "great stones from heaven" (Joshua 10:11). Other passages may describe meteorites also (see Matthew 24:29; Ezekiel 38:22; Exodus 9:18–33; Psalm 18:13,14).

What scientists denounced as heresy for two thousand years, they have come to discover to be fact. As Scripture affirms, stones fall from the sky! Meteor Crater stands as a monument to extraterrestrial power.

Petrified Forest National Park

The Petrified Forest was never really a forest at all, but a region where tree trunks, in battered condition, with limbs and roots broken off and bark stripped away, were rafted in by water and buried quickly beneath volcanic ash and fine-grained sediment. The logs are almost all found resting horizontally. The scenario seems more akin to modern deposits adjacent to Mount St. Helens than to the traditional view of sluggish streams and occasional volcanism operating over a period of millions of years. The fossil logs occur throughout the Chinle Formation of the Painted Desert, which owes its variegated color to ash contained within the beds.

Volcanic ash, composed of tiny, puffed-up particles of once-molten silica glass, is notorious for its tendency, in the presence of water, to decompose rapidly to clay. As it does, dissolved silica is released into groundwaters which, when encountering organic material such as the wood of buried tree trunks, gradually replaces the cellulose (wood) in a type of fossilization called silicification. The process need not take long periods of time. For example, approximately 100 miles to the southeast is Fossil Creek which drains a terrain of volcanic rocks and where modern-day tree leaves can be found silicified. Thus the rate of *silicification* can actually exceed the rate of *decomposition*! Laboratory experiments have also silicified wood rapidly.

Other fossils preserved in these same strata besides the most common conifer trunks include a great variety of plant fossils from fern fronds to leaves of deciduous trees, as well as crocodile-like phytosaurs and dragonflies. Although some of the fossil vertebrates are alleged to be amphibian "links" that support the evolutionary transition from water to land, such a vertical succession of fossils has never been found in any one rock sequence. Those vertebrates which have no modern-day representatives can be satisfactorily explained by extinction—a phenomenon (unlike evolution) we can observe today. As for the plants and insects, the fossil forms are very nearly identical to modern ones, and so do not demonstrate the kind of progression that one would predict if evolution were true.

The logs at Petrified Forest are recognized, by most geologists, to have been deposited in flood conditions. R. C. Moore (*Introduction to Historical Geology*, McGraw-Hill, 2nd ed., 1958, pp. 401,402) says:

> There lie thousands of fossilized logs, many of them broken up into short segments, others complete and unbroken. . . . The average diameter of the logs is 3 to 4 feet, and the length 60 to 80 feet. Some logs 7 feet in greatest diameter and 125 feet long have been observed. None are standing in position of growth but, with branches stripped, lie scattered about as though floated by running water until stranded and subsequently buried in the places where they are now found. The original forests may have been scores of miles distant. The cell structure and fibers have been almost perfectly preserved by molecular replacement of silica.

The park is also rich in archaeological finds. The Puerco River area in Petrified Forest National Park was situated between the Anasazi plateau cultures and the Mogollon mountain cultures. The native Americans who lived here acquired cultural traits from both the Anasazi and the Mogollon. Within the Park, 109 archaeological sites have been located, dating from 300 to 1400 A.D.

Agate House, located at the southern end of the Park, is an eight room pueblo. What makes it truly unique is that it is constructed of chunks of colorful agatized wood.

The Puerco Ruin, located on a bluff south of the Puerco River, contains 125 rooms. Thirty-three rooms have been excavated and three kivas discovered. It was arranged in two or three tiers around a central plaza. Points, scrapers, and other tools were made from the petrified wood found

locally and flakes can still be found scattered around the ruin. To the east, just below the bluff, numerous Indian petroglyphs are still visible.

Utah and Arizona

Zion National Park, Utah

The first white man to see Zion Canyon, a deep chasm with near-vertical walls, was the fur trapper and part-time evangelist Jedediah Smith in 1825. Smith was perhaps the most peculiar of the celebrated "Mountain Men," yet was also the most widely respected. His dealings with the Indians were with integrity, and he has been portrayed with a rifle in one hand and a Bible in the other.

There are many geological features at Zion that stimulate one's imagination. One may wonder, for example, if the White Cliffs that rise 3,500 to 4,000 feet above the valley floor can be explained solely by modern rates of erosion; or did they demand more catastrophic processes? Of course, this is a rhetorical question. We can never know for sure, but we can examine the present processes of erosion to get some perspective. The perennially turbid Virgin River, named after Tom Virgin of the Smith party, can remove up to three million tons of rock per year. At Zion, we see many hanging valleys (e.g., Refrigerator Canyon just west of Angel's Landing) and their lovely waterfalls. The road into the park ends at "The Narrows" where the canyon is in places only a few feet wide yet whose walls rise nearly vertically for a remarkable 1,500 feet. Tours are led up the narrows in the summer months, but, even then, the prospects of wading up the icy Virgin River, where sunlight shines for but a few brief moments each day, is too chilling for most. During flash floods which frequent this region, the river in the narrows has been known to rise 25 feet in just 15 minutes!

Another important process to ponder is called "spring sapping." Sandstone, such as the Navajo Sandstone which forms the steep walls, is, despite its very solid appearance, quite porous and is able to conduct water very readily. Beneath the Navajo sandstone, at a level just above the valley floor, lies the top of the Moenave Formation, which, in contrast, is a very poor conductor of water. Now, because these strata tilt ever so slightly one or two degrees to the east, springs tend to occur along the western wall. The outflow of water from the sandstone loosens the cement, particularly between the sand grains, and causes grains to be removed, especially at the base of the slope. This process is known as *sapping*. The effect is to break off the wall in large blocks leaving the western wall with an irregular, scalloped outline in contrast with to the relatively straight eastern wall. The water action has a third effect: it leaches hematite (which commonly occurs as a red stain on sand grains) from the upper portions, concentrating it in the

Figure 11.6 *Checkerboard Mesa in Zion National Park, Utah.*

lower ones, thus giving a white-over-red look to the sandstone walls.

A final process to consider while in Zion is the origin of the peculiar cross-bedding in the Navajo Sandstone. This is best displayed at Checkerboard Mesa, a very beneficial place to stop. At the visitors' center, and in most literature, "the experts" are quite sure that, like the Coconino Sandstone in the Grand Canyon, the Navajo Sandstone represents "fossil" sand dunes accumulated in a vast desert. The alternative view, that these were water-laid deposits requiring vast currents, has actually been suggested by several geologists. Were these sandstone strata the product of the Flood or from slowly migrating sand dunes over the millennia? Many investigators get a heightened appreciation of the Flood when they view the wonders at Zion National Park.

Bryce Canyon National Park, Utah

The first people to inhabit this area, as well as that of Zion Canyon, were of the mysterious Basket Maker Indian culture. They were followed by the Pueblos, who, in turn, were followed by the peaceful Paiutes. Ebenezer Bryce, for whom the canyon was named, was a Mormon rancher there in the late 1870's. He had little romance for the area because of the endless frustration he experienced in locating his lost cows among the myriad columns and spires!

Bryce Canyon is not a canyon in the literal sense of the word; it is the very unevenly eroded edge of a plateau that has assumed a bowl-shaped outline. Approximately two to four miles to the east of this edge is the Paunsaugunt Fault, from which the 800-foot plateau edge presumably has been back-worn. Because the estimated current erosion on the plateau edge is two feet every 100 years, the uniformitarian geologist reasons that the onset of erosion at the time of fault motion began 700,000 years ago. Can you check his assumptions?

The Pink Cliffs that form the edge of the plateau and the associated erosional forms are composed of the Wasatch Formation. Various systems of joints create the many arches, windows, and bridges; and pinnacles were produced by variations in erosional resistance of the various sandstone, limestone and shale layers that compose the Wasatch. The reddish and brown hues are due to hematite, the yellows to limonite, the purples to manganese oxide, and white to the bleaching out of all pigments. The fossils entombed in these rocks include various mammals, plants, and invertebrates.

Marble Canyon National Monument, Arizona

Prior to the completion of Navajo Bridge in 1928, southern Utah and northernmost Arizona were extremely remote

Figure 11.7 *Bryce Canyon National Park, Utah.*

areas. This is because the Colorado River was virtually uncrossable in all of Arizona. There were river crossings, such as Pierce Ferry beneath present-day Lake Mead at the west end of Grand Canyon, and one near Hite, Utah, 300 miles upstream, but even these were far too perilous for most pioneers. Then, in the 1850's, a ferry at Lees Crossing was discovered to be practical, for here, the monocline known as Echo Cliffs, allowed for passage around the treacherous Triassic, cliff-forming strata. The site became famous in 1869 when Major John Wesley Powell and party passed through in three small wooden boats. Finally, in 1928, the 616-foot-long Navajo Bridge was completed, and the west was penetrable in a new way.

The bridge abuts on both sides in a very hard, cherty Kaibab Limestone, and within the gorge, the Toroweap and Coconino Sandstones are exposed. It might seem puzzling that the Kaibab Limestone on which we stand at the bridge is the very same formation that forms so much of the rim of Grand Canyon, but it should be noted that the depth of the gorge here is a mere 470 feet while in Grand Canyon proper it is 5,000 feet. Does this mean that the Colorado River drops 4,500 feet between here and Grand Canyon? No, this is an illusion—otherwise John Wesley Powell would never have survived the waterfalls! The strata have been bent so greatly along the East Kaibab Monocline that the elevation difference at the top of the Kaibab—between Grand Canyon and Marble Canyon—accounts for the seeming discrepancy.

Lake Powell and Glen Canyon Dam

Lake Powell, named for geologist and explorer John Wesley Powell, is by far the largest of the six reservoirs in the upper Colorado River basin, holding 80% of the water supply. The lake's water is held behind Glen Canyon Dam. Beneath the still waters of the lake lie the flooded cataracts of Glen Canyon which, together with Marble Gorge and Grand Canyon, long stood as one of the greatest obstacles to the settlement of the western United States. The cliff-forming Navajo Sandstone is responsible for the steep walls of Glen Canyon for most of its 180-mile length.

Construction of the Glen Canyon Dam began in 1956. First, 75-foot-long bolts were anchored into the sandstone; then concrete was poured continuously for a period of three and a quarter years at an average rate of over five tons per minute! By 1963 the 600-foot-high, 350-foot-thick (at its base) dam was in operation. Eight giant turbine generators produce power at a maximum rate of 1,336 megawatts, supplying the energy needs of many cities of the Southwest. Unlike coal generators, hydroelectric plants like this one can be easily adjusted for power output ,by regulating the flow through the turbines to meet the lucrative mid-day peak demands, only to be cut back again at night. Hydroelectric-power generation was only one of the reasons for justifying the dam; the other two were the reclamation of the arid "wastelands" of the Utah desert and flood control.

Other unforeseen changes took place, however, that are interesting from an ecological standpoint. For example, the now lush belt of riparian (streamside) vegetation downstream from the dam would not have been possible before, because of the scouring action of annual floods. On the other hand, replenishment of many of the sand beaches is *not* taking place for the same reason, and so many are slowly being eroded away. Also, the artificial ebb and flow of the daily "tides," produced by changes in dam discharge, help support a unique combination of aquatic insects, fish, and birds. The river water, consistently cold, silt free, and of controlled discharge, promotes the growth of diatoms (single-celled plants) and algae which, in turn, are food for aquatic insect-and-fish species, especially the introduced carp and trout. These non-native species have come to dominate the system at the expense of native species, so a trade-off has taken place. Here, natural selection seems to have very rapidly changed the entire ecosystem, yet without the evolution of *anything* new!

Rainbow Bridge, Utah

Rainbow Bridge, which President Theodore Roosevelt once characterized as the greatest natural wonder in the world, is hidden away in an obscure canyon in southern Utah, nearly on the slopes of nearby Navajo Mountain. Located at an elevation of 3,750 feet in one of the most remote and inaccessible regions of the United States, it was not discovered until 1909. Today most visitors travel to the bridge by boat on Lake Powell. The discoverer of the bridge, Byron Cummings, described it well:

> *This remarkable freak of nature in the earth's crust is hardly a bridge in the true sense of the term, but is more properly termed an enormous flying buttress that has been chiseled out by the ages and left as a specimen of the handiwork of the master Builder.*

The bridge is, indeed, half an arch, which abuts the canyon wall on one side, and, on the other end, resembles the graceful arch of a rainbow. This structure of brilliant, salmon-pink sandstone rises 309 feet above the ravine and has a span of 278 feet, making it probably the largest of its kind in the world.

The bridge itself and the canyon walls are composed of the Navajo Sandstone, the same great rock layer that extends in the subsurface and is exposed in Zion National Park. The bridge was clearly the work of the meandering stream that once occupied the valley, except that it didn't require the "ages" of Cummings' description. Because of the predominant northeasterly jointing pattern, or "cracks," one would predict that eroded promontories would develop, which, with the undercutting action of a meandering stream, could eat through the wall of hardened rock in a relatively short process, and with time, sideward erosion would have formed the bridge. Scour marks on the canyon walls unmistakably testify that the now abandoned arm of the

Figure 11.8 *Rainbow Bridge, Utah.*

creek did the work. Along the canyon wall, springs support a diversity of plants, including wild orchids and maidenhair fern.

Indians have lived in the area for the last 2,000 years, at least. Unfortunately, we may never know the richness of the area's archaeology, because the best sites no doubt were covered beneath the waters of Lake Powell beginning in 1963. At the foot of the bridge, fire-blackened stones mark the remains of a possible old fire shrine. The bridge, as well as nearby Navajo Mountain, are revered to this day as sacred by the Indians.

Monument Valley, Arizona–Utah

The dramatic spires, buttes, and mesas of Monument Valley have given it legendary fame, and attract visitors from around the world, even the motion-picture industry has been captivated by its austere beauty. Beginning in 1938 with the film, "Stagecoach," many major Hollywood productions have been filmed in this Valley. Today, television shows and commercials continue to promote it's popularity.

Monument Valley is a broad upwarped structure on the state line dividing Arizona from Utah. As the valley is approached by road from the south, easily eroded red shales of the Moenkopi and Chinle formations give way to massive spires of thick sandstone strata which upwarp from beneath. It's striking monuments are created by soft shales of the Cutler Formation, which have eroded, providing the most meager structural support and leaving massive, vertically jointed slabs of DeChelly Sandstone above the Cutler Formation. The DeChelly Sandstone is roughly correlated with the Coconino Sandstone—the prominent cliff-forming sandstone of Grand Canyon. The Cutler Formation is the apparant equivalent of the Hermit Formation and Supai Group shales of Grand Canyon.

Visitors often ponder the erosional process which has left these spires, buttes, and mesas, but which accommodate no year-long-flowing creeks or streams in this arid valley. Could modern erosional processes, continuing at present rates, create the broad valleys and imposing monuments between? Most mesas have no extensive buildup of talus at the margins, as would be required by a continuing slow process. Many geologists believe these erosional features are relict forms, owing their formation to ancient, energetic, erosion processes when the climate was much more humid. Creationist geologists have proposed that an ancient lake shore existed in this area (see discussion in chapter 5). The rapid drainage of Canyonlands Lake, which occupied a major area of Arizona, Utah, Colorado, and New Mexico, would have caused intense shoreline erosion. It appears to have been the major cause of cliff formation and the broad valley development.

This Valley is located within the jurisdiction of the Navajo Nation and has been declared a "Navajo Tribal Park." There are many ways to tour Monument Valley. You can take the self-guided auto tour, the commercial-vehicle tour, or the horseback tour. A small fee is charged. From the visitors' center, a seventeen-mile, unpaved road winds through the park. Along the way are eleven, numbered, scenic stops. A campground is located within the park, and motel accommodations are available nearby.

HOW TO INTERPRET GEOLOGIC FACTS

Rocks do not talk. Neither do fossils, strata, canyons, nor even isotope ratios. These features simply exist; they are what they are! We can observe them, measure them, and describe their properties, and we try to understand all about them, but never will a rock actually tell us how old it is or how it got to be the way it is. All the geological observer can do is to observe present properties of the rock and interpret them, particularly as they relate to the history of the rock.

Because rocks don't talk, and because no one was present to observe and record most past geologic events, we can never be absolutely certain of our interpretation. Our interpretation process is not without foundation, however. Described below are five concepts which are helpful in guiding the observer into interpretations which are the most plausible.

1. ***Recognize the primary role that bias plays in interpretation.*** Suppose a deluge geologist and a uniformitarian geologist studied the same outcrop of fossil-bearing rock. Each would make all appropriate measurements and gather all pertinent facts. They could even share or swap their data, but, in all likelihood, they would come to different interpretations of the origin of the rocks. Why? How? Because they started their study with different models, assumptions, presuppositions, or bias. Each will interpret the facts within the framework they had when they started, which they "knew" to be true. The rocks themselves are, to varying degrees, compatible with either general

bias. Each bias cannot be *proven*, but each can be *compared*. Then, the one most likely correct, should be adopted. Deluge geologists usually recognize *their* bias and are convinced that the facts fit *their* model better than they do the evolution-uniformity model. Unfortunately, few traditional geologists are aware of their own bias, assuming that long ages of evolutionary development are proved. They acknowledge no other potential framework.

2. ***Evaluate competing models:*** Once competing models are identified, with the underlying bias of each fully set forth, "predictions" can be made to test the adequacy of each model. The proponent of each model might say, "If my model is correct, I would expect to see A, B, and C (or D, E, and F) in the real world." The model which provides the better fit to the data would be more likely correct.

Consider the fossil record as an example: The *creation model* would predict that, because each animal type was created and not descended from other animal types, the fossils should show the distinctness of each kind. The *evolution model* would predict that, because all life comes from a

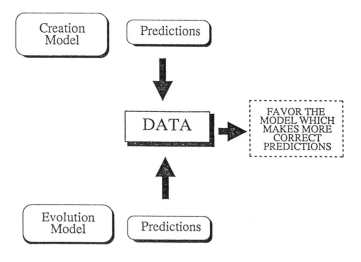

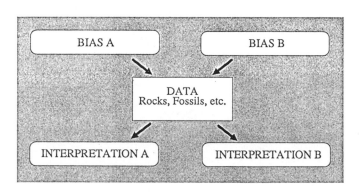

Figure A.1 *Biases affect our interpretations of data.*

Figure A.2 *How to select models.*

common ancestor, there should be innumerable transitional forms between basic types.

The example just given illustrates how facts are used to evaluate competing models. Fossil types appear abruptly, fully formed, and are easily classified into taxonomic groups. Transitional forms have not been found. This exactly matches the prediction of the creation model. Evolutionists usually modify their model and claim that a small, isolated group of animals evolved rapidly to a higher, stable group, leaving no transitional fossils. Others hope the transitional forms will one day be found. They speculate that erosion may have destroyed most of the crucial fossil forms. Clearly, the creation model fits facts better, because it needs no secondary modifications.

PROCESSES

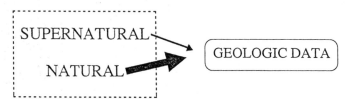

Figure A.3 *Prefer natural processes for geologic data.*

3. **Prefer known processes**: Interpreters of past events should prefer those interpretations which are in accord with the laws of physics and chemistry, and shun those which are statistically improbable. Supernatural causes should be invoked only when the evidence, carefully considered, dictates, or where the statements of Scripture specify. God's work of creation was completed at the end of six days, after which the earth's systems were to run in accordance with the natural laws He established, and it is these laws which govern geologic processes. The Biblicist is justified in ascribing certain geologic formations to "ex nihilo" creation on Day One and possibly Day Three of Creation Week, but even these rocks probably were altered by later processes. The Flood of Noah was both a natural and a supernatural event. Natural processes were used, such as erosion, deposition, faulting, and folding. These were not miraculous. However, a supernatural element appears to be present. These events occurred after God's command to Noah, and God's care and provision were vital.

4. **Apply the principle of least astonishment**: Geologists should prefer interpretations of ancient

geologic events which explain the greatest number of facts with the fewest assumptions. In short, the simpler, more straightforward, intuitive interpretation is preferred over the complex interpretation, all things being equal.

For example, cross beds in sandstone usually are considered to be a result of moving water depositing sand grains on an inclined surface. Others might consider the features to be due to crystalline rock fracture as pressure is released by overburden removal. The sedimentary origin clearly requires fewer assumptions and handles more data as well.

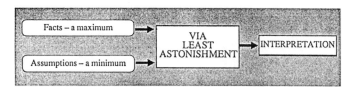

Figure A.4 *Principle of least astonishment.*

5. **Infer, by analogy, from modern processes and products**: Geologists should prefer explanations of the origin of geologic products that agree with geologic processes which they know or can infer to have occurred, without making the unlikely assumption that such processes have always acted at the same rate, scale, or intensity as at present. Observed geologic processes produce geologic products similar to, although usually of lesser extent, than geologic products of the past. By analogy, we can infer the type, rate, scale, and intensity of the processes responsible for products in the geologic record.

Consider, for example, the recent eruptions of Mount St. Helens. Although it was a

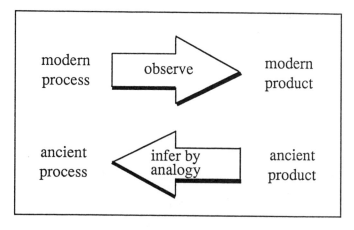

Figure A.5 *Make geologic inferences by analogy to modern processes and products.*

small-to-average volcano—much smaller than many that have operated in the past—it accomplished a great deal of geologic work. In places, finely laminated deposits many tens of feet thick were deposited; elsewhere huge canyons were eroded. A layer of peat is still being deposited and trees are being buried in upright positions, although not in the place of their growth, etc. All of these "products," which were formed catastrophically, are similar to products of the past, thus providing analogies which we can use to interpret past events.

HIKING FROM SOUTH RIM

Dozens of trails descend into Grand Canyon, and those from the south rim continue to be the most popular. No permit is required for *day* hikes on Grand Canyon National Park trails, but overnight camping within the park requires a permit. These must be obtained in advance. You should obtain the permit reservation form through the mail, by writing to the Grand Canyon Backcountry Reservations Office (address is given in appendix C). This office also provides trail-and-campsite information to assist in planning your hike.

The Havasupai Indians, whose reservation is located just west of Grand Canyon Village, allow hiking within Havasu Canyon by permit. This area offers extraordinary scenery and waterfalls in a remote section of Grand Canyon. For more information, write to Havasupai Tribal Enterprises (address has been listed in appendix C). Havasu Canyon is the home of this tribe which farms and raises cattle within the Canyon.

Three trails in the vicinity of Grand Canyon Village provide an excellent introduction to the Canyon. Each trail offers a different perspective on the geology, biology, and human history of Grand Canyon.

1. *Bright Angel Trail*: This has been called the "world's most famous footpath" and is, without doubt, the most traveled trail within the Canyon. It descends from Grand Canyon Village into Garden Creek Canyon, along the Bright Angel Fault. Water stops are frequent. Indian Gardens, a very popular campground, is only 4.6 miles, by trail, from the south rim. The Colorado River is 9.5 miles, by trail, below the rim. Suspension bridges provide easy crossing of the Colorado River. Bright Angel trail offers an "up-close-and- personal" view of the Canyon. It follows the side canyon so you can see rock formations in close proximity.

2. *South Kaibab Trail*: If spectacular vistas are what you desire, the South Kaibab Trail might be your first choice. The trailhead is near Yaki Point, just east of Grand Canyon Village. The trail descends on a ridge, allowing remarkable panoramic views of the Canyon. The river is only seven miles by trail, making this route one of the steepest. However, the trail is well constructed, very wide, and is well maintained. No water is available until you get to the river. A suspension bridge leads to campgrounds and Phantom Ranch on the north side of the Colorado River. Overnight campers often make a loop hike, going down the South Kaibab Trail and coming out the Bright Angel Trail.

3. *Grandview Trail*: One of the best-constructed backcountry trails is Grandview Trail. The trailhead is at Grandview Point, nine miles east of Grand Canyon Village. The trail was built by John Hance, a hundred years ago, to support mining activities within the Canyon. The trail provides access to primitive campsites and various backcountry trails.

From the trailhead, it is a three-mile hike to Horseshoe Mesa, a major promontory thrusting northward into the Canyon. Designated primitive campsites are maintained on the mesa, but no water is available. However, water can be obtained at a spring just a short distance east of the mesa. From Horseshoe Mesa, you have access to Cottonwood Creek (west of Horseshoe Mesa) and Hance Creek (east of Horseshoe Mesa). From Hance Creek, a trail descends to the Colorado River, through a superb exposure of Precambrian strata. These remote areas offer seclusion not experienced on the Bright Angel and South Kaibab Trails.

Backcountry Use Regulations For Grand Canyon National Park

1. A Backcountry Use Permit is required for all overnight backcountry use and must be in your possession while in the Backcountry.

2. Wood or charcoal fires are prohibited. However, the use of sterno or a backpack stove is permitted.

3. Carry out your trash. Burning or burying of trash or toilet paper is prohibited.

4. Firearms, bows and arrows are prohibited.

5. Pets are prohibited below the rim.

6. Leaving a trail or walkway to shortcut between portions of the same trail or walkway, or to shortcut to an adjacent trail or walkway is prohibited.

7. Throwing or rolling rocks or other items inside caves or caverns, into valleys, or canyons, down hillsides or mountainsides is prohibited.

8. Feeding, touching, teasing, frightening or intentional disturbing of wildlife nesting, breeding, or other activities is prohibited.

9. Possessing, destroying, injuring, defacing, removing, digging, or disturbing from its natural state any plants, rocks, animals, mineral, cultural or archaeological resources is prohibited. Walking on, entering, traversing or climbing an archaeological resources is prohibited.

10. The use of motorized vehicles or wheeled vehicles, such as motorcycles, baby buggies, bicycles, and similar vehicles, on trails below the rim is prohibited.

11. Fishing requires a valid fishing license or nonresident permit.

12. Writing, scratching, or otherwise defacing signs, buildings, or other property is prohibited.

13. Overnight private stock use requires a Backcountry Use Permit. Use is restricted to trails and campsites designated for stock.

14. More than one party/group from the same organization camping in the same designated campground or non-Corridor Use Area per night is prohibited. Violating a closure, designation, use or activity restriction or condition, schedule of visiting hours, or use limit is prohibited.

15. Use of soap in creeks or camping within 100 feet of any water source is prohibited.

16. The Backcountry Use Permit is valid only for the campsites and dates specified on the permit.

17. Commercial use of the backcountry must be authorized by concession permit or commercial use license.

Figure B.1 *Bright Angel Trail and South Kaibab Trail below the south rim at Grand Canyon Village. These trails offer the best general introduction to Grand Canyon below the rim. Because suspension bridges here cross the Colorado River, hikers have access to the north rim. Base map by U.S. Geological Survey at scale 1:62,500 (one inch equals one mile).*

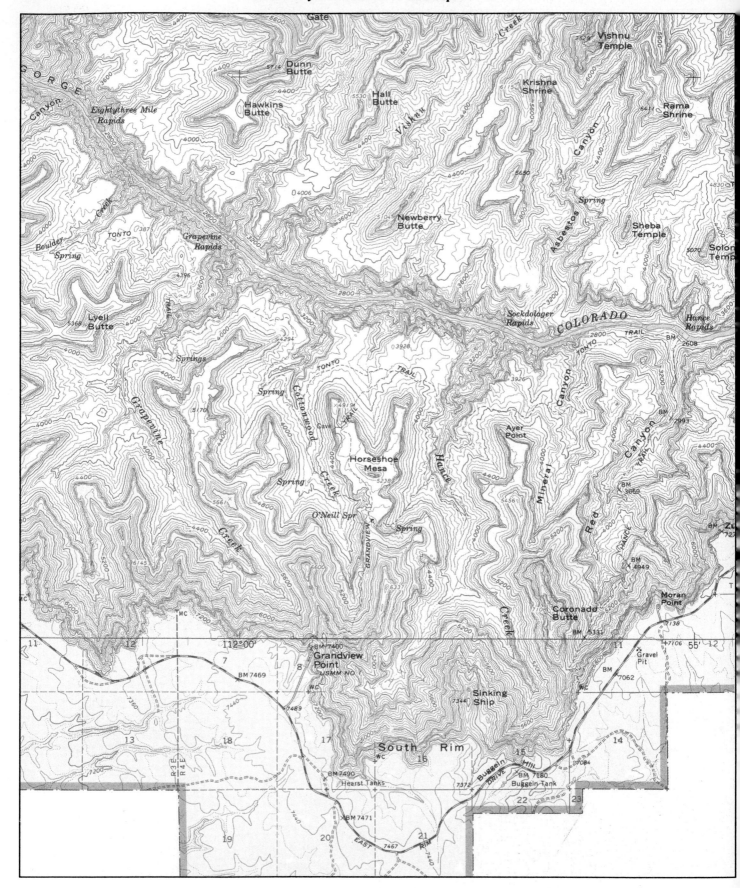

Figure B.2 *Grandview Trail below the south rim. This trail offers access to a more remote area of Grand Canyon. Horseshoe Mesa is three miles, by trail, below the rim. Base map by U.S. Geological Survey at scale 1:62,500 (one inch equals one mile).*

SOURCES OF INFORMATION

The national parks, monuments, recreation areas and attractions described in this book provide additional information and services. All provide brochures, with maps, which are very helpful in planning your visit. Addresses and phone numbers are provided so you can obtain this published information. Some of the information sources listed provide evolutionary interpretations of these features, without balanced creationist interpretations. Care must be exercised in distinguishing information from interpretation.

Grand Canyon Tour
Institute for Creation Research
10946 Woodside Avenue North
Santee, California 92071
(619) 448-0900
Conducts yearly creationist tour of Grand Canyon in April of each year, featuring raft trip, hiking groups, and bus tour. Two thousand Christians have participated in these yearly tours.

Grand Canyon National Park
P.O. Box 129
Grand Canyon, Arizona 86023
(520) 638-7888
General information on Grand Canyon. This phone has a computer switching service, which directs your call to the appropriate office.

Grand Canyon Backcountry Reservations Office
P.O. Box 129
Grand Canyon, Arizona 86023
(520) 638-7888
Overnight camping below the rim requires a permit, which is obtained by mailing in a reservation form. Phone reservations are **not** *accepted. You can request the reservation form by phone.*

Grand Canyon River Permits Office
P.O. Box 129
Grand Canyon, Arizona 86023
(520) 638-7888
Provides a current list of licensed companies offering river trips.

Grand Canyon Daily Weather Recording
(520) 638-7888
Updated daily, and very helpful for planning your activities while at Grand Canyon.

Grand Canyon National Park Lodges
P.O. Box 699
Grand Canyon, Arizona 86023
(520) 638-2401
Lodging, tours, and mule services within the national park.

Grand Canyon Airlines
P.O. Box 3038
Grand Canyon, Arizona 86023
(800) 528-2413
Daily overflight of Grand Canyon, weather permitting.

Grand Canyon Natural History Association
P.O. Box 399
Grand Canyon, Arizona 86023
(520) 638-2481
Books and maps on Grand Canyon which can be purchased through the mail.

Grand Canyon Theatre
P.O. Box 1397
Grand Canyon, Arizona 86023
(520) 638-2203
The theatre is located in Tusayan, just south of Grand Canyon Village, and features the motion picture, "Grand Canyon—The Hidden Secrets," projected on a seventy-foot-high screen.

Havasupai Tribal Enterprises
Havasupai Indian Reservation
Supai, Arizona 86435
(520) 448-2121
For permission to hike into the reservation in western Grand Canyon. They provide printed materials describing the hikes, camps, and natural features. An entry fee is charged.

Kaibab National Forest
800 South 6th Street
Williams, Arizona 86046
(520) 635-2681
Information on the national forest lands north and south of Grand Canyon.

Wupatki National Monument
HC33, Box 444A
Flagstaff, Arizona 86001
(520) 556-7040

Sunset Crater Volcano National Monument
Route 3, Box 149
Flagstaff, Arizona 86004
(520) 556-7042

Walnut Canyon National Monument
Walnut Canyon Road
Flagstaff, Arizona 86004
(520) 526-3367

Meteor Crater Enterprises, Inc.
P.O. Box AC
Winslow, AZ 86047
(520) 289-2362

Petrified Forest National Park
Holbrook, Arizona 86028
(520) 524-6228

Zion National Park
Springdale, Utah 84767
(801) 772-3256

Bryce Canyon National Park
Bryce Canyon, Utah 84717
(801) 834-5322

Glen Canyon National Recreation Area
P.O. Box 1507
Page, Arizona 86040
(520) 645-8404

Lake Powell Resorts and Marinas
ARA Leisure Services, Inc.
P.O. Box 56909
Phoenix, Arizona 85079
(800) 528-6154

Rainbow Bridge National Monument
P.O. Box 1507
Page, Arizona 86040
(520) 645-8404

Monument Valley
Navajo Tribal Park
P.O. Box 93
Monument Valley, Utah 84536
(801) 727-3287

In addition to the sources of information mentioned above, six inexpensive books may be found helpful in getting more familiar with things to see and do in Grand Canyon:

Aitchison, Stewart *A, Naturalist's Guide to Hiking the Grand Canyon* (Englewood Cliffs, N.J., Prentice-Hall, 1985).
In-depth information on hiking thirty Grand Canyon trails.

Belknap, Buzz and Loie Evans, *Grand Canyon River Guide* (Evergreen, Colorado, Westwater Books, 2nd edition, 1989).
Well-illustrated rafter's guide to Grand Canyon.

Carothers, Steven W. and Bryan T. Brown, *The Colorado River Through Grand Canyon: Natural History and Human Change* (Tucson, University of Arizona Press, 1991).
Stream ecology and human impact on the Colorado River.

Stevens, Larry, *The Colorado River in Grand Canyon: A Comprehensive Guide to its Natural and Human History* (Flagstaff, Arizona, Red Lake Books, 2nd edition, 1983).
Another rafter's guide. Contains more detail than the previous river guide and has stronger evolutionary bias.

Thybony, Scott, *A Guide to Hiking the Inner Canyon* (Grand Canyon, Arizona, Grand Canyon Natural History Association, 1980).
Introduction for hiking the most popular Grand Canyon trails.

Whitney, Stephen A., *A Field Guide to the Grand Canyon* (New York, William Morrow and Co., 1982).
Especially helpful guide to plants and animals of Grand Canyon.

1. In what ways is study of Grand Canyon relevant to the major humanist versus theist debate of our generation?

   _____

   _____

   _____

   _____

2. How does one's interpretation of the geology and biology of Grand Canyon affect one's acceptance of foundational Christian doctrines?

   _____

   _____

   _____

   _____

3. How can our understanding of Grand Canyon be used to communicate the truths of the Lord Jesus Christ as Creator, Redeemer, and Coming King?

   _____

   _____

   _____

   _____

   _____

4.   Explain how the "interpretive framework" determines or biases a person's
      understanding of rock strata and fossils of Grand Canyon.

      _____

      _____

      _____

      _____

      _____

      _____

      _____

5.   Describe several geologic structures which can be seen in Grand Canyon.

      _____

      _____

      _____

      _____

      _____

      _____

      _____

6.   Into which phases of the panorama of Earth history presented, in Genesis 1-10, does
      each part of Grand Canyon fit?

      _____

      _____

      _____

      _____

      _____

      _____

7. What evidences can you cite indicating catastrophic flood processes formed strata of Grand Canyon?

_____

_____

_____

_____

_____

_____

_____

8. Do analyses of radioisotopes in Grand Canyon rocks prove great age? Explain your answer.

_____

_____

_____

_____

_____

_____

_____

9. Did long periods of time occur on erosion surfaces separating successive formations? Explain the different interpretations of evolutionists and creationists.

_____

_____

_____

_____

_____

_____

10. What are three theories for the erosion of Grand Canyon?

_____

_____

_____

_____

_____

_____

11. Explain how fossils of Grand Canyon distinctly illustrate each of these:
Creation, Fall, and Flood.

_____

_____

_____

_____

_____

_____

_____

12. Are the Kaibab and Abert squirrels evidence of evolution? Why, or why not?

_____

_____

_____

_____

_____

_____

_____

13. What is the major environmental factor at Grand Canyon determining the distribution of plants?

_____

_____

_____

_____

_____

14. In what ways do plants and animals at Grand Canyon show evidence of economy and efficiency, as they "live at peace" with their environment? Contrast these observations to Darwin's view of "struggle for survival."

_____

_____

_____

_____

_____

15. Why does the general circulation of the atmosphere occur, and what does it produce?

_____

_____

_____

_____

_____

16.   What scientific evidence indicates that a pre-Flood vapor canopy existed?

_____

_____

_____

_____

_____

_____

_____

17.   Can you offer a Scriptural explanation for the religion, culture, and history of the
       first people who inhabited the Southwest desert?

_____

_____

_____

_____

_____

_____

18.   What are four research projects creationists have conducted on Grand Canyon?

_____

_____

_____

_____

_____

_____

Abrasion—The mechanical wearing of a **rock** by friction, rubbing, or grinding. One of four agents of **erosion**. The other three agents are **solution, plucking,** and **cavitation.**

Absorption—The process in which incident radiant energy is retained by a substance and converted into some other form of energy. **Absorption** of solar **radiation** at the earth's surface results in warming of the surface and emission of longer-wavelength terrestrial **radiation.**

Adaptation—An adjustment in the structure or function within the genetic range of an organism so that the organism benefits.

Alluvium—A general term describing all river-deposited **sediment** of recent times. The term includes **sediment** deposits of riverbeds, river flood plains, river deltas, and alluvial fans.

Algal—Of, pertaining to, or composed of algae.

Alcove—A small, wide canyon with an arched, often overhanging, wall at its head. Where greatly enlarged, an **alcove** forms an **amphitheater-headed canyon.**

Amphibole—A group of silicate minerals often with abundant iron and magnesium. Hornblende is the most common rock-forming amphibole. It has dark color and cleavage angles of 60° and 120°.

Amphitheater-headed canyon—A steep-sided valley with a wide upper end (head), not a narrow upper end beginning in a **gully.** The Grand Canyon's side canyons are often **amphitheater-headed,** and are believed to have formed by the process of **sapping.**

Anasazi—"The Ancient Ones," the early immigrant native Americans who occupied the Grand Canyon before 800 A.D. The **Anasazi** flourished within Grand Canyon by 1100 A.D. They are the ancestors of the **Hopi, Zuni,** and **Pueblo** tribes.

Andesite—A fine-grained **igneous rock** composed of the minerals **amphibole** (25% to 40%), biotite, and **plagioclase feldspar,** but no **quartz** or **orthoclase feldspar.** It forms from **lava** flows (probably derived from fractionation of partially melted basaltic material), and is a common **volcanic rock** in mountains bordering the Pacific Ocean. San Francisco Peaks, south of Grand Canyon, contain andesitic flows.

Angle of repose—The maximum slope or angle at which a material such as soil, sand, or loose rock remains stable. When the angle is exceeded, mass movement occurs. **Talus** slopes in Grand Canyon illustrate the **angle of repose.** Talus, composed of blocks one foot in diameter, has an **angle of repose** of 35°.

Angular unconformity—An **erosion** surface which has older **strata** below, dipping at a different (usually steeper) angle than the younger **strata** above. Compare to **disconformity, nonconformity,** and **paraconformity.** The word **unconformity** describes the general class to which the four **erosion** surfaces described above belong.

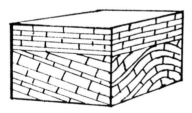

Antecedent River theory—Explanation for **erosion** of Grand Canyon by the ancestral Colorado River. The river maintained its course while uplift of the plateau occurred during tens of millions of years. The theory is now unpopular among geologists.

Anticline—A fold structure in which the **strata** flex in two directions dipping away from the fold. Compare with **syncline** and **monocline.**

Anticyclone—A closed atmospheric **circulation** of air which moves in a clockwise direction around a high-pressure center in the northern hemisphere.

Apatite—A group of calcium phosphate minerals, the most common of which is fluorapatite, $Ca_5(PO_4)_3F$. Teeth and bones of vertebrates are dominated by **apatite**.

Aphelion—The point on the earth's elliptical orbit around the sun which is farthest from the sun. The opposite to **perihelion**.

Aragonite—A **mineral** composed of calcium carbonate ($CaCO_3$) with a packing structure more dense than **calcite**. **Aragonite** is the most important component of the shells of clams and snails.

Arthropod—An organism belonging to Arthropoda, the diverse **phylum** of animals encased in an external chitinous skeleton with jointed legs. **Trilobites** are a class of the **arthropods**.

Artifact—A man-made object providing evidence of ancient culture.

Atlatl—A throwing stick used by prehistoric people before development of the bow and arrow.

Atmosphere—The gaseous envelope surrounding the earth.

Atmospheric stability—The tendency for vertical displacement of air not to occur. If the **atmosphere** is *stable*, displaced parcels of air will tend to *return to their level of origin*. If the **atmosphere** is *unstable*, displaced parcels of air will tend to *accelerate to positions away from their level of origin*. The greater the instability of the **atmosphere** the more likely is **cloud** formation, precipitation, and severe weather.

Augite—See **pyroxene**.

Autotroph—An organism which supplies its own food, needing only carbon dioxide or carbonates as a source of carbon and a simple inorganic nitrogen compound for metabolism. Contrast with **heterotroph**.

Backcutting—A style of **erosion** in which the cutting action is directed in a lateral or horizontal direction, not in a downward direction. Contrast with **downcutting**.

Ball court—A structure built by native American tribes where players propelled a rubber ball around the court. The game originated in Mesoamerica and had a ritual as well as sporting significance.

Basalt—A dark-colored, fine-grained **igneous rock** composed of **plagioclase feldspar** (greater than 50%) and **pyroxene**. The mineral **olivine** may or may not be present. **Basalt** forms from **lava** flows, and, with **andesite**, represents 98% of all volcanic **rocks**. The Precambrian Cardenas Basalt of Grand Canyon is a deeply buried **basalt** flow. On the north rim of Grand Canyon, **basalt** occurs as flows around recent volcanoes.

Basket maker—The prehistoric culture of the early pre-pueblo stages of the **Anasazi**, so called for the many woven vegetal baskets found at their habitation sites.

Bed—A layer of **sediment** which is greater than one centimeter thick. (Compare with **lamina**.)

Bedded—Containing numerous beds superimposed. Compare with **laminated**.

Bedding plane—The surface forming the boundary between two successive layers of **sedimentary rock**. A **bedding plane** may show **fossils**, **ripple marks**, or **shrinkage cracks**.

Bedrock—Solid **rock** exposed at the earth's surface or overlain by unconsolidated materials.

Bench—A narrow strip of relatively level earth or **rock** between higher and lower slopes.

Benthonic—Living on the floor of the deep ocean.

Beryl—A beryllium-aluminum silicate mineral which occurs mainly in **pegmatites** associated with **granite**. Emerald and aquamarine are gem varieties of beryl.

Bioherm—A mound-like or reef-like structure composed of sedentary marine creatures. Compare to **reef**.

Biome—A restricted geographic province delineated by a dominant plant species.

Biota—All the living plants and animals of an area.

Biotite—See **mica**.

Birefringent—Property of many crystals which cause a beam of light to be divided into two beams.

Blue-green algae—See **cyanophytes**.

Body fossil—A remain or impression which preserves the material or form of the actual body of a once-living organism. Contrast with **trace fossil**.

Boulder—A rock fragment whose diameter is more than 25.6 centimeters (ten inches). This rock fragment is larger than a **cobble**, or bigger than a standard volleyball.

Brachiopod—An organism belonging to Brachiopoda, the **phylum** of shelled marine animals with two unequal shells, each of which is bilaterally symmetrical.

Breached Dam theory—Theory proposing that Grand Canyon was eroded by catastrophic drainage of a lake after failure of a dam.

Breccia—**Sediment** or **sedimentary rock** composed of large angular fragments in a matrix of finer particles. Four types are recognized: sedimentary **breccia**, volcanic **breccia**, fault **breccia**, and impact **breccia**. If the fragments are well rounded, the rock is called **conglomerate**.

Bryozoan—An organism belonging to Bryozoa, the **phylum** of tiny, colonial, marine animals that build **calcareous** structures. They occur in the modern sea and are called "moss animals."

Burrow—A cylindrical tube-shaped biological structure, often filled with **sand** or **clay** which may occur along a single **bedding plane**, or may penetrate through various **bedding planes** within a **sedimentary rock**.

Butte—An isolated hill, usually capped by a flat-lying resistant layer of rock. A **butte** is the erosional remnant of **strata**, which were once more extensive. May be contrasted with a **mesa** which is much more broad then it is tall.

Calcareous—Containing **calcium carbonate** (primarily the minerals **calcite** or **aragonite**).

Calcite—A **mineral** composed of calcium carbonate ($CaCO_3$), with a packing structure less dense than **aragonite**. **Calcite** is a primary **mineral** forming **limestone**.

Calcium carbonate—Chemical name given to the solid $CaCO_3$ which occurs naturally within the earth as the minerals **calcite** and **aragonite**.

Cambrian System—Lowest, flat-lying **strata** system in Grand Canyon. It includes the Tapeats Sandstone, Bright Angel Shale, and Muav Limestone. It contains the earliest-known multicellular fossil organisms with hard parts. Compare to **Precambrian**. See also **system** and **geologic column**.

Canyon—A steep-walled chasm, gorge, or ravine cut by **erosion** into the surface of the earth.

Carbon dating—Technique used to obtain the "age" of a once-living thing, or artifacts containing carbon, using the proportion of radioactive carbon-14 to nonradioactive carbon-12. Because of the short **half-life** of radioactive carbon (5,730 years), the method only gives ages of thousands of years.

Carbonate—Broad class of minerals and rocks containing large amounts of carbon and oxygen.

Cast—Type of **fossil**, preserving simply the surface impression of an organism, or its track.

Catastrophe—A natural geologic event of high magnitude (energy), wide extent (area), short duration (power), and low frequency (probability).

Catastrophism—The doctrine that ancient geologic changes occurred largely in response to rapid and catastrophic processes, which were interposed between periods of slow and gradual change. Compare to **uniformitarianism**.

Catastrophist—A person who believes in the doctrine of **catastrophism**. Contrast with **uniformitarian**.

Cavitation—A catastrophic agent of **erosion** associated with high-velocity fluid flow, where vacuum bubbles form in the fluid and then collapse. **Cavitation** has been demonstrated to create pressures of many thousands of pounds per square inch and is able to pulverize rapidly the hardest of rocks. Catastrophic water-flow events usually create important **erosion** structures by **cavitation**. **Plucking** and **abrasion** are other catastrophic agents of **erosion**.

Cement—Minerals which have precipitated in between the grains of **sediment** and which bind the individual particles together to produce a **sedimentary rock**.

Channeled Scabland—A 16,000-square-mile area of eastern Washington State, containing a variety of landforms eroded and deposited by catastrophic drainage of ancient **Lake Missoula**, in Montana. More than 50 cubic miles of soft silt, **sediment**, and solid-rock lava flows were carved out to make a vast and elaborate network of scabland channels. The abandoned, usually dry, erosional channels are called **coulees**. The largest erosional feature of the **Channeled Scabland** is **Grand Coulee**, a trench 50 miles long, two miles wide, and up to 900 feet deep, chiseled into solid **basalt.**

Chaparral—A **biome** of semiarid evergreen shrubs.

Chemical weathering—Chemical reactions which decompose rocks exposed at the earth's surface. Water and the **atmosphere** are the primary agents which react with rocks. Specific **chemical-weathering** processes are **oxidation**, hydrolysis, carbonation and direct **solution**. **Chemical weathering** is also called chemical decomposition or **degradation.**

Chert—A **sedimentary rock** composed of crypto-crystalline silicon dioxide. It occurs often as nodules in Grand Canyon **limestones**. It has various colors (white, red, and black are common) but is best distinguished from **limestone** by its greater hardness. Steel will not scratch **chert.**

Chitinous—Composed of *chitin*, a resistant organic compound of the same structure as cellulose. Chitin composes the exoskeletons of insects, crabs, and many other marine creatures.

Cinder cone—A cone-shaped volcanic hill composed of loose fragments ejected by the volcano. Sunset Crater, north of Flagstaff, Arizona, is an excellent example.

Circulation—The flow or motion of a fluid such as air. There are **circulation** patterns for the entire earth or for local storms such as **cyclones.**

Clast—An individual fragment within a **sedimentary rock** which has been produced by physical disintegration of a larger mass.

Clastic—Consisting of rocks or of organic components which have been moved individually from their place of origin. The individual fragments are called **clasts.**

Clay—Sedimentary material composed of very small particles less than 1/256 millimeter in diameter. **Clay** minerals are chiefly hydrous aluminum silicates weathered from **feldspar**, **pyroxene** or **amphibole.** A **clay** particle is smaller than **silt.** **Clay** is an important component of the rock called **shale.**

Climate—The long-term manifestations of **weather.** The **climate** of a specified area is represented by a statistical collection of **weather** conditions during a specified interval of time (usually several decades).

Climax—The terminal stage in an ecological succession of communities. Contrast with **sere.**

Cloud—The visible mass of water or ice particles suspended usually at considerable height in the **atmosphere.**

Cobble—A rock fragment with diameter between 64 millimeters and 256 millimeters (tennis-ball-to-volleyball size). A cobble is larger than a **pebble**, but smaller than a **boulder.**

Coelenterate—Any organism belonging to the Phylum Cnidaria of solitary or colonial animals whose soft bodies consist of a single cavity with fleshy feeding tentacles. These organisms include the **hydra** and sea anemone. **Coral** is a common coelenterate **fossil** of Grand Canyon.

Cogenetic—Pertaining to an assemblage of geologic structures which have been produced by similar physical processes and formed during a short interval of time.

Cohonina—Native American hunters and gatherers who entered the western Grand Canyon about 700 A.D. They may be the ancestors of the **Havasupai**, who, today, farm and raise cattle in the Canyon.

Compaction—Decrease in volume of sediment by the application of compressive stress. Compaction can be induced in sediment by (1) continued deposition above, (2) drying, (3) by energetic events such as earthquakes and (4) by **syneresis.** See **evulsion.**

Competition—The negative interaction between organisms for food, space, or breeding, which inhibits life processes. Contrast with **cooperation** and **mutualism.**

Condensation nuclei—Particles upon which water vapor begins to condense in the **atmosphere.** Such particles are necessary in order that condensation may take place with **relative humidities** near 100%.

Conglomerate—A **sedimentary rock** composed of rounded fragments of **pebbles**, **cobbles**, or **boulders.** If the fragments are angular, the rock is called **breccia.**

Constellation—Any one of 88 groups of stars used to divide the areas of the night sky.

Convolution—A geologic form or structure which has been produced by folding.

Cooperation—The particular interactions of organisms that benefit each. A synonym of **mutualism.**

Coral—A subgroup of the soft-bodied **coelenterates**.

Coriolis force—An apparent force on air moving relative to the earth's surface. The **coriolis force** is a result of fixing one's frame of reference to the earth's surface, which is itself experiencing an acceleration relative to a frame of reference fixed to the stars. The **coriolis force** causes air to turn to the right of its path in the northern hemisphere.

Coulee—A long, steep-walled, trenchlike gorge or canyon representing an abandoned outflow channel eroded rapidly by catastrophic drainage of water. The largest **coulee** in Washington is **Grand Coulee.**

Creation—The doctrine that both living and nonliving things came into existence by the supernatural acts of God. The idea that things were formed by an **intelligent cause**. Contrast with **evolution.**

Creation Week—The six-day period of time in which God created the heavens, earth, and living things, along with the seventh day, on which God rested. See Genesis chapters 1 and 2.

Creationist—A person who believes in the doctrine of **creation**. Contrast with **evolutionist.**

Cretaceous—See **geologic column.**

Crinoid—A type of sea lily (animal) consisting of a cup or "head" containing vital organs, radiating arms, jointed stem, and roots by which it is attached to the sea floor. **Crinoids** belong to the **echinoderms.**

Cross-bedding—A type of **stratification** in which sediment grains accumulate along a surface that is inclined with respect to the prevailing current direction. For example, this bedding is observed on the down-current slope of both a desert **dune** and a subaqueous **sand wave**. **Cross-bedding** is common in the Coconino Sandstone, Supai Group sandstones, and Kaibab Limestone.

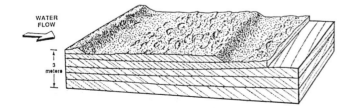

Cross-cutting relationships, principle of—Any feature which breaks the continuity of structure or cross-cuts **strata** must postdate the structure or **strata**. Canyons, faults, impact craters, and related features postdate the rocks containing them. A **fault** buried beneath an **unconformity** is older than the **unconformity**. This principle gives sequence in time—not absolute age or duration.

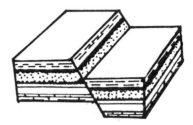

Crystalline—Texture of a rock consisting wholly of crystals or fragments of crystals which have an interlocking arrangement. This texture applies to **igneous rocks** which have cooled from a molten state and **metamorphic rocks** which have undergone recrystallization at high temperatures or pressures. Contrast with **clastic**.

Cyanophytes or **Cyanobacteria**—The technical name for "blue-green algae." Now usually classified with bacteria, these organisms do not have a central nucleus. Like plants, they perform **photosynthesis**.

Cyclone—A closed atmospheric **circulation** of air which moves in a counterclockwise direction around a low-pressure center in the northern hemisphere. The term **cyclone** is also used in other parts of the world to refer to what are called hurricanes in the United States.

Dating—see **radioisotope dating.**

Deformation—The group of processes that, because of application of pressure, change the form or volume of a **rock**. Folding, faulting, and solid flow are specific processes leading to deformation.

Degradation—Processes operative in the present world which tend to lower in grade, rank, or status, things we see.

Delta—A deposit of **sediment**, which is usually triangular in map view, formed where a river enters either a lake or the ocean.

Dendritic—Resembling in map view the branching pattern of certain trees. River drainage basins often have a **dendritic** pattern of streams.

Dendrochronology—A system of dating based on the growth-ring pattern in trees.

Density—The ratio of the mass of any substance to its volume.

Deposition—The process whereby **sediment** is accumulated at the earth's surface. Also called **sedimentation**. Contrast with **erosion**.

Desert—A geographic region characterized by less than ten inches of rainfall per year.

Desert varnish—Darkened chemical coating covering the surface of a rock in the **desert**. Although the interior of the rock may be light colored, the hard, sometimes shiny coating of brown-to-black manganese oxide and clay minerals is built up or deposited on the rock surface over hundreds of years. **Desert varnish** indicates a long period of stability—not continuous, slow **erosion**. It is useful in spotting **relict** landforms.

Desiccate—To dry up or exhaust of moisture.

Desiccation crack—A **shrinkage crack** formed on the surface of a **clay** or clayey bed due to drying under the sun's heat. Loosely called "**mud crack**." Contrast with **syneresis crack**.

Design—Particular order or form which, by the "principle of uniform experience," requires an **intelligent cause**. See **uniform experience, principle of.**

Detritus—Surface material which has been produced by disintegration and **weathering** of rocks, and which has been moved from its original position.

Devonian—See **geologic column**.

Diabase—A type of igneous **intrusive rock** with composition similar to **basalt**.

Diagenesis—All of the chemical, physical, and biologic changes undergone by **sediment** after it is deposited, and through its existence as a rock.

Dike—A tabular body of **intrusive rock** that cuts across the structural features (e.g., **stratification**) of the surrounding rock. Contrast to **sill**. **Dikes** of Zoroaster Granite penetrate the Vishnu Schist in the inner gorge of Grand Canyon.

Disaggregate—To break up or break apart, especially to separate into component parts.

Discharge—The volume of water moving through a given cross section of a stream channel during a given unit of time.

Disconformity—A type of **unconformity** where **erosion** has occurred, producing discordance of bedding on a surface between **strata** which are parallel above and below the surface. Compare to **unconformity, angular unconformity, nonconformity,** and **paraconformity**.

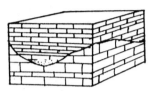

DNA—The basic chemical molecule that determines the traits inherited by living things. **DNA** is the abbreviation for deoxyribose nucleic acid.

Dolomite—A **mineral** composed of calcium and magnesium carbonate. The chemical formula for **dolomite** is $CaMg(CO_3)_2$.

Dolomite—A **sedimentary rock** composed mainly of calcium magnesium carbonate. Also the name of the **mineral** with the same composition.

Downcutting—Stream **erosion** in which the cutting action is directed in a downward direction, not in a lateral or horizontal direction. Contrast with **backcutting**.

Downwarp—A subsidence or downward bend of a part of the earth's crust. The opposite of **upwarp**.

Drainage basin—The total area of the earth's surface that contributes water to a river.

Dune—A low hill or mound of fine-grained material that has accumulated from **sediment** transported by a current of wind or water. A **sand wave** is an underwater **dune** composed of **sand**.

Duricrust—A hard crust on the surface of, or layer in the upper horizons of, a soil of a semiarid climate. The consolidation of the soil is caused by upward migration and precipitation of mineral-bearing solutions by capillary action and evaporation at the surface during the dry season. The most common type of duricrust is a caliche, a soil cemented by calcareous materials.

Echinoderm—An organism belonging to Echinodermata, the **phylum** of exclusively marine invertebrate animals which have radial and five-rayed symmetry. **Crinoids** of Grand Canyon are **echinoderms**.

Ecliptic—The great circle on the celestial sphere which is the apparent annual path of the sun around the earth. The plane in which this circle lies is called the "plane of the **ecliptic**." The angle this plane makes with the plane passing through the earth's equator is called the "obliquity of the **ecliptic**."

Ecological niche—The location where an organism lives. It is characterized by specific conditions of the environment and available food.

Ecology—The study of the relationships between organisms and their environments.

Effigy—Lifelike representation, especially of a living being.

Encyst—To form or become enclosed within a cyst.

Equinox—Either of the two points of intersection of the sun's apparent annual path around the earth and the plane of the earth's equator. These two points occur at the intersection of the **ecliptic** and the earth's equator. At the two equinoxes, day and night are of equal length.

Erathem—Body of strata composed of several **systems** thought to be deposited during a geologic era.

Erosion—A large group of processes that loosen or remove surface material and transport it from one place on the earth's surface to another. Water, ice, wind, and gravity are important agents of **erosion**. **Cavitation**, **plucking**, and **abrasion** are three catastrophic mechanisms of water **erosion**. A fourth agent of erosion is **solution**. Contrast with **deposition**.

Eucaryotes—Single-celled organisms whose cells show internal membranes and organized chromosomes. Compare to **procaryotes**.

Evolution—The notion that both living and nonliving things came into existence by the unaided activity of natural processes and without an **intelligent cause**. Contrast with **creation**.

Evolutionist—A person who believes in the doctrine of **evolution**. Contrast with **creationist**.

Evulsion—The act of plucking or pulling out by force. **Compaction** of wet **sediment** causes water to be driven out of the spaces between mineral grains, often catastrophically as a result of an earthquake.

Extinction—The total elimination of distinct populations of organisms.

Extrusive rock—**Igneous rock** which, in a fluid state, was accumulated on the earth's surface. Compare to **intrusive rock**.

Facies—A distinctive group of characteristics (such as composition, grain size, fossil assemblage) within part of a **rock** body or **strata** unit that differ as a group from those characteristics found elsewhere within the same **rock** body or **strata** unit.

Fault—A surface within the earth along which breakage and displacement of rock has occurred.

Fauna—Entire animal population living in a given area.

Feldspar—A group of **minerals** composed of silicon, oxygen, and aluminum (aluminum silicate) with one or more of the metals sodium, potassium or calcium. **Feldspar** is the most abundant group of minerals occurring in the earth's crust. Sodium and calcium substitute for each other in plagioclase **feldspars**. Potassium **feldspar** is called **orthoclase**.

Fetish—A charm or object made by man and regarded as possessing consciousness, volition, supernatural qualities, or magic powers.

Firmament—A Biblical term referring, at least in part, to the earth's **atmosphere**. It was created on the second day of **Creation** and was placed between the waters above and the waters beneath. **Firmament** also includes the space above the atmosphere. See Genesis 1:6,7,8,14–17.

Flake—A small fragment of stone, discarded while chipping or fashioning a tool, scraper, or projectile point.

Flocculate—To cause to be aggregated into small lumps. Clay minerals and other very fine **sediments** are especially susceptible to the formation of aggregates after being dispersed in water. Charged surfaces on clay minerals are the primary cause of **flocculation**.

Flood—See **Noah's flood**.

Flood erosion—The complex of processes which rapidly remove **sediment** and **rock**. See **cavitation** and **plucking**.

Flood plain—The level area bordering a river or stream that is occasionally flooded.

Fluvial—Of, or pertaining to, rivers.

Fold—A bend or zone of flexure in a rock. Examples of folds are **anticlines**, **synclines**, and **monoclines**.

Foraminifera—Unicellular marine organisms which secrete a very small shell of calcium carbonate. Although considered "primitive," **foraminifera** are *not* found in the lowest **strata** of Grand Canyon. **Foraminifera** are classified among the **protozoan**.

Formation—A body of **rock strata** which has distinctive character for study and mapping. Two or more **formations** are called a **group**. A *division* of a **formation** is a **member**. Usually, a **formation** possesses one hundred feet or more thickness of **strata** so it can be shown on a map.

Fossil—A naturally occurring remnant or evidence of ancient life. Two broad categories are recognized: the **body fossil** (bone, shell, etc.), and the **trace fossil** (trail, **burrow**, etc.).

Front—The interface or transition zone between two air masses of different temperatures.

Fusulinid—Any **foraminifera** belonging to the suborder Fusulinina.

Galaxy—A large collection of stars, dust, and gas which is regarded as the building block of the universe. Our **galaxy**, the Milky Way Galaxy, contains approximately 100 billion stars.

Gene pool—The sum total of all genes in an interbreeding **population** of organisms.

Genetic code—The specific molecular arrangement of **DNA** that is responsible for passing on information. It governs the development of organisms.

Geochronology—The study of time and its relationship to the history of the earth.

Geologic block diagram—A drawing depicting the three-dimensional structure and arrangement of **rocks** as they would occur on the surfaces of a block cut from the earth.

Geologic column—Idealized or complete sequence of **strata** which is constructed by superimposing **strata**

systems. The conventional, or popular North American "geologic column" is given in the following sequence of twelve "systems."

"System"	"Erathem"
Quaternary Tertiary	Cenozoic
Cretaceous Jurassic Triassic	Mesozoic
Permian Pennsylvanian Mississippian Devonian Silurian Ordovician Cambrian	Paleozoic
"Precambrian" (no specific systems recognized)	Proterozoic Archeozoic

Geologic cross section—A drawing depicting the structure and arrangement of rocks as they would appear in a vertical plane below the surface of the earth.

Geomorphic—Of, or pertaining to, the form of the earth's surface, including its landforms.

Glacier—A mass of ice formed from compacted snow which is thick enough to flow plastically.

Glauconite—A dull-green, amorphous, and earthy or granular mineral, or group of minerals, belonging to the **mica** group. It consists of hydrous silicates of potassium and iron, and occurs in sedimentary strata from Cambrian to the present.

Gneiss—A **metamorphic rock** possessing alignment of light-colored and dark-colored minerals which have segregated into distinct layers.

Gorge—A narrow passage with very steep rocky cliffs enclosed between elevated terrain. The inner **gorge** of Grand Canyon provides the passage for the Colorado River.

Graded bedding—A type of bedding in sedimentary deposits in which each layer possesses a decrease in grain size from the bottom to the top of the **bed**. Many graded beds resemble **turbidites**, beds which formed from sediment gravity flows.

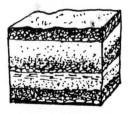

Grand Coulee—The largest **coulee** of the **Channeled Scabland** of eastern Washington. **Grand Coulee** is 50 miles long, two miles wide, and 900 feet deep. Its volume is almost 10 cubic miles and was eroded through solid **basalt**. Most geologists have been convinced by the evidences offered by J Harlen Bretz, who proposed that Grand Coulee was eroded by catastrophic drainage of **Lake Missoula**.

Granite—A coarse-grained, crystalline **intrusive**, **igneous rock** which is composed of **orthoclase** (K-feldspar), **plagioclase**, **quartz** and small amounts of ferromagnesian minerals (usually **biotite**).

Gravel—Unconsolidated, rounded **rock** fragments consisting of particles larger than **sand** and possessing diameters from 2 millimeters (1/12 inch) to 76 millimeters (3.0 inches). Compare with **pebble**.

Greenhouse effect—The heating effect exerted by the **atmosphere** upon the earth by virtue of the fact that water vapor, carbon dioxide, and ozone absorb and reemit **infrared radiation**. The shorter wavelengths of the sun's **radiation** are transmitted rather freely through the **atmosphere**, to be **absorbed** at the earth's surface. The earth then reemits this as long-wavelength **infrared radiation**, a portion of which is **absorbed** by the **atmosphere** and reemitted. The mean-surface temperature of the earth is higher by this effect than the required equilibrium temperature for a blackbody at the earth's mean distance from the sun.

Group—A geological map unit consisting of two or more **formations**.

Growth position—Used to describe fossils which are in the same orientation relative to the layers of **strata** as when the organisms were living.

Gully—A very narrow valley worn in the earth by running water confined to a channel. Contrast with **amphitheater-headed canyon**.

Gypsum—**Mineral** composed of calcium and sulfate with added water. The chemical formula for gypsum is $CaSO_4.2H_2O$. Gypsum is used in the manufacture of plaster.

Half-life—The theoretical period of time that would be required for one-half of the quantity of a **radioactive isotope** to decay, assuming constant rate of decay.

Havasupai—The native American culture which today occupies a reservation within Grand Canyon. The **Havasupai** farm the fertile soil in Havasu Canyon and profit from tourism. They are believed to be the descendants of the **Cohonina**.

Heterotroph—An organism which cannot supply its own food, but requires complex compounds of carbon and nitrogen for metabolism. Contrast with **Autotroph**.

Hiatus—Time value represented by **strata** which are now missing at a physical break or **unconformity** within a succession of **strata**. **Creationists** and **evolutionists** have different ideas about the magnitude of time represented by a **hiatus**.

Hierarchy—A graded or ranked series allowing all-encompassing things to be placed above things which are rather small and restricted.

History—The chronology of significant events of the past, usually with an explanation of causes.

Hogan—The traditional home of the **Navajo**, usually made of logs and mud assembled in a circular fashion, with a domed, mud roof, dirt floor, and doorway facing east.

Hopi—A present-day native American tribe, most likely descended from the **Anasazi**, who live in northeastern Arizona.

Hornblende—See **amphibole**.

Hydra—A member of numerous small tubular polyps having at one end a mouth surrounded by tentacles.

Hydroid—One of the hydrozoans of the class of **coelenterates**.

Hydrostatic equilibrium—The state of a fluid, such as air, when its surfaces of constant pressure and density coincide and are horizontal throughout. Under such conditions, the fluid will remain at rest or move at constant velocity.

Hypolimnon—The lowermost layer of water in a lake, characterized by uniform temperature that is generally colder than the water layer above it. Lake Powell has a distinctive **hypolimnon**, and Glen Canyon Dam draws this 45°F water into the Colorado River in Grand Canyon.

Ice age—Period of earth history following **Noah's flood** when global cooling occurred, allowing the buildup of continental and valley **glaciers**. The "Ice age" appears to have coincided with the Tower of Babel in the history of the Bible. At this time, when sea level was lower, peoples were dispersed widely upon the earth.

Ichnofossils—**Fossils** which provide only indirect traces of life. Examples include trackways, **burrows**, and resting sites. Also called **trace fossils**. Contrast with **body fossil**.

Icthyostegid—A type of four-footed amphibian known from the **fossil** record.

Igneous rock—**Rock** which has formed from cooling and solidification of molten material. These rocks form by cooling of **lava** or **magma**. See also **volcanic rock** and **intrusive rock**.

Impact crater—Any bowl-shaped structure in **rock** or **sediment** formed by the impact of an unspecified projectile. Meteor Crater in Arizona is believed to have formed by the impact of a meteorite.

Incised meander—A deep, tortuous valley, or canyon, which was cut into a **plateau** because of excessive discharge by an ancient, large stream. An example of a **relict landform**.

Infrared—Thermal (heat) radiation with wavelengths longer than those of visible light.

Intelligent cause—Logical conclusion from the "principle of uniform experience" explaining the extraordinary information content of living things. See **uniform experience, principle of.**

Intertongue—The disappearance of a **sedimentary** body within laterally adjacent **sedimentary strata** owing to the splitting into many thin units (tongues), each of which independently terminates by pinching out.

Intrusive rock—**Igneous rock** which penetrated across or between other rocks while in a fluid state and then solidified. Compare to **extrusive rock**.

Isobar—A line of constant pressure. The pattern of **isobars** on a surface weather chart is one major tool in analyzing and forecasting the weather.

Isochron—A line on an **isotope** plot thought to represent rocks of equal age.

Isochron age—The "age" obtained for a suite of **rocks** after multiple analyses have been performed for radioactive parent **isotopes** and nonradioactive daughter **isotopes**. The assumption must be made that the suite of **rocks** when formed was sufficiently mixed with respect to the daughter **isotope** for the "age" to be valid. The "age" is obtained from the slope of the line on an isotope graph, assuming the suite of **rocks** evolved by radioactive decay from points on a horizontal line. Compare to **model age.**

Isotope—One of the forms of a chemical element that have the same number of protons in the nucleus, but a different number of neutrons. Isotopes of the same element have different atomic weights, allowing them to be distinguished by their weights. Examples for lead (*Pb*) are ^{204}Pb, ^{206}Pb, ^{207}Pb and ^{208}Pb.

Jasper—A variety of **chert,** noted for red, yellow, brown, and green colors.

Joint—A fracture plane in a **rock** along which there has been little or no movement (contrast with **fault**).

Jurassic—See **geologic column**.

Kachina—A spirit of the invisible life forces of the **Pueblo** Indians. The **Kachinas** are impersonated by elaborately costumed, masked, male dancers who visit the **Pueblos** during the first half of the year. Although they are not worshipped, they are greatly revered, and one of their main purposes is to bring rain for the spring crops. "Kachina" also refers to the cottonwood dolls made by the **Hopi** and Zuni that are carved, painted and dressed like the dancers. These dolls were originally designed to instruct children about the hundreds of **Kachina** spirits.

Karst—A type of topography formed by solution or dissolving over **limestone, dolomite** or **gypsum**. The topography of a **karst** is characterized by closed depressions, sinkholes, caves, and underground drainage.

Kerogen—Various solid hydrocarbon substances which are soluble in carbon bisulfide. **Kerogen** is especially abundant in oil **shale**, and can be removed by destructive distillation of the **shale**.

Kimberlite pipe—A vertical tube of **rock** representing the neck of a **volcano** composed of **mica** peridotite (especially the minerals **olivine** and phlogopite). An economically important accessory mineral in kimberlite pipes is diamond.

Kind—A Biblical term, referring to a distinctive type of animal or plant which has remained genetically isolated since **Creation**. God's plan was that every organism should produce "after his," or "after their kind."

Kiva—A circular or rectangular, subterranean, religious and social structure containing an encircling bench, central fire pit, ventilator shaft for fresh air, roof-support posts, roof entrance, and a **sipapu**.

Kolk—A turbulent vortex of water; the underwater equivalent of a tornado. A **kolk** is able to cause significant **erosion** of **rock** because of hydraulic **plucking**. A **kolk** exerts tremendous lifting forces on **bedrock**.

Lake Missoula—An ancient "Ice age" lake in western Montana which formed by a glacier blocking the Clark Fork River Valley in northern Idaho. The site of the town of Missoula was apparently under 950 feet of water, as is suggested by the prominent shoreline markings on the hill east of town. The town of Kalispel was under 1,000 feet of water. The lake is estimated to have had a volume of 500 cubic miles of water—about half the volume of Lake Michigan. The ice dam appears to have failed catastrophically, causing more than 300 cubic miles of water to be discharged into the Columbia River Basin, eroding 50 cubic miles of **sediment** and **bedrock**, and forming the **Channeled Scabland** of eastern Washington. There is evidence that more than one lake formed behind the ice dam. **Grand Coulee** is the largest erosional structure formed by catastrophic drainage of the lake.

Lamina—A layer of **sediment** less than one centimeter thick. The plural of **lamina** is **laminae**.

Laminated—Containing numerous laminae superimposed. Compare with **bedded**.

Landform—A specific element, or feature, which composes part of the landscape. Examples of landforms include broad features, such as mountains, plains, and plateaus, as well as restricted features, such as hills, valleys, slopes, canyons, arroyos, and alluvial fans.

Laramide Orogeny—The main uplift event on the Colorado Plateau. Because Cretaceous and overlying **strata** are tilted or **faulted**, the uplift is assigned an "age" of **Cretaceous** to Oligocene.

Lava—Molten rock which has reached the earth's surface.

Lichen—A group of encrusting, poorly shaped plants composed of an alga and a fungus growing in symbiotic association on a solid surface (such as a rock). See **symbiosis**.

Life zone community—A particular grouping of plants and animals described by the dominant type of plant or plants. On the south rim of Grand Canyon, two life zone communities occur: ponderosa pine forest and the pinyon-juniper woodland. Other **life zone communities** occur within Grand Canyon.

Lime mud—Fine-grained, loose **sediment** composed of **calcium carbonate**. It is common on the floors of tropical seas.

Limestone—A **sedimentary rock** composed mainly of **calcium carbonate**.

Limiting factor—A chemical or physical phenomenon which restricts an organism's life activities.

Lithified—Changed to a rock.

Lophophore—A feeding and breathing organ of **brachiopods** and **bryozoans** consisting of a circular or horseshoe-shaped fleshy ridge with tentacles or filaments surrounding the mouth.

Macroevolution—The hypothesis that, given enough time, small-scale genetic changes (**microevolution**) could accumulate to produce large-scale changes, leading to new levels of complexity.

Mafic—A rock which is rich in iron and magnesium.

Magma—A molten, mobile mass of silicate material which is contained within the earth.

Mano—A hand stone used for grinding seeds or corn. It is used on a **metate**.

Mass wastage—Group of processes by which large masses of earth material are moved downward by gravity.

Meander—A broad bend in a river.

Mechanical weathering—The breakdown of rocks by various physical processes (especially frost wedging) into smaller fragments. Contrast with **chemical weathering**.

Member—A division of a **formation**, generally of distinctive **rock** and **mineral** composition. A layer of strata that is easily traced laterally.

Mesa—A steep-sided, flat-topped highland, capped by a resistant **rock** formation. A **mesa** is smaller than a **plateau** and larger than a **butte**.

Metamorphic rock—A **rock** which has been reformed from preexisting rocks by the application of temperature and pressure and by gain or loss of chemical components by the chemical action of fluids.

Metate—A large, trough-shaped stone on which seeds or corn were ground by a **mano**.

Metazoan—A member of a diverse group of animals (Metazoa) which possess a body composed of cells differentiated into tissues and organs. Contrast with **protozoan**.

Mica—A group of common **minerals** consisting of sheetlike layers of silicon and oxygen atoms. Black mica is called biotite while transparent mica is called muscovite.

Micrite—Very small particles of **calcite mud** whose crystal diameter is less than 4 microns. Micrite is a dominate component of many **limestones**. It is thought to have been chemically precipitated.

Microevolution—Small-scale, hereditary changes, resulting in slightly new varieties of a species. The term is simply equivalent to variation, but is used by evolutionists to indicate the process which evolutionists believe could eventually derive new species. The term is especially relevant to discussions of the tassel-eared squirrels of Grand Canyon. Contrast with **macroevolution**.

Micron—A unit of length equal to one-millionth of a meter, or one-thousandth of a millimeter. Also called a micrometer.

Milky Way—The band of light which occurs across the night sky because of the stars and gas in the plane of our **galaxy** (the Milky Way Galaxy).

Mineral—A naturally occurring substance with definite crystal structure, fixed chemical composition (or varying over small range), and diagnostic physical properties.

Mississippian—See **geologic column**.

Model age—The "age" of a **rock** obtained after a single analysis is performed for the radioactive parent **isotope** and nonradioactive daughter **isotope**. Specific assumptions must be made concerning the initial quantity of daughter **isotope** for the "age" to be valid. Compare to **isochron age.**

Mollusk—An organism belonging to Mollusca, the **phylum** of diverse marine and fresh-water animals. Divisions of Mollusca include clams (pelecypoda), snails (gastropoda) and squid (cephalopoda).

Monocline—A **fold** structure in gently dipping strata in which the **strata** flex in only one direction from the horizontal. Compare with **syncline** and **anticline**. The East Kaibab Monocline, in the extreme eastern Grand Canyon, forms a north-south-trending structure that elevates **strata** on the west by almost 3,000 feet, forming the Kaibab and Coconino Plateaus.

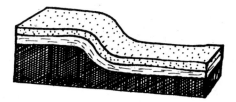

Moraine—Landform composed of **sediment** deposited directly by a **glacier**. A **moraine** is usually a linear ridge of coarse sediment at the front or sides of a glacier.

Mud—**Sediment** composed of **clay**- and **silt**-size **mineral** grains.

Mud crack—A popular name for **shrinkage crack**, a type of crack occurring in a layer of clay, mud, or silt that resulted from contraction accompanied by loss of water. See the technically correct term **shrinkage crack**. Compare to **synersis crack** and **desication crack**. **Mud cracks** in the Hermit Shale are claimed to indicate long time periods of **sediment**-drying by uniformitarians, but the features may be formed by spontaneous throwing off of water (**synersis crack**).

Mudstone—A **sedimentary rock** dominated by **clay** and **silt**.

Mutualism—The particular interactions of organisms that benefit each. A synonym of **cooperation.**

Naturalism—A philosophy denying that any event has supernatural influence or significance.

Navajo—Largest Native American tribe in the U.S. Migrated from northwestern Canada between 1200 and 1400 A.D. and settled in the southwest.

Nebula—An opaque or reflective collection of gas and dust occurring in interstellar space.

Noah's Flood—Year-long, global flood which profoundly affected the earth and life. This Flood is described in Genesis, chapters 6–9.

Nonconformity—A type of **unconformity** in which stratified **rocks** rest upon eroded **metamorphic** or **igneous rocks**. Compare with **unconformity**, **angular unconformity**, **disconformity**, and **paraconformity**.

Olivine—A group of **silicate** minerals dominated by abundant iron and/or magnesium. Olivine lacks cleavage.

Oncolite—A small, generally spheroidal-shaped, concentrically laminated, calcareous sedimentary structure which is accreted by successive layers of gelatinous sheaths of blue-green algae. These concentric spheres generally are less than 10 centimeters in diameter and provide evidence of rolling by water current. Compare with **stromatolite**.

Ordovician—See **geologic column**.

Original continuity, principle of—The principle stating that **strata** continue in all (horizontal) directions until ending by thinning or being blocked by an obstruction.

Original horizontality, principle of—The principle stating that **strata** were originally deposited horizontally (or very nearly horizontally) with tilting being subsequent to **deposition**. Deviations from true horizontality include **cross-bedding** in dunes, deposits on point bars in rivers, and accumulation of air-fall tuffs on slopes.

Orthoclase—See **feldspar**.

Overtopping—Process causing catastrophic failure of natural and man-made dams, in which water spills over the dam and rapidly enlarges a notch in the dam. Contrast with **piping**.

Oxidation—Chemical combination of oxygen with another substance.

Ozone—Three atoms of oxygen which form the molecule O_3.

Ozone layer—A stratum of our **atmosphere** 30 km above the earth, where **ozone** (O_3) is abundant. The **ozone** is formed by the dissociation of molecular oxygen by **ultraviolet radiation** and the recombination of the single atoms of oxygen with molecular oxygen to form **ozone**.

Paleontology—The study of ancient life.

Paraconformity—An obscure or uncertain **erosion** surface buried in the earth in which no **erosion** surface is able to be seen, or in which the contact is a simple **bedding plane**, where the beds above and below the suspected break are parallel. Uniformitarian geologists often use this term to admit that physical evidence of long ages of **erosion** between **rock strata** layers is missing. It should be thought of as a special type of **disconformity**. Compare to **unconformity**, **angular unconformity**, and **nonconformity**.

Parting lineation—A series of parallel ridges or grooves (a few millimeters wide and several centimeters long) occurring on the **bedding plane** within sandstone. These form parallel to the current of flowing water.

Pebble—A **rock** fragment with diameter between two millimeters and 64 millimeters (match head to tennis ball size). A **pebble** is larger than **sand** but smaller than a **cobble**. A deposit dominated by pebbles is called **gravel**.

Pegmatite—**Igneous rock** containing very large minerals, frequently large crystals are found as **dikes** or "veins" in other **rocks**.

Pennsylvanian—See **geologic column.**

Perihelion—The point on the earth's elliptical orbit around the sun which is nearest the sun. The opposite of **aphelion.**

Permian—See **geologic column.**

Permineralization—A fossilization process where the original hard parts of an animal or plant have had minerals deposited within pore spaces.

Petroglyph—An ancient carving or inscription on a **rock,** made by using another **rock.**

Photosynthesis—Process within the chlorophyll-containing tissues of plants whereby light is used to convert water and carbon dioxide to carbohydrates.

Phylum—A major unit of the **taxonomy** of animals, ranking below "kingdom" but above "class." The plural of **phylum** is phyla.

Pictograph—An ancient drawing or painting on a **rock.**

Pinnacle—A tall spire-shaped, or cone-shaped, pillar of **rock.**

Piping—A **process** causing catastrophic failure of natural and man-made dams in which water enlarges tunnels through the dam. Contrast with **overtopping.**

Pit house—A semi-subterranean dwelling made of poles, brush, and mud.

Plagioclase—See **feldspar.**

Planktonic—Said of aquatic organisms which drift or swim weakly.

Plateau—A broad and extensive upland area which is considerably elevated above the adjacent country.

Plucking—The **process** of **erosion** caused by the impact of water on **rock. Plucking** of **rock** usually occurs on **joint** surfaces subjected to high-velocity flow. A **kolk** is a macroturbulent flow structure in which significant **plucking** occurs.

Polar front—The semi-permanent, semi-continuous **front** separating global air masses of tropical and polar origin. This is the major **front** in terms of air-mass contrast and susceptibility to **cyclonic** disturbance.

Population—A group of organisms which can interbreed.

Potassium-argon dating—Technique for obtaining an "age" for a **rock** using the proportions of radioactive potassium-40 to stable decay product argon-40. The method makes an assumption about the initial quantity of argon-40 when the rock formed.

Potsherd—A fragment or piece of pottery found on sites or in refuse deposits where pottery-making peoples have lived.

Precambrian—All **strata** and **rocks** which were part of the earth's crust before the **Cambrian System** was deposited. The **Precambrian** strata of Grand Canyon lack indisputable, multicellular, **fossil** organisms with hard parts. See **geologic column.**

Pressure gradient—The rate of pressure change as a function of distance. The greater the pressure gradient, the stronger the wind will blow.

Procaryotes—Single-celled organisms without internal membranes or organized chromosomes. Compare to **Eucaryotes.**

Process—A complex series of actions occurring in accordance with physical and chemical laws and producing a change in composition, position, form, or state. That a **process** has occurred is usually obvious, because of the change which has occurred.

Productid—A suborder of **brachiopods** including the largest and most aberrant forms yet discovered.

Protist—A single-celled organism of the kingdom Protista, with affinities to both plants and animals. Includes protozoans, bacteria, some algae, fungi, and viruses.

Protozoan—A single-celled organism of kingdom Protista and phylum Protozoa with a characteristic lack of tissues and organs. Some members of the phylum are characterized by skeletons of **calcium carbonate** (**foraminifera**) or **silica** (radiolarians). Contrast with **metazoan.**

Pueblo—Flat-roofed stone or adobe apartment house built by the **Anasazi** after 700 A.D. Also the name given the later stage of the **Anasazi** culture which built these large houses.

Pyroxene—A group of **silicate minerals,** often with abundant iron, calcium and magnesium. **Augite** is the most common **rock**-forming, pyroxene mineral. It has dark color and cleavage angles near 90°. Pyroxene is abundant in **basalt.**

Quartz—A common **rock**-forming **mineral** composed of a framework structure of silicon and oxygen atoms. There are two oxygen atoms for each silicon atom. **Quartz** is an important component of **sandstone** and **granite**. The primary component of beach sand is quartz.

Quartzite—The **metamorphic rock** formed from **sandstone**.

Quaternary—See **geologic column**.

Radiation—The propagation of electromagnetic energy through space or a specified medium, such as air, by virtue of the oscillation of its electric and magnetic fields. Solar radiation comes from the sun and is characteristic of its high temperature ($6000°K$). Terrestrial radiation comes from the earth and is characteristic of its cooler temperature ($300°K$).

Radioisotope dating—Estimation of the "age" of a **rock** or **mineral** by measuring the proportions of the radioactive material (parent) and the stable decay product (daughter) and making certain assumptions concerning the initial proportions. Two types of "ages" are the **model age** and the **isochron age**. The term "radiometric dating" is not preferred.

Radioactivity—The spontaneous disintegration of the nucleus of an atom with the emission of energy.

Reef—A large, organically bound framework composed of organisms bound on top of organisms. **Reefs** would indicate long periods of organic growth but are not known in the **limestones** of Grand Canyon.

Refraction—The process in which the direction of energy propagation is changed as the result of a change in the **density** within the propagating medium. For example, the position of the sun near the horizon appears to be higher than it is in reality due to **refraction** of light through the longer path near sunrise or sunset.

Relative humidity—The ratio of the actual vapor pressure of air to the saturation vapor pressure expressed in percent. Another way of stating the meaning of relative humidity is the percentage of water vapor a parcel of air holds at a given temperature and pressure relative to the maximum amount it could hold at the same temperature and pressure.

Relict—Any **landform** which has survived decay and disintegration, being left behind after disappearance or greatly reduced activity of the formative agent. A **plateau** and an **underfit valley** are examples of landforms often considered **relict**.

Relict forms—Any feature, object, or living thing which has remained essentially unchanged after other features, objects, or living things have changed or disappeared.

Relief—The difference in elevation between the low and high portions of a landscape area.

Rhythmites—A rhythmically layered succession of sedimentary beds. Each rhythmite bed has thickness, composition, and structure similar to other beds within the succession. An individual rhythmite bed may be recognized to be a **turbidite**.

Ridge—An atmospheric term referring to an elongated area of relatively high atmospheric pressure. Contrast with **trough**.

Rill—One of the first and smallest channels eroded into soft **sediment** as water runs off a surface. **Rills** combine to form a **gully**.

Riparian—Adjacent to, or living on the bank of a body of water.

Ripple marks—Small ridges produced on the surface of **sand** or **silt** by the movement of water current or wind. When the **ripple marks** are asymmetrical, the steeper side is the down-current side, indicating direction of flow.

Rock—An aggregation of **minerals** or **mineral**-like materials.

Rubidium-strontium dating—Technique for obtaining an "age" for a **rock** using the proportions of radioactive rubidium-87 to stable decay product strontium-87, and making assumptions concerning the initial condition of the **rock**.

Rugosa—Order of solitary **corals** which forms a exoskeleton which is cone-shaped or cylindrical.

Sand—A **rock** particle whose diameter ranges from 0.0625 to 2.0 millimeters. **Quartz** grains are important components of **sand** because of their abundance and resistance to chemical and mechanical disintegration. These particles are larger than **silt**, but smaller than a **pebble**.

Sand wave—A large, underwater hill or **dune** of **sand** moved by the flow of the water. Movement of a **sand wave** produces diagonally inclined **stratification** called **cross-bedding**.

Sandstone—A clastic **sedimentary rock** composed of **sand**-sized particles.

Sapping—A natural **process** of **erosion** at the base of a cliff, by the removal of softer layers, resulting in the removal of support from, and breaking off of large masses above, from the cliff face. **Sapping** can be greatly accelerated where water seeps from **sediment** or **rock** at the base of a slope or cliff. Extensive **sapping** can produce a grotto or **amphitheatre-headed canyon.**

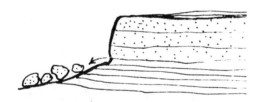

Savanna—A grassland **biome** characterized by scattered trees.

Scattering—The **process** affecting light propogation, by which small particles suspended in a medium diffuse a portion of the incident **radiation** in all directions. In **scattering**, no energy transformation results, only a change in the spatial distribution of the radiation. Rayleigh scattering produces the blue sky of our atmosphere.

Schist—A coarse-grained, **metamorphic rock** with parallel orientation of platy **minerals** (**mica**, chlorite or talc) without obvious segregation of light-colored and dark-colored **minerals** into layers as in **gneiss**. The Vishnu Schist is a prominent **rock** of the inner gorge of Grand Canyon.

Sediment—Material which is transported and deposited by water, wind, ice, or gravity. There are three classes of sediment: clastic (**clay, sand, gravel,** etc.), composed of broken **rocks**; chemical (salt, **chert, gypsum,** etc.), precipitated from solution; and organic (**lime mud,** peat, etc.), accumulated by biological activity.

Sedimentary rock—**Rock** formed by the accumulation and cementation of **sediment**. Usually these **rocks** form from transported **mineral** grains, but they can also form by chemical precipitation at the depositional site or by amassment of organic detritus.

Sedimentation—See **deposition**.

Seep—A spot where water oozes from the earth, often forming the source for a very small stream. Compare with **spring**.

Septa—Various radially disposed calcareous plates or partitions within the exoskeleton of a **coral**.

Sere—A stage in the succession of ecological communities. Contrast with **climax**.

Shale—A **clastic sedimentary rock** composed of **clay**-sized particles.

Shrinkage crack—The general name for a crack occurring in a layer of **clay** or **silt** that resulted from contraction caused by spontaneous throwing off of water (**syneresis**) or drying (desiccation). **Shrinkage cracks** can form under air by drying (see **desiccation crack**), under water by spontaneous dewatering, or within buried **sediment** layers by **compaction** and dewatering (see **syneresis crack**).

Silica—Chemical name for the variety of minerals composed of dioxide of silicon (SiO_2). The most common **mineral** form is **quartz**. The cryptocrystalline form is chalcedony. The amorphous and hydrated type is opal. Other less pure forms of silica are **sand**, diatomite, **chert**, and flint.

Sill—A tabular body of **intrusive rock** that penetrates parallel to layers of the enclosing rock without cutting across the layers. Contrast to **dike**.

Silt—**Rock** particles whose diameters range from 1/256 to 1/16 millimeter. These particles are larger than **clay**, but smaller than **sand**.

Siltstone—A **clastic sedimentary rock** composed of **silt**-sized particles.

Silurian—See **geologic column**.

Sipapu—A small hole constructed by Indians in the floor of a **kiva**, symbolizing the entrance to the spirit world.

Solstice—Either of the two points on the sun's apparent annual path around the earth, where it is displaced farthest north or south from the earth's equator. For example, at the summer solstice (about June 22) in the northern hemisphere, the sun will appear directly overhead at noon, along the 23-1/2° parallel.

Solution—Chemical process by which **rocks** are dissolved by a liquid (usually water). See **chemical weathering**.

Sorting—The separation of particles during transportation according to size, shape, and density. Fast-moving flows are able to separate particles according to size, shape, and density, and deposit them in distinctive **strata**.

Sponge—An organism belonging to Porifera, the phylum of the simplest multicelled animals. Although considered "primitive," sponges are *not* found in the lower strata of Grand Canyon, but are most abundant in the uppermost **strata**.

Spring—A place where water flows from **rock** or soil onto the land or into a river, lake, or the ocean. Most **springs** in desert areas are called **seeps**.

Stasis—The stabilization of a **population** of organisms around a particular form or type, especially well illustrated by the long-term stability of organisms in the fossil record.

Strata—The plural of **stratum**.

Stratification—The property of **sedimentary rocks** and **volcanic rocks** where layered structure occurs.

Stratum—A layer of **sediment** or **sedimentary rock**. A **bed** is *thicker* than one centimeter, and a **lamina** is *thinner* than one centimeter. The plural of **stratum** is **strata**.

Stromatolite—Unusual **laminated** structures within **limestone** believed to have accumulated under the influence of **sediment**-binding **blue-green algae**.

Subaqueous—Beneath water.

Superposition, principle of—The principle that in any undisturbed succession of **strata**, the oldest is at the base and the youngest is at the top.

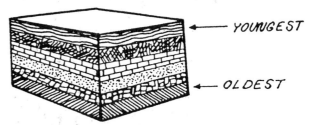

Symbiosis—The living together within close union of two dissimilar organisms in a mutually beneficial relationship. An example is **lichen**.

Syncline—A **fold** structure in which the **strata** flex in two directions dipping toward the **fold**. Compare with **monocline** and **anticline**. The **Precambrian strata** in eastern Grand Canyon form a buried **syncline**.

Syneresis—The spontaneous process where fine-grained, **clay**-rich **sediment** throws off water and decreases in volume. This dewatering of **sediments** can occur on the bottom of a water body or within deeply buried **sediment** layers. Cracking of the **sediment** usually results. **Syneresis** forms structures strongly resembling the **desiccation cracks** made when **sediment** dries. See **shrinkage crack**, **desiccation crack**, and **syneresis crack**.

Syneresis crack—A **shrinkage crack** formed on the surface of a **clay** or clayey bed by the spontaneous throwing off of water. The dewatering process, subsequent decrease in volume, and formation of the crack occur without drying or the sun's heat. Contrast with **desiccation crack**.

System—A specifically designated reference section of **strata** which is believed to provide adequate basis for correlation with other **strata** sections. **Systems** are superimposed to form the idealized complete succession of **strata** called the **geologic column**.

Talus—Broken **rock** fragments that accumulate as a sloping pile at the base of a cliff. See **angle of repose.**

Taxon—In **taxonomy**, a unit of any rank, such as a particular species, class, or family. The plural of **taxon** is taxa.

Taxonomy—The field of biology which deals with the principles of classification of living things.

Tectonics—The branch of geology dealing with the large-scale architecture of the earth, especially regional, structural, or deformational features, their history and origin.

Temperature gradient—The rate of temperature change as a function of distance or elevation.

Tertiary—See **geologic column.**

Texture—The size, shape, orientation, and packing of particles that compose a **rock.**

Theater-headed canyon—See **amphitheater-headed canyon.**

Thermoregulation—Physiological process by which animals regulate their internal temperature. An example is the jackrabbit, which uses its ears as efficient heat radiators.

Topography—The form of the earth's surface. **Topography** is conveniently expressed as contour lines on certain types of maps.

Tourmaline—A complex boron-aluminum silicate mineral which is common in **pegmatites** associated with **granite**, and in **metamorphic rocks.**

Tower of Babel—The occasion in **history** after **Noah's flood**, when peoples were dispersed widely on the earth and different languages appeared. See Genesis, chapter 11. The Tower of Babel appears to coincide with the geologic period called the "**Ice age.**"

Trace fossil—A sedimentary structure within a rock consisting of a fossilized track, trail, boring, tunnel, or tube resulting from the life activity of an organism. Contrast with **body fossil.**

Trade winds—The **wind** system, occupying most of the tropics, which blows from the subtropical highs toward the equator. These winds are northeasterly in the northern hemisphere and southeasterly in the southern hemisphere.

Travertine—A **rock** composed of **calcium carbonate** that has been chemically deposited in a cave or around a **spring.**

Triassic—See **geologic column.**

Trilobite—A **fossil** belonging to the **arthropods** which has an external, dorsal skeleton consisting of cephalon, thorax and pygidium, being divided along its length into a central axis and two pleural regions. The **fossil** is known from Cambrian to Permian **rocks** of Grand Canyon.

Trough—An atmospheric term referring to an elongated area of relatively low atmospheric pressure. Contrast with **ridge.**

Tsunami—A great sea wave produced by an ocean floor earthquake, volcanic eruption, or landslide. Often misnamed "tidal wave."

Turbidite—A sedimentary stratum composed of clay, silt, and/or sand which was accumulated rapidly from a turbulent, swiftly moving, slurrylike, underwater flow of suspended sediment which moved along the bottom slope of a standing body of water. **Graded bedding** is a common characteristic of a **turbidite.**

Turbulence—A state of fluid flow in which the instantaneous velocities exhibit irregular and apparently random fluctuations. These fluctuations often constitute major deformations of the flow and are capable of transporting momentum, energy, and suspended matter at rates far in excess of the rate of transport by the molecular processes of diffusion and conduction in non-turbulent or laminar flow.

Ultraviolet radiation—Electromagnetic **radiation** of shorter wavelength than visible light, but longer than x-rays. **Ultraviolet radiation** accounts for only four-to-five percent of the total radiation from the sun, but would be deadly to life if almost all of it were not absorbed or reflected by the upper **atmosphere.** The **ozone layer**, high above the earth's surface, is where most of the **absorption** of ultraviolet radiation occurs.

Unconformity—The general name given to a major surface of **erosion** that has been buried within the earth under **sediments** or **strata.** Specific types are **angular unconformity, disconformity, paraconformity**, and **nonconformity.**

Underfit river—A river, which because of structures on its **flood plain**, shows evidence of a history of much greater **discharge**.

Underfit valley—A valley which previously had a large amount of water flowing through it, but which now has a stream of greatly reduced size. A specific example of a **relict** landform.

Uniform experience, principle of—Principle derived from our experience with the architecture and engineering of machines which allows us to conclude that an **intelligent cause** was necessary to create the complexity of living organisms. See **design** and **intelligent cause.**

Uniformitarian—A person who believes in the doctrine of **uniformitarianism.** Sometimes these people are called "gradualists." Contrast with **catastrophist.**

Uniformitarianism—The doctrine that ancient geologic changes occurred largely in response to slow and gradual processes, without significant periods of rapid and catastrophic change. Compare to **catastrophism.**

Upwarp—A domelike structure formed in the earth where **strata** rise in elevation relative to the surrounding **strata.**

Vapor canopy—A hypothetical, spherical layer of water vapor surrounding the earth and resting on top of the current **atmosphere** prior to **Noah's flood.** This canopy would have caused a more uniform, warm climate before the Flood, likely preventing **clouds** and precipitation. Its collapse, during the time of Noah, may have contributed to the waters of the Flood and to the cooling of the earth following the Flood.

Varve—A pair of thin, sedimentary layers—one fine and dark colored and the other relatively coarse and light colored—formed as the result of one year's **deposition** in a lake. The coarse layer represents spring runoff into the lake.

Volcanic rock—A **rock** which formed by the process of **volcanism.** The most common **volcanic rock** is **basalt.** Contrast to **intrusive rock.**

Volcanism—The **process** by which molten **rock** within the earth (**magma**) and gases within the earth are transferred from the earth's interior to its surface. Steam within **magma** is a primary cause of explosive **volcanism.** More-tranquil **volcanism** is associated with a deficiency of steam.

Water table—Upper surface of the zone of water saturation within the earth. For a well to produce water, it must penetrate the **water table. Springs** are located where the **water table** intersects the earth's surface.

Weather—The state of the **atmosphere,** mainly with respect to its effects upon life and human activities. As distinguished from **climate, weather** consists of short-term (minutes'-to-months') variations of the **atmosphere.**

Weathering—The processes by which **rocks** are physically broken into fragments, or chemically altered, as a result of exposure to atmospheric agents at or near the earth's surface. **Weathering** involves little or no transport of loosened or altered debris. Two types of **weathering** are recognized: **mechanical weathering** and **chemical weathering.**

Westerlies—The dominant west-to-east motion of the **atmosphere,** centered over the middle latitudes of both hemispheres. This is the dominant **wind** pattern at Grand Canyon.

Wind—Air in motion, relative to the surface of the earth.

Zenith—The point that lies directly above an observer when looking upward at the sky.

Zodiac—A band of the night sky containing the 12 **constellations** through which the sun appears to move in the course of a year.

Zonation—The condition of being arranged or formed in zones; usually in reference to living or fossil organisms. For example, the arrangement of a pinyon–juniper community is restricted to certain zones of Grand Canyon, according to its temperature and moisture needs.

Flood legend (Havasupai), 205
Flood model, 36, 51, 52, 69, 150
Flood plain, 74, 98, 246
Flood strata, 215
Flood theory, 26
Flora, 6, 164
Florida, 38
Florida-Bahamas, 25
Flower, 161
Fluid evulsion structures, 64
Fluvial, 246
Fold, 9, 14, 224, 246
Fold structure, 16
 Carbon Canyon, 18
Footprint, 74, 75
Footprint experiment, 31
Forager, 198
Foraminifera, 72, 141, 147, 246
Forbs, 164
Formation, 12, 211, 246
Fortification Hill Basalt, 90
Fossil, 2, 3, 4, 5, 6, 21, 26, 27, 51, 65, 66, 70, 72, 74, 76, 95, 139, 218, 224, 246
 abrupt appearance, 147–150
 accumulation rate, 28
 age of, 134
 creationist view, 133, 149, 150
 disparity precedes diversity, 148–150
 environment of deposition, 147
 evidence for stasis, 149, 150
 evolutionist view, 133, 147, 148
 order of appearance, 147, 148
 rapid deposition, 134, 147
 stasis, 147
 types of, 133
Fossil-bearing rock, 2, 223
Fossil Creek, 217
Fossil-footprint trackway, 29
Fossil log, 79, 217, 218
Fossil record, 147–150
Fossil soils, 51
Fossil tracks, 31
Fossilization, 26, 133, 134, 217
Founder Principle, 178
Fountains of the great deep, 72, 194
Four-winged saltbush, 170
Framework of Scripture, 57, 80, 81, 150
Fremont cottonwood, 171
Friction, 189
Front, 189, 246
Frontal zone, 192
Fruit fly, 162
Funerary offering, 198

Fusulinid, 72, 246

Galaxy, 183, 246
Galeros Formation, 65, 66, 135
Gambel oak, 167, 168
Game trail, 207
Garden Creek Canyon, 212, 227
Gas molecules, 187
Gastropod, 71, 139, 142
Gemini, 181
Gene pool, 176, 177, 246
Genera, 149
General circulation, 187, 190, 192
General isochron-age equation, 118, 119
General model-age equation, 115
General radioactive dating equation, 114
Genetic code, 6, 153, 246
Genetic language, 154
Genetics, 154
Geochronology, 246
Geologic age, 8, 42, 45
Geologic block diagram, 9, 10, 13, 246
Geologic column, 246
Geologic cross section, 11, 12, 14, 15, 58, 246
Geologic formation, 211
Geologic map, 9, 11, 15, 16
Geologic process, 24
Geologic record, 224
Geologic structure, 9, 85
Geological museum, 211
Geologist, 21
Geomorphic, 246
Germany, 26
Germination, 162
Gigantism, 193, 194
Glacier, 194, 246
Glauconite, 246
Glen Canyon, 220
Glen Canyon Dam, 84, 105, 106, 165, 172, 173, 214, 220
Glen Canyon National Recreation Area, 232
Global circulation, 185, 192
Global flood, 22
Glorieta Sandstone, 36, 75
Glossopleura, 70, 143
Gneiss, 12, 59, 81, 246
God's judgment ,150
God's mercy, 150
Golden shiner, 171
Goldfish, 171
Good news, 4
Goosenecks of the San Juan River, 98, 99, 103
Gorge, 1, 246

NAME INDEX

SCRIPTURE INDEX